THE DIVINE ELECTION OF ISRAEL

THE DIVINE ELECTION
OF ISRAEL

by

Seock-Tae Sohn

WILLIAM B. EERDMANS PUBLISHING COMPANY
GRAND RAPIDS, MICHIGAN

Library of Congress Cataloging-in-Publication Data

Sohn, Seock-Tae.
The divine election of Israel / by Seock-Tae Sohn.
p.   cm.
Revision of thesis (Ph.D.) — New York University, 1986.
Includes bibliographical references.
ISBN 0-8028-0545-0 (pbk.)
1. Jews — Election, Doctrine of — Biblical teaching.   2. Bible. O.T. —
Theology.   I. Title.
BM613.S64   1991
296.3'11 — dc20   91-24602
                                                      CIP

Contents

Foreword

The Divine Election of Israel by Seock-Tae Sohn is a fine application of the philological method to the investigation of a major theme in the Hebrew Bible, the election of Israel as God's people. I am honored to have been Seock-Tae Sohn's teacher, and gratified that we learned so much from each other!

This valuable study shows us the proper way to comprehend theological concepts. The scholar must return to the actual terms, formulae, and metaphors which the Hebrew Bible itself employs to express the special relationship between God and Israel. These terms and formulae lead us to the *Sitz im Leben* of the ideas themselves. The scholar thereby permits the text to speak for itself and is able to grasp the genuine ideas expressed therein.

Seock-Tae Sohn complements his incisive analysis of the text by presenting a literary-historical review of the development of the idea of election, showing how it originated in the pre-monarchic period of Israel's history. As the collective experience of Israel, in its land, and later exiled from it, underwent radical changes, different interpretations of Israel's election emerged. In a fascinating manner, Seock-Tae Sohn illustrates the doing, undoing, and ultimate restoration of the process of election, weaving an intimate pattern of human-divine relationships. He emphasizes the integral importance of collective restoration, of the redemption of the remnant of Israel in postexilic times, by a forgiving God whose covenant endures.

Finally, Seock-Tae Sohn carries the theme of election, with its various metaphors, through the New Testament. In an unprecedented treatment, he illustrates the continuity of thought from Israelite-Jewish expression to the Christian experience of God.

Without compromising modern methodology, Seock-Tae Sohn provides us with a guide to theological inquiry. He epitomizes the compatibility of disciplined, scholarly inquiry with religious faith. For, after all, the struggle is not over, and the drama is far from complete! A great challenge remains until all of God's children will be united as one great family, performing His will with a perfect heart, in a world of peace and love.

Baruch A. Levine
New York University

Preface

This is an investigation of Israel's understanding of her election as the people of Yahweh, the development of the idea of election in her history, and its relationship with other major themes of the Old Testament with the New Testament reflections. It was originally submitted to the faculty of the Graduate School of Arts and Science in partial fulfillment of the requirements for the degree of Doctor of Philosophy at New York University in 1986. Parts of the dissertation have been reworked and chapter IV has been expanded in the process of publication.

Thanks are due to many people who have helped me in the course of research and in preparing this book. A particular expression of gratitude should be given to Professor Baruch A. Levine of New York University. He suggested this topic and patiently supervised my research. He spent hours reading page by page, discussing the material with me and making numerous valuable suggestions. More than that he taught me reverence for the Holy Scripture. I acknowledge, also, Professors Lawrence H. Schiffman of NYU and Tremper Longman III of Westminster Theological Seminary, whose generosity and kindness continually overwhelmed me. Professor Seyoon Kim of the Asian Center for Theological Studies and Mission (Asia United Theological College) read chapter IV and made many useful suggestions.

I owe much of my education to the members of the Korean Joong Bu Presbyterian Church of New York. Their prayer and financial assistance brought my formal study to completion. I extend gratitude to Professors Michael L. Brown of the Institute of Biblical Studies (Christ For The Nations) and Ruth Eshenaur of ACTS for their efforts to improve the style of my poor English. I wish to express my deep gratitude to Mr. William Eerdmans, the President of Wm. B. Eerdmans Publishing Co., who willingly accepted my manuscript for publication.

Most of all, I want to express my gratitude to my wife, Hee-Sook Koh, and my two children, Sooyun and Sunyong. They tried to understand why their father spent so much time away from them working on his research. In particular, Hee-Sook was very patient while I completed my studies in the United States. I dedicate this book to them.

Seoul, May 1990   Seock-Tae Sohn

Abbreviations

AASOR	*Annual of the American Schools of Oriental Research*
AB	Anchor Bible
AHw	W. von Soden, *Akkadisches Handwörterbuch*
Aistl.	J. Aistleitner, *Wörterbuch der Ugaritischen Sprache* (Berlin: Akademie, 1963)
AJSL	*American Journal of Semitic Languages and Literatures*
AnBib	Analecta biblica
ANEP	J.B. Pritchard, ed., *The Ancient Near East in Pictures*
ANET	J.B. Pritchard, ed., *Ancient Near Eastern Texts*
AP	A. Cowley, *Aramaic Papyri of the Fifth Century B.C.* (Oxford: Clarendon, 1923)
ARM	*Archives royales de Mari,* vol. 3 = G. Boyer, *Textes Juridiques* (Paris: Imprimerie nationale, 1963)
AThANT	*Abhandlungen Theologie des Alten und Neuen Testaments*
AUSS	*Andrews University Seminary Studies*
BA	*The Biblical Archaeologist*
BASOR	*Bulletin of the American Schools of Oriental Research*
BDB	F. Brown, S.R. Driver, and C.A. Briggs, *Hebrew and English Lexicon of the Old Testament*
BHS	*Biblia Hebraica Stuttgartensia*
BibOr	Biblica et orientalia
BMAP	E.G. Kraeling, *Brooklyn Museum Aramaic Papyri* (New Haven: Yale, 1953)
BWANT	*Beiträge zur Wissenschaft vom Alten und Neuen Testament*

BZ	*Biblische Zeitschrift*
BZAW	Beihefte zur *ZAW*
CAD	*The Assyrian Dictionary of the Oriental Institute of the University of Chicago*
CBOT	Coniectanea Biblica, Old Testament Series
CBQ	*The Catholic Biblical Quarterly*
CH	Code of Hammurabi
CTA	A. Herdner, *Corpus des tablettes en cunéiformes alphabétiques*
EA	J.A. Knudtzon, *Die El-Amarna Tafeln.* 2 vols. = *VAB* 2 (Leipzig: Hinrichs, 1915)
EG	E. Grant, *Babylonian Business Documents of the Classical Period* (Philadelphia: Dept. of Assyriology, University of Pennsylvania, 1919)
FRLANT	*Forschungen zur Religion und Literatur des Alten und Neuen Testaments*
GKC	*Gesenius' Hebrew Grammar,* ed. E. Kautsch (Oxford: Clarendon, 1910)
HAL	W. Baumgartner et al., *Hebräisches und aramäisches Lexikon zum Alten Testament*
HG	J. Köhler and A. Ungnad, *Hammurabis Gesetz.* 6 vols. (Leipzig: Hinrichs, 1909)
HSM	Harvard Semitic Monographs
HSS	Harvard Semitic Studies
HTR	*Harvard Theological Review*
HUCA	*Hebrew Union College Annual*
ICC	International Critical Commentary
IDB(Sup)	G.A. Buttrick, ed., *Interpreter's Dictionary of the Bible.* 4 vols. (Nashville: Abingdon, 1962). Supplementary Volume, ed. K. Crim (1976)
JAOS	*Journal of the American Oriental Society*
JBL	*Journal of Biblical Literature*
JCS	*Journal of Cuneiform Studies*
JEA	*Journal of Egyptian Archeology*
JJS	*Journal of Jewish Studies*
JNES	*Journal of Near Eastern Studies*
JPSV	Jewish Publication Society Version
JSOT	*Journal for the Study of the Old Testament*
JSOTSup	Journal for the Study of the Old Testament–Supplement Series

JSS	*Journal of Semitic Studies*
JTC	*Journal for Theology and the Church*
KAI	H. Donner and W. Röllig, *Kanaanäische und aramäische Inschriften*
KAJ	E. Ebeling, *Keilschrifttexte aus Assur juridischen Inhalts = Wissenschaftliche Veröffentlichungen der Deutschen Orient-gesellschaft* 50 (Leipzig: Hinrichs, 1927)
KD	Keil-Delitzsch, *Commentary on the Old Testament*
KJV	King James Version
Meissner, *Beiträge*	B. Meissner, *Beiträge zum altbabylonischen Privatrecht* (Leipzig: Hinrichs, 1893)
MVAG	*Mitteilungen der vorderasiatisch-ägyptischen Gesellschaft*
NASB	New American Standard Bible
NCBC	New Century Bible Commentary
NICNT	New International Commentary on the New Testament
NICOT	New International Commentary on the Old Testament
NIV	New International Version
NRVGL	M. San Nicolo, A. Ungnad, *Neubabylonische Rechts- und Verwaltungsurkunden- (Glossar)* (Leipzig: Hinrichs, 1935/37)
OBT	Overtures to Biblical Theology
OTL	Old Testament Library
PTMS	Pittsburgh Theological Monograph Series
R	Rabbinic Commentary
Rép Mari	*ARM XV, Répertoire Analytique* (Paris, 1954)
RSV	Revised Standard Version
SBLDS	Society of Biblical Literature Dissertation Series
SBLMS	Society of Biblical Literature Monograph Series
SBT	Studies in Biblical Theology
Schorr, *Urkunden*	M. Schorr, *Urkunden des altbabylonischen Zivil- und Prozessrechts = VAB 5* (Leipzig: Hinrichs, 1913)
TCL	G.Dossin, *Letters de la premiére dynastie babylonienne* (Paris: Geuthner, 1933-34)
TDNT	G. Kittel and G. Friedrich, eds., *Theological Dictionary of the New Testament*

TDOT	G.J. Botterweck and H. Ringgren, eds., *Theological Dictionary of the Old Testament*
TEV	Today's English Version
THAT	E. Jenni and C. Westermann, eds., *Theologisches Handwörterbuch zum Alten Testament*
TWOT	R.L. Harris, G.I. Archer, and B.K. Waltke, eds., *Theological Wordbook of the Old Testament*
UT	C.H. Gordon, *Ugaritic Textbook*
VAB	*Vorderasiatische Bibliothek*, vol. 5
VS	*Vorderasiatische Schriftdenkmäler* (7 vols.; Leipzig: Hinrichs, 1907-1916)
VT	*Vestus Testamentum*
VTSup	Vetus Testamentum, Supplements
WTJ	*Westminster Theological Journal*
YOS	Yale Oriental Series. 12 vols. (New Haven: Yale, 1915-1978)
ZAW	*Zeitschrift für die alttestamentliche Wissenschaft*
ZKT	*Zeitschrift für Katholische Theologie*
ZS	*Zeitschrift für Semitik und Verwandte Gebiete*

Introduction

1. THE IMPORTANCE OF THIS STUDY

The divine election of Israel is one of the major themes of the Hebrew Bible. Yahweh chose Israel to be his people and dealt with it as his own throughout biblical history. Since this idea was of central importance to the biblical writers, it is not easy to grasp the message of the Bible without a proper understanding of this theme.[1]

Furthermore, major themes of the Hebrew Bible, such as covenant, mission, rejection (exile), remnant, and restoration, are directly related to this election idea, and they presuppose the concept. Therefore, the doctrine of election is of fundamental importance to both Judaism and Christianity, since both trace their roots to Yahweh's election of Old Testament Israel. This book, however, concerns itself mainly with the subject of election in the context of the Hebrew Bible, although I am fully aware of the later transformation which affected the doctrine of election in traditional Christian theology.

Yet in comparison with the importance of our subject, research in this area has been very limited. Even though most writers have dealt with this subject in their books on Old Testament theology, the meaning of election has not yet been fully defined. In particular, Old Testament scholars have failed to explain how and in what circumstances the people of Israel came to realize that they were in

1. G.E. Wright describes the importance of the theme in this way: "The all-pervading sense of election and covenant, therefore, is the chief clue for the understanding of Israel's sense of destiny and of the meaning of existence" (*The Old Testament Against Its Environment*, SBT 1/2 [London: SCM, 1968], pp. 62-63).

1

fact chosen, and Israel's own understanding of its chosenness has not been adequately explored. Moreover, the organic unity and continuity which exists between election and the other themes mentioned above has been ignored.

Therefore, my primary purpose is to discover the meaning of election by examining the words and phrases which pertain to this idea, since the idea of election is described not by only one or two stock phrases but by a variety of words and metaphors. And each description has its own linguistic background against which its meaning has come to be understood. However, modern scholars usually put their emphasis on certain words or ideas and try to reconstruct the theology of election from these specific concepts only.

Thus, Th.C. Vriezen recognizes בחר as the only verb in the Hebrew Bible which adequately expresses the concept of election. Other Hebrew words such as ידע, קרא, or לקח may express some particular aspect of election, but they are secondary to בחר in denoting the idea of election.[2]

With Vriezen, K. Koch presupposes that בחר is the election word par excellence, and he therefore eliminates other verbs from consideration. After examining the "Wortfeld von בחר" only in Psalms, Deuteronomy, and Deutero-Isaiah, he concludes that "election thought" is expressed in the credo-hymns of the Psalms, in the discourse of Deuteronomy, and in the salvation oracles of Deutero-Isaiah.[3] He thus works from a limited vocabulary in a limited text to a general understanding of election.

P. Altmann criticizes both Vriezen and Koch for ignoring the role of universalism in the process of shaping Israel's view of election. He attempts to understand the particularism of election in the context of the principle of universalism. He notes that, as Israel's concept of God's role in the world is enlarged, so its understanding of election expands. But Altmann's thesis is dominated by his dog-

2. Th. C. Vriezen, *Die Erwählung Israels nach dem Alten Testament* (Zurich: Zwingli, 1953), pp. 35-41. See also R.G. Rogers, "The Doctrine of Election in the Chronicler's Work and the Dead Sea Scrolls" (Ph. D. Dissertation, Boston University, 1969), pp. 88-90; G.E. Mendenhall, "Election," *IDB*, 2:76-82.

3. Klaus Koch, "Zur Geschichte der Erwählungsvorstellung in Israel," *ZAW* 67 (1955): 205-26. See also Rogers, "Doctrine of Election," pp. 90-91.

matic presuppositions, and he does not even seriously consider the importance of the related election terms.[4]

Other scholars agree on the centrality of בחר in the election vocabulary of the Hebrew Bible, and they share nearly the same ideas with one or all of the above three writers. As R.G. Rogers correctly points out, since the centrality of בחר in the theology of election has too easily dominated the thinking of scholars, the whole picture of the biblical idea of election has not been properly apprehended.[5] According to my research, בחר does not necessarily play the central role in the election idea.[6] The idea of election has its origins in a variegated and changing life setting, and it is expressed in a variety of literary terms and styles. It seems clear, then, that scholarly research on election until now has not fully illuminated the original meaning of the idea and the original setting from which the idea sprang. These facts indicate to me the need to do fresh research on this topic from an entirely different perspective in order to remedy the deficiency of previous studies.

Along with discovering the meaning of election, research on the development of the idea is indispensable. Those who emphasize the importance of בחר as an election term come inevitably to the conclusion, by their examination of the occurrences and usages of the word, that Yahweh's choosing Israel is a concept not demonstrably earlier than Deuteronomy. According to G.E. Mendenhall, "Religious convictions frequently do not lend themselves to precise definition. There can hardly be any doubt that almost everything intended by the Deuteronomist is also specific or implied in the earlier religious traditions, yet we have no evidence that Israel was ever said to be 'chosen' by Yahweh before *ca.* 623 B.C." He therefore suggests that the religious expression of the conviction that there was a permanent relation between Yahweh and Israel should be placed after the destruction of the nation by Nebuchadnezzar in 587 B.C.[7] W.A. Irwin holds that the idea of election came into existence only after the settlement in Canaan, and he

4. Peter Altmann, *Erwählungstheologie und Universalismus im Alten Testament* (Berlin: Alfred Töpelmann, 1964). See also Rogers, "Doctrine of Election," pp. 91-93.

5. Rogers, "Doctrine of Election," p. 93.

6. See also H. Seebass, "בחר *(bāchar)*," *TDOT,* 2:82,84.

7. G.E. Mendenhall, "Election," *IDB,* 2:76.

offers no suggestion as to what brought it into existence.[8] At this point an examination is required to unveil the truthfulness of their assertions. I regard the concept of election as having originated from various of Israel's life settings, and it is described in figures and metaphors. Furthermore, it is not to be seen as the product of one generation. Therefore, tracing the development of the idea of election will be an important part of this book.

The idea of election is so deeply rooted in the mind of ancient Israel that the major themes of the Hebrew Bible are inseparably linked to it. In particular, the theme of election-rejection-restoration underlies much of the organic frame of history and theology in the Hebrew Bible. The covenant puts election into legal effect. Election entails mission, the purpose of Yahweh's choosing. The remnant are the bearers of election during the period between rejection and restoration. Thus, these later themes presuppose the concept of election in their progressive development. However, research in these areas has not been comprehensive to date. Therefore, it is incumbent on us to examine these themes with respect to election.

2. A DEFINITION OF ELECTION

Election refers to an exclusive relationship between Yahweh and his people, Israel. Yahweh's choice of Israel is a part of this relationship. More precisely, it is Yahweh's act in initiating this relationship. The main concern of election in the Bible is not in reference to a past event when Yahweh chose Israel as his people. Rather, election is directed to the existing relationship between Yahweh and Israel. The people of Israel looked back on what Yahweh had done for them in the past and then tried to describe and explain their relationship with him in their present situation. Therefore, the definition of election in this book will be more comprehensive and extensive than what has been traditionally offered.[9]

8. W.A. Irwin, in H. Frankfort, et al., *The Intellectual Adventure of Ancient Man* (Chicago: University of Chicago Press, 1946), pp. 329-30.
9. Cf. Edmond Jacob, *Theology of the Old Testament* (New York and Evanston: Harper & Row, 1958), pp. 201-9.

Since our definition of election is concerned more with the existing relationship between Yahweh and his people, the terms and metaphors denoting this relationship will be examined, even though they do not explicitly convey the concept of initiating the relationship. Most of these terms and metaphors presuppose the fact of election, though they describe only the existing relationship which resulted from it.

3. THE METHODOLOGY OF THIS STUDY

The basic methodology controlling this research will be philological and semantic. My basic presupposition is that the election ideas did not spring out of a vacuum. They came into being in the organic social and cultural context of the biblical community. Through their experiential knowledge of Yahweh at a certain point in history, the people of Israel became conscious of their special relationship with their God, and they tried to explain it in their everyday language, often in terms of typical human relationships.[10]

The first task, then, is to find those terms, phrases, parables, and metaphors which describe this relationship between Yahweh and Israel. Thus, היה ל־, קרא, ידע, בחר, לקח, etc., will be analyzed. The next stage is to research how, and in what kind of life setting, the specific terms were used. For example, the election terms בעל, לקח, נשא, ישב, and ידע are mostly found in the marriage context, and each term represents a certain characteristic nuance of marriage. The third step is to deduce the particular aspects of election contained in these words and descriptions. Since certain election terms are borrowed from marriage terminology, we can safely say, for example, that the people of Israel tried to explain the idea of election from the perspective of human marriage. They understood Yah-

---

10. P.C. Craigie already mentioned this phenomena as follows: "The living experience of the immanent God is to be found within the fabric of human history. The experience of God in human existence can only be expressed in human terms, for otherwise God (ultimately transcendent) could not be known at all. As a learned rabbi put it in the Talmud: 'We describe God by terms borrowed from his creation, in order to make him intelligible to the human ear'" (*The Problem of War in the Old Testament* [Grand Rapids: Eerdmans, 1978], p. 39).

weh's choosing Israel to be Yahweh's taking Israel as his bride. Since there is no more intimate social metaphor than that of a husband's choosing his bride, it is evident that Yahweh's choosing Israel was considered to be indicative of a close, familial relationship of great import. In addition to this, both a syntactical comparison of the marriage/election formulae and a philological analysis of their Semitic cognates confirm this thesis in detail. With this as a foundation, we can expand our understanding of the related themes of covenant, rejection, remnant, and restoration.

With these same principles, the metaphoric description of the Yahweh-Israel relationship as that of a divine warrior and his levied army (פקד, קרא, בחר), a father and his son (היה ל־, בחר, לקח), a potter and his clay (חיל, ילד, בנה, כון, ברא, עשה, יצר), a master and his servant (עבד), a farmer and his vineyard (שתל, זרע, נטע), a shepherd and his sheep, etc., will be investigated. Thus, chapter I will explore the meaning of election, and this understanding will then be foundational for the subsequent research.

In chapter II, we will consider the development of the election concept throughout biblical history. If my proposal that the election idea sprang from Israel's experiences with Yahweh is correct, then we can trace the historical events which influenced Israel's consciousness of its election by Yahweh. As we determine this, we will also pay attention to the different modes of expression and the varying emphases regarding election, according to the biblical writers. As our subject is confined to "people" only, the election of individuals, kings, places, and cities will not be taken into account. Additionally, the period of the patriarchs, as well as the period following the collapse of Israel as a nation, will not be dealt with here. This section will be mostly exegetical in nature.

Chapter III is closely associated with chapter I. Specifically, the themes of covenant, mission, rejection, remnant, and restoration will be viewed based on what we have found in chapter I. The main emphasis of this portion will be on the continuity of the election idea in the related themes which developed in a later period. We will, thus, find a consistency of theological thought in the mind of ancient Israel.

In the last chapter, the continuity of the themes in the New Testament will be surveyed in order to find out how the New Testament writers took them up and modified and developed them to describe the relationship between God and believers.

Note that for the Hebrew Scripture citations I have followed *BHS*, while the New American Standard Bible (NASB) was used for the English, unless otherwise specified. However, יהוה (the LORD in NASB) is translated as "Yahweh" in order to avoid confusion with אדני, which is rendered as "my lord" or "the Lord" in this book.

CHAPTER I

The Meaning of Election

The election idea is a reflection of the national and theological concerns of the people of Israel throughout their history. Since the people of Israel recognized their exclusive relationship with Yahweh in terms of their national events and then tried to explain these events in their everyday language, the meaning put forth by one generation could be changed and developed by the next generation according to their particular historical experience. Thus we can say that the idea of election arose in a variety of life settings and carries a variety of meanings. The idea of election is not unvaried and fixed; rather it is harmonized and composite. Therefore, the task of this chapter is to determine the various meanings of election and present a picture of the whole.

1. THE TERMS FOR ELECTION

The most common Hebrew words for Yahweh's initiating his relationship with Israel are בחר (to choose), לקח (to take), and היה לי לעם (to be My people). All these are widely recognized as election terms. For the description of an exclusive relationship, ידע (to know), הבדיל (to separate), and הפלה (to make a distinction) are also noteworthy. Sometimes, Yahweh says he made, formed, and created (עשה, יצר, ברא) Israel and even gave birth to (ילד) her. As a metaphorical description, Yahweh says that he planted (שתל, נטע) and sowed (זרע)

Israel. Besides these verbs, certain nouns are also used to portray the image of Yahweh-Israel relations. For example, father-son, master-servant, shepherd-sheep, potter-clay, and farmer-vineyard all occur in this context.

At this point one observation may be made. Figurative expressions are very often employed to describe the idea of election.[1] Even the verbal forms carry metaphorical imageries which describe the Yahweh-Israel relationship. This is mainly because the people of Israel became conscious of their special relationship with Yahweh through their experiential knowledge of him, and they tried to explain it in their everyday language in terms of typical human relationships. Thus, we must carefully examine these metaphorical descriptions and terms.

2. ISRAEL, THE BRIDE OF YAHWEH

In describing the idea of election, i.e., the comprehensive terms denoting the Yahweh-Israel relationship, the biblical writers employ the marriage terms and their related formulae. Yahweh is viewed as a husband and Israel as his wife.[2] Yahweh chooses Israel for his wife and enters into the marriage relationship with her. Yahweh, who as a groom provides totally for his bride, requires faithfulness and loyalty from her. However, the Israelites repeatedly betrayed Yahweh and rebelled against him in following and worshiping foreign gods. For this reason, the prophetic indictment against the Israelites was directed toward this broken relationship. A detailed analysis of the biblical references to the marriage relationship now follows.

1. According to G.E. Wright, "The images or symbols are abstractions of experienced realities by which and within which thinking and action take place" *(The Old Testament and Theology* [New York: Harper & Row, 1969], p. 147).

2. Edmond Jacob also noted out that the marriage union of Yahweh with Israel is an election theme in the OT *(Theology of the Old Testament* [New York and Evanston: Harper & Row, 1958], p. 202).

(1) The Terms for Marriage

In the Bible, several marriage terms are found. Among them, the verbs לקח, בעל, נשא, ידע, ארש, and היה לאשה are considered here as related to the election idea.

1) לקח

Because of its extensive usage, לקח is difficult to analyze and explain. In order to grasp the essential meaning of the term, we are required to look at the original context in which it is used. Conventionally, scholars have taken the verb לקח to mean "to take." However, we are more interested in how the verb came to carry the meaning "to marry." First of all, לקח is in most cases found in a military context. Usually a military campaign reaches its height by the taking (לקח) of land,[3] city,[4] men and people,[5] and various booty,[6] among which women were included. The Israelites were given special commandments with regard to captive women. In Dt. 20:13-14, they were to strike all male opponents in war with the edge of the sword, but were further instructed that:

רק הנשים והטף והבהמה וכל אשר יהיה בעיר כל־
שללה תבז לך ואכלת את־שלל איביך אשר נתן יהוה אלהיך לך:

> Only the women and the children and the animals and all that is in the city, all its spoil, you shall take as booty for yourself; and you shall use the spoil of your enemies which Yahweh your God has given you. (Dt. 20:14; cf. Judg. 5:30)

If an Israelite warrior were to see a beautiful woman among the captives and were to desire her as a wife, he would be permitted to take her after having fulfilled the required procedures (Dt. 21:11-

3. Dt. 3:8; 29:7; Josh. 11:16,23; Judg. 11:13,15.
4. Dt. 3:4; 1 Sam. 7:14; 1 Kgs. 20:34; 22:3; 2 Kgs. 13:25; Amos 6:13; 1 Ch. 2:23; 18:1.
5. Dt. 19:11; Josh. 7:24; 1 Sam. 19:14,20; 2 Sam. 20:3; 2 Kgs. 6:13; 10:7; 15:29; 20:18; 24:12; 25:18,19; 39:7; Jer. 27:20; 31:26; 38:6; 39:5; 40:2; 41:16; 52:24,25,26; Ezek. 16:20; 23:10, 25; Job 1:17; 40:24; 1 Ch. 19:4; 2 Ch. 36:4.
6. Num. 31:11; Judg. 5:19; 8:21; 14:9; 18:17,18,24,27; 1 Sam. 5:1; 26:11,12; 30:16,18; 2 Sam. 8:7,8; 12:30; 1 Kgs. 20:2; 2 Kgs. 24:7; Jer.20:5; Ezek. 22:25; 38:13,25; Zech. 12:9.

11

12). This suggests that taking a wife among the captives was an acknowledged social practice in ancient Israel. Even though the incident of the Benjamite's taking wives from the daughters of Shiloh during feast time is an unusual case in the Bible (Judg. 21:19-24), the dialogue between the tribal leaders illustrates that they had a custom to take (לקח) women as wives in war.

והיה כי־יבאו אבותם או אחיהם לרוב אלינו ואמרנו
אליהם חנונו אותם כי לא לקחנו איש אשתו במלחמה
כי לא אתם נתתם להם כעת תאשמו:

And it shall come about, when their fathers or their brothers come to complain to us, that we shall say to them, "Give them to us voluntarily, because we did not take for each man of Benjamin a wife in battle, nor did you give them to them, else you would now be guilty." (Judg. 21:22)

In the course of taking a wife, a procedure of selection is usually involved. The term לקח itself implies the meaning "to select" or "to choose."

קחו לכם מן־העם שנים עשר אנשים איש־אחד איש־אחד משבט:

Take for yourselves twelve men from the people, one man from each tribe. (Josh. 4:2)

The NASB rendering of קחו, the Qal imperative masculine plural form of לקח, as "take" is not appropriate here. Rather, RSV "choose" or JPS "select" is preferable, since the verb לקח obviously connotes the idea of choosing or selecting the tribal leaders from among the people.[7] Especially in Gen. 6:2 and Dt. 21:11, a man chooses a woman for his wife from among many others according to his own desire.[8]

Another important meaning of לקח is "to have for oneself," "to possess for oneself." In 2 Sam. 24:22-23, David, the king of Israel, wanted to buy a threshing floor from Araunah in order to build an altar there to Yahweh, and so he proposed its sale to him.

ויאמר ארונה אל־דוד יקח ויעל אדני המלך הטוב בעינו
ראה הבקר לעלה והמרגים וכלי הבקר לעצים: הכל
נתן ארונה המלך למלך ויאמר ארונה אל־המלך יהוה אלהיך ירצך:

7. Cf. Gen. 6:21; 32:13; 47:2; Dt. 21:3; 26:2; Judg. 6:25; 1 Sam. 7:9,12; 2 Sam. 3:15; 12:4; 1 Kgs. 18:31; 2 Kgs. 7:14; Is. 44:15; Ezek. 16:16,17; 17:15.
8. According to Rogers's analysis, the twenty occurrences of לקח in the Dead Sea Scrolls generally refer to taking wives ("Doctrine of Election," p. 167).

And Araunah said to David, "Let my lord the king take and offer up what is good in his sight. Look, the oxen for the burnt offering, the threshing sledges and the yokes of the oxen for the wood. Everything, O king, Araunah gives to the king." And Araunah said to the king, "May Yahweh your God accept you."

The verb נתן is suggestive with regard to the meaning of לקח here.[9] Araunah wanted to give the threshing floor to the king so that David would possess (לקח) it for himself. This nuance is found also in Ex. 29:26; Josh. 6:18; 7:1,11, 21; 1 Sam. 15:21; 2 Sam. 19:31 (E.30); 1 Kgs. 20:6; 2 Kgs. 12:6 (E.5). In this usage, לקח is often followed by the preposition ל, designating the one(s) who will take possession.

> יקחו להם הכהנים איש מאת מכרו והם יחזקו את־בדק
> הבית לכל אשר־ימצא שם בדק:

Let the priests take it for themselves, each from his acquaintance; and they shall repair the damages of the house wherever any damage may be found. (2 Kgs. 12:6 [E.5]; cf. Dt. 7:25; 1 Sam. 2:16; 21:19,20; 1 Kgs. 11:31; 1 Ch. 21:23)

The money for the sacred things which was brought into the house of Yahweh could thus be taken by the priests for themselves (להם). The preposition ל usually takes the pronoun of the subject as its object: לי, לו, להם, etc., and it clarifies and emphasizes the meaning of לקח. More than that, it signifies the transference of ownership to the subject. Sometimes, לקח takes the preposition ל twice:

> ואשה אחת מנשי בני־הנביאים צעקה אל־אלישע לאמר
> עבדך אישי מת ואתה ידעת כי עבדך היה ירא את־יהוה
> והנשה בא לקחת את־שני ילדי לו לעבדים:

Now a certain woman of the wives of the sons of the prophets cried out to Elisha, "Your servant my husband is dead, and you know that your servant feared Yahweh; and the creditor has come to take my two children to be his slaves." (2 Kgs. 4:1)

"The creditor took [לקח] my two children to himself for slaves" would be a literal translation. While the transference of ownership is made clear by לו (to himself), the intention of the creditor's act of taking two children is specified by adding לעבדים (for slaves). This syntactical peculiarity (לקח taking double ל) is also applied to

---

9. The parallel usage of נתן and לקח is found in Ezek. 18:8; Hos. 13:11; Ps. 15:5; Job 1:21; 35:7. In Ugaritic, *ytn* and *lqḥ* are also used in parallel. Cf. 2 Aqht VI:18-19 (*CTA* 17.VI.18-19).

the marriage formula and suggests the meaning of marriage as the husband's possessing his wife as his own (as one possesses property).

When לקח takes a woman for an object, it means "to marry" or, infrequently, "to adopt."

ויקח־לו למך שתי נשים שם האחת עדה ושם השנית צלה:

And Lamech took to himself two wives: the name of the one was Adah, and the name of the other, Zillah. (Gen. 4:19)

ויקח עמרם את־יוכבד דדתו לו לאשה

And Amram took to wife Jochebed his father's sister. (Ex. 6:20, RSV)

With reference to adoption, examples are found only in Esther.

ויהי אמן את־הדסה היא אסתר בת־דדו כי אין לה
אב ואם והנערה יפת־תאר וטובת מראה ובמות אביה
ואמה לקחה מרדכי לו לבת:

And he was bringing up Hadassah, that is Esther, his uncle's daughter, for she had neither father nor mother. Now the young lady was beautiful of form and face, and when her father and her mother died, Mordecai took her as his own daughter. (Esth. 2:7; cf. 2:15)

Thus, לקח carries the meanings "to capture," "to select," "to marry," and "to adopt." When it has a person as its object, it establishes a relationship between subject and object. And this term basically carries the meaning of marriage from the perspective of man as the initiator.

According to some, the Akkadian cognate of לקח is *leqû,*[10] which has similar meanings: "to take a wife," "to adopt," and "to take what belong to one."

RN *mārat* RN₂ *ana* DAM-*ut-ti-šu il-te-qè*

Ammistamru took the daughter of Bentešina as his wife.[11]

ša kaspam ana PN *išaqqulu bitam i-lá-qé*

Whoever pays the (owed) silver to PN (the creditor) takes for himself the (pledged) house.[12]

However, the Akkadian *leqû* does not carry the meaning "to select"

10. *HAL*, p. 507.
11. *CAD, L*, 9:137.
12. Ibid., p. 142.

or "to choose." Also, *lqḥ,* the Ugaritic cognate of לקח, shows the same usages as Akkadian *leqû.*

(203) *hm. ḥry. bty* (204) *iqḥ*
aš'rb. ǵlmt (205) *ḥzry.*
ṭnh. wspm (206) *atn.*
w. ṭlṭh. ḥrṣm.

If I may take Huray (into) my house,
introduce the lass to my court,
I will give twice her (weight) in silver
and thrice her (weight) in gold.[13]

(21) *a [ṭt. tq]ḥ ykrt*
aṭt (22) *tqḥ btk*
ǵlmt tš'rb (23) *ḥqrk*
tld šb' bnm lk

The [wife whom you] take o Keret,
the wife whom you take (into) your house,
the lass whom you introduce to your court,
shall bear you seven sons.[14]

Therefore, in Semitic society לקח was used as a marriage term.

Among the many usages of this term in the Hebrew Bible, the most significant one is to describe the idea of Yahweh's election of Israel.

ולקחתי אתכם לי לעם והייתי לכם לאלהים וידעתם כי
אני יהוה אלהיכם המוציא אתכם מתחת סבלות מצרים:

Then I will take you for My people, and I will be your God; and you shall know that I am Yahweh your God, who brought you out from under the burdens of the Egyptians. (Ex. 6:7)

Here לקח obviously describes Yahweh's initiating a relationship with Israel. In Dt. 4:34 this term clarifies the idea of Yahweh's election of Israel.

או הנסה אלהים לבוא לקחת לו גוי מקרב גוי במסת באתת
ובמופתים ובמלחמה וביד חזקה ובזרוע נטויה ובמוראים
גדלים ככל אשר־עשה לכם יהוה אלהיכם במצרים לעיניך:

---

13. *CTA* 14.203-206. J.C.L. Gibson suggests that *iqḥ* is used with the same meaning as לקח in Gen. 24:67 and Ruth 4:11,13 (*Canaanite Myths and Legends* [Edinburgh: T. & T. Clark, 1978], pp. 87-88). The same usage is also found in *CTA* 23.35-36.

14. *CTA* 15. col. ii. 21; Gibson, *Canaanite Myths,* p. 91.

Or has a god tried to go to take for himself a nation from within another nation by trials, by signs and wonders and by war and by a mighty hand and by an outstretched arm and by great terrors, as Yahweh your God did for you in Egypt before your eyes?

The idea of choosing conveyed by לקח becomes clearer in the phrase "from within another nation" (מקרב גוי). This rhetorical question expects the negative answer, for only Yahweh took for himself one nation out of another nation. Yahweh's taking one nation out of another is his divine act of election.

לקח is used for Yahweh's election of an individual as well as of Israel.

ביום ההוא נאם־יהוה צבאות אקחך זרבבל בן־
שאלתיאל עבדי נאם־יהוה
ושמתיך כחותם כי־בך בחרתי נאם יהוה צבאות:

"On that day," declares Yahweh of hosts, "I will take you, Zerubbabel, son of Shealtiel, my servant," declares Yahweh, "and I will make you like a signet ring, for I have chosen you," declares Yahweh of hosts. (Hag. 2:23)

Obviously, לקח and בחר are here used synonymously.

2) בעל

The marriage term בעל supplies a significant meaning in the husband-wife relationship. בעל means "owner" or "possessor," e.g., בעל השור (the owner of an ox; Ex. 21:28), בעל הבור (the owner of a pit; Ex. 21:34), בעל הבית (the owner of a house; Ex. 22:7; Judg. 19:22,23). The Semitic cognates carry the same meaning of the Hebrew: Akkadian *bēlu* (e.g., *bēl bitti*), Ugaritic *b'l* (e.g., *b'l bqr*), and Aramaic *ba'lā'* (e.g., *b'ly rkb*).

In idiomatic usage, the following instances are found. איש בעל שער (a hairy man, 2 Kgs. 1:8), כל־בעל כנף (all the possessors of wings, i.e., all the birds, Prov. 1:17; Ecc. 10:20), האיל בעל הקרנים (the ram, owner of two horns, i.e., the ram that has two horns, Dan. 8:6, 20), and נפש בעלו (the owner of life, Job 31:39; Prov. 23:2).

When בעל is followed by אשה or the feminine pronominal suffix, it means "her owner," i.e., "her husband."

16

אם־בגפו יבא בגפו יצא אם־בעל אשה הוא ויצאה אשתו עמו:

If he comes alone, he shall go out alone; if he is the husband of a
wife, then his wife shall go out with him. (Ex. 21:3)

לא־יוכל בעלה הראשון אשר־שלחה לשוב לקחתה
להיות לו לאשה אחרי

then her former husband who sent her away is not allowed to take
her again to be his wife. (Dt. 24:4)[15]

בעל as a verb carries the meaning "to marry."

לא־יאמר לך עוד עזובה ולארצך לא־יאמר עוד שממה
כי לך יקרא חפצי־בה ולארצך בעולה
כי־חפץ יהוה בך וארצך תבעל:
כי־יבעל בחור בתולה יבעלוך בניך
ומשוש חתן על־כלה ישיש עליך אלהיך:

It will no longer be said to you, "Forsaken,"
Nor to your land will it any longer be said, "Desolate";
But you will be called, "My delight is in her,"
And your land, "Married,"
For Yahweh delights in you;
And to Him your land will be married.
For as a young man marries a virgin,
So your sons will marry you;
And as the bridegroom rejoices over the bride,
So your God will rejoice over you. (Is. 62:4-5; cf. Dt. 24:1)

בעל also has the meanings "to rule" as a verb and "ruler" or
"lord" as a noun (Num. 21:28; Is. 16:8; 26:13; 1 Ch. 16:8).

ויוקים ואנשי כזבא ויואש ושרף אשר־בעלו למואב
וישבי לחם והדברים עתיקים:

And Jokim, the men of Cozeba, Joash, Saraph, who ruled in Moab,
and Jashubi-lehem. And the records are ancient. (1 Ch. 4:22)

According to the verb בעל, the marriage relationship implies
that a husband becomes the owner of the woman he took, and she
becomes the possession of her husband. By marriage a husband
becomes a ruler, master, and owner of his wife.[16] The husband is

15. Cf. 2 Sam. 11:26; Esth. 1:17,20; Prov. 31:11,23,28.
16. R. de Vaux, *Ancient Israel,* 2 vols. (New York: McGraw-Hill, repr. 1965),
1:26.

17

called בעל of the wife just as he is בעל of house or field. The Decalogue lists a wife among a man's possessions, along with his servants, his ox, and his ass (Ex. 20:17).[17]

In speaking of marriage as ownership, however, Millar Burrows, following Koschaker, pointed out that the wife was not meant to be her husband's property in exactly the same sense that a slave or an animal is his property. According to him, the husband's "ownership" of his wife was determined by the wife's place and function in the family. Beyond this, the husband's power did not go. He could not, for example, sell his wife to another man or put her to death, though he could divorce her if she did not fulfil her function as a wife for him.[18] However, a woman did not inherit her husband's property[19] and she could not ask for a divorce.[20] Thus, we can say that a wife was never merely a possession; rather, she was a special possession, special property of her husband. A wife's status in the family was very peculiar.

In relation to this, however, the verb קנה draws our special attention essentially to the nature of Hebrew marriage. In Ruth 4:10, Boaz said: וגם את־רות המאביה אשת מחלון קניתי לי לאשה (I have also acquired Ruth the Moabitess, Mahlon's widow, as my wife). Here, קנה seems to suggest that the Israelites practiced a form of marriage by purchase. L. Ginzberg and J.N. Epstein examined the usage of קנה and קדש and substantiated the presence of the practice of marriage by purchase in biblical times as well in post-biblical times.[21] David Halivni Weiss further defined the use of קנה in marriage contexts:

Hence, the technical term for betrothal in the Bible is ארש, and for marriage נשא, לקח אשה. However, when marriage (or betrothal) is discussed in conjuction with salable object (like the belongings of Eli-

17. Ibid., p. 39.

18. Millar Burrows, "The Ancient Oriental Background of Hebrew Levirate Marriage," *BASOR* 76 (Dec. 1939): 8.

19. Baruch A. Levine, "In Praise of the Israelite *Mišpāḥâ:* Legal Themes in the Book of Ruth," in *The Quest of the Kingdom of God: Studies in Honor of George E. Mendenhall,* ed. H.B. Huffmon et al. (Winona Lake: Eisenbrauns, 1983), p. 103.

20. R. de Vaux, *Ancient Israel*, 1:35.

21. J.N. Epstein, *Prolegomena Ad Litteras Tannaiticas* (Hebrew) (1957), pp. 53, 414.

melech, etc., or the field of Naomi), biblical Hebrew, just as Mishnaic, uses a term which will embrace the latter [קדש] as well; hence, the term קניתי in Ruth 4:10.[22]

If we are correct in concluding that there is a concept of ownership in marriage, we can safely say that by marriage the husband proclaimed his ownership of the woman to others, and he entered into a state of exercising ownership over her. He became her בעל. Therefore, M.A. Friedman suggests that the reconstructed marriage proclamation pronounced by the groom on the wedding day was as follows: היא אשתי ואנכי בעלה, or היא אשתי ואנכי אישה (She is my wife, and I am her husband). Evidence for this is found in the Aramaic Jewish marriage documents from Elephantine (הי אנתתי ואנה בעלה מן יומא זנה ועד עלם:, "She is my wife and I am her husband from this day forth and forever").[23] This could be said to be a proclamation of lordship of the husband over his wife. In this respect, marriage was a legal contract which required a witness.

Not only in the Bible but also in the Akkadian marriage texts this ownership concept is found. When Ereshkigal was threatened by Nergal, she pleaded for her life and said,

Attā lū mutīma anāku lū aššatka . . .
Attā lū bēlu anāku lū bēltu.

You are my husband, I will be thy wife . . .
Be thou master, I will be thy mistress. (EA 375:82-85)

Here the husband-wife and master-mistress terms constitute parallelisms, and the latter expand the meaning of the former.

However, it is noteworthy that בעל is used for the Yahweh-Israel relationship.

והיה ביום־ההוא נאם־יהוה
תקראי אישי ולא־תקראי־לי עוד בעלי:

"And it will come about in that day," declares Yahweh,
"That you will call Me Ishi

---

22. David Halivni Weiss, "The Use of קנה in Connection with Marriage," *HTR* 57 (1964): 248.
23. Mordechai A. Friedman, "Israel's Response in Hosea 2:17b: 'You are my Husband,'" *JBL* 99/2 (1980): 199-204.

And will no longer call Me Baali." (Hos. 2:18 [E.16])[24]

ואנכי בעלתי בם נאם־יהוה:

"Although I was a husband to them," declares Yahweh. (Jer. 31:32b)

כי בעליך עשיך יהוה צבאות שמו
וגאלך קדוש ישראל אלהי כל־הארץ יקרא:

For your husband is your Maker,
Whose name is Yahweh of hosts;
And your Redeemer is the Holy One of Israel,
Who is called the God of all the earth. (Is. 54:5)[25]

נשא (3

נשא means "to take away," "to carry away."

ושכבתי עם־אבתי ונשאתני ממצרים וקברתני בקברתם
ויאמר אנכי אעשה כדברך:

"but when I lie down with my fathers, you shall carry me out of Egypt and bury me in their burial place." And he said, "I will do as you have said." (Gen. 47:30)[26]

Sometimes it can mean "to bring."

וישאו אתו על־הסוסים ויקבר בירושלם עם־אבתיו בעיר דוד:

Then they brought him on horses and he was buried at Jerusalem with his fathers in the city of David. (2 Kgs. 14:20)

However, when the term is used for marriage, it has the same meaning as לקח.

וישאו להם נשים מאביות שם האחת ערפה ושם השנית
רות וישבו שם כעשר שנים:

---

24. Both *Ishi* (אשי) and *Baali* (בעלי) mean "my husband." See below, pp. 137-38, for the exposition of this verse.

25. See also Jer. 3:14.

26. Cf. Gen. 45:27; 46:5; 50:13; 1 Sam. 10:3; 18:12; 2 Kgs. 4:20; Is. 40:11,24; 41:16; 57:13; Hos. 1:6; 5:14; 1 Ch. 10:12.

And they took for themselves Moabite women as wives; the name of
the one was Orpah and the name of the other Ruth. And they lived
there about ten years. (Ruth 1:4)[27]

Therefore, marriage connotes the idea of carrying or taking a
woman away. Marriage involved the woman's moving from the
house of her father to her husband's house. In marriage, either a
man actually went to bring back the girl he wanted (Ex. 2:1), or he
sent a messenger to her on his behalf (Ex. 24:1; Judg. 14:3; 1 Sam.
25:25-39).

ויעבר האבל וישלח דוד ויאספה אל־ביתו ותהי־לו
לאשה ותלד לו בן וירע הדבר אשר־עשה דוד בעיני יהוה:

When the time of mourning was over, David sent and brought her to
his house and she became his wife; then she bore him a son. But the
thing that David had done was evil in the sight of Yahweh.
(2 Sam. 11:27)

Thus, in describing the marriage event the verbs הלך, בוא, and אסף
(2 Sam. 11:27) are frequently used with the same meaning as נשא.

It is noteworthy that Yahweh's bringing of Israel to the land of
Canaan is explained in terms of this marriage concept.[28]

ולקחתי אתכם לי לעם והייתי לכם לאלהים וידעתם
כי אני יהוה אלהיכם המוציא אתכם מתחת סבלות מצרים:
והבאתי אתכם אל־הארץ אשר נשאתי את־ידי לתת אתה
לאברהם ליצחק וליעקב ונתתי אתה לכם מורשה אני יהוה:

Then I will take you for My people, and I will be your God; and you
shall know that I am Yahweh your God, who brought you out from

27. Cf. Ezr. 9:2,12; 10:44; Neh. 13:25; 2 Ch. 11:21; 13:21; 24:3.
28. נשא is rarely used for describing the Yahweh-Israel relationship in terms
of marriage. Even Hos. 1:6 shows ambiguity.

ותהר עוד ותלד בת ויאמר לו קרא שמה לא רחמה כי
לא אוסיף עוד ארחם את־בית ישראל כי־נשא אשא להם:

Then she conceived again and gave birth to a daughter.
And Yahweh said to him, "Name her Lo-ruhamah, for I
will no longer have compassion on the house of Israel,
that I should ever forgive them."

LXX reads נשא אשא as αντιτασσόμενος αντιτάξομαι (I will surely set myself
in array against [them]), and BHS has proposed to read שנא אשנא (I surely hate
them). However, I propose that it is possible to translate it as "I am indeed married
to them."

21

under the burdens of the Egyptians. And I will bring you to the land which I swore to give to Abraham, Isaac, and Jacob, and I will give it to you for a possession; I am Yahweh. (Ex. 6:7-8)

Obviously verse 7 announces Yahweh's election using the marriage term לקח. In verse 8, the Hiphil form of בוא clearly connotes the marriage concept in his bringing Israel to the promised land.

In Jer. 3:14, this imagery is further developed.

שובו בנים שובבים נאם־יהוה כי אנכי בעלתי בכם ולקחתי
אתכם אחד מעיר ושנים ממשפחה והבאתי אתכם ציון:

"Return, O faithless sons," declares Yahweh;
"For I am a master to you,
And I will take you one from a city and two from a family,
And I will bring you to Zion." (Jer. 3:14)

Here "faithless sons" (בנים שובבים) clearly refers to Israel. Thus, the Yahweh-Israel relationship is viewed in terms of the father-son relation. However, in the next clause this relationship is changed into that of husband-wife. The rendering of בעלתי as "husband" makes more sense than as "master."[29]

Thus, Yahweh's bringing Israel from Egypt to Canaan and Israel's following him in the desert (הלך אחרי, Jer. 2:2-3)[30] may possibly be viewed from the perspective of marriage.

הושיב (4

The Hiphil form of ישב is used to denote the idea "to marry." However, this usage is found only in Ezra and Nehemiah.

ולכם הנשמע לעשת את כל־הרעה הגדולה הזאת למעל
באלהינו להשיב נשים נכריות:

Do we then hear about you that you have committed all this great

---

29. "master" in RSV, NASB, and TEV. However, JPS reads בעלתי as בחלתי and renders it as "I rejected." This reading has no textual proof and entirely misconstrues the text. Cf. Dt. 1:31; 32:11; Ezek. 3:14; 11:24.

30. See Michael DeRoche, "Jeremiah 2:2-3 and Israel's Love for God during the Wilderness Wandering," *CBQ* 45 (1983): 364-76.

evil by acting unfaithfully against our God by marrying foreign women? (Neh. 13:27)[31]

Primarily, the Hiphil form of ישׁב bears the meaning "to settle."

ויושׁב יוסף את־אביו ואת־אחיו ויתן להם אחזה בארץ
מצרים במיטב הארץ בארץ רעמסס כאשׁר צוה פרעה:

So Joseph settled his father and his brothers, and gave them a posses-sion in the land of Egypt, in the best of the land, in the land of Rameses, as Pharaoh had ordered. (Gen. 47:11)

From this we can see that marriage implies the meaning "to pro-vide a domicile for a woman." Marriage can be understood in terms of settling a woman in a permanent place. Gen. 24:67 gives us our clearest illustration, even though the specific term ישׁב is not used.

ויבאה יצחק האהלה שׂרה אמו ויקח את־רבקה
ותהי־לו לאשׁה ויאהבה וינחם יצחק אחרי אמו:

Then Isaac brought her into his mother Sarah's tent, and he took Rebekah, and she became his wife; and he loved her; thus Isaac was comforted after his mother's death.

We can also find the same concept in the Canaanite and Egyp-tian literatures. In Canaanite mythology, for example, marriage is portrayed as a woman's going into the man's house.

tn nkl y (18) *rḥ ytrḫ.*
ib t'arbm bbh (19) *th.*
watn mhrh la (20) *bh.*

Give Nikkal (that) Yarikh may marry (her),
(give) Ib (that), she may enter into his mansion;
and I will give as her bride-price to her father. . . (*CTA* 24.17-20)[32]

---

31. Cf. Neh. 13:23; Ezr. 10:2,10,14,17,18. Acording to H.G.M. Williamson, following T. Witton Davies, this term is applied only to mixed marriage. Thus, the women whom the Israelites had living with them were harlots, not wives (*Ezra, Nehemiah,* Word Biblical Commentary [Waco, Texas: Word Books, 1985], p. 185). However, the contexts never say so, neither were their children called "sons of harlotry" (ילדי זנונים) as in Hos. 1:2. If the women were harlots and their children sons of harlots, Nehemiah would not have rebuked them, beat them, and pulled out their hair because they could not understand Hebrew (Neh. 13:25).

32. The translation is from Gibson, *Canaanite Myths,* p. 128.

In Egypt, marriage is referred to simply as the woman's founding of a house (*grg pr*) or entering into the partner's house (*'qr pr*).[33]

When Yahweh is the subject of ישב, as a Hiphil form in most cases, he causes Israel to dwell in the land of Canaan (1 Sam. 12:8), in cities (2 Kgs. 17:24,26; Ezek. 36:33; 54:3; 2 Ch. 8:2), and in houses (Hos. 11:11; 12:10; Lev. 23:43).

5) ידע

Generally, ידע has been rendered as "to know." The objects of ידע cover almost all areas of knowledge and information. Strictly speaking, it is not a marriage term. However, it is a relationship term. When used with regard to people, it denotes the concept of a personal and close relationship. Especially with regard to man and woman or husband and wife, the term describes the sexual relation, i.e., the most intimate human relation.

וישכמו בבקר וישתחוו לפני יהוה וישבו ויבאו אל־
ביתם הרמתה וידע אלקנה את־חנה אשתו ויזכרה יהוה:

Then they arose early in the morning and worshiped before Yahweh, and returned again to their house in Ramah. And Elkanah had relations with Hannah his wife, and Yahweh remembered her.
(1 Sam. 1:19)[34]

Sometimes the meaning of ידע also describes the special relationship between Yahweh and his favored one.

כי ידעתיו למען אשר יצוה את־בניו ואת־ביתו אחריו
ושמרו דרך יהוה לעשות צדקה ומשפט למען הביא יהוה
על־אברהם את אשר־דבר עליו:

For I have chosen him, in order that he may command his children and his household after him to keep the way of Yahweh by doing righteousness and justice; in order that Yahweh may bring upon Abraham what He has spoken about him. (Gen. 18:19)

The NASB here renders ידע as "to choose." Speiser renders the term

33. See C.J. Eyre, *JEA* 69 (1983): 92-105.
34. Cf. Gen. 4:17,25; 19:8; 24:16; Num. 31:17,18,35; Judg. 11:39; 19:22,25; 21:11,12; 1 Kgs. 1:4.

24

with the similar idea of "to single out."[35] Hence, ידע implies the notion of Yahweh's predestination of Abraham.

The call narrative of Jeremiah begins with the description of Yahweh's foreknowing the prophet before he was even formed in his mother's womb.

בטרם אצורך בבטן ידעתיך ובטרם תצא מרחם
הקדשתיך נביא לגוים נתתיך:

Before I formed you in the womb I knew you, and before you were born I consecrated you; I have appointed you a prophet to the nations. (Jer. 1:5)

In this verse, ידעתיך, הקדשתיך, and נתתיך are all synonymous and delineate Yahweh's choice of Jeremiah for the office of prophet.

But Yahweh's ידע is not limited to the individual as in the case of Abraham and Jeremiah. Yahweh knew (ידע) Israel exclusively.

רק אתכם ידעתי מכל משפחות האדמה
על־כן אפקד עליכם את כל־עונתיכם:

You only have I known of all the families of the earth: therefore I will punish you for all your iniquities. (Amos 3:2, KJV)

Consequently, Yahweh asks Israel to know him only.

ואנכי יהוה אלהיך מארץ מצרים
ואלהים זולתי לא תדע ומושיע אין בלתי:

Yet I have been Yahweh your God
Since the land of Egypt;
And you were not to know any god except Me,
For there is no savior besides Me. (Hos. 13:4)

And so, Hosea exhorts his people to know Yahweh alone.

ונדעה נרדפה לדעת את־יהוה כשחר נכון מוצאו
ויבוא כגשם לנו כמלקוש יורה ארץ:

So let us know, let us press on to know Yahweh.
His going forth is as certain as the dawn;
And He will come to us like the rain,
Like the spring rain watering the earth. (Hos. 6:3)

One should note, however, that *idû,* the Akkadian cognate of

---

35. E.A. Speiser, *Genesis,* AB (Garden City: Doubleday, 1964), p. 133.

ידע, does not carry the same meaning as its Hebrew counterpart.[36]

6) היה לאשה

The verb היה itself does not denote the idea of marriage. It simply means "to be" or "to become." However, with the help of the preposition ל, the phrase היה לאשה can mean "to marry."

וגם־אמנה אחתי בת־אבי הוא אך לא בת־אמי ותהי־לי לאשה:

Besides, she actually is my sister, the daughter of my father, but not the daughter of my mother, and she became my wife. (Gen. 20:12)

ונתן האיש השכב עמה לאבי הנער חמשים כסף ולו
תהיה לאשה תחת אשר ענה לא־יוכל שלחה כל־ימיו:

Then the man who lay with her shall give to the girl's father fifty shekels of silver, and she shall become his wife because he has violated her; he cannot divorce her all his days. (Dt. 22:29)

36. H.B. Huffmon proposes that *idû* was used as a technical term for (legal) recognition in international treaties and related texts, and as an analogy he goes on to say that ידע is used in the Bible in the sense of recognition of a binding treaty or covenant stipulation. Therefore, he tries to explain the concept of covenant in the Bible from the perspective of an ancient Near Eastern treaty only ("The Treaty Background of Hebrew ידע," *BASOR* 181 [Feb. 1966]: 31-37). However, the biblical covenant is also understood in terms of a marriage contract, and ידע is mostly used in the Bible's linguistic field for the intimate male-female relationship within marriage. Therefore, one of the basic differences between the usage of Hebrew ידע and that of Akkadian *idû* is that the latter does not carry the meaning of sexual relationship. As for "knowing" sexually in Akkadian, *lamādu* (to know sexually) is used. Even though *idû* is used with reference to mutual legal recognition on the part of a suzerain and his vassal in the ancient Near Eastern texts, ידע does not imply any mutual legal force in the Bible. Though Huffmon explains his proposal from Gen. 18:19, 2 Sam. 7:20, and Jer. 1:5, the context of these verses does not fit with his assertion. These verses are related more with Yahweh's election of Abraham, David, and Jeremiah. And in the phrase "You have been in rebellion against Yahweh from the day He knew you" (Dt. 9:24), "from the day He knew you" does not necessarily mean "from the time Israel entered into covenant with Yahweh," as Huffmon suggests. Even before Yahweh made the covenant on Mount Sinai, Israel was rebellious. The indictment of Yahweh against Israel in Amos 3:2 and Hos. 13:4 is not to be understood with reference to a legal binding. Rather it must be viewed from the perspective of Yahweh's exclusive love relationship with Israel and Israel's betrayal of him, as the larger context of Hosea shows. The Yahweh-Israel relationship is not always a suzerain-vassal relationship. Therefore, "knowing Yahweh" does not always mean "to know Yahweh of the covenant" in its legal sense. The Yahweh-Israel relationship is a personal and intimate one, as that of husband and wife.

The sentence containing היה is usually combined with the sentence containing the marriage term לקח or בעל, and it explains the later development of a man's "taking" (לקח) a woman, i.e., into the marriage status. The subject of לקח is man and the subject of היה is woman in the marriage formula.

ואת־אחינעם לקח דוד מיזרעאל ותהיין גם־שתיהן לו לנשים:

David had also taken Ahinoam of Jezreel, and they both became his wives. (1 Sam. 25:43; cf. Gen. 24:67; Dt. 24:4; 1 Sam. 25:40,41; 2 Sam. 12:10; Ruth 4:13)

והסירה את־שמלת שביה מעליה וישבה בביתך
ובכתה את־אביה ואת־אמח ירח ימים ואחר כן
תבוא אליה ובעלתה והיתה לך לאשה:

She shall also remove the clothes of her captivity and shall remain in your house, and mourn her father and mother a full month; and after that you may go in to her and be her husband and she shall be your wife. (Dt. 21:13)

A similar formula is also used in the marriage proclamation: "You are my wife" and "you are my husband,"[37] which was used in Aramaic marriage contracts from Elephantine.

הי אנתתי ואנה בעלה מן יומא זנה ועד עלם:

She is my wife and I her husband from this day forever.[38]

Reuven Yaron suggests that this kind of formula was used in Babylon in an advanced form in the later period.[39] An equivalent formula is also found in Tob. 7:11, where Sarah's father says to Tobias: "Henceforth thou art her brother and she is thy sister." Similarly, in a contract of the second century after Christ found in the Judean desert, the formula is "Thou shall be my wife."[40]

Here we are not to disregard the fact that the usage of this phrase is also applied to the Yahweh-Israel relationship.

ולקחתי אתכם לי לעם והייתי לכם לאלהים
וידעתם כי אני יהוה אלהיכם המוציא אתכם
מתחת סבלות מצרים:

37. See Mordechai A. Friedman, *JBL* 99/2 (1980): 199-204.
38. *BMAP*, 7:4; cf. 2:4, 14:3-4; *AP*, 15:4.
39. Reuven Yaron, "Aramaic Marriage Contracts from Elephantine," *JSS* 3/1 (1958): 30-31.
40. R. de Vaux, *Ancient Israel*, 1:33.

Then I will take you for My people, and I will be your God; and you shall know that I am Yahweh your God, who brought you out from under the burdens of the Egyptians. (Ex. 6:7)

Again in Hos. 2:25 (E.23), the phrase of the marriage proclamation is directly applied to Yahweh and Israel.

וזרעתיה לי בארץ ורחמתי את־לא רחמה ואמרתי
ללא־עמי עמי־אתה והוא יאמר אלהי׃

And I will sow her for Myself in the land.
I will also have compassion on her who had not
  obtained compassion,
And I will say to those who were not My people,
"You are My people!"
And they will say, "Thou art my God!"

7) ארש

Generally, ארש is rendered as "to betroth" or "to be engaged."

ומי־האיש אשר־ארש אשה ולא לקחה ילך וישב
לביתו פן־ימות במלחמה ואיש אחר יקחנה׃

And who is the man that is engaged to a woman and has not married her? Let him depart and return to his house, lest he die in the battle and another man marry her. (Dt. 20:7)

וכי־יפתה איש בתולה אשר לא־ארשה ושכב עמה
מהר ימהרנה לו לאשה׃

If a man seduces a virgin who is not engaged, and lies with her, he must pay a dowry for her to be his wife. (Ex. 22:15[E.16]; cf. Dt. 22:23,25,27,28; 28:30; 2 Sam. 28:30)

In Hos. 2:21-22 (E. 19-20), this term is used for Yahweh.

וארשתיך לי לעולם
וארשתיך לי בצדק ובמשפט ובחסד וברחמים׃
וארשתיך לי באמונה וידעת את־יהוה׃

And I will betroth you to Me forever;
Yes, I will betroth you to Me in righteousness and in justice,
In lovingkindness and in compassion,
And I will betroth you to Me in faithfulness.
Then you will know Yahweh.

28

For וארשתיך לי, H.W. Wolff proposes another possible rendering: "I will make you my own." He understands this word as denoting "the legal act constituting marriage."[41]

8) Other Terms

The verbs קנה (Ruth 4:10)[42] and נתן (Judg. 21:7; 2 Kgs. 14:9; 2 Ch. 25:18) are also sometimes used in the marriage context.

From a consideration of the above marriage terms, we can draw the following conclusions about marriage in the Bible. Marriage implies the man's physical possession of the woman. By marriage a man acquired the ownership of his wife and became her master and ruler. In marriage, the man usually took the initiative, going to the woman's house and bringing her into his house. Thus, marriage for the woman entailed moving from her father's house to her husband's. When a husband brought his wife to him, he had to provide for her all the necessities of home. A wife was her husband's peculiar possession. What is significant here is that all these marriage terms and concepts are used to describe the existing relationship between Yahweh and Israel.

(2) The Marriage Formulae

The Hebrew syntax denoting the establishment of the marriage relationship between male and female is somewhat unusual. It is not expressed with just one word, directly, as in English or other languages, but composite expressions are used. This then constitutes the characteristic marriage formulae. Among the marriage terms, the verb לקח is dominant and is most closely related to the election idea and its formulae. In the Bible four kinds of marriage formulae are found.

41. Wolff, *Hosea*, Hermeneia (Philadelphia: Fortress, 1974), p. 46 n. h. According to Wolff, the Piel form of ארש "marks the end of the premarital status, . . . in that it denotes the act of paying the bridal price (מהר), thus removing the last possible objection the bride's father might raise." Therefore, he distinguishes this term from לקח and שגל. Especially in these verses, the threefold occurrence of the term "solemnly attests to the binding, legal act of marriage."

42. See above, pp. 10-11.

1) Formula I

X לקח (X) את־Y Z

{X: man; Y: name of woman; Z: a wife (אשה)}

ויקח אשה את־איזבל בת־אתבעל מלך צידנים

that he married Jezebel the daughter of Ethbaal king of the Sidonians (1 Kgs. 16:31; cf. 7:63)

{אשה :Z, איזבל בת־אתבעל מלך צידנים :Y ;ויקח :לקח X}

As a modification of this formula, either Y or Z is omitted.

[1] The Omission of Y

ויקח דויד עוד נשים בירושלם

Then David took more wives at Jerusalem (1 Ch. 14:3)[43]

{נשים :Z ;דויד :X}

[2] The Omission of Z

וילך איש מבית לוי ויקח את־בת־לוי:

Now a man from the house of Levi went and married a daughter of Levi. (Ex. 2:1)[44]

{בת־לוי :Y ;ויקח :לקח X}

2) Formula II

לקח(X)־ל'X X את־Y Z

{X: man; X': the pronoun of X; Y: name of woman; Z: אשה}

Formula II can be distinguished by adding the preposition ל and its object X', usually the pronoun of X.

ויקח־לו רחבעם אשה את־מחלת בן־ירימות בן־דויד
אביהיל בת־אליאב בן־ישי:

Then Rehoboam took as a wife Mahalath the daughter of Jerimoth

43. See also Gen. 25:1; 27:46; 28:1; 31:50; 36:2; Lev. 20:14; 17:21; 21:7,13,14; Num. 12:1; Dt. 22:13,14; 24:1,5; 2 Sam. 5:13; Ezr. 2:61.
44. See also Gen. 11:29; 26:34; 2 Kgs. 3:1; 2 Ch. 11:20; Hos. 1:3; Neh. 6:18.

the son of David and Abihail the daughter of Eliab the son of Jesse.
(2 Ch. 11:18)

מחלת בן־ירימות בן־דויד אביהיל בת־אליאב בן־ישי :Y, לו :X'ל, רחבעם :X};
{אשה :Z

The omissions of Y (Gen. 4:19; 28:2,6; Judg. 19:1; Hos. 1:2) and Z
(1 Ch. 2:19; Neh. 10:31; Gen. 34:16) are also found in modification
of this formula.

A third person could take a woman on behalf of someone else.

וישב במדבר פארן ותקח־לו אמו אשה מארץ מצרים:

And he lived in the wilderness of Paran; and his mother took a wife
for him from the land of Egypt. (Gen. 21:21)[45]

נשא is also used in this formula (Ruth 1:4; Ezr. 9:2).

3) Formula III

X לקח (X) את־Y ל'X ל Z
{X: man; X': the pronoun of X; Y: name of woman; Z: אשה}

This is characterized by the double preposition ל. לZ defines the
relationship between X and Y.

ויהי יצחק בן־ארבעים שנה בקחתו את־רבקה בת־
בתואל הארמי מפדן ארם אחות לבן הארמי לו לאשה:

And Isaac was forty years old when he took Rebekah, the daughter
of Bethuel the Aramean of Paddan-aram, the sister of Laban the
Aramean, to be his wife. (Gen. 25:20)

רבקה בת־בתואל הארמי מפדן ארם אחות לבן הארמי :Y; יצחק :X};
{אשה :Z; לו :X'ל

למה אמרת אחתי הוא ואקח אתה לי לאשה ועתה הנה אשתך קח ולך:

Why did you say, "She is my sister," so that I took her for my wife?
Now then, here is your wife, take her and go. (Gen. 12:19)[46]

---

45. See also Gen. 24:3,4,7,37,38,40,48; Ex. 34:16; Jer. 29:6; 1 Ch. 7:15.
46. See also Gen. 34:4,21; Ex. 6:20,23,25; Dt. 21:11; 25:5; Judg. 3:6; 1 Sam.
25:39,40; 2 Sam. 5:9; Ezek. 44:22.

Again, the omission of ל'X is found as a modification of this formula.

אחימעץ בנפתלי גם־הוא לקח את־בשמת בת־שלמה לאשה:

Ahimaaz, in Naphtali (he had taken Basemath the daughter of Solomon as his wife). (1 Kgs. 4:15, RSV)

{X: הוא, אחימעץ; Y: בשמת בת־שלמה; Z: אשה}

The subject of the verb לקח can also be a third person, other than a husband, who takes a woman on behalf of his/her son.

ויעל ויגד לאביו ולאמו ויאמר אשה ראיתי בתמנתה
מבנות פלשתים ועתה קחו־אותה לי לאשה:

So he came back and told his father and mother, "I saw a woman in Timnah, one of the daughters of the Philistines; now therefore, get her for me as a wife." (Judg. 14:2)

4) Formula IV

X לקח את־Y ותהי־ל'X ל Z

{X: man; X': the pronoun of X; Y: name of woman; Z: אשה}

This formula is characterized by the use of two verbs (לקח and היה), with the conjunction ו connecting the two sentences.

ויבאה יצחק האהלה שרה אמו ויקח את־רבקה ותהי־
לו לאשה ויאהבה וינחם יצחק אחרי אמו:

Then Isaac brought her into his mother Sarah's tent, and he took Rebekah, and she became his wife; and he loved her; thus Isaac was comforted after his mother's death. (Gen. 24:67)[47]

Sometimes, the infinitive form of היה, להיות, is replaced by ותהי. Thus, the formula becomes X לקח את־Y להיות ל'X ל Z.

ועתה לא־תסור חרב מביתך עד־עולם עקב כי בזתני
ותקח את־אשת אוריה החתי להיות לך לאשה:

Now therefore, the sword shall never depart from your house, because you have despised Me, and have taken the wife of Uriah the Hittite to be your wife. (2 Sam. 12:10; cf. 24:4)

47. See also 1 Sam. 25:43; Ruth 4:13.

The rare Hebrew syntactical peculiarity in which בעל takes this formula (Dt. 21:13) provides us with a deeper understanding of the marriage concept and of customs in biblical society. As we observed before, these formulae show, first of all, the development of Hebrew syntax. לקח carries the meaning of possession by either agreement or capture. In these cases, the choosing or selecting process is involved. By adding the preposition ל to the verb לקח the action of taking is limited and clarified. Usually the subject of the verb (לקח) takes the object for himself (לו). The concept of ownership and possession is implied in it. The addition of one more preposition (ל) explains the relationship between the subject and the object, the taker and the taken.

Surprisingly enough, this syntactical peculiarity in the Hebrew language is also employed in the election formulae. In Dt. 4:34, marriage formula II is employed in describing Yahweh as the incomparable God.

או הנסה אלהים לבוא לקחת לו גוי מקרב גוי במסת

Or has a god tried to go to take for himself a nation from within another nation by trials.

Marriage formula III (Z לֹ X'ל Y־את לקח X) is found in Ex. 6:7 in describing the Yahweh-Israel relationship.

ולקחתי אתכם לי לעם והייתי לכם לאלהים וידעתם כי
אני יהוה אלהיכם המוציא אתכם מתחת סבלות מצרים:

Then I will take you for my people, and I will be your God; and you shall know that I am Yahweh your God, who brought you out from under the burdens of the Egyptians.
{X: Yahweh [לקח X: ולקחתי]; Y: Israel [את: אתכם]; X'ל: לו; Z לֹ: לעם}

Marriage formula IV (Z לֹ X'ל להיות Y־את לקח X) occurs in Dt. 4:20.

ואתכם לקח יהוה ויוצא אתכם מכור הברזל ממצרים
להיות לו לעם נחלה כיום הזה:

But Yahweh has taken you and brought you out of the iron furnace, from Egypt, to be a people for His own possession, as today.
{X: יהוה; Y: אתכם; X'ל: לו; Z: עם נחלה}

This term and formula are used not only for the election of the people but also for the election of the Levites and other specific individuals.[48] Therefore, we can say that the election formulae are basically derived from the marriage formulae.

However, the Z elements (אשה and עם) in the formulae need explanation as to how they agree with each other in their respective meanings. In both formulae, the Z elements supply the meaning or purpose of X's taking Y. A woman was taken to be the wife of a man, the special possession of her husband. Then what does עם mean to Yahweh in the election formulae? First of all, the concept of "wife" is directly applied to the election formulae.

שובו בנים שובבים נאם־יהוה כי אנכי בעלתי בכם
ולקחתי אתם אחד מעיר ושנים ממשפחה והבאתי אתכם ציון:

"Return, O faithless sons," declares Yahweh;
"For I am a master [בעל] to you,
And I will take you one from a city and two from a family,
And I will bring you to Zion." (Jer. 3:14)

The first part of Jer. 3 deals with Yahweh's indictment against Israel's harlotry. In 3:8, Yahweh said that he sent Israel away and gave her a writ of divorce because of all her adulteries. Thus, the rendering of בעל in verse 14 as "husband" is more plausible than "master" (NASB).

In Is. 54:5, Israel is more explicitly mentioned as "a wife of Yahweh."

כי בעליך עשיך יהוה צבאות שמו
וגאלך קדוש ישראל אלהי כל־הארץ יקרא:

For your husband is your Maker,

48. For the Levites,

כי נתנים נתנים המה לי מתוך בני ישראל תחת פטרת
כל־רחם בכור כל מבני ישראל לקחתי אתם לי:

For they [the Levites] are wholly given to Me from among the sons of Israel. I have take them for Myself instead of every first issue of the womb, the first-born of all the sons of Israel. (Num. 8:16; cf. 8:9)
{לי:י'ל'X; אתם :Y; לקחתי :X לקח}

And for individuals,

ועתה כה־תאמר לעבדי לדוד כה אמר יהוה צבאות
אני לקחתיך מן־הנוה מאחר הצאן להיות נגיד על־עמי על־ישראל:

Now therefore, thus you shall say to My servant David, "Thus says Yahweh of hosts, 'I took you from the pasture, from following the sheep, that you should be ruler over My people Israel.'" (2 Sam. 7:8)
{(לקחתי)ך :X; לקח :X לקחתי; Y: אני :X}

Whose name is Yahweh of hosts;
And your Redeemer is the Holy One of Israel,
Who is called the God of all the earth.

This idea is also richly displayed in Hosea.

However, עַם must be specifically defined in order to grasp the election idea clearly. According to R.M. Good, the noun *'m(m)* designates the flock in terms of early Semitic development.[49] However, he proposes that we are to understand it in multiple perspectives (that is, as a nomadic company, a war alliance, a community of faith, a kinship concept, etc.) if we are to portray accurately Israel's concept of "people." Good maintains that a single key will not unlock the rich meaning of this word in the Bible,[50] and with this we agree. Thus, we must examine the context in which the term is used in order to grasp its proper meaning.

When Yahweh sent Moses to the Israelites to deliver them, Yahweh called them "my people."

ועתה לכה ואשלחך אל־פרעה והוצא את־עמי בני־ישראל ממצרים:

Therefore, come now, and I will send you to Pharaoh, so that you may bring My people, the sons of Israel, out of Egypt. (Ex. 3:10)

The Israelites were already constituted as a people in the land of Egypt while they served Pharaoh. However, they were Pharaoh's possession, for he owned them. Then through Moses Yahweh claimed his ownership over and above Pharaoh's: "Let My people go!" (Ex. 5:1; 7:4,16,26; 8:4,16,18; 9:1,13; 10:3,4). Yahweh desired to take Pharaoh's slaves for himself to be his people. Against this claim, Pharaoh replied, "Who is Yahweh that I should obey his voice to let Israel go? I do not know Yahweh, and besides, I will not let Israel go" (5:2). Pharaoh did not recognize Yahweh's ownership over the people of Israel. Furthermore, Pharaoh used the same genitive case "my" for the people of Egypt (9:27; 14:6) as Yahweh did when he made a distinction between the two peoples—My people and your people (8:23; 9:14). This suggests that the citizens were the property of a king in ancient societies (cf. Ex. 21:33,34,35; 24:14; Josh. 7:5; 8:1,16,20,33; Judg. 5:11;11:18,20,21; 1 Sam. 9:16,17; 14:20; 15:1; 30:4, etc.). Therefore, in the election

49. Robert M. Good, *The Sheep of His Pasture: A Study of the Hebrew Noun 'Am(m) and Its Semitic Cognates,* HSM 29 (Chico: Scholars Press,1983), p. 142.
50. Ibid., p. 145.

formulae the Z element is amplified to specify this meaning of "possession" or "property," as in עם נחלה (Dt. 4:20; 1 Kgs. 8:53) and עם סגלה (Dt. 7:6; 14:2; 26:18; cf. Ex. 19:5; Mal. 3:17; Ps. 135:4).

נחלה is often derived from the verb נחל, which means "to possess."[51]

מעט מעט אגרשנו מפניך עד אשר תפרה ונחלת את־הארץ:

I will drive them out before you little by little, until you become fruitful and take possession of the land. (Ex. 23:30)[52]

In many cases, נחל also denotes the idea "to inherit" and נחלה as a noun denotes "inheritance." Israel as the people of Yahweh was to inherit the land (Num. 26:55; 34:29; Dt. 3:28; 12:10; 19:3; 31:7; Josh. 13:32; 14:1; 19:51), territories (Josh. 14:1; 13:32), cities (Num. 35:8; Ps. 69:36), honor (1 Sam. 2:8), and testimony (Ps. 119:111).

The Ugaritic cognate *nhlt* appears not only in economic texts, where its apparent meaning is akin to the tribal concept "patrimony," but also in mythological texts, where it assumes a cosmic dimension. The realm of the god Mot is described as *arṣ nhlt* (the land of his possession),[53] and Sapan, Baal's holy mountain of sanctuary, is called *ǵr nhlty* (the mountain of my possession).[54] Thus, from the marriage point of view it would be more desirable to render עם נחלה as "the people of possession" than as "the people of inheritance."[55]

סגלה ("valued property," "peculiar treasure") has basically the same meaning as נחלה. According to Rogers's research, סגלה is always used in the Hebrew Bible to refer to the elect group only, but נחלה is not.[56] The Akkadian cognate *sug/kulu* carries the meaning

---

51. For the semantic development of נחלה as a biblical term expressing land tenure, see Baruch A. Levine, "Late Language in the Priestly Source: Some Literary and Historical Observations," *Proceedings of the Eighth World Congress of Jewish Studies, Panel Sessions, Biblical Studies and Hebrew Language* (Jerusalem, 1983), pp. 69-82.

52. Cf. Ex. 34:9; Ps. 69:36; 82:8; Zech. 2:16.

53. *CTA* 4.VIII.13-14.

54. *CTA* 3.III.27.

55. However, when we think of עם נחלה from the perspective of Yahweh-Israel as a father-son relationship, "the people of inheritance" would be more desirable, because Israel was the people of Yahweh who were to inherit his land. See below, pp. 58-65.

56. Rogers, "Doctrine of Election," p. 108.

of "herd."[57] In ancient Near Eastern nomadic society, the herd or flock would be counted as valuable property. Therefore, we can safely say that עם נחלה and עם סגלה are used with the same meaning in the election formulae to specify the Z element (לעם) and carry the concept of property or possession. Accordingly, we can draw the conclusion that the election formulae employed exactly the same terms, the same meanings, and the same formulae as those used in marriage. This enables us to understand the theology of election in the Hebrew Bible in the light of the marriage customs and traditions in biblical society.

(3) The Marriage Relationship in Israel

The character of the husband-wife relationship in the Bible must be properly understood in order to appreciate fully the Yahweh-Israel relationship. The essential character of this relationship can be explained through the concept of the possessor and the possessed.

Once a woman was taken, she was to call her taker "husband" (בעל, Hos. 2:18 [E.16]; Gen. 20:3; Ex. 21:3,22; Lev. 21:4; Dt. 22:24; 24:4; 2 Sam. 11:26; Joel 1:18), and she was to be called by the name of her husband (Is. 4:1). As they entered into the marriage relationship, the husband was to love his wife, and not surprisingly, אהב is the love term used in most cases within this context (Gen. 24:67; 29:18,30,32; Judg. 14:16; 16:15; 1 Sam. 1:15; 1 Kgs. 11:1; Esth. 2:17). The husband "went into his wife" in order "to know her."[58] קרב

57. *AHw*, 2:1053 f; cf. 1 Ch. 29:3; Eccl. 2:8; Mal. 3:17. See also Moshe Greenberg, "Hebrew *segullā*: Akkadian *sikiltu*," *JAOS* 71 (1951): 172-74. Greenberg discussed the word סגלה against its Near Eastern background.

58. The phrases here "to go in to her" and "to know her" carry the meaning "to have sexual relation." בוא אליה means "to enter a woman's tent (or room)." In Judg. 15:1, when Samson visited his wife and said to his father-in-law, אבאה אל־ אשתי החדרה ולא־נתנו אביה לבוא ("'I will go in to my wife in her room.' But her father did not let him enter"). Boling renders this verse as "Let me go in to my bride! Into the bridal chamber!" (R.G. Boling, *Judges*, AB [Garden City: Doubleday, 1975], p. 234). Jacob's story gives us a more explicit context. After seven years of service, Jacob approached his uncle, Laban. ויאמר יעקב אל־לבן הבה את־אשתי כי מלאו ימי ואבואה אליה ("Then Jacob said to Laban, 'Give me my wife, for my time is completed, that I may go in to her'" [Gen. 29:21]). E.A. Speiser suggests rendering בוא here as "united with," "cohabited with" *(Genesis*, pp. 44, 225). Thus, בוא is used to describe the action of the bridegroom entering into the bedroom where his bride awaits him the evening of the wedding day. The same usage is found in Gen. 6:4; 16:2; 29:23; 30:3,16; 38:8,9,16; 39:14; Dt. 22:13; Judg. 16:1; 2 Sam. 12:24; 16:21; 20:3; Ezek. 23:44; Prov. 6:29.

also carries the same meaning as בוא (Is. 8:3). ידע is more direct in expressing the relations than בוא, and is used in most cases within the marriage.[59] Thus, ידע is followed by הרה (to conceive) and ילד (to give birth to).

והאדם ידע את־חוה אשתו ותהר ותלד את־קין ותאמר
קניתי איש את־יהוה:

Now the man had relations with his wife Eve, and she conceived and give birth to Cain, and she said, "I have gotten a man with the help of Yahweh." (Gen. 4:1)

A wife was responsible for bearing children for her husband. This was especially true in regard to the bearing of a son, which was considered a primary obligation in this matter.

ושרי אשת אברם לא ילדה לו ולה שפחה מצרית ושמה הגר:

Now Sarai, Abram's wife had borne no children, and she had an Egyptian maid and her name was Hagar. (Gen. 16:1)

לא ילדה לו suggests that Sarai had an obligation to bear children for Abram, but she could not. This was the reason why Sarai took the initiative in solving this problem, giving her maid to Abram.

ותלד הגר לאברם בן ויקרא אברם שם־בנו אשר־ילדה הגר ישמעאל:

So Hagar bore Abram a son; and Abram called the name of his son, whom Hagar bore, Ishmael. (Gen. 16:15)

Hagar bore a son to (or, for) Abraham (cf. Gen. 16:16). Here we can clearly see the implication that a woman should bear children for her husband out of duty or obligation. Y ל ילדה בן X (X has borne a son to Y) is one of the the frequent phrases suggesting the responsibility of the woman as a wife.[60] If she was barren, she had to get a woman for her husband.[61]

59. שכב is used to denote sexual relationships mostly outside marriage and between illegal partners in the Bible (Gen. 19:32,34,35; 26:10; 34:2,7; 35:22; 39:7,12,14; Ex. 22:15; Dt. 22:22; 2 Sam. 11:4,11; 12:11,24; 13:11,14).
60. Only in Genesis, 22:23; 24:24,47; 25:3; 34:1; 41:50; 44:27; 46:15,20.
61. According to E.A. Speiser, this custom is found in a text from Nuzi. "If Gilimninu bears children, Shennima shall not take another wife. But if Gilimninu fails to bear children, Gilimninu shall get for Shennima a woman from the Lullu country (i.e., a slave girl) as concubine. In that case, Gilimninu herself shall have authority over the offspring" *(HSS* V [1929], No. 67; for translation see *AASOR* 10 [1930]: 31ff.; cf. Speiser, *Genesis,* p. 120).

Another important obligation required of the woman was "faithfulness." She was not allowed to know (ידע) another man. The Seventh Commandment prohibits adultery (Ex. 20:14; Dt. 5:18). In Lev. 20:10 (cf. 18:20),

ואיש אשר ינאף את־אשת איש אשר ינאף את־אשת
רעהו מות־יומת הנאף והנאפת:

If there is a man who commits adultery with another man's wife, one who commits adultery with his friend's wife, the adulterer and the adulteress shall surely be put to death.

Capital punishment was imposed upon the couple who committed adultery. When some indecency was found in his wife, a man could divorce her by writing a certificate of divorce and sending her out from his house.

כי־יקח איש אשה ובעלה והיה אם־לא תמצא־חן בעיניו
כי־מצא בה ערות דבר וכתב לה ספר כריתת ונתן
בידה ושלחה מביתו:

When a man takes a wife and marries her, and it happens that she finds no favor in his eyes because he has found some indecency in her, and he writes her a certificate of divorce and puts it in her hand and sends her out from his house. (Dt. 24:1)

Here, ערוה, derived from the verb ערה (Piel, to lay bare), is the term for improper behavior, usually related to the woman.[62] When Judah was informed that his daughter-in-law, Tamar, played the harlot and bore a child by her harlotry, he commanded that she be brought out and burned (Gen. 38:24). A Levite's concubine who played the harlot went away from her husband to her father's house in Bethlehem (Judg. 19:2). Her flight perhaps highlights her fear of punishment. Therefore, for a married woman to play the harlot was almost unthinkable in biblical society.[63] Perfect loyalty to her husband was required and it was considered the virtue of a wife. In this connection, the case of Gomer, the wife of Hosea, will be discussed in detail later.[64]

---

62. Cf. Lev. 18:6,7,8,9,10,17,18,19,20,21; Dt. 23:15; 1 Sam. 20:30; Is. 20:4; Ezek. 22:10.
63. F.I. Andersen and D.N. Freedman, *Hosea,* AB (Garden City: Doubleday, 1980), pp. 158-59,161.
64. See Chap. II below, pp. 131-38.

(4) Yahweh Takes Israel for His Bride

The biblical writers illustrated the theme of election through the analogy of the human marriage relationship. They employed the marriage terms and marriage formulae to explain the relationship between Yahweh and Israel. Thus, the Hebrew verb לקח plays an important role in denoting the idea of election.

When Moses returned from his first encounter with Pharaoh, the Israelites were very angry at him and blamed him for their hardships at the hand of their Egyptian taskmasters. With a frustrated heart Moses went into the presence of Yahweh. In this meeting, having introduced himself as the God of Abraham, Isaac, and Jacob, Yahweh explained his great plan to redeem Israel from the bondage of Egypt (Ex. 6:1-6). And he said,

ולקחתי אתכם לי לעם והייתי לכם לאלהים וידעתם כי
אני יהוה אלהיכם המוציא אתכם מתחת סבלות מצרים:

Then I will take you for My people, and I will be your God; and you shall know that I am Yahweh your God, who brought you out from under the burdens of the Egyptians. (Ex. 6:7)

Yahweh was about to take the Israelites for his people so as to become their God. For this purpose, Yahweh would deliver the people of Israel from Egypt and settle them in Canaan. Here, we can observe that the marriage term לקח and the marriage formula III (X לקח את־Y לי X ל Z) are employed. These facts force us to conclude that Yahweh's election of Israel was itself a marriage between Yahweh and Israel. Yahweh as a bridegroom took the initiative in taking Israel to be his bride. Furthermore, Is. 54:5 explicitly proclaims that "your husband is your Maker, whose name is Yahweh of hosts."

From this perspective, the exodus and conquest are to be perceived as follows: Yahweh, the bridegroom, went (Dt. 4:34) and brought his bride, Israel, to his place, Canaan, and settled her there (Dt. 4:37,38; Ex. 15:13). Yahweh took Israel to be his own and to exercise his lordship over her. Thus, the prophet Jeremiah understands the covenant between Yahweh and Israel on Mount Sinai as the establishment of a marriage relationship between them.

הנה ימים באים נאם־יהוה וכרתי את־בית ישראל
ואת־בית יהודה ברית חדשה: לא כברית אשר כרתי
את־אבותם ביום החזיקי בידם להוציאם מארץ מצרים
אשר־המה הפרו את־בריתי ואנכי בעלתי בם נאם־יהוה:

"Behold, days are coming," declares Yahweh, "when I will make a new covenant with the house of Israel and with the house of Judah, not like the covenant which I made with their fathers in the day I took them by the hand to bring them out of the land of Egypt, My covenant which they broke, although I was a husband to them," declares Yahweh. (Jer. 31:31-32)

In these verses, the covenant which he made with their fathers in the day he took them by the hand to bring them out of the land of Egypt, and which was now broken, clearly points to the Sinai covenant in Ex. 24:6-8. The translation of the phrase ואנכי בעלתי בם as "then I was a husband to them" is more correct than as "although I was their Lord."[65] Thus, Yahweh as a bridegroom took Israel for himself to be his bride at the time of the making of the covenant. Also, Jeremiah's words show that he understood the making of the covenant on Mount Sinai as a wedding ceremony between Yahweh and Israel in terms of establishing and sealing the relationship.[66] Ezekiel also understands the Sinai covenant as a marriage covenant between Yahweh and Israel.[67]

Based on this special relationship, a moral principle was established and an ethical responsibility was consequently demanded of Israel. They were commanded neither to have other gods before Yahweh (Ex. 20:1,2,23) nor to worship or serve them (Ex. 20:5; Dt. 6:14). Yahweh's zealousness (Ex. 20:5; 34:14; Dt. 4:24; 5:9; 6:15) and anger or wrath are basically rooted in and derived from this relationship. As a husband, Yahweh both promised and provided the land in which Israel was to dwell, thereby giving them food to eat, prosperity to enjoy, and security and protection from their enemies. Conversely, he required absolute loyalty and faithfulness from his bride.

However, Israel was not faithful to Yahweh, her husband. This is the reason why one of the central themes of the prophetic message is the indictment of Israel's adultery and of her playing the harlot. In Ex. 23:32-33, the Israelites were prohibited from making

65. John Bright translates it "though I was their Lord." However, he suggests as a possible translation "though I was a husband to them" *(Jeremiah,* AB [Garden City: Doubleday, 1965], p. 283). In this sentence, the conjunction ו also carries an important meaning. Rendering it as "then" (i.e., at the time of making the covenant) is much more acceptable than as "although" or "though." See BDB, p. 253.

66. Jewish tradition also understands the giving of the Law on Mount Sinai as the "Day of Espousals"; *Song of Songs* R. 3.11.2.

67. Ezek. 16:1-14. See Chap. II below, pp. 141-44, for the explanation of this phrase.

a covenant with the Canaanite gods because this would lead them
to sin against Yahweh, and would prove to be a snare to them. After
the Israelites made the golden calf they were told to tear down their
altars, smash their sacred pillars, and cut down their Asherim
(34:13):

פן־תכרת ברית ליושב הארץ וזנו אחרי אלהיהם
וזבחו לאלהיהם וקרא לך ואכלת מזבחו:
ולקחת מבנתיו לבניך וזנו בנתיו אחרי אלהיהן
והזנו את־בניך אחרי אלהיהן:

lest you make a covenant with the inhabitants of the land and they
play the harlot with their gods, and sacrifice to their gods, and someone invite you to eat of his sacrifice; and you take some of his daughters for your sons, and his daughters play the harlot with their gods,
and cause your sons also to play the harlot with their gods.

(Ex. 34:15-16)

Here, Israel's worship of other gods is equated with playing the harlot since they had already entered into the marriage relationship
with Yahweh. Without a commitment to a legal marriage bond, no
one could accuse anyone of adultery or harlotry.

Numbers 25:1-9 deals with another case of Israel's betrayal of
the marriage bond.

While Israel remained at Shittim, the people began to play the harlot
with the daughters of Moab. For they invited the people to the sacrifices of their gods, and the people ate and bowed down to their
gods. So Israel joined themselves to Baal of Peor, and Yahweh was
angry against Israel. (Num. 25:1-3)

The Israelites played the harlot with the daughters of Moab and
this led them to join in the worship of Baal of Peor.[68] This incident
incurred the anger of Yahweh and 24,000 Israelites were slain by
the priests, the sons of Aaron, and by the plague of Yahewh. In the
book of Judges, all Israel played the harlot with an ephod that Gideon made (8:27), and after his death "the sons of Israel again played
the harlot with the Baals and made Baal-berith their god" (8:33).

68. The title resembles a number of divine titles found in Phoenician inscrip-
tions and in the Old Testament. However, the nature of the cult of Ba'al Pe'or is
not much known. G.B. Gray suggests that "local Ba'als . . . were worshiped as the
beneficent sources of fertility, with agricultural festivals and often with immoral
rites" (A Critical and Exegetical Commentary on Numbers, ICC [Edinburgh:
T. & T. Clark, 1903], p. 382).

This theme of adultery is understood more comprehensively by the prophets Hosea, Jeremiah, and Ezekiel. Hosea explicitly compares his tragic marriage with the harlot Gomer to that of Yahweh's marriage with the harlot Israel. God commands Hosea to name his son "Lo-ammi [לֹא עַמִּי], for you are not My people and I am not your God" (Hos. 1:9). Yahweh seems to have in mind the election of Israel as a marriage and the rejection of them as a divorce. According to Friedman, this is a modification of the divorce formula.[69] Since Israel had broken the bond of marriage by playing the harlot, they were no longer to be called the people of Yahweh.

Recalling the "honeymoon" period enjoyed by Yahweh and Israel, Jeremiah accuses both Israel and Judah of faithlessness.

וָאֵרֶא כִּי עַל־כָּל־אֹדוֹת אֲשֶׁר נִאֲפָה מְשֻׁבָה יִשְׂרָאֵל
שִׁלַּחְתִּיהָ וָאֶתֵּן אֶת־סֵפֶר כְּרִיתֻתֶיהָ אֵלֶיהָ וְלֹא יָרְאָה
בֹּגֵדָה יְהוּדָה אֲחוֹתָהּ וַתֵּלֶךְ וַתִּזֶן גַּם־הִיא:

And I saw that for all the adulteries of faithless Israel, I had sent her away and given a writ of divorce, yet her treacherous sister Judah did not fear; but she went and was a harlot also. (Jer. 3:8)

The fall of the northern kingdom and its exile to Assyria are compared to a divorced woman who was driven out of the house because of her faithlessness to her husband (cf. Dt. 24:1-2).

סֵפֶר כְּרִיתוּת (a writ of divorce) suggests the essential nature of divorce. כְּרִיתוּת seems to come from the verb כרת (to cut) and appears only in Dt. 24:1,2; Is. 50:1; and Jer. 3:8. In the Bible, כרת is not only used for making a covenant but also for breaking the marriage treaty. Good extensively researched the penalty of כרת.[69] According to him, "to be cut off from one's 'ammîm" (as a Niphal form) was used as a penalty clause in the cultic community with the meaning: "to be eradicated from the community of Yahweh's worshippers." Thus, Yahweh's writing of a certificate of divorce for those who played the harlot by worshiping other gods can be understood in terms of corresponding retribution, i.e., eradicating them from the community of Yahweh's worshipers and sending them away from his presence.

Ezekiel's indictment against Israel for playing the harlot comes from a somewhat different angle.

69. Mordechai A. Friedman, *JBL* 99/2 (1980): 199-204.
69. Robert M. Good, *Sheep of His Pasture*, pp. 85-90.

And you poured out your harlotries on every passer-by who might be willing. (16:15ᵇ)

You also played the harlot with the Egyptians, your lustful neighbors, and multiplied your harlotry to make Me angry. (16:26)

Moreover, you played the harlot with the Assyrians because you were not satisfied; you even played the harlot with them and still were not satisfied. (16:28)

Thus you are different from those women in your harlotries, in that no one plays the harlot as you do, because you give money and no money is given you; thus you are different. (16:34)

Israel's harlotry was indiscriminate, unceasing, and voluntary, but never satisfying in character. Ezekiel extends the concept of playing the harlot from Israel's worship of other gods to her dependence on her neighboring countries for military defense. The Israelites did not absolutely depend on Yahweh, but they sought shelter from Assyria and Egypt. Ezekiel saw this as playing the harlot, a behavior which revealed their contempt for the lordship of their בעל, Yahweh. Israel should have requested the military help from Yahweh of hosts, their God.

The concept of the restoration of Israel is also noteworthy. Yahweh's restoration of Israel is described by the metaphor of remarriage. In Hos. 2:16-25 (E.14-23), Yahweh calls Israel and takes her back after his rejection.[70]

As we have seen, the idea of election is portrayed by that of the most intimate human relationship: marriage terms, wording, and syntax in the Hebrew Bible are those of human marriage and married life. Therefore, we must understand the doctrine of election from the perspective of the marriage customs in biblical society.

3. ISRAEL, THE LEVIED ARMY OF YAHWEH

It is not surprising that the idea of election also arose from Israel's confrontations with the surrounding countries, since Yahweh as Israel's national God always played a very important role in the his-

---

70. See the details in Chap. III below, pp. 292-296.

tory of Israel's wars.[71] The Hebrew terms for "to choose," בחר, קרא, and פקד, are found in the context of war in the Old Testament. Yahweh, as a warrior, levied Israel as his army and engaged in cosmic wars against pagan gods. Thus, Yahweh was always understood as being intimately involved in the Israelites' wars, fighting on their behalf. Through these war experiences the Israelites realized the peculiarity of their relationship with Yahweh. It is, therefore, significant that election terms are derived from military terminology. This aspect leads us to examine these war terms in order to grasp clearly the concept of election.

(1) The Terms for War

We do not need to examine here all the words related to war. Instead we will focus on those war terms whose words carry the meaning of election (to choose, to call, to appoint, to gather together, etc.).

בחר (1

בחר is regarded as one of the most important terms representing the theology of election in the Hebrew Bible. The root and its derivatives occur 198 times. בחר is mostly understood to mean "to choose," "to select."

However, בחר in many cases is found in the context of war with the meaning "to levy" or "to recruit (soldiers)." After the Exodus, when Israel was to fight for the first time against Amalek at Rephidim, Moses commanded Joshua:

ויאמר משה אל־יהושע בחר־לנו אנשים וצא הלחם
בעמלק מחר אנכי נצב על־ראש הגבעה ומטה האלהים בידי:

So Moses said to Joshua, "Choose men for us, and go out, fight against Amalek. Tomorrow I will station myself on the top of the hill with the staff of God in my hand." (Ex. 17:9)

According to Moses' commandment, Joshua as a field marshal was to choose soldiers from among the Israelites to meet Amalek in battle. The choice of a man by the leader was the process by which

71. Cf. G.E. Wright, *The Old Testament and Theology,* pp. 121-22.

the chosen would be sent into the battle. This was usually done after a general summoned his troops to war. Pharaoh (Ex. 15:4), Moses (Ex. 18:25), Joshua (Josh. 8:3), Saul (1 Sam. 17:1), Joab (2 Sam. 10:9; 1 Ch. 19:10), and Ahithophel (2 Sam. 17:1) are said to have chosen soldiers for war.

The Akkadian cognate of Hebrew בחר is *beḫēru* or *bêru*.[72] According to *CAD*, *beḫēru* means "to select," "to levy (troops)."[73]

> *ultu* MN *adi* MN₂ *rab bīti ina Akkadi bi-ḫir-ti ib-te-ḫir*

from Ajaru until Ṭebētu the *rab bīti*-official levied troops in Akkad.

bêru is also rendered "to select" or "to choose [men for a military purpose]."[74]

> *u mundaḫṣī ēpiš qabli u tāḫazi . . . [aḫ]īt a-bir-ma ana kiṣir šarrūtija akṣur*

I looked over and selected fighters, combat troops, and organized them into my royal regiment.

The Ugaritic *beḫru* was also used as a military term with the meaning of "an elite soldier."[75] From the above usages, it is obvious that בחר was understood as a military term in ancient Near Eastern societies.

The point which we would like to make from this observation is that this sense of בחר as selecting and choosing is extended to the theological concept of election.

> כי עם קדוש אתה ליהוה אלהיך בך בחר יהוה אלהיך
> להיות לו לעם סגלה מכל העמים אשר על־פני האדמה:

For you are a holy people to Yahweh your God; Yahweh your God has chosen you to be a people for His own possession out of all the peoples who are on the face of the earth. (Dt. 7:6)

The interesting point to be noted here is that בחר takes the same syntax as לקח. And בך בחר יהוה אלהיך להיות לו לעם סגלה is identical

---

72. *HAL*, p. 115. See also Horst Seebass, "בָּחַר (*bāchar*)," *TDOT*, 2:74. The Egyptian word *stp* and Akkadian *(w)atû* also carry the meaning of choosing. However, both terms seem to be particularly associated with divine royal election, but *bêru* is never used to describe divine royal election. Thus, *stp* and *(w)atû* do not closely approximate the meaning and usage of בחר. See B.E. Shafer, "The Root *bhr* and Pre-Exilic Concepts of Chosenness in the Hebrew Bible," *ZAW* 89 (1977): 23.

73. *CAD, B,* 2:186.

74. Ibid., p. 212.

75. Rép Mari 193.

with the marriage formula (X: לו :ל'X ;לו :ל' ;Z :לעם ;Y־את: בך ;יהוה אלהיך
סגלה) except for the variation of verb and preposition.[76] This usage
is found in Dt. 14:2; 1 Sam. 2:28; Ps. 33:12; 135:4; 1 Ch. 28:4,6; 2
Ch. 6:6. In Ps. 78:70, בחר and לקח are used with same meanings and
are interchangeable.

ויבחר בדוד עבדו ויקחהו ממכלאת צאן:

He also chose David His servant, and took him from the sheepfolds.

The Z element in the election formula (לעם סגלה) which defines the
relationship between X (the chooser) and Y (the chosen) is identical with that of the marriage formula meaning "possession."

In relation to בחר, עם is also used in similar terms in the Semitic
cognates. R. M. Good proposed that in Epigraphic South Arabian
a "people" (*'mm*) carries the signification of "muster," and *'amma*
carries the meaning "to levy troops," denoting a militia.[77] In sum-
marizing his findings about *'mm* in the Semitic cognates, he writes:

> Particularly interesting is the extent to which the noun is linked to
> martial contexts. In virtually all of the Semitic languages in which
> the noun occurs it seems that it can designate a group with military
> obligations, whether those obligations be conceived as an encum-
> brance of kingship, as in Arabic, or whether the group itself is a
> militia, as in Phoenician.[78]

Thus, we can see that בחר and עם are used in the same linguistic
field in the area of war.

בחר is used not only for the election of a people but also for the
election of a priest (1 Sam. 2:28), as well as for the choosing of
David (1 Ch. 28:4; 2 Ch. 6:6) and Solomon (1 Ch. 28:6).

One of the significant usages of this verb is that in many cases
בחר is followed by love terms, such as אוה, חפץ, רחם, חמד, חשק, אהב,
and רצה, which supplement the reason for Yahweh's election of
Israel.[79]

(a) אהב *(to love)*

ותחת כי אהב את־אבתיך ויבחר בזרעו אחריו ויוצאך
בפניו בכחו הגדל ממצרים:

76. In many cases ב, like את, is used to introduce the object in Biblical Hebrew, e.g., רעה בצאן (Gen. 37:2), "קרא ב (Gen. 13:4). See *GKC*, pp. 379-80.

77. Robert M. Good, *Sheep of His Pasture*, p. 32. Note Akkadian *Ummanu*
(people or troop).

78. Ibid., p. 42.

79. See also G. E. Wright, *The Old Testament Against Its Environment*, SBT
1/2 (London: SCM, 1968), pp. 46,49.

Because He loved your fathers, therefore He chose their descendants after them. And He personally brought you from Egypt by His great power. (Dt. 4:37; cf. Dt. 10:15; Is. 41:8; 43:4; Mal. 1:2; Ps. 47:5; 78:68)

The reason for the election of Israel was the deep love of Yahweh for Israel's ancestors.

(b) חשק (to love, to desire)

לא מרבכם מכל־העמים חשק יהוה בכם ויבחר בכם
כי־אתם המעט מכל־העמים:

Yahweh did not set His love on you nor choose you because you were more in number than any of the peoples, for you were the fewest of all peoples. (Dt. 7:7)

Here, the progressive line of thought between חשק and בחר is seen. Yahweh's setting his love upon Israel resulted in his choosing Israel. חשק can be understood as a synonym of בחר in this context.[80] This is more clear in Dt. 10:15.

רק באבתיך חשק יהוה לאהבה אותם ויבחר בזרעם
אחריהם בכם מכל־העמים כיום הזה:

Yet on your fathers did Yahweh set His affection to love them, and He chose their descendants after them, even you above all peoples, as it is this day.

(c) חמד (to desire, to find pleasure in)

כי יבשו מאילים אשר חמדתם
ותחפרו מהגנות אשר בחרתם:

Surely, you will be ashamed of the oaks which you have desired, and you will be embarrassed at the gardens which you have chosen.

(Is. 1:29)

Here, the same idea is repeated through the same structural pattern in order to emphasize the future condition of the subject (you). Therefore, יבשו (or, following some Heb. Mss and the Targum: תבשו) and תחפרו, מאילים and מהגנות, חמדתם and בחרתם are parallel components. Furthermore, חמדתם and בחרתם are used synonymously to convey the same idea.

---

80. According to Leonard J. Coppes, חשק emphasizes that which attaches to something or someone; in the case of emotions it is that love which is already bound to its object ("חשק," *TWOT,* 1:332).

(d) רחם *(to show love for, to have compassion on)*

כי ירחם יהוה את־יעקב ובחר עוד בישראל והניחם
על־אדמתם ונלוה הגר עליהם ונספחו על־בית יעקב:

When Yahweh will have compassion on Jacob, and again choose Israel, and settle them in their own land, then strangers will join them
and attach themselves to the house of Jacob. (Is. 14:1)

Out of compassion, Yahweh will again choose and restore Jacob.

(e) אוה *(to be lovely)*

כי־בחר יהוה בציון אוה למושב לו:

For Yahweh has chosen Zion; He has desired it for His habitation.
(Ps. 132:13; cf. Dt. 18:6)

אוה is the reason for Yahweh's choosing (בחר) Zion.

(f) רצה *(to be pleased with)*

הן עבדי אתמך־בו בחירי רצתה נפשי
נתתי רוחי עליו משפט לגוים יוציא:

Behold, My servant, whom I uphold, My chosen one in whom My
soul delights. I have put My Spirit upon Him; He will bring forth
justice to the nations. (Is. 42:1; cf. 1 Ch. 28:4)

רצה is closely related to בחר. בחירי is the delight (רצתה) of his soul.

(g) חפץ *(to take pleasure in, to desire)*

כי־כה אמר יהוה
לסריסים אשר ישמרו את־שבתותי
ובחרו באשר חפצתי ומחזיקים בבריתי:

For thus says Yahweh, "To the eunuchs who keep My sabbaths, and
choose what pleases Me, and hold fast My covenant." (Is. 56:4)

חפץ[81] is also closely related to בחר. Usually Israel chooses what can
not please Yahweh (Is. 66:3-4; 65:12).

As we have observed, the usage of בחר is very striking in view of the
accompanying love terms which explain the reason for בחר. The
reason for Yahweh's election of Israel is not found in Israel herself;

81. The basic meaning is to feel great favor toward an object. The subject is
easily attracted to it because it is desirable. The object solicits favor by its own
intrinsic qualities. See Leon J. Wood, "חפץ," *TWOT,* 1:310-11.

rather it is the sovereign grace of Yahweh. Out of his love, compassion, desire, and delight, Israel was chosen. There was no merit in Israel herself to be chosen as his own.

In relation with בחר, בחור is noteworthy. According to B.E. Shafer, בחיר is a title denoting some such status as "first among the equals in the ranks of Yahweh's covenantal warriors." Thus, a military prince (נגיד), Saul, was chosen by Yahweh and possibly called בחיר and his warriors איש בחור (tribal militia). In the same way, Shafer said, David the בחור became David the בחיר.[82]

II-קרא, I-קרא (2

Whereas קרא-I means "to call," "to name," or "to cry out," קרא-II, a by-form of קרה, is an important military term meaning "to meet" or "to encounter."

After Gideon and his 300 men attacked the Midianite camp and the army of the Midianites fled as far as Beth-Shittah, he summoned the men of Israel.

> ומלאכים שלח גדעון בכל־הר אפרים לאמר רדו
> לקראת מדין ולכדו להם את־המים עד בית ברה ואת־הירדן

And Gideon sent messengers throughout all the hill country of Ephraim, saying, "Come down against Midian and take the waters before them, as far as Beth-barah and the Jordan. (Judg. 7:24)

Here, רדו לקראת מדין must be translated as "come down to meet (or to encounter) Midian." When קרא is used as a military term, usually it takes a Qal infinitive form and follows the verb implying the meaning of coming and going: יצא (Gen. 14:17; Num. 20:18,20; 21:23,33; Dt. 1:44; 2:32; 3:1; 29:6; Josh. 8:5,14; Judg. 4:18,22; 20:25,31; 1 Sam. 4:1; 2 Kgs. 9:21; 2 Ch. 35:20; Jer. 41:6), עלה (Judg. 6:35), ילד (Judg. 7:24), ערך (1 Sam. 4:2; 17:2,21; 2 Sam. 10:9,10,11, 17), הלך and קרב (1 Sam. 17:48; 1 Kgs. 20:27; 2 Kgs. 10:15; 16:10; 23:29), and רוץ (1 Sam. 17:48). Thus, קרא describes the scene of the army coming out and forming in array to confront the enemy.

However, קרא-I is also another important election term, carrying the meaning "to choose," "to appoint," and "to call." The book of Numbers begins with the command of Yahweh to take a census

82. B.E. Shafer, *ZAW* 89 (1977): 37.

of all the congregation of the sons of Israel. In this census, every male from twenty years old and upward who was able to go out to war in Israel was to be counted for their armies (1:3). After listing the name of each tribal leader (vv. 5-15), verse 16 reads:

אלה קריאי העדה נשיאי מטות אבותם ראשי אלפי ישראל הם:

These are they who were called of the congregation, the leaders of their fathers' tribes; they were the heads of divisions of Israel. (Num. 1:16; cf. Num. 26:9)

In preparation for war, a census was taken, and war leaders for each tribe were appointed. Thus, we see that קרא carries the meaning of "to appoint" or "to elect."

In Hosea and Isaiah, קרא is used for Yahweh's election of Israel.

כי נער ישראל ואהבהו וממצרים קראתי לבני:

When Israel was a youth I loved him, and out of Egypt I called My son. (Hos. 11:1)

קרא here gives the impression of Yahweh's deliverance of Israel from Egypt, but לבני, the adoption term, forces us to understand this term in the context of election.[83] Is. 41:9 provides further evidence for the understanding of this usage.

אשר החזקתיך מקצות הארץ ומאציליה קראתיך
ואמר לך עבדי-אתה בחרתיך ולא מאסתיך:

You whom I have taken from the ends of the earth, and called from its remotest parts, and said to you, "You are My servant, I have chosen you and not rejected you."

Here, קראתיך, החזקתיך and בחרתיך bear the same meaning.

Particularly in the sense of election, Yahweh as creator says that he has called Israel by name and they are his (קראתי בשמך לי־אתה, Is. 43:1).

שמעו איים אלי והקשיבו לאמים מרחוק
יהוה מבטן קראני ממעי אמי הזכיר שמי:

Listen to me, O islands, and pay attention, you peoples from afar.

83. Andersen and Freedman follow the reading of the Targum and translate the verse: "When Israel was a youth, I loved him. From Egypt, I called him 'My child.'" They understand this as an act of election which makes Israel Yahweh's child. See F.I. Andersen and D.N. Freedman, *Hosea*, pp. 574, 576.

Yahweh called Me from the womb; from the body of My mother He named Me. (Is. 49:1; cf. v. 5)

In Is. 54:6, Israel is compared to a wife forsaken and grieved in spirit, but later called again by her husband.

כי־כאשה עזובה ועצובת רוח קראך יהוה
ואשת נעורים כי תמאס אמר אלהיך:

"For Yahweh has called you, like a wife forsaken and grieved in spirit, even like a wife of one's youth when she is rejected," says your God.

This verse is directed to the restoration of post-exilic Israel.[84] However, the point to be noticed here is that the call of Israel is described by the metaphors of marriage, divorce, and remarriage.

So, as we have seen, קרא is not only a military term but also an election term. Yahweh called Israel before her birth and named her, just as a military leader called his officers by name to appoint them to their special assignment.

פקד (3

פקד carries a variety of meanings, including "to choose (appoint)," "to number, or muster," "to visit," "to miss" (1 Sam. 20:6; 25:15; Jer. 3:16), and "to examine" (Job 7:18). Generally, it is used with the meaning "to visit." When it is used of Yahweh, he visits his people in his grace[85] and sinners in his anger, in order to punish them.[86] Moreover, פקד is a military term. When war breaks out, the military leader summons the people and musters (פקד) the soldiers, and appoints or chooses (פקד) the captains and officers for them.

וישכם יהושע בבקר ויפקד את־העם ויעל הוא וזקני ישראל לפני העם העי:

Now Joshua rose early in the morning and mustered the people, and

84. Primarily, the wife here refers to Zion, which ultimately points to the inhabitants in it. See Claus Westermann, *Isaiah 40-66*, OTL (Philadelphia: Westminster, 1970), p. 271; E. J. Young, *The Book of Isaiah* (Grand Rapids: Eerdmans, 1972), 3:360-61. Cf. Is. 42:6.
85. Gen. 21:1; 50:24,25; Ex. 4:31; Ruth 1:6; 1 Sam. 2:21; Ps. 8:5; Zeph. 2:7.
86. Ex. 32:34; 1 Sam. 15:2; Is. 10:12; 13:11; 26:14,16; 27:1; Jer. 5:9,29; 6:15; 9:8, 25; 13:21; 14:10; 13:34; 25:12; 27:8; 30:20; 36:31; 44:13; 49:8.

he went up with the elders of Israel before the people to Ai.

(Josh. 8:10)

Here, פקד is used with the meaning "to muster."[87]

והיה ככלת השטרים לדבר אל־העם ופקדו שרי צבאות בראש העם:

And it shall come about that when the officers have finished speaking to the people, they shall appoint commanders of armies at the head of the people. (Dt. 20:9)

והאיש ירבעם גבור חיל וירא שלמה את־הנער כי־
עשה מלאכה הוא ויפקד אתו לכל־סבל בית יוסף:

Now the man Jeroboam was a valiant warrior, and when Solomon saw that the young man was industrious, he appointed him over all the forced labor of the house of Joseph. (1 Kgs. 11:28)

The appointment of commanders in the army or over the forced labor is expressed by the term פקד.[88]

In particular, Yahweh is represented as the one who mustered his army. He commanded Moses to muster Israel. The census of Num. 1 concerns only "the men from twenty years old and upward, whoever is able to go out to war" (Num. 1:2,3,20).[89] Therefore, it was more than a census; it was an organizing of troops for battle. In Is. 13:4, we can clearly see Yahweh's mustering of his army for battle.

קול המון בהרים דמות עם־רב
קול שאון ממלכות גוים נאספים
יהוה צבאות מפקד צבא מלחמה:

A sound of tumult on the mountains,
Like that of many people!
A sound of the uproar of kingdoms,
Of nations gathered together!
Yahweh of hosts is mustering the army for battle.

When פקד is used of Yahweh, it is mostly in the context of

87. See also Ex. 30:12; Num. 1:3,19,44,49; 3:10,15,16,39,42; 4:23,27,29,30,34, 37,41,45,46,49; 26:63,64; 1 Sam. 11:18; 14:17; 15:4; 2 Sam. 18:1; 24:4; 1 Kgs. 20:15,26; 2 Kgs. 3:6; 1 Ch. 21:6; 25:5.

88. See also Num. 1:50; 31:14,48; Josh. 10:18; 2 Kgs. 11:15; 25: 22, 23; 1 Ch. 23:14; 26:32; Esth. 2:3; Jer. 40:5,7,11; 41:2,18; Neh. 7:1; 12:14.

89. Cf. P.D. Miller, *The Divine Warrior in Early Israel*, HSM 5 (Cambridge: Harvard University Press, 1973), p. 161.

election. In Jer. 1:10, Yahweh said that he appointed (פְּקַדְתִּיךָ) Jeremiah over the nations and kingdoms as a prophet. Cyrus king of Persia said that Yahweh, the God of heaven, appointed (פָּקַד) Cyrus to build a house in Jerusalem for him (2 Ch. 36:23). At the end of his life, Moses asked Yahweh to appoint (פָּקַד) his successor after him.

יפקד יהוה אלהי הרוחת לכל־בשר איש על־העדה:

May Yahweh, the God of the spirits of all flesh, appoint a man over the congregation. (Num. 27:16)[90]

Therefore, we can safely say that פָּקַד is also an election term that is borrowed from war terminology. Yahweh as a commander appointed his officers over his army, Israel, and commanded them to summon and organize the troops for battle. As an Akkadian cognate of פָּקַד, *paqādu* also carries the same meaning of "mustering."[91]

To sum up our findings about war terms, we may state that the idea of election borrowed from the war practices of Israel. Summoning, choosing, recruiting, mustering, appointing, and encountering were due processes in preparation for battle. The concept of election itself contains all the various aspects of that process.

Furthermore, in terms of syntax, when war terms describe the idea of election, they are similar in form to the parallel marriage formulae. בחר in particular is important because it carries the most significant theological aspects of election, that is, the meaning of election, the reason for election, and the syntax of election formulae. Thus, we are now able to understand the concept of election from the perspective of war.

(2) Yahweh and Israel in War

Israel's wars are closely associated with Yahweh. The entire nation of Israel was called to be an "army" at the time of the exodus and

90. See also Jer. 49:19; 50:44.
91. *HAL*, p. 900. *AHw*, 2:824ff. For further discussion of פקד as a military and administrative term, see J. Scharbert, "Das Verbum PQD in der Theologie des Alten Testaments," *BZ* 4 (1960): 209-26.

the conquest. When Yahweh gave the instructions concerning the
Feast of the Unleavened Bread, he regarded the Israelites as an army.

וּשְׁמַרְתֶּם אֶת־הַמַּצּוֹת כִּי בְּעֶצֶם הַיּוֹם הַזֶּה הוֹצֵאתִי אֶת־
צִבְאוֹתֵיכֶם מֵאֶרֶץ מִצְרָיִם וּשְׁמַרְתֶּם אֶת־הַיּוֹם הַזֶּה
לְדֹרֹתֵיכֶם חֻקַּת עוֹלָם:

You shall also observe the Feast of Unleavened Bread, for on this
very day I brought your hosts out of the land of Egypt; therefore you
shall observe this day throughout your generations as a permanent
ordinance. (Ex. 12:17)[92]

This designation can be explained in terms of their national situation and task, which was integrally related to war. Again, in Ex. 7:4
Israel is called to be an army of Yahweh.

וְלֹא־יִשְׁמַע אֲלֵכֶם פַּרְעֹה וְנָתַתִּי אֶת־יָדִי בְּמִצְרָיִם
וְהוֹצֵאתִי אֶת־צִבְאֹתַי אֶת־עַמִּי בְנֵי־יִשְׂרָאֵל מֵאֶרֶץ
מִצְרַיִם בִּשְׁפָטִים גְּדֹלִים:

When Pharaoh will not listen to you, then I will lay My hand on
Egypt, and bring out My hosts, My people the sons of Israel, from
the land of Egypt by great judgments.

Here, צבאתי, עמי, and בני־ישראל are all designations of the people of
Israel. Yahweh calls Israel "My hosts." After the exodus, the narrator says that "all the hosts of Yahweh" (כל־צבאות יהוה) went out
from the land of Egypt (Ex. 12:41). And in the Song of Deborah,
the people of Yahweh are identified with warriors (גבורים, Judg.
5:13).

If the people of Israel are the army of Yahweh, how is Yahweh
described in relation to them in this respect? In contrast to גבורים,
the singular גבור is used for Yahweh.

כִּי יְהוָה אֱלֹהֵיכֶם הוּא אֱלֹהֵי הָאֱלֹהִים וַאֲדֹנֵי הָאֲדֹנִים הָאֵל
הַגָּדֹל הַגִּבֹּר וְהַנּוֹרָא אֲשֶׁר לֹא־יִשָּׂא פָנִים וְלֹא יִקַּח שֹׁחַד:

For Yahweh your God is the God of gods and the Lord of lords, the
great, the mighty, and the awesome God who does not show partial-
ity, nor take a bribe. (Dt. 10:17)

Here, the rendering of הגבר as "the mighty warrior" would be more

92. See also Ex. 6:26; 12:51; Num. 2; 10:14-18; 33. In Josh. 5:4, all the people
of Israel who came out of Egypt are called to be כל אנשי מלחמה (all the men of
war). Cf. Josh. 5:6.

acceptable.[93] In Ps. 24:8, Yahweh is described as יהוה עזוז וגבור יהוה גבור מלחמה (Yahweh *is* strong and mighty, Yahweh *is* mighty in battle). גבור מלחמה means simply "warrior." In Zeph. 3:17, Yahweh is described as גבור יושיע (a victorious warrior, lit., a warrior who saves). In Is. 42:13, Yahweh is described as גבור (a warrior) and איש מלחמות (a man of war). In the Song of the Sea, Yahweh is represented as איש מלחמה (a warrior), the war leader of Israel.

יהוה איש מלחמה יהוה שמו:

Yahweh is a warrior, Yahweh is His name. (Ex. 15:3)

Yahweh is said to have cast Pharaoh's chariot into the sea (Ex. 15:4) and to have shattered the enemy with his right hand (15:6). Furthermore, the force opposing Israel is viewed as an enemy of Yahweh rising up against him (קמיך, 15:7). So the war against Israel was against Yahweh himself. This was clearly understood by the enemies of Israel. When the Egyptians met difficulties as they pursued Israel into the sea, they cried out:

ויאמר מצרים אנוסה מפני ישראל כי יהוה נלחם להם במצרים:

So the Egyptians said, "Let us flee from Israel, for Yahweh is fighting for them against the Egyptians." (Ex. 14:25)

And when the Philistines came to know that the ark of Yahweh had arrived in the camp of Israel, they also cried:

אוי לנו מי יצילנו מיד האלהים האדירים האלה אלה
הם האלהים המכים את־מצרים בכל־מכה במדבר:

Woe to us! Who shall deliver us from the hand of these mighty gods? These are the gods who smote the Egyptians with all kinds of plagues in the wilderness. (1 Sam. 4:8)

Thus, the enemies of Israel considered their battle to be not only against the Israelites but also against Yahweh.

In the same way, Yahweh himself considered a war against the enemies of Israel as a battle against their gods as well.[94] In this case, Yahweh as the supreme God is described as having the character of one who punishes the gods of their enemies. So the killing of the

93. The Canaanite deities El and Baal are also leaders of cosmic armies. See B.E. Shafer, *ZAW* 89 (1977): 37; F.M. Cross, *Canaanite Myth and Hebrew Epic*, p. 89.

94. See Judg. 5:31.

first-born of Egypt is said to be a judgment on the gods of Egypt by Yahweh himself.

וְעָבַרְתִּי בְאֶרֶץ־מִצְרַיִם בַּלַּיְלָה הַזֶּה וְהִכֵּיתִי כָל־בְּכוֹר
בְּאֶרֶץ מִצְרַיִם מֵאָדָם וְעַד־בְּהֵמָה וּבְכָל־אֱלֹהֵי מִצְרַיִם
אֶעֱשֶׂה שְׁפָטִים אֲנִי יְהוָה:

> For I will go through the land of Egypt on that night, and will strike down all the first-born in the land of Egypt, both man and beast; and against all the gods of Egypt I will execute judgments— I am Yahweh. (Ex. 12:12)[95]

Thus, in the Bible a war on earth is understood as a replica of the cosmic battles between the gods above. A people engaged in war comprised the army of gods whom they served.[96] Therefore, a victory of one nation is also a triumph of its gods over others. We can see this also in the Babylonian story of creation, *Enuma Elish*. Marduk engaged in battle with the encroaching powers of chaos, represented by the goddess Tiamat, and by his victory Marduk ensured the perpetuity of the ordered cosmic state. According to P.C. Craigie, this Babylonian creation story reflected the level of the nation state. Any threat to the maintenance of the order in the state was a threat of impending chaos. Thus, "as the nation state was within the realm of the god Marduk, the continuance of the ordered structure of the state against the impending threat of an external power had to be maintained by military means. Victory was inherent in military exploits of this nature, for the earthly war was based on the pattern of the victorious activities of the heavenly Marduk."[97]

From this perspective, the relationship between Yahweh and

95. See also Ex. 33:4; Num. 33:4; Jer. 46:25; Ps. 78:53-55; 80:9-12 (E. 8-11).
96. P.D. Miller suggests that "a god or gods are engaged in battle with human beings." As evidence for this, he points out that "the figures slaughtered by 'Anat, *lim* and *adm* are human, not divine beings [*CTA* 3.IV.7-8]. . . . Furthermore, the human beings are characterized as warriors" *(mhrm, ġzrm)* in *CTA* 3.IV.14-15, 21-22. Therefore, he concludes "that the pattern of the cosmic battle is sometimes projected onto the realm of human life, producing conflict and battle between human and divine elements" *(Divine Warrior,* p. 47). See also G.E. Wright, *The Old Testament and Theology,* p. 141; F.M. Cross, *Canaanite Myth and Hebrew Epic,* pp. 58-59, 105ff.
97. P.C. Craigie, *The Problem of War in the Old Testament* (Grand Rapids: Eerdmans, 1978), pp. 120-21. He also demonstrates this point by the development of Ashur as a national god in Assyria to Ashur as a world god through the move towards universalism at the religious level in accordance with imperialism at the political level.

Israel in war is made clearer.[98] As it were, Yahweh was a divine warrior and the Israelites were his levied hosts. Yahweh had chosen (בחר) Israel as his army, just as the military leaders chose (בחר) and mustered (פקד) their armies from among the people when they went out to battle. Ps. 60:8-9 (E. 6-7) strongly supports this idea.

> God has spoken in His holiness:
> "I will exult, I will portion out Shechem and measure out the valley of Succoth.
> Gilead is Mine, and Manasseh is Mine;
> Ephraim also is the helmet of My head [מאוז ראשי];
> Judah is My scepter [מחקקי]."

These verses present Yahweh as a warrior whose helmet is Northern Israel and whose commander's staff is Judah. Both Ephraim and Judah are introduced as the instruments of Yahweh in his battle (cf. Ps. 108:8-9; Zech. 9:13).[99] And in Jer. 51:20, Yahweh said to Israel: "You are My war-club, My weapon of war. And with you I shatter nations, and with you I destroy kingdoms." Thus, a war for Israel was a war of, with, and for Yahweh.

98. Miller also says that the imagery of Yahweh as a warrior god, a leader of cosmic armies, was an imagery central to Israel's religion from earliest times and a basic aspect of the concept of deity in the ancient Near East *(Divine Warrior,* p. 63). For this ancient Near Eastern concept, see W. H. Schmidt, *The Faith of the Old Testament* (Philadelphia: Westminster, 1983), pp. 96-97. According to Egyptian sources, the gods joined in battle on behalf of their nation, and the victors owed their success to their god. Rameses III assigns all power to his god, Amun-Re, alone: "You make the victory of the land of Egypt, your own land, without the hand of a soldier or of any human being involved, but only your great strength which delivers it." See S. Morenz, *Gott und Mensch im Alten Ägypten* (Leipzig, 1964), pp. 18,66.

As for Canaanite sources, the inscription of King Mesha of Moab shows that the king conducted war against Israel according to the counsel of his god Chemosh: "Now the men of Gad had always dwelt in the land of Ataroth, and the king of Israel had built Ataroth for them; but I fought against the town and took it and slew all the people of the town as satiation (intoxication) for Chemosh and Moab. And Chemosh said to me: 'Go, take Nebo from Israel!' (15) So I went by night and fought against it from break of dawn until noon, taking it and slaying all, seven thousand men, boys, women, girls and maid-servants, for I had devoted them to destruction for (the god) Ashtar-Chemosh. And I took from there the [...] of Yahweh, dragging them before Chemosh" *(ANET,* p. 320).

According to M. Weippert's suggestion, this kind of "divine war" was known from Assyria ("'Heilige Krieg' in Israel und Assyrien," *ZAW* 84 [1972]: 460-93).

99. For the exegesis of this verse, see Chap. II below, pp. 162-165. G. E. Wright also pointed out the role of Israel as Yahweh's agent in his overall purposes *(The Old Testament and Theology,* p. 126).

David had a special insight into this aspect of Israelite war. When he accepted the challenge of Goliath and confronted him, David said to the Philistine:

אתה בא אלי בחרב ובחנית ובכידון ואנכי בא־אליך
בשם יהוה צבאות אלהי מערכות ישראל אשר חרפת:

You come to me with a sword, a spear, and a javelin, but I come to you in the name of Yahweh of hosts, the God of the armies of Israel, whom you have taunted. (1 Sam. 17:45)

Furthermore, David referred to the armies of Israel as the armies of the living God (מארכות אלהים היים, 1 Sam. 17:26,36) and he was said to fight Yahweh's battle (מלחמות יהוה, 1 Sam. 18:17; 25:18).

Isaiah 13, the oracle about Babylon, gives us another aspect of Yahweh as a warrior. In verses 3-4, Yahweh summons his warriors.

3 אני צויתי למקדשי
גם קראתי גבורי לאפי עליזי גאותי:
4 קול המון בהרים דמות עם־רב
קול שאון ממלכות גוים נאספים
יהוה צבאות מפקד צבא מלחמה:

3 I have commanded My consecrated ones,
I have even called My mighty warriors,
My proudly exulting ones,
To execute My anger.
4 A sound of tumult on the mountains
Like that of many people!
A sound of the uproar of kingdoms,
Of nations gathered together!
Yahweh of hosts is mustering the army for battle.

Here, Yahweh is seen as the commander-in-chief in his headquarters who possesses standing armies specially dedicated to him.[100] At his command, kingdoms and nations are gathered together on the mountains with a sound of tumult and uproar. Then Yahweh begins to master his army for battle (v. 4). These hosts of Yahweh are pictured as coming to destroy the whole land from a far country, even from the end of heaven (v. 5). Thus, the day of Yahweh is near. When the day of Yahweh comes, it will be the day of destruc-

---

100. Following von Rad, Miller sees מקדש as a term "which belongs to the practice of holy war, in which the soldiers were purified and set under certain taboos before battle" (Divine Warrior, p. 136).

tion (v. 6), the day of terror (v. 8), and the day of cruelty (v. 9). On that day, there will be unusual cosmic phenomena because of Yahweh's wrath.

10 כי־כוכבי השמים וכסיליהם לא יהלו אורם
חשך השמש בצאתו וירח לא־יגיה אורו:

For the stars of heaven and their constellations
Will not flash forth their light;
The sun will be dark when it rises,
And the moon will not shed its light.

13 על־כן שמים ארגיז ותרעש הארץ ממקומה
בעברת יהוה צבאות וביום חרון אפו:

Therefore I shall make the heavens tremble,
And the earth will be shaken from its place
At the fury of Yahweh of hosts
In the day of His burning anger.

Yahweh as a divine warrior brings a human army as well as one comprising cosmic divine hosts.[101] In verses 17-22, Yahweh is going to use the Medes as his instrument to destroy Babylon, the beauty of kingdoms, the glory of the Chaldeans' pride. On that day Babylon would be as those whom God overthrew in Sodom and Gommorah. The day of the fall of Babylon would be the day of deliverance for Israel. Israel would be chosen again and settled in its own land (14:1).

Thus, Is. 13 represents Yahweh as the sovereign ruler of the universe and the divine warrior fighting for Israel. Israel is not Yahweh's army here, but rather the Medes. Thus he not only uses Israel as his army, but he also employs other nations to do his will. Consequently, he could say of Assyria that she was "My rod of anger" (שבט אפי) sent against a godless nation (10:5-6; cf. 30:32). Indeed, Yahweh is above all the nations and above all gods. And this supreme God chose Israel among all the nations of the world as his supreme army on earth.

Therefore, the election idea can be seen to have been expressed in the context of war. And the designation of Yahweh in the Bible as "refuge," "rock," "shield," and even "deliverance and salvation" is a metaphorical description of a divine warrior who is fighting for them. Yahweh was their ultimate security. Their victory or de-

101. Cf. Gen. 32:1-2; Judg. 5:14; 1 Kgs. 6:17; 22:19; Ps. 34:8 (E. 7); 68:18 (E. 17); Hab. 3:8. See also G.E. Wright, *The Old Testament and Theology,* p. 130.

feat in battle was entirely dependent upon the will of God. This was why they had to sanctify their army before battle (Jer. 6:4; 22:7; 51:27,28; Mic. 3:5; Joel 3:9). Whenever they went out to fight, an oracle would be consulted (Judg. 20:18ff.;1 Sam. 14:37; 23:2; 28:6; 30:8), and the priests were to speak to the people: "Hear, O Israel, you are approaching the battle against your enemies today. Do not be fainthearted. Do not be afraid, or panic, or tremble before them, for Yahweh your God is the one who goes with you, to fight for you against your enemies, to save you" (Dt. 20:3-4).

The military leaders also had to encourage their armies in the name of Yahweh and assure them that Yahweh was fighting for them.[102] Because of the nature of this relationship between Yahweh and Israel, seeking the national security from any agent other than Yahweh was absurd and was regarded as a betrayal of Yahweh. Often such a rebellion was severely condemned by the prophets.[103] It was even regarded as playing the harlot in Ezekiel (16:26,28). One of the main reasons that King Ahaz was labelled as evil among the kings was his dependency upon Tiglath-pileser king of Assyria, when Rezin of Syria and Pekah of Israel came up to Jerusalem to wage war (2 Kgs. 16:1-10). By contrast, Hezekiah was miraculously saved from the siege of Sennacherib by Yahweh and was regarded as a good king because he trusted Yahweh firmly in national crisis. In the context of rejection, Yahweh deserts Israel and fights against her. He employs Assyria and Babylon to destroy Israel and has them taken into captivity. In restoration, Yahweh will choose Israel again and deliver them from the exile.[104] He will use them again as his levied army. Therefore, we can conclude that the election of Israel is the election of Yahweh's army on earth.

4. ISRAEL, THE SON OF YAHWEH

The father-son relationship is another characteristic aspect describing Yahweh's election of Israel. Yahweh adopts Israel as his own

102. Ex. 14:14; Dt. 1:30; 3:22; 7:23; 9:3; 20:4; Josh. 23:3,10; Judg. 11:32; 12:3; Is. 30:32; Zech. 14:3; Dan. 10:20; Neh. 4:14; 2 Ch. 18:31; 20: 29; 32:8. See G.H. Jones, "'Holy war' or 'Yahweh war'?" *VT* 25 (1975): 642-58.

103. Is. 30:1-5; 31:1-3; 36:56; Jer. 2:18,19; 37:1-10; Ezek. 17:15; Hos. 7:11.

104. See Chap. III below, pp. 196-201, 217-20.

son and appoints him as his heir.[105] Thus, we need to examine the terms, meaning, and customs of adoption as practiced in Israel. Then we shall look at the relationship between Yahweh and Israel from the perspective of the father-son relationship.

(1) The Terms for Adoption

From the viewpoint of the adopter, לקח or בחר is used as an adoption term. However, from the viewpoint of the adoptee, the phrase היה ל- is generally used. Therefore, "A (the adoptee) became a son to B (the adopter)" is a typical formula for adoption.

1) היה לו לבן

היה simply means "to be," "to become." According to G.S. Ogden's research, היה is mainly used (1) as a copula, (2) to indicate the existence of a subject, and (3) to indicate the transition from one sphere of existence to another.[106] According to his classification, the usage of היה is transitional in describing the concept of adoption. In this case היה takes the preposition ל, or sometimes double ל as in the marriage formulae, to specify the direction of transition. Therefore, the phrases "A היה לבן B ל" (A became a son to B) and אני אהיה־ לו לאב והוא יהיה־לי לבן (I will be his father and he shall be my son) are found as a general adoption formula.

ויגדל הילד ותבאהו לבת־פרעה ויהי־לה לבן ותקרא
שמו משה ותאמר כי מן־המים משיתהו:

And the child grew, and she brought him to Pharaoh's daughter, and he became her son. And she named him Moses, and said, "Because I drew him out of the water." (Ex. 2:10)

In the Bible, the practice of adoption on a human level is rarely mentioned. However, on a theological level many examples are

---

105. Gerald Cooke asserts that the father-son figure is one of the best expressions of the special favor expressed in Israel's elective covenantal relationship to Yahweh. See "The Israelite King as Son of God," *ZAW* 73 (1961): 217.

106. G.S. Ogden, "Time, and the Verb היה in O.T. Prose," *VT* 21 (1971): 451.

found. Yahweh promised David that he would raise up his descendant after him to build a temple and then said:

אני אהיה־לו לאב והוא יהיה־לי לבן אשר בהעותו
והכחתיו בשבט אנשים ובנגעי בני אדם:

I will be a father to him and he will be a son to Me; when he commits iniquity, I will correct him with the rod of men and the strokes of the sons of men. (2 Sam. 7:14; cf. 1 Ch. 17:13; 22:10)[107]

In Jer. 31:9, this adoption formula: "I will be a father to him and he will be a son to Me," is also found on the national level.[108]

כי־הייתי לישראל לאב ואפרים בכרי הוא:

For I am a father to Israel, and Ephraim is My first-born.

Here, Yahweh is introduced as the Father of Israel.

Another important aspect of this usage is found in the context of the covenant. In his covenant with Abraham, Yahweh says:

והקמתי את־בריתי ביני ובינך ובין זרעך אחריך
לדרתם לברית עולם להיות לך לאלהים ולזרעך אחריך:
ונתתי לך ולזרעך אחריך את ארץ מגריך את כל־ארץ
כנען לאחזת עולם והייתי להם לאלהים:

And I will establish My covenant between you and Me and you and your descendants after you throughout their generations for an everlasting covenant, to be God to you and to your descendants after you. And I will give to you and to your descendants after you, the land of your sojournings, all the land of Canaan, for an everlasting possession; and I will be their God. (Gen. 17:7-8)

Speaking of the Israelites, Yahweh said:

והתהלכתי בתוככם והייתי לכם לאלהים ואתם תהיו־לי לעם:

I will also walk among you and be your God, and you shall be My people. (Lev. 26:12)[109]

In the prophetical books, the phrase "I will be your God and

---

107. G. Cooke asserts that this verse should be regarded as adoptional and he interprets it as such ("The Israelite King as Son of God," *ZAW* 73 [1961]: 211).

108. "I will be a father to him and he will be a son to me" is generally acknowledged to be an adoption formula. See S.M. Paul, *MAARAV* 2/2 (April 1980): 178.

109. See also Ex. 29:45; Lev. 11:45; 22:33; 26:45; Num. 15:41; Dt. 26:19; 29:12; 2 Sam. 7:24; 2 Kgs. 11:17; Jer. 7:23; 11:4; 13:11; 24:7; 30:22; 31:1,33; 32:38; Ezek. 11:20; 14:11; 34:24; 36:28; 37:23,27; Zech. 2:15; 8:8; 1 Ch. 17:22; 2 Ch. 23:16.

you will be My people" (והייתי לכם לאלהים ואתם תהיו־לי לעם) is a common covenant formula. Therefore, this covenant formula is closely
associated with that of adoption,[110] and thus with that of election.[111]

2) בחר and לקח

As adoption terms, לקח appears twice and בחר once in the Hebrew
Bible, with the same syntax as that of the marriage formulae.

ויהי אמן את־הדסה היא אסתר בת־דדו כי אין לה אב
ואם והנערה יפת־תאר וטובת מראה ובמות אביה ואמה
לקחה מרדכי לו לבת:

Now the young lady was beautiful of form and face, and when her
father and her mother died, Mordecai took her as his own daughter.
(Esth. 2:7; cf. 2:15)

ויאמר לי שלמה בנך הוא־יבנה ביתי וחצרותי כי־
בחרתי בו לי לבן ואני אהיה־לו לאב:

And He said to me, "Your son Solomon is the one who shall build
My house and My courts; for I have chosen him to be a son to Me,
and I will be father to him." (1 Ch. 28:6)

1 Ch. 28:6 is worthy of special attention because the election formula and the adoption formula are combined together, and this
shows the close affinity of election with adoption in their formulae.
Solomon was chosen to be Yahweh's son. Since we have already
discussed לקח and בחר as election terms, we do not need to repeat
our findings again here. However, it is noteworthy that *leqû,* the
Akkadian cognate of לקח, and its Sumerian equivalent are frequently used in the adoption formula: *ana mārūti leqû* (to take into
the status of sonship);[112] NAM · DUMU · NI · ŠÈ ŠU · BA · AN ·
TI · EŠ (to take into sonship).[113] The nominal forms *liqû* (adoption
[*KAJ* 167:4] and *liqûtu* (adoptive child [*YOS* 2, 50:6]) are also note-

---

110. See Good's *Sheep of His Pasture,* pp. 65-68, for an extensive discussion
about the life setting of this formula היה ל־ . . . ל־.

111. See below, pp. 175-81.

112. *šumma awilum siḥram ina mešu ana marutim ilqi* (If a man has taken a
young boy in adoption [he is to be called] by his name). CH 185:34-35; 186:41;
190:67-68. See S.M. Paul, *MAARAV* 2/2 (April 1980): 181.

113. *EG* 68:7 = YOS 8:152.

worthy. Thus the similarity between the phrase *ana mārūti leqû* and לקחה לבת (Esth. 2:7,15) is striking and has already been recognized.[114]

3) שים בנים

As a unique expression, שים בנים in Jer. 3:19 is used for describing the idea of Yahweh's adoption of Israel as his son.

> ואנכי אמרתי איך אשיתך בבנים
> ואתן־לך ארץ חמדה נחלת צבי צבאות גוים
> ואמר אבי תקראו־לי ומאחרי לא תשובו:

According to S.M. Paul, Hebrew שים בנים is the semantic equivalent of Akkadian *ana mārūti šakānu*[115] (Sum. NAM · DUMU · NI · ŠÙ · IN · GAR,[116] to establish sonship relations, i.e., to adopt). Thus he translates the above verse as follows: "I thought, I will surely adopt you as my child and give you a desirable land, the most beautiful heritage of the nations; then I reckoned you would call me 'Father,' and you would not turn away from me."[117]

4) נתן

In very rare cases נתן is used for Yahweh's adoption of David as his son.

> אף־אני בכור אתנהו עליון למלכי־ארץ:

I also shall make him My first-born,
The highest of the kings of the earth. (Ps. 89:28 [E. 27])

Paul again suggests that בכור אתנהו is the Hebrew interdialectal counterpart of Akkadian *ana mārūti nadānu* (to appoint/designate sonship).[118] However, נתן is not used of the Yahweh-Israel relation.

---

114. S.M. Paul, *MAARAV* 2/2 (April 1980): 180,182.
115. *VAB* 5, 29:5; *TCL* 18, 153:21.
116. Meissner, *Beiträge,* 97:5 = *HG* 3:23 = Schorr, *Urkunden,* 10.
117. S.M. Paul, *MAARAV* 2/2 (April 1980): 184.
118. See S.M. Paul, *MAARAV* 2/2 (April 1980): 182-83.

(2) Adoption in the Bible

The custom of adoption is rarely found in the Old Testament. Only two cases are explicitly mentioned: Moses was adopted by Pharaoh's daughter (Ex. 2:10), and Esther was adopted by her uncle (Esth. 2:7,15). Since these two events took place outside biblical society, the existence of such a practice in Israel is suspect. However, we can hardly exclude the possibility of its existence, because the Bible itself hints in that direction. When the promise of Yahweh to give a son to Abram was delayed, he complained to God.

ויאמר אברם אדני יהוה מה־תתן־לי ואנכי הולך ערירי
ובן־משק ביתי הוא דמשק אליעזר: ויאמר אברם הן לי
לא נתתה זרע והנה בן־ביתי יורש אתי:

And Abram said, "O Lord Yahweh, what wilt Thou give me, since I am childless, and the heir of my house is Eliezer of Damascus?" And Abram said, "Since Thou hast given no offspring to me, one born in my house is my heir." (Gen.15:2-3)

These verses suggest that Abram considered adopting Eliezer as his son.

In ancient Near Eastern society, a childless couple adopted a son, sometimes a slave, to serve them in their lifetime and to bury them and to mourn for them when they died. In return for this service, the adopted son was designated as their heir (i.e., of house and property). But if a child should subsequently be born to the couple, he would be the chief heir, and the adopted son would be second to him.[119] Abraham's case is apparently an example of this practice.

1 Ch. 2:34-41 is another possible hint for the case of adoption.

ולא־היה לששן בנים כי אם־בנות ולששן עבד מצרי
ושמו ירחע: ויתן ששן את־בתו לירחע עבדו לאשה ותלד לו את־עתי:

Now Sheshan had no sons, only daughters. And Sheshan had an Egyptian servant whose name was Jarha. And Sheshan gave his

---

119. According to Hurrian family law, which might also have been normative for the patriarchs, there were two types of heir: *aplu* and *ewuru*. *aplu* was a direct heir and *ewuru* was an indirect heir, whom the law recognized when normal inheritors were lacking. Thus, Eliezer "was juridically in the position of an *ewuru*" (E.A. Speiser, *Genesis*, p. 112). See also Jeffrey Howard Tigay, "Adoption," *Encyclopaedia Judaica* (Jerusalem: Keter, 1971), 1:298.

daughter to Jarha his servant in marriage, and she bore him Attai.
(1 Ch. 2:34-35)

Jarha seemed to be manumitted, adopted by Sheshan, and then married to his master's daughter.[120] Unfortunately, we know nothing about Jahra. In Ezr. 2:61, we find a priest who is said to have taken a wife from the daughters of Barzillai the Gileadite, who was called by their name, Barzillai. The fact that this man obviously changed his name and bore his wife's name alludes to adoption into his wife's family.

Besides these cases, we have no explicit evidence for the practice of adoption in Israel. The strong tribal consciousness, the practice of polygamy, and even the levirate marriage[121] seemed to have obviated the necessity of adoption.[122] However, we can safely conclude that the idea of adoption existed throughout the biblical period. The one adopted became the heir who inherited his adopter's property and bore his name.

(3) Yahweh-Israel as Father-Son

The father-son relationship is another metaphorical description of the relationship between Yahweh and Israel. Even though the practice of adoption in biblical society was very limited, the Yahweh-Israel union was described as a father-son relationship in which Yahweh calls Israel "My son" and "My first-born":

ואמרת אל־פרעה כה אמר יהוה בני בכרי ישראל:
ואמר אליך שלח את־בני ויעבדני

Then you shall say to Pharaoh, "Thus says Yahweh, 'Israel is My son, My first-born.' So I said to you, "Let My son go, that he may serve Me.'" (Ex. 4:22-23; cf. Is. 43:6; Hos. 11:1)

120. Tigay, "Adoption," p. 300.
121. Levirate marriage was instituted by an entirely different system of law. However, its basic motive is similar to that of adoption in the sense of raising up offspring to inherit the name and property of the deceased. Therefore, Boaz made this purpose clear to the people when he acquired the right to redeem Ruth. "Moreover, I have acquired Ruth the Moabitess, the widow of Mahlon, to be my wife in order to raise up the name of the deceased on his inheritance, so that the name of the deceased may not be cut off from his brothers or from the court of his birth place; you are witnesses today" (Ruth 4:10). See also R. de Vaux, *Ancient Israel*, 1:51.
122. G. Cooke, "The Israelite King as Son of God," *ZAW* 73 (1961): 215.

Not only does Yahweh call Israel "My son," but Yahweh also asks Israel to call him "My father."

ואמר אבי תקראו־לי ומאחרי לא תשובו:

And I said, "You shall call Me, My father,
And not turn away from following Me." (Jer. 3:19; cf. 3:4; 31:20)

And in Is. 63:16 (cf. 64:7 [E.8]), Israel calls Yahweh "our Father."

כי־אתה אבינו כי אברהם לא ידענו וישראל לא יכירנו
אתה יהוה אבינו גאלנו מעולם שמך:

For Thou art our Father, though Abraham does not know us,
And Israel does not recognize us.
Thou, O Yahweh, art our Father,
Our Redeemer from of old is Thy name.

The Bible even asserts that Yahweh gave birth to Israel.

צור ילדך תשי ותשכח אל מחללך:

You neglected the Rock who begot you,
And forgot the God who gave you birth. (Dt. 32:18)

In Is. 1:2, Yahweh said that he nourished and brought up Israel. Therefore, the Bible portrays the intimacy of Yahweh's relationship with Israel in terms of a father-son imagery (cf. Is. 46:3-5; 49:15).[123]

Adoption is not established by any agreement between the adopter and adoptee. Usually it is according to the adopter's choice and will; the adoptee is passive in the process of adoption. The adopter is active and sets his favor on the one whom he wants for his child,[124] and proclaims him to be his son. According to S.M. Paul's research, "the creation and dissolution of adoptive ties were accompanied by solemn declarations (as was also the case in the field of marital relations)."[125] It is expressed by means of judicial

123. In Jeremiah Yahweh calls Israel "My daughter My people" (בת־עמי, 6:26; 8:11,19,21,22,23 [E.9:1]; 9:6 [E.7]) and "the virgin daughter, My people" (בתולת בת־עמי, 14:17).

124. However, the adopter provided a document for his adopted son. We see this provision particularly in Ugaritic texts. See I. Mendelsohn, "An Ugaritic Parallel to the Adoption of Ephraim and Manasseh," *Israel Exploration Journal* 9 (1959): 180-83.

125. Thus he listed those declaration: "You are my son" (*māru^meš-ú-á*, CH 170:45); "He is your son" (*lú-u māru-ki, VS* 7:10-11 = *HG* 3.32); "I, the king, called him my son" (LUGAL-*ru* [*al*]-*si-šu-ma* DUMU(?)-*am*"); "Behold, Muršiliš is now my son" (*a-nu-um-ma* ¹*mu-ur-šil-li* DUMU-*ri* [the Hittite-Akkadian bilingual text, I, lines 2-4,37]). See S.M. Paul, *MAARAV* 2/2 (April 1980): 179.

formulations well known from Mesopotamian documents.

Thus, Yahweh's adoption of Israel as his son also carries this aspect. Yahweh did not need any consent or agreement with Israel in order to choose and adopt him as his son. This is the reason why Yahweh called Israel "My son" without any previous notice, asking the nation to call him "My father."

As a son of Yahweh, Israel was bestowed with many special privileges. First of all, Israel was called by the name of Yahweh.

וראו כל־עמי הארץ כי שם יהוה נקרא עליך ויראו ממך:

So all the peoples of the earth shall see that you are called by the name of Yahweh; and they shall be afraid of you. (Dt. 28:10)

עמי אשר נקרא־שמי עליהם ("My people who are called by My name," 2 Ch. 7:14) is Yahweh's special designation for Israel.[126] The literal rendering of "My people upon whom My name is called (or proclaimed)" makes more sense than the paraphrase. According to S.R. Driver, this phrase expresses the fact of ownership coupled with protection, as in 2 Sam. 12:28.[127] Thus, we can say that Israel is a bearer of Yahweh's name together with Jerusalem (Is. 62:2,4,12; Jer. 25:29) and the Temple (Jer. 7:10,11,30; 32:34; 34:15), because Yahweh caused his name to dwell there (לשכן שמו שם שמה, Dt. 12:11) and Yaweh God has chosen to put his name there (יבחר יהוה אלהיך לשום שמו שם, Dt. 12:21). Therefore, this privilege entails responsibility on the part of Israel. Israel was to honor, glorify, and proclaim the name of Yahweh (Dt. 32:2). The Third Commandment deals with the law concerning his name (Ex. 20:7), and Yahweh gave strong warnings against profanation of his name (Lev. 18:21; 19:12). If anyone blasphemed the name of Yahweh, he was to be put to death (Lev. 20:3; 24:16).

Deuteronomy 28:58-64 gives us a clearer picture of the relationship between sonship and bearing the name.

אם־לא תשמר לעשות את־כל־דברי התורה הזאת
הכתובים בספר הזה ליראה את־השם הנכבד והנורא
הזה את יהוה אלהיך:

126. See also Is. 43:7; 63:19; Jer. 14:9; 15:16; Dan. 9:19.
127. S.R. Driver, *A Critical and Exegetical Commentary on Deuteronomy,* ICC (Edinburgh: T. & T. Clark, 1895), p. 306. Also see E.L. Curtis and A.A. Madsen, *A Critical and Exegetical Commentary on the Books of Chronicles,* ICC (Edinburgh: T. & T. Clark, 1910), p. 344. They comment that Yahweh's responsibility for Israel's welfare is involved.

If you are not careful to observe all the words of this law which are written in this book, to fear this honored and awesome name, Yahweh your God . . . (Dt. 28:58)

ונסחתם מעל האדמה אשר־אתה בא־שמה לרשתה:
והפיצך יהוה בכל־העמים מקצה הארץ ועד־קצה הארץ

and you shall be torn from the land where you are entering to possess it. Moreover, Yahweh will scatter you among all peoples, from one end of the earth to the other end of the earth. (Dt. 28:63-64; cf. 4:25-27)

The way of honoring the name of Yahweh was to obey and keep his words. If Israel did not, the people would be torn out and scattered from the land which Yahweh gave them as an inheritance. The failure to meet the responsibility as a son was immediately followed by the withdrawal of a privilege, viz., the withdrawal of their inheritance.

Besides bearing the name, another privilege bestowed upon Israel as Yahweh's son was to be his heir, to be a people of inheritance (Dt. 4:20-21). As a son, he had a right to the inheritance, particularly since the eldest son had a privileged position and received a double share of his father's property (Dt. 21:17). Thus, Israel as Yahweh's first-born was entitled to an inheritance from Yahweh and was even called the tribe of his inheritance (Jer. 10:16).[128]

The Song of Moses (Dt. 32) provides us with a clue which helps us understand the background of how Israel became a people of inheritance.

8   בהנחל עליון גוים בהפרידו בני אדם
    יצב גבלת עמים למספר בני ישראל:
9   כי חלק יהוה עמו יעקב חבל נחלתו:

8   When the Most High gave the nations their inheritance,
    When He separated the sons of man,
    He set the boundaries of the peoples
    According to the number of the sons of Israel.
9   For Yahweh's portion is His people;
    Jacob is the allotment of His inheritance.

Yahweh is called עליון (Most High), which is an honorific epithet for Yahweh, glorifying him as the one and only Most High God. This title expresses the sovereignty and authority of Yahweh over

128. Cf. S.M. Paul, *MAARAV* 2/2 (April 1980): 178.

all nations.[129] When Yahweh separated the people and set their boundaries according to the number of the sons of God[130] and gave the nations their inheritances, Israel was Yahweh's portion and allotted inheritance. Thus, he says, "I have set you apart from the peoples to be Mine" (Lev. 20:26). Israel became a special people for Yahweh. According to these verses, Yahweh's election of Israel is to be dated back to the time of creation.

Yahweh is the owner of the land (ליהוה הארץ, Ps. 24:1). He wanted to give the most pleasant portion of it to his people as an inheritance.[131] "Hence I have said to you, 'You are to possess their land, and I Myself will give it to you to possess it, a land flowing with milk and honey.' I am Yahweh your God, who has separated you from the people" (Lev. 20: 24).

Jeremiah 3:19 gives us more information about the relationship between sonship, inheritance, and land.

ואנכי אמרתי איך אשיתך בבנים
ואתן־לך ארץ חמדה נחלת צבי צבאות גוים
ואמר אבי תקראו־לי ומאחרי לא תשובו:

Then I said,
"How I would set you among My sons,
And give you a pleasant land,
The most beautiful inheritance of the nations!"
And I said, "You shall call Me, My Father,
And not turn away from following Me."

129. For a legitimate function of the national gods, see J. J. M. Roberts, "Zion in the Theology of the Davidic-Solomonic Empire," in *Studies in the Period of David and Solomon and Other Essays,* ed. Tomoo Ishida (Winona Lake: Eisenbrauns, 1982), pp. 97-98.

130. MT reads "sons of Israel" and LXX "angels of God," which seems to reflect an original בני אל or בני אלים. See P.C. Craigie, *The Book of Deuteronomy,* NICOT (Grand Rapids: Eerdmans, 1976), pp. 378-79; W.H. Schmidt, *The Faith of the Old Testament,* pp. 101-2. See Loewenstamm, "נחלת ה," in *Studies in Bible,* Scripta Hierosolymitana 31, ed. Sara Japhet (Jerusalem: Magnes, 1986), pp. 179-80.

131. According to Gen. 17:7-8, the promise of the land is given to Abraham and his descendants within the context of election and covenant. Therefore, the promise of the land is not simply understood as a gift, as W. Eichrodt asserted in *Theology of the Old Testament,* OTL (Philadelphia: Westminster, 1967), 2:372. Rather, it must be seen as an inheritance. H.O. Forshey rightly pointed out over against Eichrodt that the parallelism of נחלה//עם is not synonymous but rather supplementary ("The Construct Chain *naḥ*lat YHWH/ *lōhim,*" *BA* 20 [1957]: 51-53).

This verse suggests that the land is Yahweh's gift to his son as an inheritance (cf. Dt. 4:37-38). According to S. M. Paul, the phrase "I would set you among My sons" (אשׁיתך בנים) is the unique technical expression of adoption whose Mesopotamian counterparts are Akkadian *ana mārūti šakānu* and Sumerian NAM · DUMU · NI · ŠÙ · IN · GAR, "to establish sonship relations," i.e., "to adopt."[132] Since adoption was an expression of election, the possession of the land for Israel was the sure mark of their sonship and their election. The visible sign of sonship was possession of the land which Yahweh gave them as an inheritance. Thus, the phrase "the land which Yahweh your God is giving you as an inheritance to possess" (ארץ אשׁר יהוה אלהיך נתן־לך נחלה לרשׁתה) as well as "the people of inheritance" (עם נחלה) must be understood in the context of adoption and election.[133]

Therefore, as a son of Yahweh Israel had two privileges, that is, to bear the name of Yahweh and to inherit the land. However, Israel neglected its responsibility as a son. Israel profaned and polluted the name of Yahweh (Jer. 34:16; Ezek. 20:39; 36:20; 39:7; Amos 2:7). The people even forgot the name of Yahweh (Jer. 23:27) and Yahweh himself (Is.17:10; 51:13; Jer. 2:32; 3:21; 13:25; 18:15; Ezek. 23:35; Hos. 2:15). Because of this rebellion of Israel, Yahweh had to reject the nation as his son. Yahweh had to scatter them from the land which he gave them as an inheritance (Jer. 12:7-8;13:24-25; Ezek. 12:9-16). Since the exodus is compared to the adoption of a son and the possession of the land is regarded as an inheritance, the exile equals the rejection of sonship and the dispossession of the land. Therefore, without exception Yahweh's rejection of Israel is equated with deportation from the land. In the same way, the restoration of sonship means bringing back the people to the land (Jer. 12:15; 16:15; 30:3; Amos 9:13-15). Ezek. 36:24-28 gives us a good example of this. "For I will take you from the nations, gather you from all the lands, and bring you into your own land" (36:24); "And you will live in the land that I gave to your forefathers; so you will be My people, and I will be your God" (36:28).

132. S. M. Paul, *MAARAV* 2/2 (April 1980): 184. He also pointed out that the phrase שׁים בנים is found 4Q Dib Ham 3:4-6.
133. Dt. 15:4; 19:10; 20:16; 21:23; 24:4; 25:19; 26:1; Is. 19:25; Ps. 135:12. Cf. also Ps. 33:12; 78:71; 105:10-11, 43-44; 136:22.

The restoration of the relationship between Yahweh and Israel is followed by the return of Israel to the land, i.e., the restoration of the inheritance. And the restoration of Israel is the restoration of the name.

ונתתי להם בביתי ובחומתי יד ושם טוב מבנים ומבנות
שם עולם אתן־לו אשר לא יכרת:

To them I will give in My house and within My walls a memorial,
And a name better than that of sons and daughters;
I will give them an everlasting name which will not be cut off.

(Is. 56:5)

As we have seen, the election idea in the Bible is expressed in terms of adoption. Therefore, election must also be understood from the perspective of adoption.

5. ISRAEL, THE SERVANT OF YAHWEH

In Lev. 25:55, Yahweh proclaims:

כי־לי בני־ישראל עבדים עבדי הם אשר־הוצאתי אותם
מארץ מצרים אני יהוה אלהיכם:

For the sons of Israel are My servants; they are My servants whom I brought out from the land of Egypt. I am Yahweh your God.

Again, in Is. 41:8 (cf. v. 9), Yahweh says that he has chosen Israel as his servant.

ואתה ישראל עבדי יעקב אשר בחרתיך זרע אברהם אהבי:

But you, Israel, My servant, Jacob whom I have chosen, descendant of Abraham My friend.

Here, we see the master-servant relationship as another aspect of election. Israel is a chosen servant of Yahweh. Thus, our next task is to expound the meaning of the master-servant relationship.

(1) The Term עבד

עבד, the Hebrew noun for "servant," is derived from the root עבד, which means "to serve," "to till (work)." Semitic cognates of this word are Ugaritic *'bd*, Amorite *habadu*, Akkadian *abdu* ([*w*] *ardu*), and Arabic *'abd*.[134]

In about 230 out of its 290 occurrences in the Hebrew Bible the verb עבד takes "king" or "God" (or, "gods") as its object. This verb is almost never used with regard to the ordinary people except in the case of Jacob (Gen. 25:13; 29:15,18,20,25; 29:18,20,27,30; 30:26,29; 31:6,41) and in a few cases of law codes (Ex. 21:2; Lev. 25:39,40,46). Sometimes its object is the nation or people as a whole (1 Sam. 4:9; 11:1; 17:7; 2 Sam. 10:19; Jer. 40:9). Otherwise, the verb is mainly used to refer to the service of God and king.

In the call narrative of Moses, Yahweh says to him:

ויאמר כי־אהיה עמך וזה־לך האות כי אנכי שלחתיך
בהוציאך את־העם ממצרים תעבדון את־האלהים על ההר הזה:

And He said, "Certainly I will be with you, and this shall be the sign to you that it is I who have sent you: when you have brought the people out of Egypt, you shall worship God at this mountain."

(Ex. 3:12)

The literal translation of תעבדון את־האלהים (they will serve God) seems suitable. However, the later event at Mount Horeb suggests that here the word implies worship. Until now, Israel had served Pharaoh, but after the exodus they would serve Yahweh. שלח את־בני ועבדני ("Let My son go, that they may serve Me," Ex. 4:23) and שלח את־עמי ועבדני ("Let My people go, that they may serve Me," Ex. 7:16; cf. 7:26; 8:16; 9:1,13; 10:3,7,26) are repeated claims of Yahweh through Moses to Pharaoh. In Ex. 5:1, Yahweh asks Pharaoh:

כה־אמר יהוה אלהי ישראל שלח את־עמי ויחגו לי במדבר:

Thus says Yahweh, the God of Israel, "Let My people go that they may celebrate a feast to Me in the wilderness."

In the same context of Yahweh's demand for the release of Israel from Pharaoh, the verb חגג is used instead of עבד.
In Ex. 5:3, זבח is used.

נלכה־נא דרך שלשת ימים במדבר ונזבחה ליהוה אלהינו

Please, let us go a three days' journey into the wilderness that we may sacrifice to Yahweh our God.

Here, "to serve" (עבד), "to celebrate" (חגג), and "to sacrifice" (זבח)

134. *HAL*, p. 731.

all point to the same event, explaining the purpose of Israel's going out into the wilderness. Therefore, serving Yahweh implies "worship," "celebration," "sacrifice," which are the main elements of service.

Furthermore, in Is. 43:10 to be a servant of Yahweh means to be a witness of Yahweh.[135]

אתם עדי נאם־יהוה ועבדי אשר בחרתי
למען תדעו ותאמינו לי ותבינו כי־אני הוא
לפני לא־נוצר אל ואחרי לא יהיה:

"You are My witnesses," declares Yahweh,
"And My servant whom I have chosen,
In order that you may know and believe Me,
And understand that I am He.
Before Me there was no God formed,
And there will be none after Me.

Israel as the chosen servant of Yahweh was to be his witness (cf. 43:12; 44:8). Therefore, witnessing can also be seen as a way of serving Yahweh. However, serving the king is entirely different. In order to serve kings, the people had to work, labor (Ex. 5:4; 1 Kgs. 12:4-15), and pay various taxes and tributes (1 Sam. 8:11-17).

As a noun, עבד is used extensively. W. Zimmerli classified the secular uses of the word into five categories: עבד as a slave, in the service of the king, as a description of political submission, as a humble self-description, and as a sanctuary servant.[136]

As for the religious realm, עבד is used for the individual as well as for Israel in relation to Yahweh.[137] Abraham, Isaac, and Jacob are called servants of Yahweh (Ex. 32:13; Dt. 9:27; Ps. 105:6,42). Moses is most frequently designated as a servant of Yahweh,[138] and next to Moses, David.[139] Caleb and Joshua are also called servants of Yahweh (Num. 14:24; Judg. 2:8). Prophets are usually regarded

135. This seems to be a later idea; see Chap. III below, pp. 190-91.
136. W. Zimmerli and J. Jeremias, *The Servant of God,* SBT 1/20, rev. ed. (London: SCM Press, 1965), pp. 11-15.
137. Exegesis of the so-called *Ebed-Yahweh* texts (Is. 42:1-9; 49:1-6; 50:4-9; 52:13–53:12) always forces us to take into account the identification of the *Ebed.* Either an individualistic or collective interpretation is suggested. For a historical survey of these interpretations, see H.H. Rowley, *The Servant of the Lord and Other Essays on the Old Testament* (London: Lutterworth, 1952), pp. 1-57.
138. Ex. 14:31; Num. 12:7; 34:5; Josh. 1:1,2,7,13,15; 8:31,33; 11:12, 15; 12:6; 13:8; 14:7; 18:7; 22:2,4,5; 1 Ch. 6:34; 2 Ch. 1:3; 24:6,9; Neh. 9:14; 10:30; Ps. 105:26.
139. 2 Sam. 7:5,8,20-29; 1 Kgs. 8:66; 11:13,36,38; 14:8; Ps. 18:1 (E. superscription); 36:1 (E. superscription); 89:4 (E.3); Jer. 33:21,22,26; Ezek. 34:23; 37:24.

as servants of Yahweh (2 Kgs. 21:10; Jer. 7:25; 25:4; 35:15; 44:4; Zech. 1:6). However, most significant is that Israel is called a servant of Yahweh (Is. 41:8-9; 42:19; 44:1-2; 45:4,11).

(2) Israel as the Servant of Yahweh

When Yahweh delivered Israel from the bondage of Pharaoh, he refused to treat the Hebrews as slaves to be sold, since they were his servants (כי־עבדי הם) whom he brought out from the land of Egypt (Lev. 25:42). And in the same context, Yahweh also declares that the sons of Israel are his servants (Lev. 25:55).

Yahweh's designation of Israel as עבדי seems to be closely related to the kingship of Yahweh. When the people of Israel asked Samuel to appoint a king over them, Yahweh answered Samuel, who was displeased at the request of the people.

ויאמר יהוה אל־שמואל שמע בקול העם לכל אשר־יאמרו
אליך כי לא אתך מאסו כי־אתי מאסו ממלך עליהם:
ככל־המעשים אשר־עשו מיום העלתי אתם ממצרים ועד־היום
הזה ויעזבני ויעבדו אלהים אחרים כן המה עשים גם־לך:

And Yahweh said to Samuel, "Listen to the voice of the people in regard to all that they say to you, for they have not rejected you, but they have rejected Me from being king over them. Like all the deeds which they have done since the day that I brought them up from Egypt even to this day—in that they have forsaken Me and served other gods—so they are doing to you also. (1 Sam. 8:7-8)

The Israelites needed a king who could judge justly (1 Sam. 8:5) and who could go before them and fight their battles, i.e., a military leader (8:19-20). According to these verses, Yahweh had been recognized as the king of Israel (cf. 12:12)—the divine Judge and Warrior—from the days of the exodus, and Israel was to serve (עבד) him as such. However, the Israelites had forsaken Yahweh and served other gods as their king. Here, in view of previous events, אלהים אחרים refers specifically to the Baals and the Ashtaroth (12:10).

The Song of the Sea describes the reign of Yahweh over against Pharaoh (Ex. 15:1-7; cf. vv. 17-18). This shows that the kingship of

Yahweh was known to the people of Israel from an early date.[140]
However, the idea of his kingship can be said to be fully developed
by the psalmists. In the Psalms, Yahweh is called מלכי ואלהי ("my
King and my God," Ps. 5:3 [E.2]; 84:4 [E.3]), מלכי אלהים ("my King,
O God," 44:5 [E.4]; cf. 74:12), אלי מלכי ("my God, my King," 68:25
[E.24]), אלהי המלך ("my, God, O King," 145:1), מלך כל־הארץ אלהים
("God is the King of all the earth," 47:8 [E.7]), מלך גדול על־כל־אלהים
("a great King above all gods," 95:3). Is. 33:22 gives us a clearer
picture of this.

כי יהוה שפטנו יהוה מחקקנו יהוה מלכנו הוא יושיענו:

For Yahweh is our judge, Yahweh is our lawgiver, Yahweh is our king;
He will save us.

Therefore, the Yahweh-Israel relationship is portrayed as a king-
servant relationship, and Yahweh's choosing of Israel was a choosing of his royal servant. Is. 44:1,2,5 illustrate this idea very clearly.

1 ועתה שמע יעקב עבדי וישראל בחרתי בו:
2 כה־אמר יהוה עשך ויצרך מבטן יעזרך
   אל־תירא עבדי יעקב וישרון בחרתי בו:
. . . .
5 זה יאמר ליהוה אני וזה יקרא בשם־יעקב
   וזה יכתב ידו ליהוה ובשם ישראל יכנה:

1 But now listen, O Jacob, My servant;
   And Israel, whom I have chosen:
2 Thus says Yahweh who made you
   And formed you from the womb, who will help you,
   "Do not fear, O Jacob My servant;
   And you Jeshurun whom I have chosen."
. . . .
5 "This one will say, 'I am Yahweh's';
   And that one will call on the name of Jacob;
   And another will write on his hand, 'Belonging to Yahweh,'
   And will name Israel's name with honor."

140. For the exegesis of this song, see Chap. II below. According to S. Mowinckel, the Israelites took over the concept of the deity as king from the Canaanites. See *The Psalms in Israel's Worship* (Nashville: Abingdon, 1962), 1:114. See
also John Gray, *The Biblical Doctrine of the Reign of God* (Edinburgh: T. & T.
Clark, 1979), pp. 7-71; idem, "The Kingship of God in the Prophets and Psalms,"
VT 11 (1961): 1-29.

Israel was chosen to be the servant of Yahweh from the womb (cf. Is. 49:5). Here, the election terms בחר (43:10; 45:4), חזק, and קרא (cf. 65:15) may be noted. Besides these, יצר is used for the election of the servant (cf. 44:21; 49:5).[141] According to 44:2, the election of Israel as Yahweh's servant dates back even before her birth. And the phrases "I am Yahweh's" (ליהוה אני) and "Belonging to Yahweh" (ליהוה) completely conformed to the idea of a servant in ancient society, because a servant was a possession of his master (Ex. 21:21). Therefore, the election of Israel was the election of his servant.

In relation to this, the Lord-servant (אדון-עבד) terminology needs to be examined. The Semitic cognates of אדון (e.g., Ugaritic *adn*) carry the same meaning as the Hebrew. Even though Sarah uses this word when she speaks of her husband (Gen. 18:12), in most cases servants use this term with reference to their masters. In Gen. 24, the servant of Abraham faithfully calls him אדני אברהם, and introduces himself as אנכי עבד אברהם (Gen. 24:34). And in the story of Joseph, Potiphar is called "Joseph's master" (אדניו, Gen. 39:2,7,8,20). Eli the priest is also addressed as such by Hannah (1 Sam. 1:15). As a legal term, אדון is a counterpart of עבד (Ex. 21:4-8). In most cases, subjects address their kings by this title.

However, if אדון appears as אדני (in the special plural form with a first person singular pronominal suffix), it always refers to God. Yahweh is "the Lord of lords" (אדני האדנים, Ps. 136:3), "the Lord of all the earth" (אדון כל־הארץ, Josh. 3:11,13; Mic. 4:13; Zech. 4:14; 6:5; Ps. 97:5), and "our Lord [who] is above all gods" (אדנינו מכל־אלהים, Ps. 135:5). As in the case of the king, Yahweh as the Lord is the divine judge who executes justice (Dt. 10:17-18; Is. 3:1; 10:16), and he is also the divine protector of Israel (Ps. 8:2-3). Thus, to call Yahweh אדון means basically the same as calling him מלך.

As the Yahweh-Israel relationship is viewed in terms of the master (King, Lord)-servant relationship, the concept of Yahweh's buying-selling of the people must be understood from this election perspective. Since purchasing is one of the major methods of acquiring servants (עבדים, Gen. 17:3,12; 37:36; 39:1), along with the taking of war captives, an עבד is basically regarded as his master's property (Ex. 21:21). Thus the people of Israel are said to be Yahweh's possession purchased by him (עם־זו קנית, Ex. 15:16; עם־זו גאלת, Ex. 15:13; אביך קנך, Dt. 32:6).

141. Zimmerli, *Servant of God*, p. 17.

זכר עדתך קנית קדם גאלת שבט נחלתך הר־ציון זה שכנת בו:

Remember Thy congregation, which Thou hast purchased of old,
Which Thou hast redeemed to be the tribe of Thine inheritance;
And Mount Zion, where Thou hast dwelt. (Ps. 74:2)

כי אני יהוה אלהיך קדוש ישראל מושיעך
נתתי כפרך מצרים כוש וסבא תחתיך:
מאשר יקרת בעיני נכבדת ואני אהבתיך
ואתן אדם תחתיך ולאמים תחת נפשך:

For I am Yahweh your God, the Holy One of Israel, your Saviour;
I have given Egypt as your ransom, Cush and Seba in your place.
Since you are precious in My sight,
Since you are honored and I love you,
I will give other men in your place and other peoples in exchange
    for your life. (Is. 43:3-4)

In Ps. 74:2 above, Israel is mentioned as Yahweh's congregation
which he has purchased of old and has redeemed. Furthermore, in
Is. 43:3-4, he is said to have given Egypt as a ransom, and Cush and
Seba in place of Israel at the time of the exodus. However, in restoration he promises to give other men and other people in ex-
change for the life of his people. Here, קנה, גאל, and נתן תחת all carry
the concept of buying and paying to acquire some object. Thus,
Yahweh's buying of Israel is described as his salvation of Israel
from Egypt, and also as Yahweh's election of Israel for his people.

As a corollary to this, the rejection of his people is equated with
the concept of selling his people, as a master sells his servant (עבד)
for money. In Dt. 28:68, Yahweh gave a warning that he would sell
the people of Israel in the case of their apostasy.

והשיבך יהוה מצרים באניות בדרך אשר אמרתי לך
לא־תסיף עוד לראתה והתמכרתם שם לאיביך לעבדים
ולשפחות ואין קנה:

And Yahweh will bring you back to Egypt in ships, by the way about
which I spoke to you, "You will never see it again!" And there you
shall offer yourselves for sale to your enemies as male and female
slaves, but there will be no buyer.

When the people of Israel actually did evil in the sight of Yahweh,
they are said to be sold by him to their enemy countries.[142]

142. See Chap. III below, pp. 203-4.

וימכרם יהוה ביד יבין מלך־כנען אשר מלך בחצור
ושר־צבאו סיסרא והוא יושב בחרשת הגוים:

And Yahweh sold them into the hand of Jabin king of Canaan, who reigned in Hazor; and the commander of his army was Sisera, who lived in Harosheth-hagoyim. (Judg. 4:2)

In the context of the restoration, this concept of selling-repurchasing was realistically experienced.[143] In prohibiting the selling of Israelites for food, Nehemiah said to the people:

"We according to our ability have redeemed [קנינו] our Jewish brothers who were sold [היהודים הנמכרים] to the nations; now would you even sell [תמכרו] your brothers that they may be sold to us [ונמכרו־לנו]?" Then they were silent and could not find a word to say. (Neh. 5:8)

In conclusion, we can say that Yahweh as King and Lord chose Israel for his servant. Thus, Yahweh's election of Israel is the election of his servant. Israel as his servant was to worship Yahweh, celebrate his feasts, offer sacrifices to him, and be a witness to his name. Failure to uphold this responsibility brought rejection. Here, the concepts of election and rejection are described by the commercial terms קנה and מכר.

6. ISRAEL, THE VINEYARD OF YAHWEH

The portrait of the planter and his vineyard is used mainly by the prophets to describe the Yahweh-Israel relationship. They present Yahweh as a divine planter with Israel as his vineyard. Yahweh calls Israel "My vineyard" (Is. 5:3,5) and says that he planted the choicest vine (Is. 5:2; Jer. 2:21). The event of the exodus and the settlement of Israel is often described in terms of Yahweh's planting Israel in the land.[144] Thus, the parable of the farmer and vineyard can be said to be a figurative description of Yahweh's election of Israel.

---

143. See Chap. III below, pp. 225-27.
144. See above, pp. 75-76.

The Meaning of Election

(1) The Terms for Planting

In Hebrew, three words carry the meaning of planting and sowing: נטע, זרע, and שתל.

1) נטע

The word נטע means "to plant" and appears in the Hebrew Bible about seventy times. Nearly half of its occurrences are found in the prophetic books. Objects of this word include tree (Lev. 19:23; Ecc. 2:5), olive tree (Dt. 6:11; Josh. 24:13), and vineyard (Dt. 20:6; 28:30,39; Ps. 80:16; 107:37; Prov. 31:16; Ecc. 2:4; Is. 5:2; 65:21; Jer. 2:21; 31:5; 35:7; Ezek. 28:26; Amos 5:11; 9:14; Zeph. 1:13). In Is. 51:16, נטע means "to create (heaven)," and in Jer. 1:10; 11:17; 12:2; 18:9; 31:28, and Ps. 44:3, it means "establishing (a nation, people)." The psalmist says that Yahweh planted the ear (הנטע אזן, Ps. 94:9). Another interesting case is found in Dan. 11:45, where it means "to pitch a tent" (ויטע אהלי).

However, we are more concerned with "the people of Israel" as an object of the verb נטע. In this case, Israel is compared to a tree planted by Yahweh in a particular place. A verse from the Song of the Sea reads:

תבאמו ותטעמו בהר נחלתך מכון לשבתך פעלת יהוה
מקדש אדני כוננו ידיך:

Thou wilt bring them and plant them in the mountain of Thine inheritance,
The place, O Yahweh, which Thou hast made for Thy dwelling,
The sanctuary, O Yahweh, which Thy hands have established.
(Ex. 15:17; cf. Ps. 80:9)

This verse anticipates Yahweh's safe guidance of his people to the promised land with their subsequent settlement there. נטע portrays the imagery of Yahweh's settling Israel. In his answer through Nathan to David, who wanted to build a temple, Yahweh promised that he would appoint a place and plant his people there (2 Sam. 7:10; 1 Ch. 17:9). Specifically, in the Song of the Vineyard (Is. 5) Yahweh is compared to a planter and Israel to a vineyard. The divine planter expected Israel to produce good grapes.

But in most cases in the prophetic books, נטע is used in the context of the restoration from exile.

> ושמתי עיני עליהם לטובה והשבתים על־הארץ הזאת
> ובניתים ולא אהרס ונטעתים ולא אתוש:

> For I will set My eyes on them for good, and I will bring them again to this land; and I will build them up and not overthrow them, and I will plant them and not pluck them up. (Jer. 24:6; cf. Amos 9:15; Jer. 32:41; 42:10)

Here, בניתים and נטעתים are used synonymously, as are אהרס and אתוש. This also points to the permanent settlement of Yahweh's people after the exile.

2) זרע

This verb refers to the action of sowing seed in the fields. It appears fifty-six times in the Hebrew Bible. Objects of this verb include land (Gen. 47:23; Ex. 23:10), seed (Lev. 26:16; Ecc. 11:16), wheat (Jer. 12:13), fields (Lev. 19:19; 24:4; Ps. 107:37), and ground (Is. 30:23). In an unusual case, זרע is used for sowing salt in the captured city of Shechem (Judg. 9:45). Sometimes it is used as a figurative description of moral action, thus "sowing righteousness" (זרעו לכם לצדקה, Hos. 10:12; Prov. 11:18), "sowing iniquity" (עולה זורע, Prov. 22:8), and even "sowing wind" (יזרעו רוח, Hos. 8:7 [futility]).

However, this verb often takes Yahweh as the subject and Israel as the object.

> הנה ימים באים נאם־יהוה וזרעתי את־בית ישראל
> ואת־בית יהודה זרע אדם וזרע בהמה:

> "Behold, days are coming," declares Yahweh, "when I will sow the house of Israel and the house of Judah with the seed of man and with the seed of beast." (Jer. 31:27; cf. Hos. 2:25; Zech. 10:9)

3) שתל

שתל has the same meaning as נטע and זרע, but it is only found ten times in the Hebrew Bible. In most cases it is used figuratively. In Ps. 1:3 the righteous are compared to a tree planted (שתל) by the streams of water, and in Ps. 92:14 the righteous are likened to the ones planted in the house of Yahweh. However, Israel is said to be planted by Yahweh on the high mountain (Ezek. 17:23), by the waters (Ezek. 19:10), and in the wilderness (Ezek. 19:13).

(2) Yahweh-Israel as Farmer-Vineyard

The terms we have examined above do not refer explicitly to election, since נטע, זרע, and שתל do not carry any concept of choosing or selecting. However, the parables of the vineyard which are described by these verbs most vividly illustrate the Yahweh-Israel relationship, and in the parable itself the idea of choosing is implied.

Since ancient Israel was an agricultural society, like others in the Near East, the Israelites were so accustomed to farming that the parable of the vineyard proved to be a vivid means of expression. For them, the vineyard was important and precious as the source of their food. It was not to be sold outside the clan, because it was an inheritance from their ancestors (1 Kgs. 20:3). They sowed seeds and planted trees expecting good fruits to be produced. And so the Song of the Vineyard in Is. 5 conveys these ideas and compares the vineyard to the people of Israel and the farmer to Yahweh himself.[145] The point of this parable is that Yahweh is the owner of the vineyard (land), and he transplanted Israel onto his land so as to produce good fruit. Therefore, Israel's failure to bear good fruit was to result in rejection in the form of plucking, or uprooting, them from the land. In relation to this metaphor, נתש, שרש, and נסח are found as rejection terms.[146]

ויתשם יהוה מעל אדמתם באף ובחמה ובקצף גדול
וישלכם אל־ארץ אחרת כיום הזה:

And Yahweh uprooted them from their land in anger and in fury and in great wrath, and cast them into another land, as it is this day. (Dt. 29:27 [E. 28]; cf. 1 Kgs. 14:15; Jer. 12:14-15; Amos 9:15; 2 Ch. 7:20)

Therefore, the restoration will mean Yahweh's bringing Israel back again and planting them in the land.[147]

145. For exegesis of the Song, see Chap. II below, pp. 151-53.
146. See Chap. III below, pp. 204-5.
147. See Chap. III below, pp. 227-28.

ונטעתים על־אדמתם ולא ינתשו עוד מעל אדמתם אשר
נתתי להם אמר יהוה אלהיך:

"I will also plant them on their land,
And they will not again be rooted out from their land
Which I have given them,"
Says Yahweh your God. (Amos 9:15; cf. Jer. 24:6; 31:27-28; 42:10;
45:4)

Israel is also viewed as the shoot (נצר) which Yahweh has planted in the context of the restoration (Is. 60:21).

7. ISRAEL, THE SHEEP OF YAHWEH

In Ps. 95:6-7, the psalmist exhorts the people:

באו נשתחוה ונכרעה נברכה לפני־יהוה עשנו:
כי הוא אלהינו ואנחנו עם מרעיתו וצאן ידו
היום אם־בקלו תשמעו:

Come, let us worship and bow down;
Let us kneel before Yahweh our Maker.
For He is our God,
And we are the people of His pasture, and the sheep of His hand.
Today, if you would hear His voice.

According to this psalm, Yahweh is presented as the maker of Israel, and Israel as the sheep under his care. In fact, the people and the sheep are identified together as seen in Ps. 79:13, ואנחנו עמך וצאן מרעיתך (So we are Thy people and the sheep of Thy pasture). Both the sheep and the pasture belong to Yahweh. They are Yahweh's property.

הוי רעים מאבדים ומפצים את־צאן מרעיתי נאם־יהוה:
לוכ כה־אמר יהוה אלהי ישראל על־הרעים הרעים את־
עמי אתם הפצתם את־צאני ותדחום ולא פקדתם אתם
הנני פקד עליכם את־רע מעלליכם נאם־יהוה:

"Woe to the shepherds who are destroying and scattering the sheep of My pasture!" declares Yahweh. Therefore thus says Yahweh God of Israel concerning the shepherds who are tending My people: "You have scattered My flock and driven them away, and have not attended to them; behold, I am about to attend to you for the evil of your deeds," declares Yahweh. (Jer. 23:1-2)

In these verses, "the sheep of My pasture," "My people," and "My flock" all point to Israel. Yahweh is their owner, and he entrusts them to the shepherds' care. Therefore, Yahweh is not viewed as the shepherd of Israel, since the shepherds of Israel seem to be the leaders of Israel.

Numbers 27:16-17 gives us a clear picture. Moses, at the end of his life, went up to the mountain of Abarim where Yahweh would appoint his successor.

> May Yahweh, the God of the spirits of all flesh, appoint a man over the congregation, who will go out and come in before them, and who will lead them out and bring them in, that the congregation of Yahweh may not be like sheep which have no shepherd (ולא תהיה עדת יהוה וצאן אשר אין להם רעה:).

Moses compares the congregation of Yahweh to a flock of sheep, and his successor to a shepherd. According to Moses, the shepherd is the one who can lead the people to the promised land after him. Thus, the psalmist says that "Thou didst lead Thy people like a flock, by the hand of Moses and Aaron" (נחית כצאן עמך ביד־משה ואהרן, Ps 77:20 [E.21]). We can see this same expression in 1 Kgs 22:17; 2 Ch. 18:16; Jer. 49:16; 50:6; Ezek 37:24; Mic. 5:5; Zech. 10:3. As in the ancient Near East, kings are particularly viewed as the shepherds of the people (1 Kgs. 22:17; 2 Ch. 18:16).[148]

As Num. 26:17 suggests, the role of the shepherd is to go before the sheep and lead them to pasture or to water. Sometimes the shepherd had to protect his sheep from the wild beasts, as David did while he was tending his father's sheep (1 Sam. 17:34-36). As in the confession of Jacob (Gen. 31:38-40), the shepherd was to watch over the flocks day and night so that they would not be lost or stolen.

However, the shepherds of Israel were not faithful. Yahweh's indictment against them exposes their negligence. "Those who are

---

148. Thus Sennacherib (Königinschriften: Sanherib 1-3) and Hammurabi (*ANET*, p. 164b) were seen in this role. See G.E. Wright, "The Good Shepherd," *BA* 3/1 (Feb. 1940): 44-48. Valentine Muller suggests that the king was called "a good shepherd" in Mesopotamian literature as early as the third millennium B.C., and the Old Testament uses the same term ("The Prehistory of the 'Good Shepherd'," *JNES* 3 [1944]: 87-90).

sickly you have not strengthened, the diseased you have not healed, the broken you have not bound up, the scattered you have not brought back, nor have you sought for the lost; but with force and with severity you have dominated them" (Ezek. 34:4). These shepherds had been feeding themselves instead of feeding the flocks (Ezek. 34:3). Furthermore, they were scattering and destroying the sheep (Jer. 23:1). Thus, Yahweh's flock wandered through all the mountains and on every hill, scattered over all the earth, having become a prey and food for all the beasts of the fields (Ezek. 34:5-6), and there was no one to search or seek for them. The shepherds ignored and misled the people of Yahweh. From this perspective we can understand the repeated formula in the book of Kings indicting the kings of Israel: "And he did evil in the sight of Yahweh and walked in the way of Jeroboam the son of Nebat, who made Israel sin" (1 Kgs. 15:26;16:19; 22:52; 2 Kgs. 8:18,27, etc.). The responsibility of the leaders for the fall of Israel is also to be so explained (Hos. 8:10; Jer. 27:10). Therefore, Yahweh made them cease feeding his sheep (Ezek. 34:10) and promised to raise up new shepherds over them. "I shall also raise up shepherds over them and they will tend them; and they will not be afraid any longer, nor be terrified, nor will any be missing" (Jer. 23:4). In Ezek. 34:23-24, the shepherd whom Yahweh would raise up will be like David.

Moreover, Yahweh promised that he himself would be the shepherd of Israel.

הנה אדני יהוה בחזק יבוא וזרעו משלה לו
הנה שכרו אתו ופעלתו לפניו:
כרעה עדרו ירעה בזרעו יקבץ
טלאים ובחיקו ישא עלות ינהל:

Behold, Yahweh the Lord will come with might,
With His arm ruling for Him.
Behold, His reward is with Him,
And His recompense before Him.
Like a shepherd He will tend His flock,
In His arm He will gather the lambs,
And carry them in His bosom;
He will gently lead the nursing ewes. (Is. 40:10-11)

In Ezekiel, Yahweh says: "I will care for My sheep and will deliver them" (34:12), "I will feed them in a good pasture" (34:14), and "I will feed My flock and I will lead them to rest" (34:16). The failure of the leaders in Israel inevitably led to the raising up of a good shepherd, and so Yahweh himself had to be involved in feeding his sheep. Thus, the imagery of Yahweh as the shepherd of Israel is the result of later development. Yahweh is seen in two roles in the Bible: as the owner of the sheep and as the shepherd of sheep.

This imagery of God as the shepherd of his people seems to be a religious metaphor traditionally associated with the exodus.

52 ויסע כצאן עמו וינהגם במדבר:
53 וינחם לבטח ולא פחדו ואת־אויביהם כסה הים:
54 ויביאם אל־גבול קדשו הר־זה קנתה ימינו:
55 ויגרש מפניהם גוים ויפילם בחבל נחלה וישכן
באהליהם שבטי ישראל:

52 But He led forth His own people like sheep,
    And guided them in the wilderness like a flock;
53 And He led them safely, so that they did not fear;
    But the sea engulfed their enemies.
54 So He brought them to His holy land,
    To this hill country which His right hand had gained.
55 He also drove out the nations before them,
    And He apportioned them for an inheritance by measurement,
    And made the tribes of Israel dwell in their tents. (Ps. 78:52-55)

As this psalm suggests, the event of the exodus is viewed as Yahweh's leading his flock through the wilderness and the sea to his pasture. The same idea is also found in Ps. 77:20 (E. 21), Ps. 80:2 (E. 1), and Is. 63:11. Therefore, the election of Yahweh can be explained by Yahweh's leading and tending his flock from Egypt to a land flowing with milk and honey.

The relation of the images of the rejection and restoration to this metaphor of shepherd and his sheep should be examined. Since the idea of election was portrayed by the imagery of Yahweh's leading and tending his sheep, the concept of rejection and restoration is also described in terms of the imagery of Yahweh's scattering and gathering his sheep.

As rejection terms, פוץ, אבד, and טרף all carry the meaning of "scattering (sheep)" and "driving out." Thus, the "flock" symbolizing Israel is used as the object of פוץ in Jer. 10:21; 23:1-2; and Ezek. 34:6. But Yahweh scatters (פוץ) Israel (Dt. 4:27; 28:64; 30:3; Is. 24:1; Jer. 9:15; 13:24; 18:17; Ezek. 11:16-17; 20:34,41; 28:25; 29:13; 34:12; 36:19). Therefore, the rejection of Israel is Yahweh's scattering or driving his sheep out of his pasture and exposing them before wild beasts (Hos. 5:14; 13:8; Mic. 5:8).[149] טרף means "to tear in pieces" and is used mostly with regard to wild animals. Jacob was informed that Joseph was torn in pieces by an animal (Gen. 37:33; 44:28; cf. Ps. 7:3 [E. 2]; Nah. 2:13 [E. 12]; Ezek. 19:3,6; 22:25,27). טרף is also used for Yahweh and Israel. "Come, let us return to Yahweh. For He has torn [טרף] us, but He will heal us; He has wounded us, but He will bandage us" (Hos. 6:1; cf. 5:14; Jer. 5:6).

Following on this analogy, the restoration is Yahweh's gathering his sheep from the dispersed land and settling them again in his pasture. קבץ, אסף, and נהל are used as restoration terms in relation to the metaphor of shepherd-sheep.[150]

8. ISRAEL, THE VESSEL OF YAHWEH

The creator-creature relationship is another aspect of Yahweh's election of Israel in the Old Testament. Yahweh is portrayed as the creator of Israel, and Israel as his creature.

ועתה כה־אמר יהוה בראך יעקב ויצרך ישראל
אל־תירא כי גאלתיך קראתי בשמך לי־אתה:

> But now, thus says Yahweh, your creator, O Jacob,
> And He who formed you, O Israel,
> "Do not fear, for I have redeemed you;
> I have called you by name; you are Mine!" (Is. 43:1)

Here, Yahweh is introduced as the creator of Jacob, the fashioner of Israel, the redeemer of Israel, and the one who called Israel by name. Thus, Yahweh proclaims to Israel: "You are Mine!" ברא and יצר are employed to describe the creator-creature relationship between Yahweh and Israel. Since the relationship constitutes an important election idea, we will consider this imagery.

149. See below, pp. 206-7.
150. See below, pp. 228-29.

(1) The Terms for Creation

The key creation terms in the Old Testament are כון, בנה, עשׂה, יצר, and ברא, all found with relation to the creation of Israel. Sometimes ילד and חיל are used with reference to Yahweh's giving birth to Israel. Thus, we include these two terms in this topic.

1) יצר

יצר means "to fashion" or "to form." In regard to human activity, יצר in the participial form means a "potter," one who forms a vessel out of clay (Is. 29:16; 41:25; Jer. 18:4,6). In Is. 44:9 and Hab. 2:18, the word is used with the meaning of a carver of graven images. However, this verb is predominantly used for Yahweh as the divine potter of the earth (Jer. 33:2), universe (Is. 45:18), man (Gen. 2:7,8) and other natural phenomena (Amos 4:13; Ps. 74:17; 95:5). For example, Yahweh said to Jeremiah: "Before I formed you [בטרם אצורך] in the womb I knew you, and before you were born I consecrated you; I have appointed you a prophet to the nations" (Jer. 1:5).

Yahweh formed not only an individual, but also the people of Israel.

> ועתה שמע יעקב עבדי וישראל בחרתי בו:
> כה־אמר יהוה עשׂך ויצרך מבטן יעזרך
> אל־תירא עבדי יעקב וישרון בחרתי בו:

> But now listen, O Jacob, My servant;
> And Israel, whom I have chosen:
> Thus says Yahweh who made you
> And formed you from the womb, who will help you,
> "Do not fear, O Jacob My servant;
> And you Jeshurun whom I have chosen." (Is. 44:1-2)

The appearance of בחר and עבדי suggests that these verses belong to the context of election. Yahweh's making (עשׂה) and forming (יצר) of Israel, therefore, can be categorized under the concept of election. Particularly, the phrase "Yahweh formed Israel from the womb" is repeated in Isaiah (27:11; 43:1,21; 44:21,24; 45:11; 49:5). Thus, Yahweh is called "his [Israel's] Maker" (יצרו, Is. 45:9,11).

In order to illustrate more vividly this creator-creature relationship between Yahweh and Israel, Yahweh is compared to the potter and Israel to the clay.

ועתה יהוה אבינו אתה
אנחנו החמר ואתה יצרנו ומעשה ידך ולנו:

But now, O Yahweh, Thou art our Father,
We are the clay, and Thou our potter;
And all of us are the work of Thy hand. (Is. 64:7 [E. 8]; cf. 29:16;
45:9-13)

In Is. 49:5, יצר is employed in the election formula.

ועתה אמר יהוה יצרי מבטן לעבד לו

And now says Yahweh, who formed me from the womb to be His servant.
{X: (יהוה); Y: יצרי; X¹: לי; לו: Z¹: לל; לעבד}

2) עשה

עשה means "to do" or "to make." This word in many cases is synonymous with יצר, but the former is used more frequently than the latter. In Gen. 1:31, עשה is used for God's creation of all things. In that sense, עשה is interchangeable with ברא.

However, in Hosea this term is employed to denote the origin of the Israelites. Yahweh is said to be the maker of Israel.

וישכח ישראל את־עשהו ויבן היכלות
ויהודה הרבה ערים בצרות
ושלחתי־אש בעריו ואכלה ארמנתיה:

For Israel has forgotten his Maker and built palaces;
And Judah has multiplied fortified cities,
But I will send a fire on its cities that it may consume
    its palatial dwellings. (Hos. 8:14)

More frequently, this verb describing Yahweh as the maker of Israel is found in Isaiah (44:1,2; 51:13; 54:5) and in the Psalms (95:6,7; 100:3; 149:2).

It is also employed in the election formula.

כי לא־יטש יהוה את־עמו בעבור שמו הגדול כי הואיל
יהוה לעשות אתכם לו לעם:

For Yahweh will not abandon His people on account of His great
name, because Yahweh has been pleased to make you a people for
Himself. (1 Sam. 12:22)
{X: יהוה; Y־את :אתכם; X:לו:לי; Z :לעם :לֹ}

עשה is preceded by the verb הואיל, implying pleasure of heart as in
the case of the election term בחר.

3) ברא

ברא carries the basic meaning "to create," "bring into existence,"
and "initiate something new." It differs from יצר in that the latter
emphasizes primarily the shaping of an object, while ברא emphasizes the actual creator of the object.[151] Qal and Niphal forms of
this verb are exclusively used for God. God created the heavens and
earth (Gen. 1:1), and everything in the earth (i.e., all natural phenomena), and he will one day create new heavens and a new earth
(Is. 65:17). This word is also used for the creation of Israel.

אני יהוה קדושכם בורא ישראל מלככם:

I am Yahweh, your Holy One, the Creator of Israel, your King.
(Is. 43:15; cf. 43:1; Mal. 2:10)

4) בנה, כון

Both כון and בנה are construction terms. בנה is used for the building
of a house, altar, sanctuary, high place, and city, and כון is used for
the establishment of a kingdom and for God's creative acts. These
terms are also used with reference to Yahweh's creation of Israel.

ה־ליהוה תגמלו־זאת עם נבל ולא חכם
הלוא־הוא אביך קנך הוא עשך ויכננך:

Do you thus repay Yahweh,
O foolish and unwise people?
Is not He your Father who has bought you?
He has made you and established you. (Dt. 32:6)

151. T.E. McComiskey, "ברא," *TWOT,* 1:127.

יצר, קנה and כון establish the relationship between Yahweh the father and his people here below.

In the restoration context of Jeremiah, בנה is used for Yahweh's building Israel.

ושמתי עיני עליהם לטובה והשבתים על־הארץ הזאת
ובניתים ולא אהרס ונטעתים ולא אתוש:

For I will set My eyes on them for good, and I will bring them again to this land; and I will build them up and not overthrow them, and I will plant them and not pluck them up. (Jer. 24:6; cf. 31:4,28; 33:7; 42:10; 45:4)

Here, בנה parallels the election verb נטע. Thus, בנה and כון are creation terms which are related to election.

5) ילד and חיל

To describe Yahweh's creation of Israel, ילד and חיל are also used. ילד means "to bear" or "to beget (a child)" and חיל means (with respect to a woman) "to bring into labor (birth-pangs)." Both terms are used for Yahweh's creation of the world as well as of Israel.

בטרם הרים ילדו ותחולל ארץ ותבל ומעולם עד־עולם אתה אל:

Before the mountains were born,
Or Thou didst give birth to the earth and the world,
Even from everlasting to everlasting, Thou art God. (Ps. 90:2)

צור ילדך תשי ותשכח אל מחללך:

You neglected the Rock who begot you,
And forgot the God who gave you birth. (Dt. 32:18; cf. Ps. 2:7;
      Ezek. 16:20; Hos. 5:7)

(2) Yahweh-Israel as Potter-Clay

As we have seen, Yahweh is described as creator or maker of Israel. He built Israel as a people. He gave birth to Israel. Thus he is called their maker, builder, and father. Since all these images reflect the same concept of Yahweh as creator, we can deal with them under the heading of potter-clay. One of the best illustrations for the cre-

ator-creature relationship between Yahweh and Israel would be the
parable of the potter and the clay (Is. 29:16; 45:9-13; 64:7 [E.8]; Jer.
18:1-10). "But now, O Yahweh, Thou art our Father, We are the clay,
and Thou art our potter; And all of us are the work of Thy hand"
(Is. 64:7 [E. 8]).

Yahweh as a sovereign potter could fashion any form and make
anything he wanted. He could also break down whatever he has
made and remake it according to his will (Jer. 18:4). The same principle can be applied to Israel (Jer. 18:6). Using parental imagery,
Yahweh said that he bore and carried (עמס, נשא) Israel. Thus, Yahweh's election, rejection, and restoration of his people are expressed in this metaphor of potter-clay. The rejection terms, with
respect to the creator-creature relationship, are the negative counterparts to the concepts of making and building.

והיה כאשר שקדתי עליהם לנתוש ולנתוץ ולהרס
ולהאביד ולהרע כן אשקד עליהם לבנות ולנטוע נאם־יהוה:

"And it will come about that as I have watched over them to pluck
up, to break down, to overthrow, to destroy, and to bring disaster, so
I will watch over them to build and to plant," declares Yahweh.
(Jer. 31:28)

Here, נתש, נתץ, הרס, and אבד are all rejection terms. We have examined נתש in the previous section as an antonym of נטע. נתץ (to tear
down or to demolish), with a meaning opposite to that of Yahweh's
fashioning Israel as a potter (Jer. 1:10; 18:7; Ps. 52:7 [E. 5]), הרס (to
overthrow, Jer. 1:10; 24:6; 42:10; 45:4), and אבד (to destroy, Dt.
4:26; 8:19; 28:20, 51, 63; Josh. 23:13; Jer. 15:7; 12:17; 27:10,15; Ezek.
25:7) are in contrast to the concepts of making or building.[152]

As for the restoration,[153] the above verbs are used in an entirely
negative context.

ושמתי עיני עליהם לטובה והשבתים על־הארץ הזאת
ובניתים ולא אהרס ונטעתים ולא אתוש:

For I will set My eyes on them for good, and I will bring them again
to this land; and I will build and not overthrow them, and I will plant
them and not pluck them up. (Jer. 24:6)

152. See Chap. III below, pp. 207-8.
153. See Chap. III below, pp. 229-30.

9. ISRAEL, A HOLY PEOPLE TO YAHWEH
(עם קדוש ליהוה)

In Lev. 20:26, Yahweh commands Israel:

והייתם לי קדשים כי קדוש אני יהוה ואבדל אתכם מן־העמים להיות לי:

Thus you are to be holy to Me, for I Yahweh am holy; and I have set you apart from the peoples to be Mine.

Furthermore, in Dt. 14:2, Yahweh says:

כי עם קדוש אתה ליהוה אלהיך ובך בחר יהוה להיות
לו לעם סגלה מכל העמים אשר על־פני האדמה:

For you are a holy people to Yahweh your God; and Yahweh has chosen you to be a people for His own possession out of all the peoples who are on the face of the earth.

According to these two verses, Yahweh, who is holy, separated and chose Israel to be his own people out of all the peoples. Thus Israel became a holy people to Yahweh, and they were to be holy. We can see here that Yahweh's separation of Israel is Yahweh's election of his holy people, and the concept of Yahweh's setting them apart is closely related to that of election and holiness. Thus, we will examine the concept of election from the perspective of "separation."

(1) The Terms for Separation

Of the terms meaning "to separate" or "to set apart," הבדיל, הפלה, and קדש are found in relation to our topic.

1) הבדיל

הבדיל means "to make a distinction" or "to divide." Mostly as a ritual term, it is used with reference to making a distinction between clean and unclean things (Lev. 10:10; 11:47; 20:25; Ezek. 22:26; 42:20). Moses was commanded to hang up the veil to separate (הבדיל) between the holy place and the holy of holies when he

94

built the tabernacle (Ex. 26:33). At the time of Korah's rebellion against Moses, Yahweh spoke to Moses and Aaron to separate themselves (הבדלו) from the rebellious congregation of Korah, so that he might consume them instantly (Num. 16:21). The Israelites who returned from the exile are described as the ones who had separated themselves (הנבדל) from the impurity of the nations of the land (Ezr. 6:21), from the people of the land (Ezr. 9:1; 10:11; Neh. 10:29), and from all foreigners (Neh. 9:2). Sometimes הבדיל is used for selection for a special assignment. Moses was to separate the Levites for the service of the tent of meeting according to the commandment of Yahweh (Num. 8:14; 16:9; Dt. 10:8; 1 Ch. 23:13). David and the commanders of the army set apart (הבדיל) the sons of Asaph and of Heman and of Jeduthun for the service of singing and playing musical instruments in the house of Yahweh (1 Ch. 25:1).

However, הבדיל is also used in describing the election of Israel. As an election term, בדל is used only in the Niphal and Hiphil forms.

ואמר לכם אתם תירשו את־אדמתם ואני אתננה לכם לרשת
אתה ארץ זבת חלב ודבש אני יהוה אלהיכם אשר־הבדלתי
אתכם מן־העמים:

Hence I have said to you, "You are to possess their land, and I Myself will give it to you to possess it, a land flowing with milk and honey." I am Yahweh your God, who has separated you from the peoples.
(Lev. 20:24)

Yahweh separated Israel out of all the peoples to make them his people, and he gave them the land as an inheritance.

The purpose of Yahweh's separating Israel is more specific in Lev. 20:26. Solomon mentions Yahweh's separation of his people in his prayer for the dedication of the temple.

כי־אתה הבדלתם לך לנחלה מכל עמי הארץ כאשר דברת
ביד משה עבדך בהוציאך את־אבתינו ממצרים אדני יהוה:

For thou didst separate them from among all the peoples of the earth, to be thy heritage, as thou didst declare through Moses, thy servant, when thou didst bring our fathers out of Egypt, O Lord Yahweh. (1 Kgs. 8:53, RSV)

It is noteworthy that הבדיל is used in an election formula here.

הפלה (2

הפלה also means "to make a distinction" or "to set apart." This verb is mainly used in Exodus for Yahweh's making a distinction between Israel and Egypt when he poured out his plagues on the land of Egypt (Ex. 8:18 [E.22]; 9:4; 11:7). However, הפלה is also used for Yahweh's separation of Israel from all other peoples.

וּבַמֶּה יִוָּדַע אֵפוֹא כִּי־מָצָאתִי חֵן בְּעֵינֶיךָ אֲנִי וְעַמֶּךָ הֲלוֹא
בְּלֶכְתְּךָ עִמָּנוּ וְנִפְלִינוּ אֲנִי וְעַמְּךָ מִכָּל־הָעָם אֲשֶׁר עַל־פְּנֵי הָאֲדָמָה׃

For how then can it be known that I have found favor in Thy sight, I and Thy people? Is it not by Thy going with us, so that we, I and Thy people, may be distinguished from all the other people who are upon the face of the earth? (Ex. 33:16)

קדש (3

The verb קדש is mostly found in the sphere of cultic regulations with the meaning "to sanctify."[154] When the verb is used for a man or a special group of people, it implies the meaning "to set apart," "to be chosen," or "to be devoted." Yahweh said to Jeremiah, "Before you were born I consecrated you [הִקְדַּשְׁתִּיךָ]" (Jer. 1:5). When Samuel chose David for king, he consecrated (קדש) Jesse and his sons and invited them to the sacrifice (1 Sam. 16:5). The priests (Ex. 29:1), as well as Aaron and his sons (Ex. 30:30), were to be consecrated (קדש) in order to minister as priests to Yahweh. Yahweh said that he sanctified (קדש) the first-born of Israel as his own (Num. 8:16,17). As for the people of Israel, Yahweh repeatedly says that he is the one who sanctified them (אֲנִי יְהוָה מְקַדִּשְׁכֶם) (Ex. 31:13; Lev. 20:8; 21:8,15,23; 22:9,16,32; Ezek. 20:12; 37:28).

In particular, the adjective form קדוש is used for the elected people.

כִּי עַם קָדוֹשׁ אַתָּה לַיהוָה אֱלֹהֶיךָ בְּךָ בָּחַר יְהוָה אֱלֹהֶיךָ
לִהְיוֹת לוֹ לְעַם סְגֻלָּה מִכֹּל הָעַמִּים אֲשֶׁר עַל־פְּנֵי הָאֲדָמָה׃

154. Though the suggestion that קדש is derived from the biliteral קד (to cut) has been proposed by W. Baudissin (*Studien zur semitischen Religionsgeschichte,* II [1878]) and many others, it is tenuous in view of the uncertainties in the transition of biliteral roots to the triliteral form. See T.E. McComiskey, "קדש," *TWOT,* 2:786-87.

For you are a holy people to Yahweh your God; Yahweh your God
has chosen you to be a people for His own possession out of all the
peoples who are on the face of the earth. (Dt. 7:6)

According to this verse, the phrase "a holy people to Yahweh" does
not imply any ritual or moral holiness. It rather defines the relationship between Yahweh and his people.[155] Thus, the phrase should
be understood as "a devoted people to Yahweh" or "a consecrated
or dedicated people to Yahweh."[156] This then agrees with the meaning of the next line, that Yahweh chose Israel as his own possession.
Therefore, עם קדוש is another characteristic designation of God's
chosen people in the Hebrew Bible (Dt. 14:2,21; 26:19; Is. 62:12).
And similar phrases, גוי קדוש (a holy nation, Ex. 19:6) and קדשים צאן
(a holy flock, Ezek. 36:38), are also used.

(2) Israel as a Holy People to Yahweh

Since Yahweh set apart Israel and chose them to be a people for his
own possession, they became "a holy people," a people dedicated
to Yahweh (עם קדוש ליהוה). Anything dedicated to Yahweh must be
sanctified and hallowed, so as a people belonging to Yahweh, Israel
was required to be holy. Therefore, Yahweh commanded them:
"Thus you are to be holy to Me, for I Yahweh am holy" (Lev. 20:26).
Israel was to conform perfectly to the holiness of Yahweh in every
aspect of life. In particular, their religious life (Ex. 31:13; Lev. 20:8)
and moral behavior (Lev. 21:8,15,23) had to be different from that
of the neighboring countries. Even their food had to be sanctified
(Lev. 22:8-9,16).

However, they defiled themselves by following pagan customs
and traditions. "Her priests have done violence to My law and have
profaned [חלל] My holy things; they have made no distinction between the holy and the profane, and they have not taught the difference between the unclean and the clean; and they hide their eyes
from My sabbaths, and I am profaned among them" (Ezek. 22:26).
Therefore, Yahweh also profaned them. "I was angry with My peo-

155. Otto Procksh, "ἅγιος," TDNT, 1:91-92.
156. The phrase כי נתנים נתנים לי מתוך בני ישראל (for they are wholly given
to Me among the sons of Israel, Num. 8:16) gives the clue for our understanding of
עם קדוש ליהוה. See also P.C. Craigie, The Book of Deuteronomy, p. 179.

ple, I profaned [חללתי] My heritage, And gave them into your hand. You did not show mercy to them, On the aged you made your yoke very heavy" (Is. 47:6).

Though Israel defiled itself by obliterating the distinction between the holy and the profane, Yahweh defiled his people by delivering them into the hand of Babylon so as to be taken into exile (cf. Is. 43:28). Therefore, the reason for Yahweh's rejection of his people was because of Israel's חלל, טמא, חנף, and געל.[157] And the restoration of Israel will be a restoration of holiness.[158]

> And the house of Israel will not again defile My holy name, neither they nor their kings, by their harlotry and by the corpses of their kings when they die, by setting their threshold by My threshold, and their door post beside My door post, with only the wall between Me and them. And they have defiled My holy name by their abominations which they have committed. So I have consumed them in My anger. Now let them put away their harlotry and the corpses of their kings far from Me; and I will dwell among them forever. (Ezek. 43:7-9)

And on the day of restoration,

> Behold, Yahweh has proclaimed to the end of the earth . . .
> And they will call them, "The holy people [עם־הקדש],
> The redeemed of Yahweh [גאולי יהוה]";
> And you will be called, "Sought out, a city not forsaken."
>
> (Is. 62:11, 12)

SUMMARY

As we have seen, the idea of election is expressed by various terms and metaphors. These imageries are borrowed from the human family relationships (husband-wife, father-son), social and political institutions (warrior-his army, master-servant), and the nomadic (shepherd-sheep), agricultural (farmer-vineyard), and industrial (potter-clay) settings of life. Moreover, each of these imageries expresses a characteristic aspect of the Yahweh-Israel relationship. The people of Israel were conscious of their special relationship

157. See Chap. III below, p. 208.
158. See Chap. III below, pp. 230-31.

with Yahweh which existed throughout the whole range of their social life. Yahweh, the God of Israel, was not an abstract and theoretical deity, but rather one who could be perceived personally and practically in everyday life. Thus, this relationship is dynamic and organic in its character, not rigid or static.

The following is a summary of what we have found about the meaning of election.

1. The election idea is borrowed from the marriage idea in its terms, formulae, and relationship characteristics. Yahweh as a husband chose Israel as his bride. In particular, the exodus is compared to Yahweh's going to Egypt and bringing back his bride, while the settlement of the promised land is seen as Yahweh's providing a domicile for his wife. Yahweh initiated this exclusive relationship with Israel and demanded loyalty to himself alone. The verbs לקח, ידע, בעל, ישב, נשא, and ארש play an important role conveying the idea. Thus, the unfaithfulness of Israel to Yahweh is described as "playing the harlot," or "committing adultery." Therefore, Yahweh's election of Israel can be said to be equivalent to Yahweh's choosing a wife.

2. Election is represented as Yahweh's choosing his army. Yahweh as a divine warrior chose his army and fought for them. Thus, the election verbs בחר, קרא, and פקד are all war terms, although they employ the same syntax as was found in the marriage formulae in their description of the election idea. Since Yahweh was Israel's chief warrior, the people had to consult with him whenever they went out to war, and so they went out to battle in the name of Yahweh. Therefore, Israel's seeking its national security in anyone other than Yahweh was seen as a great rebellion against him. In those cases, Yahweh himself employed his agents and fought with them against Israel, as can be seen in the context of the exile.

3. The image of father-son is another important metaphor which portrays the election theology. Yahweh adopted Israel as his son, and thus Israel was called by his name and became his heir, the tribe of his inheritance (Jer. 10:16). Therefore, the land was given to Israel as an inheritance. However, the exile is viewed as a withdrawal of sonship with the consequent deprivation of the land.

4. In the master-servant relationship, Yahweh as a master or king chooses Israel as his servant and requires its service. Since Israel was viewed as his servant, the concept of Yahweh's "pur-

chasing" (קנה, גאל) and "selling" (מכר) Israel is applied to Israel's election and rejection.

5. Israel as Yahweh's special possession is implied in the metaphor of farmer-vineyard. Yahweh as a farmer planted Israel in the land of Canaan and expected the nation to produce good fruit. The concept of Israel's planting and uprooting, referring to the exodus and exile, is another metaphoric description of election and rejection.

6. Since Yahweh made Israel, he has the authority and power to break or to reshape the nation according to his will. The emphasis on Yahweh's sovereignty in his election and rejection of Israel is portrayed by the analogy of potter-clay.

7. The shepherd-sheep image obviously points to the issues of Yahweh's protection and feeding of Israel. Yahweh's leading Israel to a pasture and protecting it from the beasts are significant election ideas. However, Yahweh's scattering the sheep and withdrawing his protection as wild beasts attack his rebellious flock are also characteristic rejection ideas. Besides these images, the idea of Yahweh's separating Israel from the rest of the nations is also one of the important concepts of election.

Therefore, the idea of election is expressed by a variety of metaphors. We must understand this idea in the light of the composite picture portrayed by these various imageries. The idea of election is too vast and deep to be expressed by a single term or phrase. Rather, election is a composite idea with graphic imagery developed from the unique life context of Old Testament Israel.

CHAPTER II

The Development of the Idea of Election

The idea of election did not spring out of a vacuum. At a certain point in history and in a certain context of Israelite life, the nation realized that it had a special relationship with Yahweh, and so tried to explain and describe it in terms of its own life and culture.[1] The election metaphors that we have seen in the previous chapter are basically the product of this effort. Therefore, our next task is to find out in what cultural setting the idea of election arose and to determine why certain characteristic expressions were employed in describing the idea.

Many factors must have been operative in awakening the minds of the Israelites to the fact that Yahweh had chosen them as his people. In particular, the national crises which threatened the nation's existence and faith seem to be the most probable settings for the origin and development of the election idea. Israel overcomes those national crises by the help of Yahweh. The superiority of Yahweh and his wonders for his people are manifested during this period, and these stir the minds of the people to perceive that they have an exclusive relationship with Yahweh. However, certain metaphors arise as reflections of contemporary society in order to emphasize the established relationship and to issue a warning against the unfaithfulness of the people.

1. This does not necessarily mean that the Old Testament contains God's self-revelation or record of that revelation, but that it portrays man's search after God, i.e., man's endeavor to understand the revelation. Cf. P.C. Craigie, *The Problem of War in the Old Testament* (Grand Rapids: Eerdmans, 1978), p. 37.

Religious ideas are basically conditioned by their social and cultural context. Thus, we will examine the life setting from which the idea of election sprung and developed. Since we are dealing with the election of Israel as a people, the election of isolated individuals will be left out of our consideration.

1. THE PRE-MONARCHIC IDEA

Israel's pre-monarchic experience of Yahweh takes place mostly in the battlefield. As they engage in war and experience great victories, they ascribe their success to the supernatural intervention of Yahweh. The Song of the Sea, the battles of Joshua, the Song of Deborah, and the story of Gideon can be classified in this category as we examine the development of the election idea.

(1) The Song of the Sea (Ex. 15:1-18)

The Song of the Sea is regarded as one of the oldest poems in the Hebrew Bible.[2] In this poem, key ideas and terms of election are manifold.

1 אשירה ליהוה כי־גאה גאה סוס ורכבו רמה בים:

2 עזי וזמרת יה ויהי־לי לישועה
זה אלי ואנוהו אלהי אבי וארממנהו:

1 I will sing to Yahweh, for He is highly exalted;
   The horse and its rider He has hurled into the sea.

2. W.F. Albright defended a thirteenth-century dating in his *Archeology of Palestine* (Harmondsworth, Middlesex, 1949), p. 233. He was, however, forced to regard the reference to the "inhabitants of Philistia" as an anachronism. Cf. F.M. Cross, Jr., and D.N. Freedman, "The Song of Miriam" *JNES* 14 (1955): 237-50. In buttressing Albright's major arguments, F.M. Cross proposes that the poem is to be dated by (1) the typology of its language, (2) the typology of its prosody, (3) orthographic analysis, (4) the typology of the development of Israel's religion, (5) history of tradition, and (6) historical allusion *(Canaanite Myth and Hebrew Epic*, pp. 112-44). Through this cumulative evidence, he concludes that "the Song of the Sea does not derive its account from Yahwistic tradition" (ibid., p.133), and "all the evidence points to a premonarchic date for the Song of the Sea, in the late twelfth or early eleventh century B.C." (ibid., p. 124). See also his article, "The Song of the Sea and Canaanite Myth," *JTC* 5 (1968): 1-25.

2   Yahweh is my strength and song,
And He has become my salvation;
This is my God, and I will praise Him;
My father's God, and I will extol Him.

This introductory portion of the song recounts the poet's confession of faith in Yahweh. The poet describes Yahweh as "my strength" (עזי), "my song" (וזמרת),[3] "my salvation" (לי לישועה), "my God" (אלי),[4] and "my father's God" (אלהי אבי), since Yahweh had been highly exalted by hurling the horse and its rider into the sea. The phrases זה אלי and אלהי אבי are very significant. According to P.D. Miller, one of the most ancient attestations of the identification of Yahweh with the God of the fathers is found here.[5] More than that, זה אלי is a proclamation that Yahweh is the poet's God. He accepts Yahweh as his personal God, and by mentioning אבי אלהי, he tries to emphasize the continuity of his faith with his fathers. The experiential knowledge of Yahweh made him praise and extol him as his God. The idea of "adopting" God is observed here and this is, precisely speaking, the poet's recognition of his exclusive relationship with Yahweh.

3   יהוה איש מלחמה יהוה שמו:

4   מרכבת פרעה וחילו ירה בים ומבחר שלשיו טבעו
בים־סוף:

5   תהמת יכסימו ירדו במצולת כמו־אבן:

6   ימינך יהוה נאדרי בכח ימינך יהוה תרעץ איוב:

7   וברב גאונך תהרס קמיך תשלח חרנך יאכלמו כקש:

8   וברוח אפיך נערמו מים נצבו כמו־נד נזלים
קפאו תהמת בלב־ים:

9   אמר אויב ארדף אשיג אחלק שלל תמלאמו נפשי
אריק חרבי תורישמו ידי:

10   נשפת ברוחך כסמו ים צללו כעופרת במים אדירים:

3   Yahweh is a warrior;
Yahweh is His name.

4   Pharaoh's chariots and his army He has cast into the sea;
And the choicest of his officers are drowned in the Red Sea.

5   The deeps cover them;
They went down into the depths like a stone.

3. A few Mss read זמרתי.

4. This designation is clearly in contrast to that of Yahweh's "My people" (Ex. 3:7,10; 5:1; 6:7), "My son," "My first-born" (Ex. 4:22-23), and "My host, My people the sons of Israel" (Ex. 7:4).

5. Patrick D. Miller, Jr., *The Divine Warrior in Early Israel,* HSM 5 (Cambridge: Harvard University Press, 1973), p.114.

6   Thy right hand, O Yahweh, is majestic in power,
    Thy right hand, O Yahweh, shatters the enemy.
7   And in the greatness of Thine excellence Thou dost overthrow those
        who rise up against Thee;
    Thou dost send forth Thy burning anger, and it consumes them as
        chaff.
8   And at the blast of Thy nostrils the waters were piled up,
    The flowing waters stood up like a heap;
    The deeps were congealed in the heart of the sea.
9   The enemy said, "I will pursue, I will overtake, I will divide the spoil;
    My desire shall be gratified against them;
    I will draw out my sword, my hand shall destroy them."
10 Thou didst blow with Thy wind, the sea covered them;
    They sank like lead in the mighty waters.

The second paragraph of this song begins with a new description
of Yahweh. יהוה איש מלחמה (Yahweh is a warrior). Yahweh is a warrior who is fighting for Israel. Yahweh as divine warrior directs the
wind that causes the waters to pile up on Israel's behalf and then
drowns the Egyptians in the sea. We have here two opposing forces:
one is Yahweh and his people, and the other is Pharaoh and the
choicest of his officers. In this second paragraph, Yahweh's people
are not directly mentioned, but they are expressed implicitly
(v. 9), and the main concern of the third paragraph is the people of
Yahweh. We can see the counterparts of these two opposing forces:
Yahweh vs. Pharaoh; Israel vs. the choicest of Pharaoh's officers.

The Song of the Sea describes Yahweh as the great king, and
the kingship of Yahweh is one of the major themes of this poem.
Significantly, the Song of the Sea climaxes with Yahweh's enthronement in his sanctuary on his holy mountain and concludes
with the proclamation of his everlasting reign, "Yahweh shall reign
forever and ever" (v. 18). Thus, Yahweh the warrior is Yahweh the
king,[6] the counterpart of the Egyptian king in this battle.

The designation of Pharaoh's army draws our attention to its
counterpart, the people of Israel. If the army of Pharaoh is מבחר
שלשיו (the choicest of his officers), the army of Yahweh implies that
the people of Israel are Yahweh's מבחר שלשיו. Furthermore, Pharaoh
and his army are designated as the enemy of Yahweh (אויב, v. 6)
who rose up against him (v. 7). Yet strictly speaking, Pharaoh and

6. Millard C. Lind, *Yahweh Is a Warrior* (Scottdale, PA: Herald Press, 1980),
p. 50.

his army did not rise up against Yahweh but against the Israelites. They were actually the enemies of Israel, and Yahweh, identified here with Israel, is seen as a warrior who is fighting for Israel against Pharaoh and his army. Thus it seems clear that the Israelites are implicitly described as Yahweh's choicest army (מבחר שלשיו), which is a basic idea in Yahweh's election of Israel.

11 מי־כמכה באלם יהוה מי כמכה נאדר בקדש
נורא תהלת עשה פלא:

12 נטית ימינך תבלעמו ארץ:

13 נחית בחסדך עם־זו גאלת נהלת בעזך אל־נוה קדשך:

14 שמעו עמים ירגזון חיל אחז ישבי פלשת:

15 אז נבהלו אלופי אדום אילי מואב יאחזמו רעד
נמגו כל ישבי כנען:

16 תפל עליהם אימתה ופחד בגדל זרועך ידמו כאבן
עד־יעבר עמך יהוה עד־יעבר עם־זו קנית:

17 תבאמו ותטעמו בהר נחלתך מכון לשבתך פעלת
יהוה מקדש אדני כוננו ידיך:

18 יהוה ימלך לעלם ועד:

11 Who is like Thee among the gods, O Yahweh?
Who is like Thee, majestic in holiness,
Awesome in praises, working wonders?

12 Thou didst stretch out Thy right hand,
The earth swallowed them.

13 In Thy loving kindness Thou hast led the people whom Thou hast redeemed;
In Thy strength Thou hast guided them to Thy holy habitation.

14 The peoples have heard, they tremble;
Anguish has gripped the inhabitants of Philistia.

15 Then the chiefs of Edom were dismayed;
The leaders of Moab, trembling grips them;
All the inhabitants of Canaan have melted away.

16 Terror and dread fall upon them;
By the greatness of Thine arm they are motionless as stone;
Until Thy people pass over, O Yahweh,
Until the people pass over whom Thou hast purchased.

17 Thou wilt bring them and plant them in the mountain of Thine inheritance,
The place, O Yahweh, which Thou hast made for Thy dwelling,
The sanctuary, O Yahweh, which Thy hands have established.

18 Yahweh shall reign forever and ever.

The third paragraph of this song begins with the rhetorical question: "Who is like Thee among the gods, O Yahweh? Who is like

105

Thee, majestic in holiness, awesome in praises, working wonders?" According to C.J. Labuschagne, the phrase, מִי־כּ (who is like) is a typical expression of the incomparability of Yahweh, and it is to be taken as implying a negative answer.[7] Thus it means, "No one is like Yahweh among other gods." The poet's recognition of the incomparability of Yahweh reflects his sense of belonging to Yahweh and his solidarity with Yahweh. Surely this confession must have sprung out of his experience of Yahweh. Since Yahweh is the incomparable being, the poet is proud of his status of belonging to him, and thus he exalts and praises him.

However, the third paragraph is basically different from the second one. The second one (vv. 3-10) describes Yahweh as a divine warrior with respect to the forces of his army and emphasizes the destruction of Pharaoh's army by Yahweh's mighty power. The third paragraph, however, describes Yahweh as a divine redeemer with respect to his people and emphasizes the salvation of the Israelites by his strength through his lovingkindness. From this perspective, the third paragraph is also different from the first one (vv. 1-2). Whereas the first paragraph recounts the poet's individual exaltation of Yahweh and personal confession of faith (my strength, my song, my salvation, I will sing, I will praise, I will extol, etc.), in the third paragraph the description of the people is of significance. First of all, the phrase in verse 13, "the people who Thou hast redeemed" (עַם־זוּ גָּאָלְתָּ), provides a very important aspect of relationship between Yahweh and the people of Israel. The verb גאל is basically a clan term meaning "to make a claim for a person or thing" or "to redeem."[8] Here, Yahweh is portrayed as Israel's redeemer who stands up for his people and vindicates them. We find

---

7. C.J. Labuschagne, *The Incomparability of Yahweh in the Old Testament* (Leiden: E.J. Brill, 1966), p. 16.

8. According to R. Laird Harris, besides the above usage, there are three other basic situations in which the verb גאל is used. The first is the Pentateuchal legislation which refers to the repurchase of a field which was sold in time of need (Lev. 25:25ff.). The second situation is "redemption of property or non-sacrificial animals dedicated to the Lord, or the redemption of the firstborn of unclean animals" (Lev. 27:11ff.). The third situation concerns the next of kin who is the "avenger of blood" for a murdered man (Num. 35:12ff.). See Harris, "גאל," *TWOT,* 1:144. See also Baruch A. Levine, "In Praise of the Israelite *Mišpāḥâ*: Legal Themes in the Book of Ruth," in *The Quest for the Kingdom of God: Studies in Honor of G.E. Mendenhall,* ed. H.B. Huffmon et al. (Winona Lake: Eisenbrauns, 1983), pp. 95-106; A.R. Johnson, "The Primary Meaning of גאל," VTSup 1:66-77; Roland de Vaux, *Ancient Israel,* 1:11-12, 21-23.

a similar phrase in verse 16: "The people whom Thou hast pur-chased" (עַם־זוּ קָנִיתָ). The verb קנה must be viewed in relation to גאל, because גאל itself implies the meaning of קנה.[9] Thus, these two phrases suggest that the relationship between Yahweh and Israel is characteristic of kinship and further ownership. In verse 16, the word עַמְּךָ (Thy people) reinforces this concept. Yahweh is the re-deemer of Israel. He redeemed the people of Israel in his loving-kindness (חַסְדְּךָ).[10]

Another significant image portrayed in this paragraph is that of Yahweh's leading his people to a new place (אֶל־נְוֵה קָדְשֶׁךָ [to Thy holy habitation], v. 13) and planting (נטע) them in the mountain of his inheritance (בְּהַר נַחֲלָתְךָ [in the mountain of Thine inheritance], v. 17).[11] Yahweh's redemption and guidance of his people to a new habitation basically portray the idea of election as observed in the marriage metaphor when a bridegroom takes a girl for his bride and brings her into a new dwelling place.[12] The verb נטע and the noun נחל are also terms related to the concept of election. Yahweh as a farmer plants his people on the mountain of his inheritance. And the description of Yahweh as an eternal King who shall reign forever and ever (v. 18) with Israel as his royal people is also one of the figures in which the idea of election can be seen.

9. The idea of Yahweh's buying Israel from Egypt is well described in Is. 43:3-4. Yahweh is said to have given Cush and Seba to Egypt as a ransom for Israel in the past, and he is going to give other men in her place and other peoples in ex-change for her life in the future. Of course, this is not a precise historical reference; rather it describes the nature of Yahweh's deliverance of Israel in terms of com-mercial imagery, i.e., buying, paying, and exchanging.

10. See Nelson Glueck, *Hesed in the Bible* (New York: KTAV, 1975); R. Laird Harris, "חסד," *TWOT,* 1:305-7.

11. According to Loewenstamm, "the expression בְּהַר נַחֲלָתְךָ—'the mountain of thy heritage,' which precedes מִקְּדָשׁ אֲדֹנָי—'the sanctuary, O Lord,' is reminiscent of the phrase *bqdš ǵr nḥlty* in the formulary description of the 'heritage' of Baal, and the words מְכוֹן לְשִׁבְתֶּךָ—'the place...for thy abode,' recall the formula *ksu ṯbth* used to describe the 'heritages' of Mot and *Ktr-wḥss* ("נחלת ה־," in *Studies in Bible,* Scripta Hierosolymitana 31, ed. S. Japhet [Jerusalem: Magnes, 1986], p. 162). B.E. Shafer asserts that the *nḥlt* designates both a divine cosmic realm and a cosmic mountain of sanctuary in the literature of Ugarit, and Ex. 15:17 is an identical mythic extension of נחלה to the sanctuary mount of the cosmic deity ("The Root *bḥr* and Pre-Exilic Concepts of Chosenness in the Hebrew Bible," *ZAW* 89 [1977]: 37). However, even though the writer of this poem borrowed the language from Canaanite mythic imagery, נוה קדשך (Thy holy habitation) and בהר נחלתך (in the mountain of Thine inheritance) clearly point to the promised land of Yahweh.

12. Israel's wandering in the wilderness is compared to the bride's following her groom in Jer. 2:2.

(2) The Battles of Joshua

Before Joshua was engaged in the war for the conquest, he met the captain of the host of Yahweh (שר־צבא־יהוה, Josh. 5:13-15).[13] This is a very significant event for understanding both the character of the wars that Joshua had to conduct thereafter and the concept of election. When Joshua approached Jericho, he saw a mysterious person holding a drawn sword in his hand just in front of him. Joshua went to him and asked him, "Are you for us or for our adversaries?" The person answered, "No, rather I indeed come now as captain of the host of Yahweh" (לא כי אני שר־צבא־יהוה עתה באתי, 5:14). Therefore, Joshua fell on his face and bowed down, inquiring as to the message of Yahweh which he brought. The captain of Yahweh said, "Remove

13. According to M. Noth, this event is basically a type of cult legend associated with an unknown holy place near Jericho, which went back to Canaanite times but was used by the Israelites (etiological sagas of the tribe of Benjamin preserved in the Gilgal sanctuary). Thus, he proposes that Joshua is the primary figure only in the account of his grave tradition in Ephraim (24:29-30) and in the Shechem covenant story. By the time of the Deuteronomist he had became the central figure of the whole conquest tradition.

However, P.D. Miller criticized Noth's theory since his history-of-tradition analysis failed to see the associations of various traditions with other elements which may have been stronger, and he therefore proposed that it is precisely the tradition history which forces one to associate this episode primarily with the events in the conquest, presumably even before the "collector" of the tradition. See Miller, *Divine Warrior,* p. 130.

John Bright also challenged Noth's presupposition that *Ortsgebundenheit* (traditions tied to natural phenomenon or to places such as graves or to peculiar topographical features) plays a primary role in the creation of historical tradition. See Bright, *Early Israel in Recent History Writing,* SBT 1/19 (London: SCM, 1956).

Therefore, G.E. Wright rightly pointed out that the issue is the presuppositions which are brought to bear on the form and tradition-history methodology, rather than the methods themselves. If one discovers certain presuppositions embedded in the narrative itself, then, as a matter of course, one will reach different conclusions regarding the role of Joshua in the narrative. As an example, Wright proposed that the story of Josh. 5:13-15 is unique and without parallel. Yet it is surely not a composition of the Deuteronomist, but an ancient tradition in which place attachment plays no role. Instead, the story derives from holy war traditions. Yet Joshua's encounter with the cosmic commander near Jericho is clearly an account in which the centrality of Joshua in the narrative is pivotal. So also is the tradition's statement of the pivotal place which Joshua has in the sight of unseen cosmic forces behind the conquest events. A strong argument may be made, therefore, that Joshua is not a secondary figure in the Gilgal-Jericho pericopes or, for that matter, in the remainder of the narratives. See Wright, "Introduction," in Robert G. Boling and G. Ernest Wright, *Joshua,* AB (Garden City: Doubleday, 1982), pp. 71-72.

your sandals from your feet, for the place on which you are standing is holy" (המקום אשר אתה עמד עליו קדש הוא, 5:15). And Joshua did so.[14]

Here, Yahweh is presented as the one who possesses his hosts.[15] שר means a military captain (Gen. 21:22; 1 Sam. 17:18,55). Here the term refers to an angelic figure. The reason for the captain's commandment to remove the sandals implies the appearance of Yahweh himself on the land where Joshua now stands and his ownership of the land set aside for himself.[16] The place is holy because it belongs to holy Yahweh. The appearance of the captain of the host of Yahweh at this beginning moment of the conquest is not by chance. Yahweh is showing that he is with Joshua as a warrior with his hosts and he is going to fight for him.[17] Thus, Joshua did not need to fight. Even though he fought, Yahweh would join with him and help him. This is a characteristic of holy war. Here, we are required to understand the wars of Joshua and the conquest with respect to the concept of holy war. For example, the wall of Jericho was not destroyed by the force of Israel but by the power of Yahweh.

ויאמר יהוה אל־יהושע ראח נתתי בידך את־יריחו
ואת־מלכה גבורי החיל:

And Yahweh said to Joshua, "See, I have given Jericho into your hand, with its king and the valiant warriors." (Josh. 6:2; cf. 6:16)

They were to march around the city with the ark of Yahweh once a day for six days, and on the seventh day, they were only to shout when the priest blew the trumpets. Marching around the city with the ark of Yahweh thus symbolizes Yahweh's participation in the campaign.[18] Further, this march proclaims that this war belonged to Yahweh. Since this campaign was to belong to Yahweh, the city was to be under the ban.

14. Some interpreters regard this description of the event as incomplete, and some believe that v. 15 should contain more instruction that it does now. See M. Woudstra, *The Book of Joshua*, NICOT (Grand Rapids: Eerdmans, 1981), p. 104.

15. Cf. 1 Kgs. 22:19; Ps. 103:20-21; 148:2.

16. See G. von Rad, *Old Testament Theology*, 1:204ff.

17. Jacob had a similar experience as he returned from the house of Laban to meet his brother Esau. He met the angel of God in his turmoil as he fearfully prepared to meet his brother, and he named that place Mahanaim (Gen. 32:1).

18. This should not be viewed as a magical rite of circumambulation or as a ritual to bring about the desired end efficaciously. See Woudstra, *Book of Joshua*, p. 109.

והיתה העיר חרם היא וכל־אשר־בה ליהוה רק רחב הזונה
תחיה היא וכל־אשר אתה בבית כי החבאתה את־המלאכים
אשר שלחנו: ורק־אתם שמרו מן־החרם פן־תחרימו ולקחתם
מן־החרם ושמתם את־מחנה ישראל לחרם ועכרתם אותו:
וכל כסף וזהב וכלי נחשת וברזל קדש הוא ליהוה אוצר יהוה יבוא:

And the city shall be under the ban, it and all that is in it belongs to
Yahweh; only Rahab the harlot and all who are with her in the house
shall live, because she hid the messengers whom we sent. But as for
you, only keep yourselves from the things under the ban, lest you
covet them and take some of the things under the ban, so you would
make the camp of Israel accursed and bring trouble on it. But all the
silver and gold and articles of bronze and iron are holy to Yahweh;
they shall go into the treasury of Yahweh. (Josh. 6:17-19)

The Akkadian cognate of Hebrew חרם, ḥarāmu, means "to separate."[19] According to Lev. 27:28,29, חרם is a proscribed thing which
a man set apart to Yahweh out of all that he had, whether it be of
man, animal, or the fields of his own property. Thus, it was not to
be sold or redeemed. The חרם was most holy to Yahweh. It belonged
to no one but Yahweh.[20] Since the city of Jericho was proclaimed
as חרם, everything in it was to be destroyed so that no one could
take anything except for the precious metals that were to be brought
into the treasury of Yahweh, since they were holy to Yahweh. Israel
had no right to take any booty from Jericho.

Another good example of Yahweh's fighting for Israel is found
in the battle at Gibeon. As Israel made a covenant with the Gibeonites, Adoni-zedek king of Jerusalem made an alliance with the

19. *AHw*, 1:339-40; *CAD*, *Ḥ*, 6:89-90. According to Carol Meyers, the uncon-
scionable חרם perhaps can be seen as a kind of plague control. Thus, execution of
the חרם in biblical texts is frequently associated with destruction by fire as a response to epidemic disease. See Meyers, "The Roots of Restriction: Women in
Early Israel," *BA* 41 (1978): 91-103. However, חרם "was a holy war institution that
Israel held in common with other peoples of the Near East. This is evident from
the Mesha tablet where the same verbal root is used (*ḥrm*). It cannot be overem-
phasized that all of Israel's institutions of holy war as such were not held in common with Near Eastern peoples. The difference between Israelite and other Near
Eastern holy war is the radical reorientation of the holy war institutions in ancient
Israel in terms of the issue of political power. This is graphically illustrated by the
Mesha stone; 'I Mesha (the king of Moab) . . .' stands in contrast to the concept of
leadership set forth above, where the leader is Yahweh" (Millard C. Lind, *Yahweh
Is a Warrior*, pp. 81-82).

20. See further J. Bright, *The Authority of the Old Testament* (Grand Rapids:
Baker, repr. 1980), pp. 243-51; W.F. Albright, *From the Stone Age to Christianity*
(Garden City: Doubleday, 1957), pp. 279-80.

neighboring kings, Hoham of Hebron, Piram of Jarmuth, Japhi of Lachish, and Debir of Eglon, and they together attacked Gibeon. Thus, the Israelites had to be involved in this war. At the beginning of the war, Yahweh appeared to Joshua and said,

אל־תירא מהם כי בידך נתתים לא־יעמד איש מהם בפניך:

Do not fear them, for I have given them into your hands; not one of them shall stand before you. (Josh. 10:8)

So Joshua marched to Gibeon to deliver the inhabitants of the city and fought against those allied forces. In the midst of this battle Joshua and his men experienced the saving activity of Yahweh.

ויהמם יהוה לפני ישראל ויכם מכה־גדולה בגבעון
וירדפם דרך מעלה בית־חורן ויכם עד־עזקה ועד־מקדה:

And Yahweh confounded them before Israel, and He slew them with a great slaughter at Gibeon, and pursued them by the way of the ascent of Beth-horon, and struck them as far as Azekah and Makkedah. (Josh. 10:10)

The verb המם is used to describe Yahweh's aid to Israel in defeating their enemies by means of various natural phenomena (Ex. 14:24; Judg.4:15; 5:20-21; 1 Sam. 7:10; 2 Sam. 22:15; Ps. 18:14 [E.15]; 77:16-18 [E.17-19]; 114:6).[21] Here, המם refers to severe hailstones which Yahweh threw down from heaven (Josh. 10:11). Thus,

וימתו רבים אשר־מתו באבני הברד מאשר הרגו בני ישראל בחרב:

there were more who died from the hailstones than those whom the sons of Israel killed with the sword. (Josh. 10:11b)

In addition, we see a most striking incident that happened on that day. Yahweh stopped the sun in the middle of the sky to help the Israelites. Joshua spoke to Yahweh before Israel:

שמש בגבעון דום וירח בעמק אילון:
וידם השמש וירח עמד עד־יקם גוי איביו
הלא־היא כתובה על־ספר הישר ויעמד השמש בחצי
השמים ולא־אץ לבוא כיום תמים:

"O sun, stand still at Gibeon,
And O moon in the valley of Aijalon."
So the sun stood still, and the moon stopped,

21. Woudstra, *Book of Joshua*, p. 172.

111

Until the nation avenged themselves of their enemies.
Is it not written in the book of Jashar? And the sun stopped in the middle of the sky, and did not hasten to go down for about a whole day. (Josh. 10:12-13)[22]

There was no day like that before it or after it when Yahweh listened to the voice of a man; כי יהוה נלחם לישראל (for Yahweh fought for Israel, v. 14). Therefore, all the meteorological phenomena on that day were regarded as Yahweh's fighting for his people. Finally in verse 42, "Joshua captured all these kings and their lands at one time," כי יהוה אלהי ישראל נלחם לישראל (because Yahweh, the God of Israel, fought for Israel). The phrases כי יהוה נלחם לישראל (vv. 14, 42) and ויתן יהוה גם־אותה ביד ישראל (and Yahweh gave it also into the hand of Israel, vv. 8, 12,19, 30, 32) clearly emphasize that the victory of Joshua over the allied forces of the Amorite kings was won not by the power of Israel but by the help of Yahweh. Therefore, in his farewell address Joshua reminded the people:

ואתם ראיתם את כל־אשר עשה יהוה אלהיכם לכל־הגוים
האלה מפניכם כי יהוה אלהיכם הוא הנלחם לכם:

And you have seen all that Yahweh your God has done to all these nations because of you, for Yahweh your God is He who has been fighting for you. (Josh. 23:3; cf. 23:10)

Furthermore, Joshua exhorted the people of Israel to choose to serve Yahweh on the grounds of his fighting for them in the course of their exodus and settlement (24:22). As the people reaffirmed their devotion to Yahweh, Joshua made the covenant at Shechem.[23]

22. Some commentators think that Sun and Moon are supposed to have been the guardian deities of Gibeon and Aijalon, and they did not take part in the battle. See J. Blenkinsopp, *Gibeon and Israel* (Cambridge: The University Press, 1972), p. 47; and J. Dus, "Gibeon: Eine Kultstätte des ŠMŠ und die Stadt des benjamin-itischen Schicksals," *VT* 10 (1960): 353-74. However, according to Woudstra what Joshua bid the sun to do was to "stand still," because "the language that Joshua uses in addressing the sun and moon is the language of ordinary observation still used today in the scientific age" (*Book of Joshua,* p. 175). Also R. de Vaux points out that there is no indication that these cities were centers of the cult of sun and moon (*The Early History of Israel* [Philadelphia: Westminster, 1978], p. 634).

23. D.J. McCarthy examined the sources of Josh. 24:1-28 and proposed that: "It is basically old in all its parts. The locale described and the ideas involved in the description in 25-27 are antique. The introductory and concluding notice (1.28) are traditional material for assemblies. Joshua's opening speech uses the language of prophecy or treaty and old royal narrative material (2a). It reflects traditions found in J (2-4.5-7.6-8), E (*ibid.* plus 8-11aA), and Amos (6-8)." Thus

Through this covenant they bound themselves one to another to be a people of Yahweh and to worship him alone. Tribal unity was created by tribal acknowledgment of Yahweh's fighting on their behalf.

(3) The Song of Deborah (Judg. 5:1-31)

The fifth chapter of Judges is usually known as the Song of Deborah, and it has been considered by the majority of scholars as one of the earliest texts in the Hebrew Bible.[24] The poem is often thought to be practically contemporary with the events which it describes.[25] The Song of Deborah is a victory hymn celebrating Israel's military defeat of the northern Canaanite cities. In this poem, the concept of election is vividly delineated. We can divide this song into a few sections and observe the presence of our key theme.

ותשר דבורה וברק בן־אבינעם ביום ההוא:

Then Deborah and Barak the son of Abinoam sang on that day.
(Judg. 5:1)

This title indicates that the song was sung on that day, the day of victory. Thus, this poem directs our attention to the role played by Yahweh in this war.

---

he treats the text as a block of pre-Deuteronomistic material, and forbids simply assigning it a single source because of its complexity. See McCarthy, *Treaty and Covenant,* AnBib 21A (Rome: Biblical Institute Press,1978), p. 231. However, M.C. Lind thinks that it "is fundamentally made up of an ancient unified text, which may have had a few ancient supplements, followed by a Deuteronomistic editing. This latter is difficult to assess since the tradition of the Book of Deuteronomy is old (a core goes back to ancient Shechem) and is rooted in worship experiences that celebrated covenant, perhaps the Horeb (or Sinai) covenant itself." He considers that this "Shechem covenant may have formed the constitutional basis of Israel during the period of the Judges" (*Yahweh Is a Warrior,* p. 85).

24. 1150-1125 B.C. is suggested as the possible period for the composition of this song. See W.F. Albright, "The Song of Deborah in the Light of Archaeology," *BASOR* 62 (1936): 26-31; David N. Freedman, "Early Israelite History in the Light of Early Israelite Poetry," in *Unity and Diversity,* ed. H. Goedicke and J.J.M. Roberts (Baltimore, London: Johns Hopkins University Press, 1975), pp. 3-34; F.M. Cross, Jr., and D.N. Freedman, *Studies in Ancient Yahwistic Poetry,* SBLDS 21 (Missoula: Scholars Press,1975); P.D. Miller, *Divine Warrior,* pp. 87-102.

25. George F. Moore, *A Critical and Exegetical Commentary on Judges* (Edinburgh: T. & T. Clark, 1895), p. 131.

בפרע פרעות בישראל בהתנדב עם ברכו יהוה: 2

שמעו מלכים האזינו רזנים אנכי ליהוה אנכי אשירה 3
אזמר ליהוה אלהי ישראל:

יהוה בצאתך משעיר בצעדך משדה אדום 4
ארץ רעשה גם־שמים נטפו גם־עבים נטפו מים:

הרים נזלו מפני יהוה זה סיני מפני יהוה אלהי ישראל: 5

2 That the leaders led in Israel,
   That the people volunteered,
   Bless Yahweh!
3 Hear, O kings; give ear, O rulers!
   I— to Yahweh, I will sing,
   I will sing praise to Yahweh, the God of Israel.
4 Yahweh, when Thou didst go out from Seir,
   When Thou didst march from the field of Edom,
   The earth quaked, the heavens also dripped,
   Even the clouds dripped water.
5 The mountains quaked at the presence of Yahweh,
   This Sinai, at the presence of Yahweh, the God of Israel.

As the poet exhorts her hearers to praise Yahweh, she presents him as a very special figure. The first thing that attracts our attention here is the designation of Yahweh as the God of Israel (v. 3). This designation is emphasized by its repetition in verse 5. To the kings and rulers of the world she proclaims that Yahweh is the God of Israel, and she makes it clear that her song is directed to Yahweh. The second point to be noted here is that the poet describes Yahweh in the typical image of divine warrior. The coming of Yahweh is accompanied by supernatural phenomena, such as an earthquake, dripping water from the heavens, and the trembling of the mountains. The journey of Yahweh when he came to help his people in the war began at Mount Sinai. From Horeb, Yahweh would come into Canaan, from Seir, the plateau of Edom (Dt. 33:2; Hab. 3:3).[26] The primary meaning of צעד (as in the phrase בצעדך) seems to be "to walk with great steps, stride, stalk"; it is the stately march of religious pomp (2 Sam. 6:13. cf. 2 Sam. 22:37; Prov. 4:12; 7:8; Job 18:7; Jer. 10:5).[27] Thus the theophany of Yahweh is described in terms of an army. Yahweh as a warrior is coming forth from his place.

בימי שמגר בן־ענת בימי יעל חדלו ארחות 6
והלכי נתיבות ילכו ארחות עקלקלות:

26. Ibid., p. 140.
27. Ibid., p. 141.

7 חדלו פרזון בישראל חדלו
עד שקמתי דבורה שקמתי אם בישראל:
8 יבחר אלהים חדשים אז לחם שערים
מגן אם־יראה ורמח בארבעים אלף בישראל:

6 In the days of Shamgar the son of Anath,
  In the days of Jael, the highways were deserted,
  And the travelers went by roundabout ways.
7 The peasantry ceased, they ceased in Israel,
  Until I , Deborah, arose,
  Until I arose, a mother in Israel.
8 New gods were chosen;
  Then war was in the gates.
  Not a shield or a spear was seen
  Among forty thousand in Israel.

Verses 6-8 explain the miserable situation of Israel before the war. The characteristic term denoting the state of Israel is חדל, which means "to stop, to cease," or "to leave off" (Ex. 9:34; Dt. 15:11). ארחות (the travellers, the population that was settled in the open country in unfortified places)[28] had ceased. The main roads were cut off by enemy forces, and the travellers had to take roundabout routes. As a result of the broken treaty, new gods were chosen and war broke out in the gates.[29] However, the forty thousand of Israel were poorly equipped in comparison with the Canaanites.

In this difficulty, Yahweh the God of Israel performed righteous deeds for his people.

9 לבי לחוקקי ישראל המתנדבים בעם ברכו יהוה:
10 רכבי אתנות צחרות ישבי על־מדין והלכי על־דרך שיחו:
11 מקול מחצצים בין משאבים שם יתנו צדקות יהוה
צדקת פרזנו בישראל
אז ירדו לשערים עם־יהוה:

28. According to KD, פרזות means "the open flat country or hamlets" as distinguished from the towns surrounded by walls (Ezek. 38:11; Zech. 2:8), and פרזי means "the peasant population," or "the inhabitants" of the country (Dt. 3:5; 1Sam. 4:18). Thus, פרזון is taken to mean both place and population (*Judges*, p. 311). See also G.F. Moore, *Judges*, p. 144. However, other meanings such as "warriors" (R.G. Boling, *Judges*, p. 109), and even "iron" (G. Garbini, "*Parzon 'Iron' in the Song of Deborah?" *JSS* 23 [1978]: 23-24) are proposed.

29. According to Boling, since deities were regularly listed as witnesses and guarantors of a treaty, "the choice of 'new gods' may therefore derive its context from the collapse of trade route agreements and general security that brought on the warfare" (*Judges*, pp. 109, 118).

9   My heart goes out to the commanders of Israel,
    The volunteers among the people;
    Bless Yahweh!
10 You who ride on white donkeys,
    You who sit on rich carpets,
    And you who travel on the road—sing!
11 At the sound of those who divide flocks among the watering places,
    There they shall recount the righteous deeds of Yahweh,
    The righteous deeds for His peasantry in Israel.
    Then the people of Yahweh went down to the gates.

In this paragraph, the poet exhorts her people to bless and hymn
Yahweh. Firstly, she calls upon the commanders of Israel, and then
the riders on white donkeys, those who sit on rich carpets,[30] and the
travellers. These are to bless and hymn the deeds of Yahweh, his
righteous acts on behalf of the peasantry of Israel. The righteous
deeds of Yahweh point to the deliverance of his people from the
miserable condition described before he fought for them. Here, the
peasantry is described as Yahweh's. Also, עם־יהוה is mentioned
(v. 11). When the poet uses this phrase, we may assume that she had
the phrase יהוה אלהי ישראל (vv. 3,5) in mind. Thus, we can see here
that the Yahweh-Israel relationship is described in terms of the
election idea.

12 עורי עורי דבורה אורי עורי דברי־שיר
    קום ברק ושבה שביך בן־אבינעם:
13 אז ירד שריד לאדירים עם יהוה ירד־לי בגבורים:
14 מני אפרים שרשם בעמלק אחריך בנימין בעממיך
    מני מכיר ירדו מחקקים ומזבולן משכים בשבט ספר:
15 ושרי ביששכר עם־דברה ויששכר כן ברק בעמק שלח ברגליו
    בפלגות ראובן גדלים חקקי־לב:
16 למה ישבת בין המשפתים לשמע שרקות עדרים
    לפלגות ראובן גדולים חקרי־לב:
17 גלעד בעבר הירדן שכן ודן למה יגור אניות
    אשר ישב לחוף ימים ועל מפרציו ישכון:
18 זבלון עם חרף נפשו למות ונפתלי על מרומי שדה:
19 באו מלכים נלחמו אז נלחמו מלכי כנען
    בתענך על־מי מגדו בצע כסף לא לקחו:
20 מן־שמים נלחמו הכוכבים ממסלותם נלחמו עם־סיסרא:
21 נחל קישון גרפם נחל קדומים נחל קישון
    תדרכי נפשי עז:
22 אז הלמו עקבי־סוס מדהרות דהרות אביריו:

30. Boling suggests the rendering of ישבי על־מדין as "ones who sit on the judgment seat" (*Judges,* pp. 102, 110).

23 אורו מרוז אמר מלאך יהוה ארו ארור ישביה
כי לא־באו לעזרת יהוה לעזרת יהוה בגבורים:

12 Awake, awake, Deborah;
Awake, awake, sing a song!
Arise, Barak, and take away your captives, O son of Abinoam.
13 Then survivors came down to the nobles;
The people of Yahweh came down to me as warriors.
14 From Ephraim those whose root is in Amalek came down,
Following you, Benjamin, with your peoples;
From Machir commanders came down,
And from Zebulun those who wield the staff of office.
15 And the princes of Issachar were with Deborah;
As was Issachar, so was Barak;
Into the valley they rushed at his heels;
Among the divisions of Reuben
There were great resolves of heart.
16 Why did you sit among the sheepfolds,
To hear the piping for the flocks?
Among the divisions of Reuben
There were great searchings of heart.
17 Gilead remained across the Jordan;
And why did Dan stay in ships?
Asher sat at the seashore,
And remained by its landings.
18 Zebulun was a people who despised their lives even to death,
And Naphtali also, on the high places of the field.
19 The kings came and fought;
Then fought the kings of Canaan
At Taanach near the waters of Megiddo;
They took no plunder in silver.
20 The stars fought from heaven,
From their courses they fought against Sisera.
21 The torrent of Kishon swept them away,
The ancient torrent, the torrent Kishon.
O my soul, march on with strength.
22 Then the horses' hoofs beat
From the dashing, the dashing of his valiant steeds.
23 "Curse Meroz," said the angel of Yahweh,
"Utterly curse its inhabitants;
Because they did not come to the help of Yahweh,
To the help of Yahweh against the warriors."

In this section, we see the summoning of the people and their coming out as warriors. First, Deborah and Barak are called, and then

117

the tribes. Ephraim, Machir (the first-born son of Manasseh, Josh. 17:1), Benjamin, Zebulun, Issachar, Reuben, Dan, Asher, and Naphtali came to join in the battle. Following LXX A, *BHS* suggests reading עם יהוה ירד-לי בגבורים (the people of Yahweh came down to me as warriors) rather than עם יהוה ירד-לו בגבורים (the people of Yahweh came to him as warriors) in verse 13.[31] However, in verse 23 the angel of Yahweh beckons the people to curse Meroz and its inhabitants, "because they did not come to the help of Yahweh" (לעזרת יהוה),[32] "to help against the warriors" (לעזרת יהוה בגבורים). Therefore, ירד-לו is a more plausible reading than ירד-לי. Here, we see two parties in this battle: Yahweh and his people, and their opponents, Sisera and Meroz. As in verses 3 and 4, Yahweh is accompanied by supernatural phenomena; the stars from heaven fought against Sisera (v. 20), and the torrent of Kishon was also a terrifying force against him (v. 21). Thus, Yahweh is described here as a divine warrior and the people of Israel as the joint forces of Yahweh in the battle. Meroz and its inhabitants are condemned not because they did not help Israel but because they did not help Yahweh. Obviously the basic conviction in Israel's thought is that they are the army of Yahweh fighting against his enemy, Sisera.

The last paragraph (vv. 24-31) shows the contrasting scenes of two women: the most blessed one, Jael who killed Sisera in the tent (vv. 24-27), and the lamenting one, the mother of Sisera who awaits his return in the palace (vv. 28-30). At the conclusion of this song, the poet prays to Yahweh, "Thus, let all Thine enemies perish, O Yahweh, but let those who love him be like the rising of the sun in its might." Again Sisera is regarded as an enemy of Yahweh.

As we have seen, the thought of election is implied all through the song. The poet has a clear conviction of her people as Yahweh's army, with Israel's enemies being Yahweh's enemies.

31. See also G.F. Moore, *Judges,* p. 150; J.A. Soggin, *Judges,* OTL (Philadelphia: Westminster, 1981), p. 82.

32. The place "Meroz" is not known. Mostly, Yahweh comes to the help of man (Ps. 22:20 [E. 19]; 27:9; 35:2; 38:23 [E. 22]; 40:14 [E. 13], 18 [E. 17]; 44: 27 [E. 26]; 46:2 [E. 1]; 60:13 [E. 11]; 63:8 [E. 7]; 70:2 [E. 1]; 71:12; 94:17; 108:13 [E. 12]). However, in one rare ancient Near Eastern record, the king helps the gods. See D.D. Luckenbill, "The Oriental Institute Prism Inscription (H2)," Col. III,1,2, *The Annals of Sennacherib* (Chicago: University of Chicago Press, 1924), p. 31. Von Rad sees this coming "to the help of Yahweh" as the ancient reality of holy war, a reality which was later changed by theological reflection (*Der Heilige Krieg im alten Israel,* 3rd ed. [Göttingen: Vandenhoeck & Ruprecht, 1969], pp. 12ff.). See also M. Lind, *Yahweh Is a Warrior,* pp. 71, 191 nn. 23,24.

(4) The Battle of Gideon

Gideon's story is significant in helping us to understand the role played by Israel in its battle under Yahweh. Gideon was instructed by Yahweh when he attacked the Midianites. After he spied the camp of Midian and heard the account of the dream and its interpretation from a Midianite, he came back to the camp of Israel and said:

קומו כי־נתן יהוה בידכם את־מחנה מדין:

Arise, for Yahweh has given the camp of Midian into your hands.
(Judg. 7:15)

He divided his three hundred men into three companies and gave them special instructions for their attack against the camp of Midian. "Look at me, and do likewise. And behold, when I come to the outskirts of the camp, do as I do. When I and all who are with me blow the trumpet, then you also blow the trumpets all around the camp, and say, 'For Yahweh and for Gideon [ליהוה ולגדעון]'" (Judg. 7:17-18). Therefore, according to Gideon's signal they cried: "A sword for Yahweh and for Gideon!" (חרב ליהוה לגדעון, Judg. 7:20b)

In this narrative we can observe that they had a sense that they fought for Yahweh. Thus they cried: "For Yahweh and for Gideon," "A sword for Yahweh and for Gideon," as they attacked their enemies; these phrases mean that "the cause of Israelites against foreign foes is Yahweh's cause; and he who smites for Gideon, smites for Yahweh."[33] Boling understands חרב ליהוה as being synonymous with מלחמה ליהוה (Yahweh's battle).[34] This requires further explanation.

In this attack, there is no mention that the Israelites carried a sword. They each carried only a trumpet and a torch inside a pitcher. When the companies of Gideon cried out, "A sword for Yahweh and for Gideon," it was with reference to the torches hidden in the pitchers and to the sound of the trumpets. The torches and sounding of the trumpets should clearly be seen as the symbolic military equipment of Yahweh in his battle. Judg. 7:22 supports this idea further.

ויתקעו שלש־מאות השופרות וישם יהוה את־חרב
איש ברעהו ובכל־המחנה וינס המחנה עד־בית
השטה צררתה עד שפת־אבל מחולה על־טבת:

33. G. E. Moore, *Judges*, p. 210.
34. R.G. Boling, *Judges*, p. 147.

119

And when they blew 300 trumpets, Yahweh set the sword of one against another even throughout the whole army;[35] and the army fled as far as Beth-shittah toward Zererah, as far as the edge of Abel-meholah, by Tabbath.

When the Gideonite companies blew their trumpets and raised their torches, the Midianites in panic began killing each other in their tents. Here we learn that the Israelites did not use their swords that night. And the narrator writes that "Yahweh set the sword of one against another." Therefore, חרב ליהוה לגדעון is not to be understood as "a sword for the sake of Yahweh and Gideon." It must be rendered as "the sword of Yahweh and Gideon," which implies the meaning of possession. Gideon and his men are not a voluntary group fighting for the sake of Yahweh. Rather they are Yahweh's chosen army (Judg. 7:7) to be used by him in this battle.

In this battle, the Israelites clearly perceived their role as an army or instrument of Yahweh against his enemy. The Israelites were participating in Yahweh's war as his army. This was the nature of their self-understanding in relation to Yahweh through this experience of battle.

Summary

Israel's pre-monarchic experience of Yahweh took place mostly on the battlefield. In the course of the exodus, conquest, and following settlement, they had to conduct wars against the neighboring countries. In a very real way, war was a part of their life. War seems to have been the greatest pressure which they had to survive in their ancient migratory society.

According to their war experience, Yahweh was the God who was fighting for them. Whenever they went out to battle, Yahweh was there and led them into victory. Through his guidance and their consequent victory in war, they realized their special relationship with Yahweh, and sang songs and praises to him.

The exodus experience seems to be the earliest event in which Israel as a nation realizes its election by Yahweh, particularly as his

---

35. The NASB rendering of המחנה is confusing and unclear. Boling's suggestion of "tent" (*Judges*, pp. 143, 147-48), or even Moore's suggestion of "comrade" (*Judges*, p. 211), is more acceptable.

army.[36] Even though the Song of the Sea presents Yahweh as a "warrior" (יהוה איש מלחמה, Ex.15:3) and Israel as "Thy people" (עמך, v. 16) and the people "whom Thou hast purchased" (עם־זו קנית, v. 16), the exodus narrative (Ex. 1–14) is more specific in the description of this relationship. Yahweh's designation of Israel is replete with election terms. Yahweh calls Israel "My people" (עמי, 3:7; 5:1; 6:7), "My people, the sons of Israel" (עמי בני־ישראל, 3:10), and "My son, My first-born" (בני בכרי, 4:22,). In relation to this designation, Yahweh is described as "the God of Israel" (7:4,16; 8:1,20,21,22; 9:1,3,13,17; 12:31) or "the God of the Hebrews" (7:16; 9:1,13; 10:3). Furthermore, in 6:7 this designation constitutes an election formula.

> ולקחתי אתכם לי לעם והייתי לכם לאלהים וידעתם כי
> אני יהוה אלהיכם המוציא אתכם מתחת סבלות מצרים:

> Then I will take you for My people, and I will be your God; and you shall know that I am Yahweh your God, who brought you out from under the burdens of the Egyptians.

However, the most striking designation of the nation in relation to our topic is "My army" (צבאתי).

> ולא־ישמע אלכם פרעה ונתתי את־ידי במצרים והוצאתי את־
> צבאתי את־עמי בני־ישראל מארץ מצרים בשפטים גדלים:

> When Pharaoh will not listen to you, then I will lay My hand on Egypt, and bring out My hosts, My people the sons of Israel, from the land of Egypt by great judgments. (Ex. 7:4)

"My hosts" clearly refers to "My people, the sons of Israel" in the same verse. Also, the phrase "all the hosts of Yahweh" (כל־צבאות יהוה) is used in Ex. 12:41. Thus, the people of Israel recognized Yahweh as the divine warrior who was fighting for them, and they perceived themselves to be "the army of Yahweh" through the exodus experience.

The election idea based on the pre-monarchic experience basically shares the same characteristic as this one. However, both a minor variation and a further development of the concept are observed. In the Song of the Sea, the description of Israel as Yahweh's army is explicit, while the idea of "chosenness" is only indirectly

---

36. According to John Bright, "The exodus was the act of a God who chose for himself a people that they might choose him" (*The Kingdom of God* [Nashville: Abingdon, 1953], p. 28).

121

implied. Yahweh's role as a divine warrior is emphasized. Yahweh himself and his right hand alone fought against Pharaoh and his army (Ex. 15:5-6). Israel did nothing but cross the Red Sea.

In the story of Joshua, however, Israel's wars were conducted according to Yahweh's guidance, and the concept of חרם was employed. Since the angels of Yahweh joined in the battle and the supernatural help of Yahweh is emphasized, the human role in the battle was minimized, as seen in the stories of Jericho and Gideon. The confessional description "Yahweh fought for Israel" (Josh. 10:14,42; 23:3,10) is noteworthy here.

In the Song of Deborah, the participation of the people in Yahweh's war is emphasized. Those who did not come to the help of Yahweh were utterly cursed (Judg. 5:23). Even though Yahweh's coming is described in terms of a divine warrior who is accompanied by earthquake and rain (5:3-5), with even the celestial bodies joining in the battle, the main concern of the song is the participation of the human army in Yahweh's war. In contrast to the two previous cases, the war is Yahweh's and Israel is seen as a "helper of Yahweh." Therefore, the activity of a human army is more positive and volitional here than in the two previous cases. Israel had the impression that they contributed something to Yahweh's war. In particular, "the people of Yahweh" (5:11,13) are described as warriors for Yahweh.

In the story of Gideon, this idea is expanded further, and we can see the choosing of Yahweh's army. They had a clear understanding that they were fighting for Yahweh, and they themselves were part of his war machine.

In any event, Yahweh worked together with Israel in war. Yahweh was a divine warrior and Israel was his army. Thus the premonarchic election idea is mostly found in the war context. No other significant description of the idea is found. Therefore, we can conclude that the idea of election originated in Israel's war experience and dated back to the beginning of Israel's history.

2. THE EARLY MONARCHIC IDEA

The election idea occurs frequently in the literature describing the early monarchic events. In this period we see the activities of Samuel and David, the preeminent worshipers of Yahweh. The idea of Yahweh's election of Israel seems to have been the foundational ideology which united the tribes and led to the building of the Temple.

(1) The Activities of Samuel

After the collapse of Eli's family, Samuel assumed the religious leadership of Israel. Unlike his predecessor, he was totally Yahweh-centric, and the people of Israel listened to his voice. Since he upheld worship of Yahweh alone, he urged his people to remove the alien gods from among them and return to Yahweh with all their heart (1 Sam. 7:3-4). Therefore, the convention at Mizpah was seen as a kind of return-to-Yahweh movement in the eyes of the author of this book.[37] They fasted on that day and repented of their polytheism.

This national convention precipitated a national crisis, however, because the Philistines heard the news and went up to attack Israel. The Israelites were afraid and they asked Samuel to pray to Yahweh to help them. Thus, Samuel took a suckling lamb and offered it for a whole burnt offering to Yahweh and cried out to him on behalf of the nation. As the Philistines drew near to battle against Israel, "Yahweh thundered with a great thunder on that day against the Philistines and confused them, so that they were routed before Israel" (וירעם יהוה בקול־גדול ביום ההוא על־פלשתים ויהמם וינגפו לפני ישראל, 1 Sam. 7:10). The battle, therefore, ended with Israel's victory. The intervention of Yahweh for his people by means of thunder is a characteristic phenomenon of a holy war. In particular, the verb

37. Many scholars agree that even though the language of this passage may be younger and Deuteronomistic, the idea is not. According to M.C. Lind, this passage "deals with the first commandment, which is fundamental to the earliest 'rîb' poetry, in which Yahweh's case against the people is presented, and to the 'rîb' oracles of the ancient prophets." Furthermore, the intercession of Samuel is linked with that of Moses, and the role of Samuel as a judge is concerned with Israel's sin and her relationship with Yahweh. See Lind, *Yahweh Is a Warrior,* p. 98.

המם, which means "to throw into confusion and panic," is usually found in a holy war context (Ex. 14:24; Josh. 10:10; Judg. 4:15). Once again, Israel experienced the miraculous help of Yahweh in the war, an immediate result of their return to him.

We do not see any specific war leader here. Samuel only prayed and Yahweh answered. Even without any human leader in battle, Israel could win and overcome a national crisis. Israel viewed this event differently, however, for they thought they needed a visible human war leader. The main reason for requesting a king was to have a warrior who could lead them out to war and fight their battles (1 Sam. 8:5, 20). So they demanded a warrior-king. Samuel was displeased at their request for a king. Yahweh also regarded it as the rejection of his kingship over Israel (8:7). However, Yahweh listened to them and commanded Samuel to give a king to them. Thus, Saul was anointed as the first human king of Israel, and he was, eventually, acknowledged by the people as such when he defeated Nahash the Ammonite (chap. 11).

After this, Samuel again called for a national convention at Gilgal (12:1-25), which is known as the occasion for his farewell address. In his speech, Samuel first recounted his honesty and fidelity (vv. 1-5), and second, he repeated the absurdity of Israel's request for a king in spite of their experience of Yahweh's kingship over them (vv. 6-12).[38] Thus, he said,

ותראו כי־נחש מלך בני־אמון בא עליכם ותאמרו לי
לא כי־מלך ימלך עלינו ויהוה אלהיכם מלככם:

When you saw that Nahash the king of the sons of Ammon came against you, you said to me, "No, but a king shall reign over us," although Yahweh your God was your king. (1 Sam. 12:12)

38. J.R. Vannoy comprehensively summarizes the divergent opinions of the literary criticism concerning 1 Sam. 11:14–12:25 in *Covenant Renewal at Gilgal* (Cherry Hill: Mack Publishing Co., 1978), pp. 95-126. While not denying Deuteronomistic influence in the narrative, he argues that it is not to be considered the result of late editorializing, or exilic or even postexilic authorship, but rather the reflection of a vital theological dynamic operative in and contemporaneous with the events which are here described (pp. 237-38). D.J. McCarthy assigns 1 Sam. 12 to a pre-Deuteronomistic stage, "because it is *not quite* deuteronomistic." According to him, "a phrase not *exactly* deuteronomistic must simply be non-deuteronomistic, for example, 'dwell in safety (v. 11b: בטח)' for deuteronomistic 'quiet (שקט),' 'making a people for yourself (v. 22b)' for deuteronomistic 'be a people . . . ,' or מקום for 'land' (v. 8b) and not deuteronomistic 'Temple'" ("Compact and Kingship: Stimuli for Hebrew Covenant Thinking," in *Studies in the Period of David and Solomon and Other Essays,* ed. Tomoo Ishida [Winona Lake: Eisenbrauns, 1982], pp. 89-90).

Therefore, Samuel called for a demonstration of thunder and rain, showing them that Yahweh was still their king over and above any human king. Thus Yahweh's thunder and rain manifested here in the harvest season were not salvific (as they were at Mizpah); rather they were to awaken the sons of Israel who had asked for a king besides Yahweh (v. 17). Responding in terror, Israel repented and asked Samuel to pray to Yahweh for them.

> התפלל בעד־עבדיך אל־יהוה אלהיך ואל־נמות כי־יספנו
> על־כל־חטאתינו רעה לשאל לנו מלך:

Pray for your servants to Yahweh your God, so that we may not die, for we have added to all our sins this evil by asking for ourselves a king. (1 Sam. 12:19)

In response to their repentance (vv. 20-25), Samuel exhorted the people to serve Yahweh in truth with all their heart. Quite significantly, he stated,

> כי לא־יטש יהוה את־עמו בעבור שמו הגדול
> כי הואיל יהוה לעשות אתכם לו לעם:

For Yahweh will not abandon His people on account of His great name, because Yahweh has been pleased to make you a people for Himself. (1 Sam. 12:22)

Here we see an unusual rejection term as well as an important election formula. נטש is a rejection term meaning "pluck up" or "throw off,"[39] and it was especially utilized by Jeremiah in the rejection context (Jer. 12:14,15,17; 18:7,14; 31:28,40; 42:10; 45:4). The verb עשה in its participial form is sometimes used for Yahweh as the Maker of Israel (Ps. 95:6; Is. 44:2; 51:13; 54:5; Hos. 8:14). However, its use here in an election formula is unique. The combination of the love term הואיל with the election term suggests the later origin of this usage.

The institution of kingship seemed to have been socially indispensable if Israel was to survive in its hostile surroundings. The struggle between the prophetic defense of Yahweh's kingship and the people's demand of a human king resulted in the people's victory. In the process of asking for and choosing a king, however, they had to realize that Yahweh was still their king who fought for them. The keen concern of the people of Israel during the days of Samuel seemed to have been directed at finding a real human king for

---

39. See Chap. III below, p. 205.

them.[40] The social need created a new image of Yahweh as their king. Thus, the image of Yahweh as a warrior-king who was to rule Israel and fight for them was the product of this transitional period from the age of the Judges to the monarchy. However, this image of Yahweh as a warrior-king is alluded to in the Song of the Sea.

(2) The Battles of David

David seems to be one of the most zealous worshipers of Yahweh throughout biblical history. Even though David was anointed by Samuel (1 Sam. 16:1-13), he did not receive any national attention until he killed Goliath, the Philistine. When he returned from killing the Philistine, the women came out of all the cities of Israel, singing and dancing with tambourines and other musical instruments, saying:

הכה שאול באלפו ודוד ברבבתיו:

Saul has slain his thousands, and David his ten thousands.

(1 Sam. 18:7)

Since this song was known even to the people of Gath, when David fled from Saul to Achish king of Gath, the servants of Achish said to him, "Is this not David the king of the land? Did they not sing of this one as they danced, saying, 'Saul has slain his thousands, and David his ten thousands'"? (1 Sam. 21:11). Again, when the allied forces of the Philistines gathered together against Saul, the commander of the Philistines did not like David's joining with them and reminded Achish of this very song (29:5). This indicates that the killing of Goliath and the ensuing victory over the Philistines gave David international fame. The

40. Since "in the Assyrian enthronement ritual the kingship of Ashur is significantly proclaimed prior to the crowning of the human king (K.F. Müller, *Das assyrische Ritual 1* [MVAG 41/3, 1973] 8-9 line 29)," and since "the Babylonian view is well reflected in the prologue to the Code of Hammurabi (i 1-52, v 14-24)," J.J.M. Roberts asserts that Israel followed the lines of Assyria and Babylon in viewing Yahweh as the real king, with the human king as his earthly representative or regent, "elected by the deity to carry out his earthly tasks" ("Zion in the Theology of the Davidic-Solomonic Empire," in *Studies in the Period of David and Solomon and Other Essays,* ed. Tomoo Ishida [Winona Lake: Eisenbrauns, 1982], p. 99).

background of this song (chap. 17) suggests some very important clues in our understanding of the concept of election.

In the narrative section of David's confrontation against Goliath, David himself calls the army of Israel "the armies of the living God" (מערכות אלהים חיים, 17:26, 36). And when he went out to meet the Philistines, he said:

אתה בא אלי בחרב ובחנית ובכידון ואנכי בא־אליך
בשם יהוה צבאות אלהי מערכות ישראל אשר חרפת:
היום הזה יסגרך יהוה בידי והכיתך והסרתי את־ראשך
מעליך ונתתי פגר מחנה פלשתים היום הזה לעוף השמים
ולחית הארץ וידעו כל־הארץ כי יש אלהים לישראל:
וידעו כל־הקהל הזה כי־לא בחרב ובחנית יהושיע יהוה
כי ליהוה המלחמה ונתן אתום בידנו:

> You come to me with a sword, a spear, and a javelin, but I come to you in the name of Yahweh of hosts, the God of the armies of Israel, whom you have taunted. This day Yahweh will deliver you up into my hands, and I will strike you down and remove your head from you. And I will give the dead bodies of the army of the Philistines this day to the birds of the sky and the wild beasts of the earth, that all the earth may know that there is a God in Israel, and that all this assembly may know that Yahweh does not deliver by sword or by spear; for the battle is Yahweh's and He will give you into our hands.
> (1 Sam. 17:45-47)

Here, David again calls Yahweh "Yahweh of hosts" and "the God of the armies of Israel." The battle is Yahweh's, and the battle is entrusted to David by Yahweh, so that all the earth may know that there is a God in Israel, and that all Israel may know that Yahweh does not deliver by sword or by spear. According to these words, Israel is an army of Yahweh, and David himself is a commander of this army who is about to fight for Yahweh and his honor.

These ideas seem to be prevalent among the Israelites after the war. Saul offers his daughter Merab to David to be his wife on the condition of his being a valiant man and fighting "Yahweh's battle" (מלחמות יהוה, 1 Sam. 18:17). Even though Saul had a cunning design to kill David through the hand of the Philistines, he recognized David as a man who waged the wars of Yahweh. Also, Abigail the wife of Nabal spoke similar words about David when he came to destroy the whole family of Nabal in vengeance for the latter's contempt.

שא נא לפשע אמתך כי עשה־יעשה יהוה לאדני בית נאמן
כי־מלחמות יהוה אדני נלחם ורעה לא־תמצא בך מימיך:

Please forgive the transgression of your maidservant; for Yahweh
will certainly make for my lord an enduring house, because my lord
is fighting the battles of Yahweh, and evil shall not be found in you
all your days. (1 Sam. 25:28)

Abigail believed that since David was fighting Yahweh's battle,
Yahweh would build an enduring house for David.[41] Therefore, we
can see here that the idea of Israel's being the army of Yahweh took
on a more concrete form in the days of David. This idea is also
present in the psalms of David.

Psalm 60 is considered to be genuinely Davidic.[42]

אלהים זנחתנו פרצתנו אנפת תשובב לנו:	3
הרעשתה ארץ פצמתה רפה שבריה כי־מטה:	4
הראיתה עמך קשה השקיתנו יין תרעלה:	5
נתתה ליראיך נס להתנוסס מפני קשט סלה:	6
למען יחלצון ידידיך הושיעה ימינך וענני:	7
אלהים דבר בקדשו אעלזה אחלקה שכם	8
ועמק סכות אמדד:	
לי גלעד ולי מנשה ואפרים מעוז ראשי יהודה מחקקי:	9
מואב סיר רחצי על־אדום אשליך נעלי	10
עלי פלשת התרעעי:	
מי יבלני עיר מצור מי נחני עד־אדום:	11
הלא־אתה אלהים זנחתנו ולא־תצא אלהים בצבאותינו:	12
הבה־לנו עזרת מצר ושוא תשועת אדם:	13
באלהים נעשה־חיל והוא יבוס צרינו:	14

1   O God, Thou hast rejected us. Thou hast broken us;
     Thou hast been angry; O, restore us.
2   Thou hast made the land quake, Thou hast split it open;
     Heal its breaches, for it totters.
3   Thou hast made Thy people experience hardship;
     Thou hast given us wine to drink that makes us stagger.

41. According to P.K. McCarter, 1 Sam. 17 and 25:28-31 are the Deuteronomistic additions (1 Samuel, AB [Garden City: Doubleday, 1980] pp. 16, 284-98,
388-402). However, 1 Sam. 18:17 suggests that, at the time of David, many people
regarded him as the one who fought the battle of Yahweh.
42. Moses Buttenwieser, The Psalms (New York: KTAV, 1969), pp. 67- 82.
M. Dahood also dates this psalm in the Davidic period. He, however, does not
exclude the possibility of its belonging to the Solomonic period (Psalms, AB [Gar-
den City: Doubleday, 1973], 2:76). A.A. Anderson suggests that the date would be
after 722 B.C., but hardly as late as the Maccabean period, as suggested by Hitzig
and Duhm (Psalms, 2 vols., NCBC [Grand Rapids: Eerdmans, 1981], 1:441).

4 Thou hast given a banner to those who fear Thee,
   That it may be displayed because of the truth. Selah.
5 That Thy beloved may be delivered,
   Save with Thy right hand, and answer us!
6 God has spoken in His holiness:
   "I will exult, I will portion out Shechem and measure out the valley
     of Succoth.
7 Gilead is Mine, and Manasseh is Mine;
   Ephraim also is the helmet of My head;
   Judah is My scepter.
8 Moab is My washbowl;
   Over Edom I shall throw My shoe;
   Shout loud, O Philistia, because of Me!"
9 Who will bring me into the besieged city?
   Who will lead me to Edom?
10 Hast not Thou Thyself, O God, rejected us?
   And wilt Thou not go forth with our armies, O God?
11 O give us help against the adversary,
   For deliverance by man is in vain.
12 Through God we shall do valiantly,
   And it is He who will tread down our adversaries.

The present heading of this psalm describes the historical background: "when he struggled with Aram-naharaim and with Aram-zobah, and Joab returned, and smote twelve thousand of Edom in the Valley of Salt." Aram-naharaim was the ancient home of the patriarch in northern Mesopotamia (Gen. 24:10), and Aram-Zobah was an Aramean kingdom north of Damascus, probably in the valley between Lebanon and Anti-Lebanon. David's victories over the Aramean kingdoms are described in 2 Sam. 8 and 1 Ch. 18:3ff.[43]

The first paragraph of this psalm (vv. 3-7 [E. 1-5]) begins with a lament for the defeat of Israel and ends with a petition for deliverance. According to Buttenwieser, these expressions are describing the fall of Saul after the disastrous battle on Mount Gilboa.[44] Here we observe two very important phrases: "Thy people" (עַמְּךָ) and "Thy beloved" (יְדִידֶיךָ). Even though David thinks that they are suffering hardship which Yahweh had caused, he still considers his people to be Yahweh's beloved people.

The second paragraph (vv. 8-11 [E. 6-9]) is Yahweh's answer to

43. A.A. Anderson, *Psalms*, 1:441-42. See also John Bright, *History of Israel*, pp. 197-98.
44. Buttenwieser, *Psalms*, p. 79.

David. Yahweh's dividing (חלק) Shechem and measuring (מדד) Succoth is a proclamation of his ownership of the land. And Yahweh continues to declare his ownership of Gilead, Manasseh, Ephraim, and Judah (v. 7). In particular, Yahweh calls Ephraim the helmet of his head (מעוז ראשי, lit. fortress of my head) and Judah his scepter (מחקקי, a symbol of military or royal authority). This word-picture presents Yahweh as a warrior whose helmet is Northern Israel and whose commander's staff is Judah.[45] As a corollary of the picture in this specific context, Moab and Edom are described as Yahweh's washbowl and shoe-chest, and Philistia as she who cries out because of him. This is a metaphorical picture portraying their disgraceful defeat by Yahweh and his army.

The third paragraph (vv. 12-14 [E. 10-12]) is a prayer of David asking Yahweh to go into battle with him. Even though Yahweh had rejected them before, David asks now that he should lead them to Edom and to the besieged city so as to tread down their adversary. David confesses that deliverance by man is in vain. Only Yahweh is able to help them, and only through God can they triumph. Thus, according to our interpretation of this psalm, the idea that Yahweh was a divine warrior with Israel as his army existed in the days of David, and it was prevalent as well in popular thought. In Ps. 108:8-10 (E. 7-9), Ps. 60:8-11 (E. 6-9) is inserted. This reflects the popularity of these concepts among the Israelites. The thought of Yahweh as a divine warrior in its more concrete form seems to come to ascendancy mostly in the time of David.

(3) The Oracle of Nathan

In Nathan's oracle and the following prayer of David (2 Sam. 7), the relationship between Yahweh and Israel is described in its most perfect form in relation to our topic.[46] Here, Yahweh's designation

45. A.A. Anderson, *Psalms,* 1:445.
46. Concerning the literary history of Nathan's oracle and David's prayer in 2 Sam. 7, scholars' opinions are so divergent that it is not easy to draw a firm conclusion. See P.K. McCarter, *2 Samuel,* AB (Garden City: Doubleday, 1984), pp. 209-31, 239-41. However, Gerald Cooke proposes, against R. Pfeiffer, that the poetic prophecy concerning the Davidic dynasty is part of the prophecy which stemmed from near the time of David himself. "In other words, it is at least plausible that the verses under discussion were first uttered in the context of the glories of David's rule, in the expectation of the continuation of the current level of well-

of Israel is very significant in tracing the idea of election. Yahweh calls Israel "My people" four times (vv. 7,8,10,11): "to shepherd My people Israel" (לרעות את־עמי את־ישראל, v. 7), "to rule over My people Israel" (להיות נגיד על־עמי על־ישראל, v. 8), "to appoint a place for My people Israel" (ושמתי מקום לעמי ישראל, v. 10), and "to judge over My people Israel" (שפטים על־עמי ישראל, v. 11). These phrases are all directed to David in Yahweh's response to David's wish to build a house for him. According to these phrases, Yahweh emphasizes that Israel is not David's people but Yahweh's. Nathan, the religious leader in those days, views Israel as Yahweh's people.

David's prayer in response to Nathan's oracle (2 Sam. 7:18-29) also shows David's understanding of the Yahweh-Israel relationship and his role as a king in between them.

על־כם גדלת אדני יהוה כי־אין כמוך ואין אלהים זולתך
בכל אשר־שמענו באזנינו: ומי כעמך כישראל גוי אחד
בארץ אשר הלכו־אלהים לפדות־לו לעם ולשום לו שם
ולעשות לכם הגדולה ונראות לארצך מפני עמך אשר
פדית לך ממצרים גוים ואלהיו: ותכונן לך את־עמך
ישראל לך לעם עד־עולם ואתה יהוה היית להם לאלהים:

For this reason Thou art great, O Lord Yahweh; for there is none like Thee, and there is no God besides Thee, according to all that we have heard with our ears. And what one nation on the earth is like Thy people Israel, whom God went to redeem for Himself as a people and to make a name for Himself, and to do a great thing for Thee and awesome things for Thy land, before Thy people whom Thou hast redeemed for Thyself from Egypt, from nations and their gods? For Thou hast established for Thyself Thy people Israel as Thine own people forever, and Thou, O Yahweh, hast become their God.

(2 Sam. 7:22-24)

The superiority of Yahweh, the extraordinariness of Israel in its relationship with him, Yahweh's going forth to redeem his people, and Yahweh's establishing his people are all related to the idea of election. Here we observe two unusual election formulae: הלכו־ ותכונן לך את־עמך ישראל לך לעם עד־עולם (v. 23) and אלהים לפדות־לו לעם ואתה יהוה היית להם לאלהים: (v. 24) Both פדה and כון seem to be used from the earliest times. Though פדה is spoken of in terms of the

being and favor with Yahweh" ("The Israelite King as Son of God," *ZAW* 73 [1961]: 202-25). As we have observed before, we can hardly deny the existence of the election idea in its highly developed form in the days of David, nor the preservation of its original ideas found in the oracle and prayer.

redemption of a slave girl for the purpose of marriage in Ex. 21:8 and Lev. 19:20, its root occurs in Akkadian (*padû/pedû*)[47] with the meaning "to exempt, spare," and in Ugaritic (*pdy*) it is used in the sense of "to ransom."[48] At the cost of the slaughter of every first-born of man and beast in Egypt, Yahweh delivered Israel from slavery in Egypt (Ex. 4:23; 12:29). So also Jonathan was rescued (פרה) by the people of Israel from his father's hand (1 Sam. 14:45), although most of the usage of this term is found in the books of Exodus, Leviticus, and Numbers. The root כון appears to mean "to bring something into being with the consequence that its existence is a certainty."[49] However, the Hebrew root rarely has that meaning (Ex. 15:17; Job 31:15; Ps. 119:73,90; Ezek. 16:7). The cognates in Ugaritic (*kwn*)[50] and Akkadian (*kânu*) stress existence or establishment. Many times כון is used with reference to the establishment of a dynasty (1 Sam. 13:13; 20:31; 2 Sam. 5:12; 7:12,13,16; 1 Kgs. 2:12,45,46; 1 Ch. 17: 12, 14, 24; 22:10; 28:7; Ps. 140:12 [E. 11]). According to Oswalt, this word carrying a theological significance shows a semantic development moving from the root meaning to the meanings of preparation, establishment, fixity, and rightness. Thus, the meaning of כון found here is closer to the Akkadian root meaning "to organize, create, or fashion." Therefore, we can conclude that in the days of David, the idea of election as well as the formulae of election were shaped and used particularly among political and religious leaders such as David and Nathan.

(4) Solomon Builds the Temple

During the period of Solomon we see the construction of the Temple of Yahweh, which gives a new meaning to Israel's worship of him. The erection of the Temple was planned and prepared by David, and it took seven years to build it. "Solomon levied forced laborers from all Israel; and the forced laborers numbered 30,000 men. And he sent them to Lebanon, 10,000 a month in relays; they were in Lebanon a month and two months at home. And Adoniram was over the forced laborers. Now Solomon had 70,000 transport-

47. *AHw*, p. 808b.
48. *UT*, p. 466, nr. 2013; Aistl., 2194.
49. John N. Oswalt, "כון," *TWOT*, 1:433.
50. See *UT*, p. 418, nr. 1213.

ers, and 80,000 hewers of stone in the mountains, besides Solomon's 3,300 chief deputies who were over the project and who ruled
over the people who were doing the work" (1 Kgs. 5:13-16). All
through these seven years, great number of people were forced to
join in the construction. When he levied this multitude, how could
he justify it? When Solomon asked the help of Hiram in building
the Temple, he said,

> You know that David my father was unable to build a house for the
> name of Yahweh his God because of the wars which surrounded
> him, until Yahweh put them under the soles of his feet. But now
> Yahweh my God has given me rest on every side; there is neither
> adversary nor misfortune. And behold, I intend to build a house for
> the name of Yahweh my God, as Yahweh spoke to David my father,
> saying, "Your son, whom I will set on your throne in your place, he
> will build the house for My name." (1 Kgs. 5:3-5)

According to these verses,[51] the first reason for both David and
Solomon to build a temple was for the name of Yahweh. It was out

51. M. Noth, with many other scholars, assigns the whole composition to the
Deuteronomist. See M. Noth, *The Deuteronomistic History,* JSOTSup 14 (Sheffield: JSOT, 1981); Richard D. Nelson, *The Double Redaction of the Deuteronomistic History,* JSOTSup 18 (Sheffield: JSOT, 1981). However, B. Stade saw the
whole section as practically of one piece, with a few interpolated passages, except-
ing only vv. 44-51 as a later edition (*The Book of Kings,* Sacred Books of the OT
[1904]). A. Šanda attempted a minute analysis, and found the original record of
dedication, following vv. 1-14, in vv. 22, 31-39, 54ff. He attributed the remaining
section to redactors (*Die Bucher der Könige,* 2 vols. [1911-12]). G. Hölscher found
three strata, in this chronological order: A (vv. 14- 26,28,29); B (vv. 27,30-43, 52-
61); C (vv. 45-51) (*Das Buch der Könige, Seine Quellen und seine Redaktion* [1923]).
See also James A. Montgomery, *A Critical and Exegetical Commentary on the
Books of Kings,* ICC (Edinburgh: T. & T. Clark, 1951), pp. 192-95.
    However, according to J.A. Soggin, who carefully examined the evidence of
the LXX, the prayer of consecration for the Temple (1 Kgs. 8:12ff.) has been taken
from a certain "Book of Songs," perhaps equivalent to the "Book of the Upright"
(Josh. 10:13ff., 2 Sam. 1:19ff.). And he concludes that "if the notice given in the
LXX is correct (and scholarly opinion is almost unanimous on this point), there is
an authentic kernel in the long prayer which was then considerably revised by Dtr"
(Introduction to the Old Testament, OTL [Philadelphia: Westminster, 1976],
p. 203). R.K. Harrison believes that the treaty with Hiram of Tyre and the prepa-
rations for building the Temple (1 Kgs. 5:15-32 [E. 1-18]), the construction of the
Temple and the royal palace (6:1–7:51), and the dedication of the Temple (8:1-66)
all belong to the book of the Acts of Solomon and may well have been derived from
the reliable ancient Temple archives *(Introduction to the Old Testament* [Grand
Rapids: Eerdmans, 1969], p. 725). See also S. Szikszai, "Kings, I and II," *IDB,*
3:31.

of human intention and personal zeal for their God. However, that was not enough to persuade the people to join in. The greater motivation was Yahweh's promise to David. For Solomon, it was Yahweh's will to build it because Yahweh predestined him to build it. Therefore, we can see that these two factors are emphasized.

On the day of the dedication of the Temple, Solomon spoke to all the assembly of Israel.

> Blessed be Yahweh, the God of Israel, who spoke with His mouth to my father David and has fulfilled it with His hand, saying, "Since the day that I brought My people Israel from Egypt, I did not choose a city out of all the tribes of Israel in which to build a house that My name might be there, but I chose David to be over My people Israel." Now it was in the heart of my father David to build a house for the name of Yahweh, the God of Israel. But Yahweh said to my father David, "Because it was in your heart to build a house for My name, you did well that it was in your heart. Nevertheless you shall not build the house, but your son who shall be born to you, he shall build the house for My name." Now Yahweh has fulfilled His word which He spoke; for I have risen in place of my father David and sit on the throne of Israel, as Yahweh promised, and have built the house for the name of Yahweh, the God of Israel. (1 Kgs. 8:15-20)

Here, Yahweh's choosing David, David's desire to build the Temple for the name of Yahweh, Yahweh's predestination of Solomon to build it instead of David, and Yahweh's fulfillment of his promise constitute the main body of Solomon's address. At the outset of his speech, Solomon blesssed Yahweh, who declared his will to David, and he concluded by saying, "Now Yahweh has fulfilled his word which He spoke." By ascribing the motivation, the process, and even the completion of the building of the Temple to Yahweh, Solomon had recourse to Yahweh's authority. As a corollary, the people of Israel must have had a strong attitude of devotion to Yahweh, at least during the period of Temple construction. If we take into account the political atmosphere at the beginning of the construction of the Temple, it is more understandable why he leaned on Yahweh to justify his intention. He began to build the house of Yahweh in the fourth year of his reign over Israel (1 Kgs. 6:1). This four-year period was not long enough for him to consolidate his throne. From the end of David's reign over Israel, the rebellion of Absalom (2 Sam. 13–19), Sheba's revolt (2 Sam. 20), delivering Saul's family into the hand of the Gibeonites (2 Sam. 21), the pestilence throughout the country (2 Sam. 24), Adonijah's claim of the throne after David (1 Kgs. 1), and the resulting purge of his followers (1 Kgs. 2) were significant and potentially traumatic events. Thus, even though four years might have been long enough for him to appoint new officials, including priests (1 Kgs. 3), it was too short a time in which to unite and heal the divided mind of the people. Again, we see the political adversaries and opposing forces of Hadad the Edomite (11:14-22), Rezon the son of Eliada (11:23-25), and Jeroboam the son of Nebat (11:26-40) during Solomon's reign. Therefore, we can safely say that Solomon began to build the Temple so as to bring about the unity of his people under the covering strength of Yahweh.

This is the reason why Yahweh first warned Solomon to keep his commandments. "Now the word of Yahweh came to Solomon saying, 'Concerning this house which you are building, if you will walk in My statutes and execute My ordinances and keep all My commandments by walking in them, then I will carry out My word with you which I spoke to David your father. And I will dwell among the sons of Israel, and will not forsake My people Israel'" (1Kgs. 6:11-13). Yahweh clearly gave warning regarding Solomon's political motive in building the Temple. If Solomon had built the Temple out of genuine religious motivation, he would not have fallen into the worship of alien gods so quickly (1 Kgs. 11). He took advantage of the religious mind of Israel in order to achieve his political goals. In any event, Israel must have directed its heart to Yahweh while building the Temple.

In his speech and prayer during the dedication ceremony, we can observe Solomon's other emphasis. Solomon intentionally uses the pronominal epithet for both Yahweh and people. He refers to Yahweh as "the God of Israel" (יהוה אלהי ישראל, 8:15, 17,20,23,25,26), "Yahweh our God" (יהוה אלהינו, 8:57,59,61), and "my God Yahweh" (יהוה אלהי, 8:28), and the people were "Thy people Israel" (עמך ישראל, 8:30,33,34,36, 38, 43, 51, 52), "Thy people" (עמך, 8:44,50), "His people Israel" (עמו ישראל, 8:56, 59,66), "My people Israel" (את־עמי ישראל, 8:16), and "Thine inheritance" (נחלתך, 8:51). In such a short speech, why did he repeatedly use those personal pronouns? Solomon never called Israel "my people," and he even tried to restrain from calling Yahweh "my God" (once in v. 28). He seemed to be dependent upon the authority of Yahweh, and he tried to convince the people that they were the people of Yahweh, and Yahweh was the God of Israel. He was still too young and politically unstable to claim them as his own people.[52] However, we can not disregard the fact that the weakness of Solomon contributed to Israel's awareness of their being Yahweh's people.

In this prayer a particular election formula is found. Solomon says in 8:53, "For Thou hast separated them from all the peoples of the earth as Thine inheritance" (כי־אתה הבדלתם לך לנחלה מכל עמי הארץ). This formula itself is very unusual, with a similar formula found in Lev. 20:26, "I have set you apart from the peoples to be mine" (ואבדל אתכם מן־העמים להיות לי). Even though the usage of הבדיל meaning "to separate, or to set apart" is found over a wide range of time (from Genesis to Chronicles, mainly in the Priestly Code and post-exilic literature), the employment of this term in the election formula is obviously later.

Another important phrase to be noted here is in verse 41. Solomon makes a clear distinction between the people of Yahweh and "the foreigner who is not of Thy people Israel" (הנכרי אשר לא־מעמך ישראל הוא). However, Solomon's prayer is not exclusive, but rather universalistic. The God of Solomon is the God of uniqueness, of incomparability (8:60), and the God of the whole world. Thus, Solomon asks God to bestow the same grace on the foreigner as on the Israelites (v. 41), and he further asks that "all the peoples of the earth may know that Yahweh is God; there is no one else" (למען דעת כל־עמי הארץ כי יהוה הוא האלהים אין עוד, 8:60). Solomon's consciousness of Yahweh as a universal God can be said to reflect, on the one hand, his international policy and, on the other hand, the idea of Yahweh's choosing David (8:16), Jerusalem (8:44), and the people, Israel.

Summary

Israel's early monarchic experience of Yahweh is more realistic than that of any other period. Though the request for a human king was an indispensable social need, they had to know that Yahweh was

---

52. In 1 Kgs. 22:4 Jehoshaphat the king of Judah said to Ahab the king of Israel, "I am as you are, my people as your people, my horses as your horses." Thus, kings usually seemed to call the people "my people."

their real king who was among them and fought for them. Yahweh was recognized as a warrior-king and as the one who could not be compared with any other gods.

We see here the special term "Yahweh's battle." David was known to fight Yahweh's battle (1 Sam. 18:17). He fought for Yahweh, his name, and his glory. This idea is opposite to Yahweh's fighting for Israel. However, this does not mean that Yahweh needed human help. This expression reflects David's zeal for Yahweh and his conviction that Yahweh would fight for Israel.

We see also the frequent usage of the term עַם here. In the premonarchic experience, the people of Israel were designated as "My people" by Yahweh himself. But here עַמְּךָ יִשְׂרָאֵל is spoken to Yahweh by humans. Therefore, the idea that Israel was the people of Yahweh, not the people of a king, seemed to be established in this early monarchic period particularly by Samuel (1 Sam. 12:22; 13:14), Nathan (2 Sam. 7:7, 8, 10), David (2 Sam. 7:23,24), and Solomon (1 Kgs. 3:8,9). The idea that the human king is not the ultimate owner of the people, but that Yahweh is, is a characteristic feature of kingship in Israel.[53] This could be possible because Yahweh's election of Israel as his people existed before the beginning of the monarchy.

The kingship of Yahweh over Israel is also closely associated with the building of the Temple. David as a human king living in a house compared himself with Yahweh dwelling in a tent, and he expressed his intention to build a house for Yahweh (2 Sam. 7:1). Since the Temple is called "the house of Yahweh" (1 Kgs. 6:37) and "the house for the name of Yahweh" (1 Kgs. 8:20), Yahweh was believed to dwell there, because the Temple was generally recognized as the place where heaven and earth met, the localization of heaven on earth in ancient Near Eastern thought.[54] For David, who was a king, Yahweh was also a king, and he was a greater king than David. As David sat enthroned in his house, Yahweh also needed a house in which to be enthroned. This intention of David to build a house for Yahweh reflects his genuine reverence of Yahweh as the

53. Henri Frankfort, *Kingship and the Gods : A Study of Ancient Near Eastern Religion as Integration of Society and Nature* (Chicago: University of Chicago Press, 1948), pp. 337-44.

54. Tryggve N.D. Mettinger, "YHWH SABAOTH—The Heavenly King on the Cherubim Throne," in *Studies in the Period of David and Solomon and Other Essays,* ed. Tomoo Ishida (Winona Lake: Eisenbrauns, 1982), pp. 119-23.

king over him. Even though Solomon distorted this novel intention of David and made use of it politically, the erection of the Temple brought an obvious tribal and spiritual unity centered on Yahweh. The people's devotion to the building of the Temple can be regarded as an expression of their commitment and service to Yahweh as his loyal people. Israel's awareness of their election by Yahweh seems to have reached its climax at the time of building and dedicating the Temple.[55]

Thus, we can state that the early monarchic idea of election is focused on Yahweh as the king with Israel as his people. The choosing of a human king and the legitimizing of the Davidic dynasty naturally drew national attention to the place of the kingship in Israel, while at the same time seeing Yahweh as the real king with the human king as his representative on earth provided a viable theology for the nation.

3. THE MONARCHIC IDEA AND ITS DEVELOPMENT

Most of the election metaphors are the creation of the prophets in the period between the fall of the two kingdoms. In particular, the collapse of the northern kingdom and the following deportation into Assyria created serious theological concerns for the people in the southern kingdom, such as the election of the people, national apostasy, the possession of the land, the sovereignty of Yahweh, and the restoration. In this period we see a variety of expressions of the idea of election.

(1) Husband and Wife

In the Bible, the metaphorical description of Yahweh as a husband and Israel as his wife appears in the books of Hosea, Jeremiah, and Ezekiel. However, this metaphor usually expresses a negative sense, indicting Israel of playing the harlot. Therefore, this metaphor bas-

55. B.E. Shafer also proposes that the concept of chosen people is an old one which emerged from the Solomonic period into the royal theology of the southern kingdom (*ZAW* 89 [1977]: 38-39).

ically concerns the unfaithfulness of Israel to her God, Yahweh. First of all, we need to examine the related texts as they stand.

1) Hosea 2:4-25 (E. 2-23)

Hosea's ministry covered the days of Uzziah, Jotham, Ahaz, and Hezekiah, kings of Judah, and Jeroboam, king of Israel, who are listed in the heading of the book (1:1).[56] During this period, we see the fall of the northern kingdom and the apostasy of Ahaz in the southern kingdom.

In particular, the religious policy of Ahaz was endangering the continued existence of Yahwism in Judah. This was the most threatening period for the prophetic faith since the time of Ahab. In order to escape the allied forces of Rezin king of Syria and Pekah king of Israel, Ahaz sought military aid from Tiglath-pileser the king of Assyria by offering silver and gold which was taken from the Temple and the palace (2 Kgs. 16:5-9). Due in part to this tribute, Ahaz could survive the calamity that overtook Israel, although Judah still became a vassal state of the Assyrian empire. According to ancient Near Eastern custom, Ahaz as a vassal king had to recognize his suzerain's gods and follow his directions. He went to Damascus and paid homage to Assyrian gods at a bronze altar that stood there. While he stayed there, he made a copy of the altar and sent it to Urijah the priest to build according to its pattern and model. Thus, the new altar was erected in the Temple, and the bronze altar which was before Yahweh was set aside. When he came back from Damascus, he himself cut off the borders of the stands and removed the laver from there (16:17). He also ordered the periodic offering of various kinds of sacrifices according to the custom of Assyria (16:15). Thus the Temple of Yahweh was thoroughly desecrated. According to J. Bright:

> Since Ahaz was, as all the evidence indicates, without real faith in or zeal for the national religion, he did not exert himself to keep the defenses against paganism otherwise intact. As II Kings 16:3f. al-

56. Hosea's prophetic ministry seems to begin before the death of Jeroboam II of Israel (746 B.C.) and to end after the accession of Hezekiah, king of Judah (715 B.C.). See James M. Ward, "The Message of the Prophet Hosea," *Interpretation*, 23/4 (1969): 388.

leges and as contemporary prophetic passages (e.g., Isa. 2:6-8,20; 8:19f.; Micah 5:12-14) indicate, native pagan practices flourished, together with all sorts of foreign fashions, cults, and superstitions. Ahaz is even charged, on what occasion we do not know, with offering his own son as a sacrifice in fulfillment of some vow or pledge, in accordance with contemporary pagan practice. The reign of Ahaz was remembered by later generations as one of the worst periods of apostasy that Judah had ever known.[57]

In this same period, the northern kingdom departed from Yahweh and the entire nation fell into paganism. Furthermore, the continuous power struggle in the royal court weakened the country. Soon after the reign of Jeroboam II, we see the fall of Samaria and its consequent deportation into Assyria.[58] Therefore, both kingdoms faced critical situations politically as well as religiously. In these circumstances, Hosea's ministry began in the northern kingdom.

In describing the unfaithful relationship of Israel with Yahweh, Hosea uses the metaphor of marriage based on his personal tragic experience. He portrays Yahweh as a loving husband and Israel as an adulterous wife. In particular, the second chapter of Hosea vividly describes the Yahweh-Israel relationship as that of a husband and wife.

4 ריבו באמכם ריבו כי־היא לא אשתי ואנכי לא אישה
ותסר זנוניה מפניה ונאפופיה מבין שריה:

5 פן־אפשיטנה ערמה והצגתיה כיום הולדה
ושמתיה כמדבר ושתה כארץ ציה והמתיה בצמא:

2 Contend with your mother, contend,
    For she is not my wife, and I am not her husband;
    And let her put away her harlotry from her face,
    And her adultery from between her breasts,
3 Lest I strip her naked
    and expose her as on the day when she was born.
    I will also make her like a wilderness,

57. John Bright, *History of Israel*, p. 275.
58. Tiglath-pileser III occupied the greater part of the northern kingdom, leaving only her capital city, Samaria, when he was asked by Ahaz for military help to encounter the Syro-Ephraimite coalition. Hoshea, the successor of Pekah, rebelled against Shalmanezer V at his accession, and was attacked by this emperor in 724 B.C. Sargon finally overtook Samaria in 722 B.C. (2 Kgs. 17:1-41). See Bright, *History of Israel*, pp. 273-74.

Make her like desert land,
And slay her with thirst.

This is basically an indictment speech. The word ריב (to contend or to accuse) denotes the judicial procedure in the court.[59] Yahweh asks the children of Israel to accuse their mother of her harlotry. Thus, Yahweh ascribes the reason for the fate of Israel as "Lo-ru-hamah" and "Lo-ammi" to their mother's unfaithfulness (Hos. 1:6-9). The expression "For she is not my wife, and I am not her husband" is noteworthy here. This expression presupposes the marriage relationship between Yahweh and Israel, and corresponds exactly with Hos. 1:9 (for you are not My people and I am not your God) in both form and meaning. We are not told here exactly when Yahweh entered into the marriage relationship with Israel. At the present time, however, this relationship had been broken because of Israel's harlotry and adultery. Before Yahweh imposed his punishment on her, he ordered Israel to remove her promiscuity from before her face and her breasts, since prostitutes painted their faces (Jer. 4:30; Ezek. 23:40) and used a bunch of myrrh between their breasts (Cant. 1:13) as an aphrodisiac.[60]

In verse 5 (E. 3), the Hebrew conjunction פן governs fives clauses: "I strip her," "expose her," "make her like a wilderness," "make her like a desert land," and "slay her with thirst." Therefore, NASB's rendering of ושמתיה כמדבר as "I will also make her like a wilderness" is syntactically confusing. These five clauses all governed by פן describe Israel's situation before she had a relationship with Yahweh. The phrase "to strip her naked and expose her on the day when she was born" refers to Yahweh's sending her back to her original state (Ezek. 16:6-7). Also, Yahweh's making her like a wilderness and a desert land, and even slaying her with thirst, refers to his returning the woman to the condition in which she lived during the period of her desert wandering.[61]

Therefore, the refusal to heed Yahweh's exhortation to remove

59. As H.B. Huffmon pointed out, ריב is clearly referring to the divine lawsuit against Israel for having broken the covenant. See "The Covenant Lawsuit in the Prophets," *JBL* 78 (1959): 285-95. See also D.J. McCarthy, *Old Testament Covenant: A Survey of Current Opinions* (Atlanta: John Knox, 1972), pp. 38-40; J. Limburg, "The Root ריב and the Prophetic Lawsuit Speeches," *JBL* 88 (1969): 291-304.

60. F. I. Andersen and D.N. Freedman, *Hosea*, p. 224.

61. Ibid., p. 226.

her harlotry would result in Yahweh's putting Israel back into the situation out of which he took her to be his people. The imagery of a husband sending his wife away from his house is a characteristic expression of divorce (Dt. 22:19,29; 24:1,3,4).[62] In the case of her refusal to repent, he had no choice but to take her into court and sentence her to die, since the penalty for adultery under the Mosaic code was death.

6   ואת־בניה לא ארחם כי־בני זנונים המה:

7   כי זנתה אמם הבישה הורתם
                כי אמרה אלכה אחרי מאהבי
                נתני לחמי ומימי צמרי ופשתי שמני ושקויי:

8   לכן הנני־שׂך את־דרכך בסירים
                וגדרתי את־גדרה ונתיבותיה לא תמצא:

9   ורדפה את־מאהביה ולא־תשׂיג אתם
                ובקשתם ולא תמצא ואמרה אלכה
                ואשובה אל־אישי הראשון כי טוב לי אז מעתה:

4   Also, I will have no compassion on her children,
      Because they are children of harlotry.
5   For their mother has played the harlot;
      She who conceived them has acted shamefully.
      For she said, "I will go after my lovers,
      Who give me my bread and my water,
      My wool and my flax, my oil and my drink."
6   Therefore, behold, I will hedge up her way with thorns,
      And I will build a wall against her so that she cannot find her
        paths.
7   And she will pursue her lovers, but she will not overtake them;
      And she will seek them, but will not find them.
      Then she will say, "I will go back to my first husband,
      For it was better for me then than now!"

This paragraph describes the apostasy of Israel from a different perspective. Here Yahweh is dealing with the children and mother together. However, children are mentioned only in verse 6 (E.4). The mother sinned not only against her husband but against her children as well, and the latter will bear the consequence of her conduct. The husband had to provide the basic commodities of life, such as food, clothes, and housing, for his wife even after the divorce in some cases (Ex. 21:10). However, this woman, having sought her lovers in vain for those things, came back again to her

62. See Chap. III below, pp. 193-94.

first husband. Obviously, the woman refers to Israel, her lovers refer to the foreign gods, and her first husband refers to Yahweh. Again, this parable equates the Yahweh-Israel relationship with that of marriage, emphasizing the wife's dependency on her husband in terms of her daily needs. Israel, Yahweh's wife, should have been totally dependent on him. Here, Yahweh is represented as the one who can abort her whole plan to seek her lover.

The next paragraph (vv. 10-15 [E.8-13]) amplifies Yahweh's plan to frustrate her.

10 והיא לא ידעה כי אנכי נתתי לה הדגן והתירוש והיצהר
וכסף הרביתי לה וזהב עשו לבעל:

11 לכן אשוב ולקחתי דגני בעתו ותירושי במועדו
והצלתי צמרי ופשתי לכסות את־ערותה:

12 ועתה אגלה את־נבלתה לעיני מאהביה
ואיש לא־יצילנה מידי:

13 והשבתי כל־משושה חגה חדשה ושבתה וכל מועדה:

14 והשמתי גפנה ותאנתה אשר אמרה
אתנה המה לי אשר נתנו־לי מאהבי
ושמתים ליער ואכלתם חית השדה:

15 ופקדתי עליה את־ימי הבעלים אשר תקטיר להם
ותעד נזמה וחליתה ותלך אחרי מאהביה
ואתי שכחה נאם־יהוה:

8 "For she does not know that it was I who gave her the grain, the
    new wine, and the oil,
And lavished on her silver and gold,
Which they used for Baal.

9 Therefore, I will take back My grain at harvest time
And My new wine in its season.
I will also take away My wool and My flax
Given to cover her nakedness.

10 And then I will uncover her lewdness
In the sight of her lovers,
And no one will rescue her out of My hand.

11 I will also put an end to all her gaiety,
Her feasts, her new moons, her sabbaths,
And all her festal assemblies.

12 And I will destroy her vines and fig trees,
Of which she said, 'These are my wages
Which my lovers have given me.'
And I will make them a forest,
And the beasts of the field will devour them.

13 And I will punish her for the days of the Baals

When she used to offer sacrifices to them
And adorn herself with her earrings and jewelry,
And follow her lovers, so that she forgot Me," declares Yahweh.

Baal is first mentioned here as her lover's name (vv. 10, 15 [E. 8,13]). Yahweh had been the sole provider for whatever she needed. However, Israel believed that Baal gave the necessities of life to her, and she offered sacrifice to Baal with the produce which Yahweh gave her. Therefore, Yahweh was about to take back what he gave her for food, clothing, shelter, and enjoyment. And he was going to uncover her lewdness in the sight of her lovers, so that no one would rescue her out of his hand. Here, "to uncover her lewdness" carries a different nuance from that of verse 5 (E. 3). Since "lewdness" (נבלתה) is a euphemistic expression for either the genitals or sexual intercourse,[63] "to uncover her lewdness" carries the nuance of putting her into treacherous shame. Obviously, this is Yahweh's retributive punishment corresponding to her evil behavior. Furthermore, he would like to abolish her festivals. This paragraph clearly refers to the destruction of Israel because of her apostasy. The point that merits our attention here is that the fall of the nation is compared to a woman who was divorced because of her unfaithfulness to her husband and her indiscriminate devotion to her lovers.

16 לכן הנה אנכי מפתיה והלכתיה המדבר ודברתי על־לבה:

17 ונתתי לה את־כרמיה משם ואת־עמק עכור לפתח תקוה
 וענתה שמה כימי נעוריה וכיום עלתה מארץ־מצרים:

18 והיה ביום־ההוא נאם־יהוה
תקראי אישי ולא־תקראי־לי עוד בעלי:

19 והסרתי את־שמות הבעלים מפיה ולא־יזכרו עוד בשמם:

20 וכרתי להם ברית ביום ההוא
עם־חית השדה ועם־עוף השמים ורמש האדמה
וקשת וחרב ומלחמה אשבור מן־הארץ
והשכבתים לבטח:

21 וארשתיך לי לעולם
וארשתיך לי בצדק ובמשפט ובחסד וברחמים:

22 וארשתיך לי באמונה וידעת את־יהוה:

23 והיה ביום ההוא אענה נאם־יהוה
אענה את־השמים והם יענו את־הארץ:

24 והארץ תענה את־הדגן ואת־התירוש ואת־היצהר
והם יענו את־יזרעאל:

25 וזרעתיה לי בארץ ורחמתי את־לא רחמה
ואמרתי ללא־עמי עמי־אתה והוא יאמר אלהי:

63. Andersen and Freedman, *Hosea*, p. 246.

14 Therefore, behold, I will allure her,
   Bring her into the wilderness,
   And speak kindly to her.
15 Then I will give her her vineyards from there,
   And the valley of Achor as a door of hope.
   And she will sing there as in the days of her youth,
   As in the day when she came up from the land of Egypt.
16 "And it will come about in that day," declares Yahweh,
   "That you will call Me Ishi
   And will no longer call Me Baali.
17 For I will remove the names of the Baals from her mouth,
   So that they will be mentioned by their names no more.
18 In that day I will also make a covenant for them
   With the beasts of the field,
   The birds of the sky,
   And the creeping things of the ground.
   And I will abolish the bow, the sword, and war from the land,
   And will make them lie down in safety.
19 And I will betroth you to Me forever;
   Yes, I will betroth you to Me in righteousness and in justice,
   In lovingkindness and in compassion,
20 And I will betroth you to Me in faithfulness.
   Then you will know Yahweh.
21 "And it will come about in that day that I will respond,"
      declares Yahweh.
   "I will respond to the heavens, and they will respond to the earth,
22 And the earth will respond to the grain, to the new wine,
      and to the oil,
   And they will respond to Jezreel.
23 And I will sow her for Myself in the land.
   I will also have compassion on her who had not obtained compassion,
   And I will say to those who were not My people,
   'You are My people!'
   And they will say, 'Thou art my God!'"

The last paragraph (vv. 16-25 [E. 14-23]) describes the days of the restoration after Yahweh's punishment. The first step for Yahweh's restoration of Israel was to allure her back to himself. As in the days of the exodus, he will bring her into the wilderness, and he will give her a vineyard as a bride-gift and the valley of Achor as a door of hope.[64] Thus, she will be pleased as in the days when she came up from the land of Egypt. Here we see that the exodus is viewed in the context of the Yahweh-Israel marriage. On that day, Israel

64. Ibid., pp. 272-74.

will call Yahweh "Ishi" (my husband), not "Baali" (my husband). Both אישי and בעלי are used as a woman's designation of her husband. However, the pronunciation of Baali is too similar to that of her former lovers, the Baalim. Therefore, Yahweh is going to abolish the use of this title from her mouth forever. At any rate, the reunion of Yahweh-Israel as a married couple is established by the initiative of Yahweh.

In order legally to effectuate this marriage, Yahweh will enter into a covenant relationship. First of all, Yahweh wants to provide his wife with a safe place from the attack of wild beasts and men in war. Thus he will make a covenant with various kinds of animals so that they will not attack her and he will abolish every instrument of war from the land (v. 20 [E. 18]). The providing of a dwelling place is a duty required by a husband for his bride. Then he will betroth Israel to himself with every kind of virtue: righteousness, justice, lovingkindess, compassion, and faithfulness. These qualities can be said to be a "binder" that binds the two partners in the covenant.[65] Therefore, their second betrothal and marriage will be more secure and firm than the first. Israel then will "know" (ידע) Yahweh. The term ידע connotes the most intimate human relationship. In this covenant, the heavens, the earth, and Jezreel will be the witnesses (vv. 23-24 [E. 21-22]).[66]

Finally, Yahweh will say to those who were not his people, "You are My people!" And they will reply, "Thou art my God!"[67] This is obviously the modified form of the marriage formula: "You are my wife," and "you are my husband,"[68] and the reverse of verse 4 (E. 2), "She is not My wife, and I am not her husband."

As we have seen, Hos. 2:4-25 (E. 2-23) describes the Yahweh-Israel relationship in terms of the husband-wife relationship. Yahweh's election, rejection, and restoration of Israel are all described in the marriage context. In particular, Hosea's view of the exodus from the perspective of marriage is significant.

65. Andersen and Freedman (*Hosea*, p. 283) and H.W. Wolff (*Hosea*, p. 52) regard these five qualities as Yahweh's bridal price offered to Israel. However, this explanation does not fit into the covenant context of vv. 20-24.

66. Andersen and Freedman, *Hosea*, p. 286.

67. See also Zech. 13:9.

68. Mordechai A. Freedman, "Israel's Response in Hosea 2:17b: 'You are my Husband,'" *JBL* 99/2 (1980): 199-204.

2) Jeremiah 3:6-10

More than one century after Hosea, Jeremiah took up the theme of the husband-wife relationship. But the situation in his day was entirely different from that of Hosea, as can be seen in the following passages.

6   ויאמר יהוה אלי בימי יאשיהו המלך הראית אשר עשתה
משבה ישראל הלכה היא על־כל־הר גבה ואל־תחת כל־עץ רענן ותזני־שם:

7   ואמר אחרי עשותה את־כל־אלה אלי תשוב ולא־
שבה ותראה בגודה אחותה יהודה:

8   וארא כי על־כל־אדות אשר נאפה משבה ישראל שלחתיה ואתן את־ספר
כריתתיה אליה ולא יראה בגדה יהודה אחותה ותלך ותזן גם־היא:

9   והיה מקל זנותה ותחנף את־הארץ ותנאף את־האבן ואת־העץ:

10   וגם־בכל־זאת לא־שבה אלי בגודה אחותה יהודה בכל־לבה כי אם־
בשקר נאם־יהוה:

6 Then Yahweh said to me in the days of Josiah the king, "Have you seen what faithless Israel did? She went up on every high hill and under every green tree, and she was a harlot there.

7 "And I thought, 'After she has done all these things, she will return to Me'; but she did not return, and her treacherous sister Judah saw it.

8 "And I saw that for all the adulteries of faithless Israel, I had sent her away and given her a writ of divorce, yet her treacherous sister Judah did not fear; but she went and was a harlot also.

9 "And it came about because of the lightness of her harlotry, that she polluted the land and committed adultery with stones and trees.

10 "And yet in spite of all this her treacherous sister Judah did not return to Me with all her heart, but rather in deception," declares Yahweh.

The reign of Josiah is marked by his religious reform in Judah. But he could not fully turn the hearts of the people who were so accustomed to the pagan practices. This paganism owed its prosperity to Josiah's predecessors, Ahaz and Manasseh. In particular, the reign of Manasseh played a key role in bringing about Judah's national collapse (2 Kgs. 21:10-15). The book of Kings describes Manasseh's acts as follows:

And he did evil in the sight of Yahweh, according to the abominations of the nations whom Yahweh dispossessed before the sons of Israel. For he rebuilt the high places which Hezekiah his father had destroyed; and he erected altars for Baal and made an Asherah, as Ahab king of Israel had done, and worshiped all the host of heaven

147

and served them. And he built altars in the house of Yahweh, of which Yahweh had said, "In Jerusalem I will put My name." For he built altars for all the host of heaven in the two courts of the house of Yahweh. And he made his son pass through the fire, practiced witchcraft and used divination, and dealt with mediums and spiritists. He did much evil in the sight of Yahweh provoking Him to anger. . . . But they did not listen, and Manasseh seduced them to do evil more than the nations whom Yahweh destroyed before the sons of Israel. (2 Kgs. 21:2-9)

According to Bright,

The nature of primitive Yahwism had been so widely forgotten, and rites incompatible with it so long practiced, that in many minds the essential distinction between Yahweh and the pagan gods had been obscured. It was possible for such people to practice these rites alongside the cult of Yahweh without awareness that they were turning from the national faith in doing so. The situation was one of immense, and in some ways novel, danger to the religious integrity of Israel. Yahwism was in danger of slipping unawares into outright polytheism.[69]

However, this religious crisis was temporarily checked by King Josiah, the grandson of Manasseh, who succeeded his assassinated father Amon. Aided by the weakness of Assyrian forces in the western frontier, Josiah could gain independence from foreign pressure and conduct a religious reform in the country. He purged all foreign cults and practices which had any connection with Assyrian supremacy or which came into being as a result of it, and he repaired the Temple. In the course of repairing the Temple, "the book of the law" was found (622 B.C.). He assembled the people at the Temple and read the law to them, making a covenant of obedience with them before Yahweh (2 Kgs. 23:3). All the people were commanded to celebrate the Passover, as it is written in the book of the covenant (23:21). The centralization of the cult was also a product of this period. The other places where Yahwistic sacrifice was offered were destroyed or desecrated (23:15,19,20) and the Temple in Jerusalem became the only legitimate place of worship.

Nevertheless, this vigorous reform of Josiah was not welcomed by all the people. We can see a negative attitude toward this reform among the priests of the high places in 2 Kgs. 23:8-9. In later years,

69. John Bright, *History of Israel,* p. 311.

the people even ascribed their national calamity to this reform
(Jer. 44:16-20). Jeremiah's activities as a prophet began in this crisis.

Jeremiah 3:6-10 seems to reflect this reform movement. This
is a prose monologue addressed to Jeremiah by Yahweh. Yahweh
asks Jeremiah, "Have you seen what faithless Israel did?" And Yahweh himself answers. She went up on every high hill and under
every green tree, and there she played the harlot.[70] Yahweh saw her
and waited for her to come back to him, but she did not. In verse
8, this act of playing the harlot is regarded as the act of adultery.
Adultery is the sin that can be committed only within the marriage
bond. Therefore, when Yahweh uses the term, it presupposes his
marriage relationship with Israel. This marriage relationship can
also be observed in Yahweh's sending her away and giving her the
bill of divorce in the same verse. When a husband divorced his
wife, he was to give her this bill and send her away from his house
(Dt. 24:1,3). Therefore, "sending her away" and "giving a bill of
divorce" are synonymous concepts,[71] and both images refer to the
fall of the northern kingdom and the subsequent deportation of the
people from the land to Assyria.

When Judah, the sister of Israel, saw all these tragic events, she
should have taken them seriously and repented. But she followed
the ways of her sister and committed adultery with stones and trees.
According to Jer. 2:26-27, kings, princes, priests, and prophets say
to a tree, "You are my father," and to a stone,"You gave me birth."
Thus, John Bright comments that "trees and stones" refer to the
gods of fertility to whom the people ascribed their very existence.[72]
Judah had fallen deeply into the Canaanite fertility cult and refused Josiah's reform movement. They only pretended to return to
Yahweh. Thus, Yahweh calls Judah treacherous (בגודה) and decep-
tive (שקר).

3) Ezekiel 16, 23

Ezekiel was a younger contemporary of Jeremiah. He was a priest
and one of the exiles who was taken into captivity along with Je-

70. The rendering of ותזני־שם as "there she played the harlot" is more graphic
than NASB's "she was a harlot there."
71. See Chap. III below, pp. 192-93.
72. John Bright, *Jeremiah*, pp. 16, 24.

hoiachin (598/97 B.C.). His call to a prophetic ministry took place at Tel-Abib by the river Chebar in Babylon (Ezek. 1:1–3:15; 593/92 B.C.). Therefore, his sphere of activity was limited to the exiles in Babylon, and his ministry spanned at least twenty years. In his book, we see his characteristic interpretation of Israelite history from the perspective of the Yahweh-Israel marriage relationship. He seemed to have been well versed in the messages of Hosea and Jeremiah. However, he did not copy them verbatim but rather he adapted, enriched, and expanded them for the needs of his contemporary situation.

Ezekiel's marriage metaphor begins with the origin of Israel.

ואמרת כה־אמר אדני יהוה לירושלם מכרתיך
ומלדתיך מארץ הכנעני אביך האמרי ואמך חתית:

and say, "Thus says Lord Yahweh to Jerusalem, 'Your origin and your birth are from the land of the Canaanite, your father was an Amorite and your mother a Hittite.'" (Ezek. 16:3)

Here, "Jerusalem" does not necessarily mean the city, but rather it symbolizes Israel. According to this verse, the origin and the birth of Israel were Canaanite, from an Amorite father and a Hittite mother.[73] Unfortunately, when she was born, she was abandoned and exposed miserably in the open field. Her navel cord was not cut, nor was she cleansed with water; she was not rubbed with salt or wrapped in cloths (16:4). Furthermore, no one had compassion on her (16:5). At this critical moment, Yahweh saw her as he passed by and his saving work began.

6 ואעבר עליך ואראך מתבוססת בדמיך ואמר לך
בדמיך חיי ואמר לך בדמיך חיי:
7 רבבה כצמח השדה
נתתיך ותרבי ותגדלי ותבאי בעדי עדיים שדים נכנו
ושערך צמח ואת ערם ועריה:
8 ואעבר עליך ואראך
והנה עתך עת דדים ואפרש כנפי עליך ואכסה ערותך
ואשבע לך ואבוא בברית אתך נאם אדני יהוה ותהיי לי:

---

73. This phrase should not be understood to convey historical information about the origin of Israel. It is rather referring to the status of Israel before her election, i.e., Israel belongs basically to the same category of people as the Amorites and Hittites. For a discussion of this, see Meir Weiss, *The Bible From Within* (Jerusalem: Magnes Press, 1984), pp. 113-18.

6   "When I passed by you and saw you squirming in your blood, I said to you while you were in your blood, 'Live!' I said to you while you were in your blood, 'Live!'

7   I made you numerous like plants of the field. Then you grew up, became tall, and reached the age for fine ornaments; your breasts were formed and your hair had grown. Yet you were naked and bare.

8   Then I passed by you and saw you, and behold, you were at the time for love; so I spread My skirt over you and covered your nakedness. I also swore to you and entered into a covenant with you so that you became Mine," declares Lord Yahweh.

Here, we can point out that Yahweh met the child twice and did two things to change her status. First, Yahweh rescued her and took care of her in her childhood. Second, Yahweh spread his skirt over her[74] and entered into a marriage covenant with her. Thus, we can see here that the idea of election is explained by the metaphor of marriage, which culminated in the establishment of a covenant. Thus she could enjoy all the riches and splendor of Yahweh, and so she became exceedingly beautiful (vv. 8-13).

Verse 14 summarizes her new status.

ויצא לך שם בגוים ביפיך כי כליל הוא בהדרי
אשר־שמתי עליך נאם אדני יהוה:

"Then your fame went forth among the nations on account of your beauty, for it was perfect because of My splendor which I bestowed on you," declares Lord Yahweh.

However, she betrayed her husband. Verses 15-35 describe Israel's infidelity to Yahweh. As we saw in Hosea and Jeremiah, she gave her gifts to her lovers, although these very gifts were tokens of Yahweh's goodness, and she played the harlot. The most abominable type of harlotry was the practice of child sacrifice.

ותקחי את־בניך ואת־בנותיך אשר ילדת לי ותזבחים
להם לאכול המעט מתזנתך: ותשחטי את־בני ותתנים
בהעביר אותם להם:

Moreover, you took your sons and daughters whom you had borne to Me, and you sacrificed them to idols to be devoured. Were your harlotries so small a matter? You slaughtered my children, and offered them up to idols by causing them to pass through the fire.

(vv. 20-21)

---

74. According to M. Greenberg, covering a woman with a garment is an expression of acquiring her, as in Ruth 3:9, Mishnah *Peah* 4:3, and some early Arabic literature. See Greenberg, *Ezekiel, 1-20*, p. 277.

Among the gifts that Yahweh gave to Israel, children seemed to be the most precious. However, she delivered (בהעביר) them to Baal and Molech. Obviously, this refers to the child sacrifices of kings Ahaz (2 Kgs. 16:7) and Manasseh (2 Ch. 33:6) in the Valley of Ben-Hinnom.[75]

However, there is a different perspective here of Israel's playing the harlot. Ezekiel regards Israel's military dependency on any other than Yahweh as a type of harlotry. Israel was so indiscriminate that she poured out her harlotries on every willing passerby (v. 15). She played the harlot with the Egyptians (v. 26), with the Assyrians (v. 28), with the Chaldeans (v. 29). Furthermore, whenever she played the harlot, she paid the price and gave gifts to bribe her lovers to come to her, instead of receiving money from them. This made her different from other harlots (vv. 30-34). The rest of this chapter is devoted to the description of the punishment of this unusual harlot and to her subsequent restoration.

Ezekiel 23 is similar to Jer. 3:6-10 in describing the apostasy of both kingdoms. Here, the names of two sisters are mentioned as Oholibah and Oholah, referring to Jerusalem the younger and Samaria the elder. The major difference between this metaphor and others is that these two sisters were harlots when they were in Egypt. Yahweh took these two harlots to be his, and they bore sons and daughters. However, they played the harlot while they belonged to Yahweh and lusted after their lovers. The emphasis of this chapter is on the origin of Israel's harlotry, which goes back to the time before Yahweh's election.

As we have seen, the imagery of a husband and wife in describing the Yahweh-Israel relationship has been employed to explain Israel's apostasy. Each of these contexts presupposes the Yahweh-Israel marriage relationship and proceeds from that understanding to indict and to expose the present critical situation of Israel. Their main emphasis is not laid on the Yahweh-Israel union, but rather on the broken relationship. Therefore, we can safely say that the election idea as expressed by the marriage metaphor arose in the context of Israel's paganism.

The fact that the three prophets lived in such critical moments in the history of Israel gives more evidence for such paganism. Ho-

75. Moshe Greenberg, *Ezekiel, 1-20*, p. 281.

sea lived in the days of Ahaz, the one who introduced the Assyrian cult and altar into the Temple, and soon after he saw the fall of Samaria. Jeremiah experienced both Manasseh's apostasy and Josiah's reform movement, and he himself was taken captive into Egypt and saw the fatal collapse of the nation. Ezekiel also lived as an exile, in Babylon. Thus, the election metaphor of husband and wife evolved among the circumstance of the religious corruption and the crisis of national insecurity (Hos. 5:11-19). These prophets looked back to their national history and national events and tried to interpret them in terms of the husband-wife relationship. They regarded the exodus as Yahweh's taking Israel as his wife. For Jeremiah, in particular, the Sinai covenant is understood as a wedding of Yahweh with Israel (Jer. 31:32). Their worship of foreign gods and their pagan practices on high places were seen as tantamount to committing adultery. The exile of both kingdoms is understood as a husband's sending away his unfaithful wife from his house.

Obviously, Hosea is responsible for the creation of this idea. Later, Jeremiah and Ezekiel appropriated it. Consequently, the election formula which was modified from the marriage formula should be regarded as the creation of a later redactor.

(2) Father and Son

The election idea as expressed in terms of the father-son analogy seems to be an old one. We can see Yahweh's designation of Israel as "My son" in the exodus narrative (Ex. 4:22, 23), and the use of terms related to the metaphor such as "the people of inheritance" can be traced back to an early date. However, Hosea and Jeremiah seemed to have taken over this idea and to have shaped the election theology.

1) Hosea 11:1-11

Hosea 11:1-11 describes Yahweh as the father who brought up his son, Israel.[76] The contiguous themes of election, rejection, and res-

---

76. Most scholars believe that Hos. 1–3 and 4–14 may have circulated separately, with the latter belonging to the exilic period, based on the passages expressing hope for Israel and the alleged inconsistency with Hosea's "early" teaching.

toration are delineated from the perspective of the father-son metaphor.

1 כי נער ישראל ואהבהו וממצרים קראתי לבני:

2 קראו להם כן הלכו מפניהם
לבעלים יזבחו ולפסלים יקטרון:

3 ואנכי תרגלתי לאפרים קחם על־זרועתיו
ולא ידעו כי רפאתים:

4 בחבלי אדם אמשכם בעבתות אהבה
ואהיה להם כמרימי על על לחיהם
ואט אליו אוכיל:

1 When Israel was a youth I loved him,
  And out of Egypt I called My son.
2 The more they called them,
  The more they went from them;
  They kept sacrificing to the Baals
  And burning incense to idols.
3 Yet it is I who taught Ephraim to walk,
  I took them in My arms;
  But they did not know that I healed them.
4 I led them with cords of a man, with bonds of love,
  And I became to them as one who lifts the yoke from
      their jaws;
  And I bent down and fed them.

Yahweh loved Israel from his youth (נער). Yahweh's designation of Israel as "my son" (בני) is significant. Hosea changes the image of Yahweh-Israel from husband-wife (chaps. 1–3) to father-son, and traces back the beginning of his love for the son to the time of exodus.

In verse 2 we have some textual variants. The Septuagint reads קראו as וקראי (καθὼς μετεκάλεσα) and מפניהם as מפני הם (ἐκ προσώπου μου αὐτοί). Thus Wolff renders this verse as "Yet as I call them, they strayed from me."[77] Against Wolff, however, Andersen and Freedman's rendering is more convincing: "They called to them. They

---

However, R.K. Harrison maintains that even if chapters 4–14 circulated independently for some time, it could only have been for a comparatively short period, certainly falling within the lifetime of the prophet himself. This is because there is no tradition of the book as anything but a unity, and by the time the oracles of chapters 4–14 were in writing, a knowledge of the contents of chapters 1–3 was necessary for an overall understanding of the unique prophetic emphasis of Hosea. See Harrison, *Introduction,* p. 868. See also F.I. Andersen and D.N. Freedman, *Hosea,* pp. 57-59.

77. H. W. Wolff, *Hosea,* p. 190.

departed from Me." Because the change of number to plural means a change of subject, verse 2 deals with a situation different from that in verse 1, in spite of the repetition of the verb "to call." Therefore, the object (them) can not be the Israel of verse 1 (who is called "him").[78] Those who called the Israelites refer to those who, in the next line, invited them to worship Baal. Yahweh called his son from Egypt. But Israel responded to the call of Baal. Hosea seemed to have had the events of Baal-peor (Num. 25) in his mind. Thus, this verse shows that the apostasy of Yahweh's son began at the same time as did the call to sonship.

Verses 3 and 4 describe how Yahweh brought up his son in spite of his following Baal. Yahweh took Ephraim in his arms and taught him how to walk, making him strong and whole (רפא). Furthermore, he led him with human chords and with ropes of love. According to Andersen and Freedman, the verb משך carries the meaning "to link up" (Judg. 4:6,7; 20:37), and משך and אהב go together in the language of covenant making (Jer. 31:3). Also the term "ropes" is used to describe covenant obligation (Ps. 2:3).[79] If this suggestion is correct, Yahweh's leading of his son with cords of a man and with bonds of love refers to his covenantal care for Israel.[80] Therefore, he became to them as one who lifts the yoke from their jaws and bends down to feed them. The imagery of "lifting the yoke from the jaw" is a metaphor drawn from feeding a cow. Hosea compared Israel to a heifer (4:16; 10:11). As a ploughman releases the yoke and harnesses from the animal before he feeds it, so did Yahweh. This represents Yahweh's liberation and feeding of Israel. In order to feed them, Yahweh himself bent down. Yahweh as the father was perfect in taking care of his son.

5   לא ישוב אל־ארץ מצרים ואשור הוא מלכו
כי מאנו לשוב:

6   וחלה חרב בעריו וכלתה בדיו
ואכלה ממעצותיהם:

7   ועמי תלואים למשובתי
ואל־על יקרא הו יחד לא ירוממם:

78. F.I. Andersen and D.N. Freedman, *Hosea*, pp. 574, 577-78.
79. Ibid., pp. 580-81.
80. Cf. Andreas Reichert, "Israel, the Firstborn of God: A Topic of Early Deuteronomic Theology," *Proceedings of the Sixth World Congress of Jewish Studies,* vol.1 (Jerusalem: World Union of Jewish Studies, 1977), p. 347.

5   They will not return to the land of Egypt;
    But Assyria—he will be their king,
    Because they refused to return to Me.
6   And the sword will whirl against their cities,
    And will demolish their gate bars
    And consume them because of their counsels.
7   So My people are bent on turning from Me.
    Though they call them to the One on high,
    None at all exalts Him.

Verses 5-7 describe Yahweh's dealing with Israel who yet refuses to
return to him. They will return to Assyria, and Assyria will be their
king. Their cities will be destroyed, their gate bars will be demol-
ished, and they themselves will be consumed. Nevertheless, the
people are bent on turning away from Yahweh. Though Yahweh's
prophets called Israel to the one who is on high, no one at all exalted him. The main emphasis of this paragraph is on the returning
of Yahweh's son to Assyria, not to the land of Egypt. The apostate
son had to leave the land where he now lived. And thus the land
would be desolated.

In the third paragraph (vv. 8-11), Hosea foresees Yahweh's restoration of his sons. In particular, verses 10-11 describe their return
from deportation.

אחרי יהוה ילכו כאריה ישאג   10
כי־הוא ישאג ויחרדו בנים מים:
יחרדו כצפור ממצרים וכיונה מארץ אשור   11
והושבתים על־בתיהם נעם־יהוה:

10 They will walk after Yahweh,
    He will roar like a lion;
    Indeed He will roar,
    And His sons will come trembling from the west.
11 They will come trembling like birds from Egypt,
    And like doves from the land of Assyria;
    And I will settle them in their houses, declares Yahweh.

In the time of restoration, Yahweh's mercy and compassion for his
sons will be rekindled (vv. 8-9), and his salvation will begin. In
those days, Israel will come back from the land of Assyria under
his guidance and protection and will be settled again in their land.

Hosea foresaw the Assyrian assault of Samaria and the subsequent deportation of the people from the land of inheritance to
Assyria. Now the land no more belonged to the people of Yahweh.

In these circumstances, Hosea explains this phenomena through
the metaphor of father-son. Israel was a people of inheritance. As
for Hosea, Israel was his son who had inherited the land from Yahweh. However, Israel's apostasy caused the withdrawal of sonship
and the consequent withdrawal of inheritance. This interpretation
is more explicit in Jeremiah.

2) Jeremiah 3:19; 12:14-15; 24:7-8

ואנכי אמרתי איך אשיתך בבנים
ואתן־לך ארץ חמדה נחלת צבי צבאות גוים
ואמר אבי תקראו־לי ומאחרי לא תשובו:

Then I said,
"How I would set you among My sons,
And give you a pleasant land,
The most beautiful inheritance of the nations!"
And I said, "You shall call Me, My Father,
And not turn away from following Me." (Jer. 3:19)

Since Yahweh, the God of Israel, is the creator of the world and of
all humans, all the people of the earth are his בנים. From among all
nations he has chosen Israel as עם נחלה, and he gave them a pleasant
land, the most beautiful inheritance of all. Then Yahweh said to
Israel,"You shall call Me, My father." As this verse suggests, Yahweh's endowment of the land to Israel was seen as Yahweh's inheritance being given to his heir. Therefore, the possession of the land
for Israel was the gift of Yahweh for his son.

כה אמר יהוה על־כל־שכני הרעים הנגעים בנחלה אשר־
הנחלתי את־עמי את־ישראל הנני נתשם מעל אדמתם ואת־
בית יהודה אתוש מתוכם: והיה אחרי נתשי אותם אשוב
ורחמתים והשבתים איש לנחלתו ואיש לארצו:

Thus says Yahweh concerning all My wicked neighbors who strike at
the inheritance with which I have endowed My people Israel, "Behold I am about to uproot them from their land and will uproot the
house of Judah from among them. And it will come about that after
I have uprooted them, I will again have compassion on them; and I
will bring them back, each one to his inheritance and each one to his
land." (Jer. 12:14-15)

In these verses, it is clear that the land is the inheritance with which

Yahweh has endowed his people, and the imagery of "uprooting them from their land" refers to the coming deprivation of the inheritance from Israel, i.e., the deportation.

Furthermore, we can see that the land is directly mentioned in the context of the election formula in Jer. 24:6-7.

6 ושמתי עיני עליהם לטובה והשבתים על־הארץ הזאת
ובניתים ולא אהרס ונטעתים ולא אתוש:

7 ונתתי להם לב לדעת אתי כי אני יהוה והיו־לי לעם
ואנכי אהיה להם לאלהים כי־ישבו אלי בכל־לבם:

6 For I will set My eyes on them for good, and I will bring them again
to this land; and I will build them up and not overthrow them, and I
will plant them and not pluck them up.

7 And I will give them a heart to know Me, for I am Yahweh; and they
will be My people, and I will be their God, for they will return to Me
with their whole heart.

Jeremiah had a keen interest in the land. He referred continuously to the desolation of the land and their return from the exile to the land (4:20,26,27; 7:34; 8:16; 16:11,13; 18:16; 23:8; 25:11). Therefore, in the midst of the collapse of the nation he bought a field (Jer. 32). As Hosea was a prophet at the fall of the northern kingdom so was Jeremiah at the fall of the southern kingdom. Both prophets saw and experienced the exile of a kingdom, and, therefore, they both seemed to have thought often about the meaning of the land. For them, the deportation of the people was a sign of Yahweh's disinheritance of his son.

Therefore, the election idea described in terms of the father-son metaphor is a product of a theological concern having to do with losing the land because of the exile. Even though we can not deny that the idea of representing the land as an inheritance of Yahweh existed before this critical period, we can safely conclude that Hosea originated this metaphor and that Jeremiah was his successor.[81]

81. Andreas Reichert postulated that Ex. 4:22–23, speaking of Israel as the "firstborn" of God, can not antedate Hosea's metaphor of Israel as the "son." And he asserted the notion of "Israel as the firstborn of God" should be placed somewhere between the Hosean and Deuteronomic conceptions, i.e., approximately between the mid-eighth century and 622 B.C. See ibid., p. 348.

THE DEVELOPMENT OF THE IDEA OF ELECTION

(3) Farmer and Vineyard

The parable of the vineyard is a vivid expression of Yahweh's election, as well as his rejection, of Israel. The image of Yahweh's "planting" and "uprooting" people from the land is borrowed from this parable. This metaphor is found mostly in Isaiah and Jeremiah.

1) Isaiah 5:1-7; 27:2-6

After the long description of social injustice in Judah (Is. 1–4), Isaiah illustrated it graphically in the song of the vineyard.

1 אשירה נא לידידי שירת דודי לכרמו
כרם היה לידידי בקרן בן־שמן:
2 ויעזקהו ויסקלהו ויטעהו שרק
ויבן מגדל בתוכו וגם־יקב חצב בו
ויקו לעשות ענבים ויעש באשים:
3 ועתה יושב ירושלם ואיש יהודה
שפטו־נא ביני ובין כרמי:
4 מה־לעשות עוד לכרמי ולא עשיתי בו
מדוע קויתי לעשות ענבים ויעש באשים:
5 ועתה אודיעה־נא אתכם את אשר־אני עשה לכרמי
הסר משוכתו והיה לבער פרץ גדרו והיה למרמס:
6 ואשיתהו בתה לא יזמר ולא יעדר ועלה שמיר ושית
ועל העבים אצוה מהמטיר עליו מטר:
7 כי כרם יהוה צבאות בית ישראל
ואיש יהודה נטע שעשועיו
ויקו למשפט והנה משפח לצדקה והנה צעקה:

1 Let me sing now for my well-beloved
A song of my beloved concerning His vineyard.
My well-beloved had a vineyard on a fertile hill.
2 And He dug it all around, removed its stones,
And planted it with the choicest vine.
And He built a tower in the middle of it,
And hewed out a wine vat in it;
Then He expected it to produce good grapes,
But it produced only worthless ones.
3 "And now, O inhabitants of Jerusalem and men of Judah,
Judge between Me and My vineyard.
4 What more was there to do for My vineyard that I have not
done in it?

159

> Why, when I expected it to produce good grapes did it
> produce worthless ones?

5 So now let Me tell you what I am going to do to My vineyard:
> I will remove its hedge and it will be consumed;
> I will break down its wall and it will become trampled ground.

6 And I will lay it waste;
> It will not be pruned or hoed,
> But briars and thorns will come up.
> I will also charge the clouds to rain no rain on it.

7 For the vineyard of Yahweh of hosts is the house of Israel,
> And the men of Judah His delightful plant.
> Thus He looked for justice, but behold, bloodshed;
> For righteousness, but behold, a cry of distress. (Is. 5:1-7)

According to George B. Gray's very plausible suggestion, this song was recited by Isaiah in the Temple court on a great national feast day, or at the close of the vintage season.[82] "But the year in which the poem was either written or recited cannot be even approximately determined."

This song is composed of an introduction (v. 1a), the description of the vineyard (vv. 1b-2), the owner's speech of disposal (vv. 3-6), and the interpretation of the parable (v. 7). As the song itself says, the owner of the vineyard was Yahweh, the vineyard the house of Israel, and his delightful plant the men of Judah. The vineyard and the plant are, of course, not necessarily one and the same, as the men of Judah are included in the house of Israel. "A fertile hill" (קרן בן־שמן) in verse 1 is literally "a horn, the son of oil." However, קרן means here "a small hill," and בן־שמן carries the meaning of fatness. Thus קרן בן־שמן describes the richness and fatness of the vineyard. This obviously refers to the land "flowing with milk and honey" (Ex. 3:8), which Yahweh promised and to which he brought Israel from Egypt. נטע in verse 2 is an election term. Yahweh's settling Israel in the land of Canaan is compared to a farmer's planting a vine in the vineyard. The שרק, whatever may be its precise signification, is apparently the name of a specially choice vine. In Jer. 2:21, its meaning is amplified as "a completely faithful seed" (כלה זרע אמת). Yahweh's caring for the vineyard was very meticulous, and thus his expectation of good fruit was great. However, he was betrayed. The tree produced only worthless grapes. Isaiah's

---

82. George B. Gray, *The Book of Isaiah, I-XXVII,* ICC (Edinburgh: T. & T. Clark, 1912), p. 83.

interpretation itself (v. 7) identifies the parallel: the good fruit refers
to justice, and the worthless grapes to "bloodshed" and "a cry of
distress." Yahweh's planting of the choicest vine on a fertile land is
a characteristic election metaphor. In this parable we can deduce
the purpose of Yahweh's election of Israel. He looked forward to
social justice among his people when he chose Israel. However, the
severe corruption of society had to be destroyed, just as the worthless vineyard had to be consumed by fire. The failure of Israel to
fulfill its election purpose precipitated Yahweh's anger and the subsequent desolation of the land.

In 27:2-6, however, Isaiah describes the restoration of the
vineyard.

2	ביום ההוא כרם חמד ענו־לה:
3	אני יהוה נצרה לרגעים אשקנה
	פן יפקד עליה לילה ויום אצרנה:
4	חמה אין לי מי־יתנני שמיר שית
	במלחמה אפשעה בה אציתנה יחד:

. . . .

6	הבאים ישרש יעקב יציץ ופרח ישראל
	ומלאו פני־תבל תנובה:

2　In that day,
　　"A vineyard of wine, sing of it!
3　I, Yahweh, am its keeper;
　　I water it every moment.
　　Lest anyone damage it,
　　I guard it night and day.
4　I have no wrath.
　　Should someone give me briars and thorns in battle,
　　Then I would step on them, I would burn them completely."

. . . .

6　In the days to come Jacob will take root,
　　Israel will blossom and sprout;
　　And they will fill the whole world with fruit.

In the days of restoration, Yahweh is going to sing again the forgotten song of the vineyard. Here, Yahweh is represented as the faithful tender of the vineyard. He waters it every moment, and guards
it day and night. His former wrath is now directed to the briars and
thorns, which symbolize Israel's enemies fighting against her. Thus,
the people of Yahweh will take root, sprout, and blossom, and the
whole world will be filled with their fruit.

161

2) Jeremiah 2:21

Jeremiah's metaphor of farmer-vineyard is almost the same as that
of Isaiah in its basic concepts. In Jer. 2:21, Yahweh said:

ואנכי נטעתיך שרק כלה זרע אמת
ואיך נהפכת לי סורי הגפן נכריה:

Yet I planted you a choice vine,
A completely faithful seed.
How then have you turned yourself before Me
Into the degenerate shoots of a foreign vine?

Jeremiah omitted the detailed description of Yahweh's care for his
vineyard. He dealt only with his planting a choice vine and Israel's
producing a foreign vine that is the utter inconsistency of what was
sowed versus what was reaped. "A choice vine" and "a completely
faithful seed" stand in contrast to "the degenerated shoots" and "a
foreign vine." "Planting a choice vine" is again an election metaphor.

3) Psalm 80:9-20 (E. 8-19)

Psalm 80 is particularly noteworthy because the poet describes the
history of Israel—the exodus, settlement, growth, and fall—in terms
of an allegory drawn from the relationship of the farmer to the vine.

9 גפן ממצרים תסיע תגרש גוים ותטעה:
10 פנית לפניה ותשרש שרשיה ותמלא־ארץ:
11 כסו הרים צלה וענפיה ארזי־אל:
12 תשלח קצירה עד־ים ואל־נהר יונקותיה:
13 למה פרצת גדריה וארוה כל־עברי דרך:
14 יכרסמנה חזיר מיער וזיז שדי ירענה:
15 אלהים צבאות שוב־נא הבט משמים וראה ופקד גפן זאת:
16 וכנה אשר־נטעה ימינך ועל־בן אמצתה לך:
17 שרפה באש כסוחה מגערת פניך יאבדו:
18 תהי־ידך על־איש ימינך על־בן־אדם אמצת לך:
19 ולא־נסוג ממך תחינו ובשמך נקרא:
20 יהוה אלהים צבאות השיבנו האר פניך ונושעה:

8 Thou didst remove a vine from Egypt;
Thou didst drive out the nations, and didst plant it.
9 Thou didst clear the ground before it,
And it took deep root and filled the land.

10 The mountains were covered with its shadow;
    And the cedars of God with its boughs.
11 It was sending out its branches to the sea,
    And its shoots to the River.
12 Why hast Thou broken down its hedges,
    So that all who pass that way pick its fruit?
13 A boar from the forest eats it away,
    And whatever moves in the field feeds on it.
14 O God of hosts, turn again now, we beseech Thee;
    Look down from heaven and see, and take care of this vine,
15 Even the shoot which Thy right hand has planted,
    And on the son whom Thou hast strengthened for Thyself.
16 It is burned with fire, it is cut down;
    They perish at the rebuke of Thy countenance.
17 Let Thy hand be upon the man of Thy right hand,
    Upon the son of man whom Thou didst make strong for Thyself.
18 Then we shall not turn back from Thee;
    Revive us, and we will call upon Thy name.
19 O Yahweh God of hosts, restore us;
    Cause Thy face to shine upon us, and we will be saved.

The exegetes disagree over the date and place of this poem. The mention of Israel and Joseph in verse 2 (E.1) and the tribes of Ephraim, Benjamin, and Manasseh in verse 3 (E.2) suggests to some that the psalm was composed in the northern kingdom after its destruction in 722/1 B.C.[83] Other scholars ascribe it to the Judean circles which sympathized with their northern brethren; thus it can be dated during the period of Josiah's reign (640-609 B.C.).[84] However, the mixed imagery of Yahweh as "Shepherd of Israel" (רעה ישראל, v. 2 [E.1]), "God of hosts" (אלהים צבאות, vv. 5, 8,15, 20 [E. 4,7, 14,19]), and "the planter" (v. 7 [E.8]), and of Israel as "a flock" (צאן, v. 2 [E.1]), "a vine" (גפן, vv. 9, 15 [E.8,14]), "shoot" (כנה, v. 16 [E. 15],[85] "the son" (בן, v. 16 [E. 15]), and "the son of man" (בן־אדם, v.

83. Gunkel, Leslie, Eissfeldt, M. Dahood, D. Kidner. See A.A. Anderson, *Psalms,* 2:581.
84. König, Schmidt. See A.A. Anderson, *Psalms,* 2:581.
85. כנה is found only here in the OT and its correct meaning is uncertain. The LXX reads it as a verb כון (to restore). And the NASB translates it as "shoot." However, "stock, stem, root" are also suggested, from כן ("stand" for basin). See William Holladay, *A Concise Hebrew and Aramaic Lexicon of the Old Testament* (Grand Rapids: Eerdmans, 1971), p. 160; and Anderson, *Psalms,* 2:585.

18 [E. 19]) suggest a date possibly around the imminent fall of Jerusalem or after it. Furthermore, the highly developed theology of election, rejection, and restoration indicates a date even after the exile.

This allegorical poem portrays Yahweh as a divine planter who transplanted a vine, i.e., Israel, from Egypt to Canaan. The vine became prosperous and filled the land. However, all the passersby pick its fruit, and whatever moves in the field feeds on it because he has broken its hedges. The passersby and the moving creatures refer here to the enemies of Israel, and their picking and feeding on the vine (Israel) to the destruction of the nation. In this horrible situation, they ask the favor of Yahweh to restore the nation. Thus, the poet describes Yahweh's election, rejection, and restoration of Israel in terms of the metaphor of Yahweh-Israel as a farmer-vine.

The image of "planting" and "uprooting" is not, however, the monopoly of Isaiah, Jeremiah, and the poet. Almost all the prophets used this metaphor in describing the coming fall and restoration of Israel and Judah. However, this imagery is more frequently found in the restoration context. Thus, "I will plant them in their land, and they will not again be rooted out from their land" (Amos 9:15; Jer. 24:6; 31:27-28; 42:10; 45:4) is a common formula for Yahweh's promise for the return of Israel from the exile. Therefore, we can easily conclude that the metaphor of farmer and vineyard implying the election idea is also a product of the period between the collapse of the two kingdoms and is further developed throughout the exile. In particular, this image is closely related to the land. On the one hand, the deportation of the people from the land is viewed as the uprooting of the vine from the vineyard. On the other hand, the election is portrayed as the planting and the restoration as the replanting.

(4) Shepherd and Sheep

The representation of ruler and subject by means of the image of shepherd and sheep is well known through all of Mesopotamia and Egypt. Hammurabi described himself as "the shepherd of man," "the supplier of pasture and water" in his Code.[86] Merodach Bala-

---

86. *ANET,* p. 164b.

dan in a royal inscription expresses his duty as a shepherd to collect those who were scattered. One of the oldest Egyptian royal hymns also describes a king as a shepherd who requires earnest love from his subjects.[87] As a shepherd, the king had to protect as well as feed his people. Since Israel was also a nomadic society from early times, this image must have been very familiar to them, and it appears in a wide range of texts.[88] However, the most frequent use of this metaphor is found in the prophetic literature.

1) Jeremiah 23:1-4

1 הוי רעים מאבדים ומפצים את־צאן מרעיתי נאם־יהוה:
2 לכן כה־אמר יהוה אלהי ישראל על־הרעים הרעים את־ עמי אתם הפצתם את־צאני ותדחום ולא פקדתם אתם הנני פקד עליכם את־רע מעלליכם נאם יהוה:
3 ואני אקבץ את־שארית צאני מכל הארצות אשר־הדחתי אתם שם והשבתי אתהן על־ נוהן ופרו ורבו:
4 והקמתי עליהם רעים ורעום ולא־ייראו עוד ולא־יחתו ולא יפקדו נאם־יהוה:

1 "Woe to the shepherds who are destroying and scattering the sheep of My pasture!" declares Yahweh.
2 Therefore thus says Yahweh God of Israel concerning the shepherds who are tending My people: "You have scattered My flock and driven them away, and have not attended to them; behold, I am about to attend to you for the evil of your deeds," declares Yahweh.
3 Then I Myself shall gather the remnant of My flock out of all the countries where I have driven them and shall bring them back to their pasture; and they will be fruitful and multiply.
4 I shall also raise up shepherds over them and they will tend them; and they will not be afraid any longer, nor be terrified, nor will any be missing," declares Yahweh.

As in the other ancient traditions, rulers are compared to shepherds. However, rulers are not the owners of the flock. Yahweh is introduced as the owner of the flock and pasture. Yahweh's involvement in the shepherd-sheep relationship makes for a basic difference between the biblical metaphor and that of the other ancient

87. Walther Eichrodt, *Ezekiel,* OTL (Philadelphia: Westminster, 1970), p. 469.
88. See Chap. I above, pp. 76-80. Strikingly, Jacob confesses that God has been his shepherd (הרעה) from his birth (Gen. 48:15).

traditions. Yahweh himself is not described as a shepherd of sheep. Rather, as an owner, he condemns the irresponsible shepherds of his sheep. In verse 2, "My flock" is synonymous with "My people." Also, the root פקד is used in two different senses. In ולא פקדתם אתם the verb פקד means "to take care of," as in 2 Kgs. 9:34; Gen. 21:1. However, in הנני פקד עליכם את־רע מעלליכם, the verb פקד carries the meaning of retribution or punishment, as "to avenge" (1 Sam. 15:2; Jer. 9:8 [E.9]). Since the shepherds did not take care of (פקד) the sheep, Yahweh is about to punish (פקד) them. Then Yahweh will gather his flock out of dispersion and he will raise up shepherds (רעים) over them to tend them. Therefore, in this oracle we can see the Yahweh-ruler-people relationship in terms of the owner-shepherd-sheep relationship. The image of scattering the flock and driving them away from his pasture refers to the exile. The restoration is Yahweh's bringing them back to their pasture, the land of their inheritance.

2) Ezekiel 34:1-31

Ezekiel 34 is one of the clearest pictures of the Yahweh-Israel relationship described by the metaphor of owner-shepherd-sheep. This chapter is composed of Yahweh's indictment against the wicked shepherds (vv. 1-8), Yahweh's deliverance of his flock (vv. 9-16), Yahweh's judgment on the sheep (vv. 17-22), Yahweh's setting a shepherd over his flock (vv. 23-24), and Yahweh's covenant of peace (vv. 25-31). The understanding of Yahweh as an owner, the rulers as the shepherds, and the people as the flock is still maintained here. Yahweh's main concern here is "His flock." The duties of the shepherd for the flock are specified—strengthening the sick ones, healing the diseased, binding up the broken, bringing back the scattered, and seeking for the lost (v. 4). However, they neglected all these responsibilities and only indulged in feeding themselves (v. 2). Therefore, the flock was scattered and became food for every beast of the field (v. 5). Yahweh laments the miseries of his flock.

6 ישגו צאני בכל־ההרים ועל כל־גבעה רמה ועל כל־פני
הארץ נפצו צאני ואין דורש ואין מבקש:
7 לכן רעים שמעו את־דבר יהוה:
8 חי־אני נאם אדני יהוה אם־לא יען היות־צאני לבז

ותהיינה צאני לאכלה לכל־חית השדה מאין רעה ולא־
דרשו רעי את־צאני וירעו הרעים אותם ואת־צאני לא רעו:

6 "My flock wandered through all the mountains and on every high
hill, and My flock was scattered over all the surface of the earth; and
there was no one to search or seek for them."
7 Therefore, you shepherds, hear the word of Yahweh:
8 "As I live," declares the Lord Yahweh, "surely because My flock has
become a prey, My flock has even become food for all the beasts of
the field for lack of a shepherd, and My shepherds did not search for
My flock, but rather the shepherds fed themselves and did not feed
My flock."

The irresponsibility of the shepherds brought about the downfall of
Yahweh's people. Thus, Yahweh is going to reject the shepherds of
his flock (34:10), and he himself will be a shepherd who will search
for his sheep and deliver them from all the places where they were
scattered (34:11,12,14,15,17,22). The idea of Yahweh's being the
shepherd of his flock is new. However, since the lack of good shepherds (v. 5) caused the destruction of his flock, he promised to set
over them one shepherd, David (v. 23). This does not mean that
David would be brought to life again, but rather an ideal ruler such
as David would be provided. The mention of the name of the shepherd is also a new development. Yahweh's covenant of peace made
with them emphasizes his perfect protection from the harmful
beasts (vv. 25, 28) and his faithful feeding of his flock (vv. 26,27,29).

30 וידעו כי אני יהוה אלהיהם אתם והמה עמי בית ישראל
נאם אדני יהוה:
31 ואתן צאני צאן מרעיתי אדם אתם אני
אלהיכם נאם אדני יהוה:

30 "Then they will know that I, Yahweh their God, am with them, and
that they, the house of Israel, are My people," declares the Lord
Yahweh.
31 "As for you, My sheep, the sheep of My pasture, you are men, and I
am your God," declares the Lord Yahweh.

Therefore, this chapter ends with a characteristic election formula:
"I, Yahweh, am their God, and they are My people," and "I am
your God, and You are My sheep, the sheep of My pasture."

As we observed, Jer. 23:1-4 and Ezek. 34 show both similarities
and differences in thought and expression. First of all, the basic

167

structure of the speeches is the same. In both passages, the chain of
Yahweh-ruler-people is described as that of owner-shepherd-sheep.
In Ezekiel, however, we find a new development in the image of
Yahweh as a shepherd. Both passages ascribe the scattering of the
flock to the shepherd's negligence of his duty (Jer. 23:2; Ezek. 34:3-
10). In particular, Ezekiel is specific in listing the duties of shepherds. And the scope of the scattering of the flock is expanded from
"all the countries" in Jeremiah (Jer. 23:3) to "over all the surface
of the earth" in Ezekiel (Ezek. 34:6). Both passages mention Yahweh's gathering of his flock after his rejection of the shepherds (Jer.
23:3; Ezek. 34:11-16) and his raising up a shepherd (Jer. 23:4; Ezek.
34:23-24), but only Ezekiel specified the name of the shepherd.
Finally, only in Ezekiel is Yahweh's making a covenant of peace
mentioned.

Therefore, we can safely conclude that Ezekiel modified and
expanded Jeremiah's metaphor of shepherd-sheep. Ezekiel may
possibly have heard Jeremiah's message before his exile to Babylon,
since Jeremiah may have given this message at the end of Jehoiachin's reign or early in Zedekiah's reign.[89] The threat to the national
existence, the issue of a true protector between Egypt and Babylon,
the desperate situation of the exile, etc., seemed to provide the original life setting for this metaphor.

(5) Potter and Clay

The election metaphor of a divine potter and clay is infrequently
used. Since Yahweh is generally known as the creator of all existing
things or as the maker of Israel, this general description seems to
underlie the entire concept. However, a specific social situation explains this kind of parable as it emphasizes a certain aspect of the
Yahweh-Israel relationship. In particular, Jer. 18:1-11 is noteworthy.

1 הדבר אשר היה אל־ירמיהו מאת יהוה לאמר:
2 קום וירדת בית היוצר ושמה אשמיעך את־דברי:
3 וארד בית היוצר והנהו עשה מלאכה על־האבנים:
4 ונשחת הכלי אשר הוא עשה בחמר ביד היוצר ושב ויעשהו כלי אחר
כאשר ישר בעיני היוצר לעשות:

89. Many believe that Jeremiah uttered these words early in Zedekiah's reign.
See J. Bright, *Jeremiah*, pp. 143, 145-46.

5 ויהי דבר־יהוה אלי לאמור:
6 הכיוצר הזה לא־אוכל לעשות לכם בית ישראל
נאם־יהוה הנה כחמר ביד היוצר כן־אתם בידי בית ישראל:
7 רגע אדבר על־גוי ועל־ממלכה לנתוש ולנתוץ ולהאביד:
8 ושב הגוי ההוא מרעתו אשר דברתי עליו
ונחמתי על־הרעה אשר חשבתי לעשות לו:
9 ורגע אדבר על־גוי ועל־ממלכה לבנת ולנטע:
10 ועשה הרעה בעיני לבלתי שמע בקולי ונחמתי על־הטובה אשר אמרתי
להיטיב אותו:
11 ועתה אמר־נא אל־איש־יהודה ועל־יושבי ירושלם
לאמר כה אמר יהוה הנה אנכי יוצר עליכם רעה וחשב עליכם
מחשבה שובו נא איש מדרכו הרעה והיטיבו דרכיכם ומעלליכם:

1   The word which came to Jeremiah from Yahweh saying,
2   "Arise and go down to the potter's house, and there I shall announce
    My words to you."
3   Then I went down to the potter's house, and there he was, making
    something on the wheel.
4   But the vessel that he was making of clay was spoiled in the hand of
    the potter; so he remade it into another vessel, as it pleased the potter
    to make.
5   Then the word of Yahweh came to me saying,
6   "Can I not, O house of Israel, deal with you as this potter does?"
    declares Yahweh. "Behold, like the clay in the potter's hand, so are
    you in My hand, O house of Israel.
7   "At one moment I might speak concerning a nation or concerning a
    kingdom to uproot, to pull down, or to destroy it;
8   if that nation against which I have spoken turns from its evil, I will
    relent concerning the calamity I planned to bring on it.
9   "Or at another moment I might speak concerning a nation or con-
    cerning a kingdom to build up or to plant it,
10 if it does evil in My sight by not obeying My voice, then I will think
    better of the good with which I had promised to bless it.
11 "So now then, speak to the men of Judah and against the inhabitants
    of Jerusalem saying, 'Thus says Yahweh, "Behold, I am fashioning
    calamity against you and devising a plan against you. Oh turn back,
    each of you from his evil way, and reform your ways and your
    deeds."'"

Jeremiah seemed to have delivered this message in his early ministry, posssibly before the fourth year of the reign of Jehoiakim,
since this discourse still assumes the possibility of the people's repentance, and the first Babylonian assault still seems not yet envi-
sioned. Furthermore, even though judgment is threatened, there is

no suggestion of an imminent catastrophe. Since there is no hint that Judah had become a tributary to Egypt in this chapter, Keil even assigns the prophecy to the last year of Josiah.[90]

By Yahweh's commandment, Jeremiah went down to the potter's house and watched the potter making something on the wheel. "On the wheel" (על־האבנים) means literally "on the two stones." According to J. Bright's explanation, the apparatus consisted of two stone wheels on a vertical axle, the lower of which was spun by the feet, while the upper carried the clay which the potter shaped as the wheel revolved.[91] Jeremiah observed the repeated work of the potter's shaping and reshaping of the clay to make the vessel of whatever sort seemed best to him. Then the word of God came to him explaining the meaning of this (vv. 5-6). Yahweh compared himself to the potter and Israel to the clay in his hand. He could do with Israel as the potter did with the clay. In particular, Yahweh was the divine potter of a nation or a kingdom. He could uproot (נתש), pull down (נתץ), destroy (אבד), build (בנה), and plant (נטע). These are all election terms (נטע, בנה) and rejection terms (אבד, נתץ, נתש).[92] Thus, the potter's work of making and remaking vessels refers to Yahweh's sovereign activity in the election and rejection of a nation or a kingdom.

With this parallel in mind, the next point of emphasis refers to the clay. As the quality of clay was decisive in the process of making a vessel (v. 4), the fate of Israel was entirely dependent upon her conduct (vv. 7-10). If Yahweh pronounces judgment and the people turn from their wickedness, he relents of his decree; conversely, even though he promises the people blessing and prosperity, if the people turn away from him and do wickedly, he then will change his good will toward them. Thus, Yahweh is fashioning calamity against them and devising a plan against them (v. 11). If they repent, they will still have a chance. However, the response of the people was negative (v. 12).

Besides the message in Jer. 18:1-12, the parable of the potter and clay appears in Is. 29:16; 45:9-13; 64:7 (E.8). Is. 29:16 explains that the potter (Yahweh) is not to be considered as equal with the

90. KD, *Jeremiah, Lamentations*, p. 293. According to J. Bright, this took place probably not later than the first years of Jehoiakim's reign (*Jeremiah*, p. 126).

91. Bright, *Jeremiah*, p. 124.

92. See above, pp. 73, 83, for the former; for the latter, see below, pp. 207-8.

clay (Israel) in power and wisdom. In Is. 45:9-13, Yahweh is described as the maker of all the universe and as the father of his son, Israel. In particular, Yahweh is compared to a potter and Israel to an earthen vessel. In the form of a rhetorical question, the clay is counselled not to complain about its present situation, nor to ask about its future fate, since Yahweh has aroused Cyrus to build his city Jerusalem and to set the captives free without payment or reward.

Isaiah 64:7-8 (E.8-9) is Israel's confession.

7   ועתה יהוה אבינו אתה
אנחנו החמר ואתה יצרנו ומעשה ידך כלנו:

8   אל־תקצף יהוה עד־מאד ואל־לעד תזכר עון
הן הבט־נא עמך כלנו:

8   But, now, O Yahweh, Thou art our Father,
     We are the clay, and Thou our potter;
     And all of us are the work of Thy hand.
9   Do not be angry beyond measure, O Yahweh,
     Neither remember iniquity forever;
     Behold, look now, all of us are Thy people.

The Israelites confess that Yahweh is the father as well as the potter, and they are the clay, the work of his hands; indeed, they are his people. They ask Yahweh not to be angry and not to remember their iniquity. Thus, the relationship between Yahweh and Israel is clearly recognized by the nation itself.

Therefore, there is no basic difference between the Jeremianic and Isaianic description of the Yahweh-Israel relationship in terms of the parable of the potter-clay. This image seems to be first used by Isaiah in Is. 29:16. However, the subject matter is not strictly limited to Yahweh's election of Israel. Is. 45:9-13 and 65:7-8 are a combination of two images: the potter-clay is combined with father-son. However, Jeremiah does not relate the image of father-son with that of potter-clay. Therefore, the Isaiah passages seem to be a later expansion. Thus, Jeremiah is responsible for the employment of this metaphor as an election metaphor. As he foresaw the fall of the monarchy, through this metaphor he emphasized Yahweh as the sovereign ruler of Israel's history.

(6) Master and Servant

The designation of Israel as a servant of Yahweh appears in Lev. 25:42, 55; Jer. 30:10; 46:27-28; Is. 41–49. Many scholars believe that the description of Israel as עבד יהוה originated in Deutero-Isaiah;[93] we must examine the truthfulness of this popular idea.

1) Leviticus 25:42, 55

כי־עבדי הם אשר־הוצאתי אתם מארץ מצרים לא ימכרו
ממכרת עבד:

For they are My servants whom I brought out from the land of Egypt; they are not to be sold in a slave sale. (Lev. 25:42)

כי־לי בני־ישראל עבדים עבדי הם אשר־הוצאתי אותם
מארץ מצרים אני יהוה אלהיכם:

For the sons of Israel are My servants; they are My servants whom I brought out from the land of Egypt. I am Yahweh your God.
(Lev. 25:55)

Since A. Klostermann, these verses have been classified as part of the Holiness Code, an independent entity which was incorporated into P and adapted to the source stratum.[94] According to G. Fohrer, it was first a combined collection of independent units composed in Jerusalem toward the end of the pre-exilic period, while the final redaction of the legal code H occurred during the exile.[95] If we accept Fohrer's postulate, it is not easy for us to trace the growth of the individual units. However, the special character of Lev. 25 provides a clue towards a solution. Lev. 25 contains the precepts concerning the sabbatical year to be observed every seven years and the jubilee year to be observed every fifty years. The sabbatical year is considered to have had its origin among the ancient Semitic peoples. According to J. Morgenstern, this sabbatical-year system was introduced in the so-called pentecontad calendar which was the earliest agricultural calendar and which continued to be an in-

93. W. Zimmerli and J. Jeremias, *The Servant of God,* SBT 1/20, rev. ed. (London: SCM, 1965), p. 17.
94. G. Fohrer, *Introduction to the Old Testament* (Nashville: Abingdon, 1968), p. 137.
95. Ibid., 142.

tegral element of the Canaanite agricultural civilization of Palestine. The invading nomadic and semi-nomadic Israelite clans and tribes adopted it when they conquered and established permanent residence in the land.[96] Also, the book of the covenant commanded the people of Israel to observe the sabbatical year (Ex. 23:10-19). Therefore, the precepts of Lev. 25 seem to belong to an earlier tradition. In particular, the repeated phrase מארץ מצרים אשר־הוצאתי אותם (whom I brought out from the land of Egypt) seems to be Israel's original confession of faith (so von Rad),[97] and it does not therefore suggest Israel's return from exile, the second exodus. Furthermore, Yahweh's designation of Israel as "My servant" is a reflection of the life of slavery in Egypt.

2) Jeremiah 30:4-11; 46:27-28

The Jeremiah passages deserve our special attention, because these give us a possible clue which helps explain the origin of the prophetic use of the master-servant metaphor.

4	ואלה הדברים אשר דבר יהוה אל־ישראל ואל־יהודה:
	. . . .
7	הוי כי גדול היום ההוא מאין כמהו
	ועת־צרה היא ליעקב וממנה יושע:
8	והיה ביום ההוא נאם יהוה צבאות אשבר עלו מעל צוארך
	ומוסרותיך אנתק ולא־יעבדו־בו עוד זרים:
9	ועבדו את יהוה אלהיהם ואת דוד מלכם אשר אקים להם:
10	ואתה אל־תירא עבדי יעקב נאם־יהוה ואל־תחת ישראל
	כי הנני מושיעך מרחוק ואת־זרעך מארץ שבים
	ושב יעקב ושקט ושאנן ואין מחריד:
11	כי־אתך אני נאם־יהוה להשיעך
	כי אעשה כלה בכל־הגוים אשר הפצותיך שם
	אך אתך לא־אעשה כלה ויסרתיך למשפט ונקה לא אנקך:

4   Now these are the words which Yahweh spoke concerning Israel and
    concerning Judah,
    . . . .
7   'Alas! for that day is great,
    There is none like it;

96. J. Morgenstern, "Sabbatical Year," *IDB,* 4:141-44; idem, "Jubilee," *IDB,* 2:1001-2.
97. Von Rad, *Old Testament Theology,* 1:176.

> And it is the time of Jacob's distress,
> But he will be saved from it.
>
> 8 'And it shall come about on that day,' declares Yahweh of hosts, 'that I will break his yoke from off their neck, and will tear off their bonds; and strangers shall no longer make them their slaves.
>
> 9 'But they shall serve Yahweh their God, and David their king, whom I will raise up for them.
>
> 10 'And fear not, O Jacob My servant,' declares Yahweh,
> 'And do not be dismayed, O Israel;
> For behold, I will save you from afar,
> And your offspring from the land of their captivity.
> And Jacob shall return, and shall be quiet and at ease,
> And no one shall make him afraid.
>
> 11 'For I am with you,' declares Yahweh, 'to save you;
> For I will destroy completely all the nations where I have scattered you,
> Only I will not destroy you completely.
> But I will chasten you justly,
> And will by no means leave you unpunished.' (Jer. 30:4, 7-11)

Jer. 30:10,11 is parallel to Jer. 46:27,28, but is absent in the Septuagint. Furthermore, these phrases are quite similar to the characteristic expression of Deutero-Isaiah, "Israel, My servant" (Is. 41:8; 42:1; 43:10; 44:1-2; 44:21; 45:4; 48:20; 49:3; 65:8-15). Therefore, it is believed that the Yahweh-Israel relationship expressed in terms of a master-servant metaphor started with Deutero-Isaiah, and thus the Jeremiah passages were inserted by a later redactor.[98]

Source criticism generally classifies Jer. 30–31 as the Book of Consolation. As for the authenticity of this book, however, opinions are so widely divergent that they offer us no sure answer. J.P. Hyatt believes that Jer. 30:10-11 was influenced by Deutero-Isaiah and thus, in its present form, was collected later than the Deuteronomic edition, posssibly in Nehemiah's time.[99] However, we find it difficult to isolate Jer. 30:10-11 from the corpus of Jer. 30:4-11. The motif of the "servant" and his deliverance in verse 10 actually begins in verse 7, as J.A. Thompson has rightly pointed out.[100] Jacob's distress in verse 7 is caused by his slave status, and he is seen as

98. W. Zimmerli and J. Jeremias, *The Servant of God,* p. 17.

99. J. Philip Hyatt, "The Deuteronomic Edition of Jeremiah," in *A Prophet to the Nations,* ed. Leo G. Perdue and Brian W. Kovacs (Winona Lake: Eisenbrauns, 1984), p. 266.

100. J.A. Thompson, *The Book of Jeremiah,* NICOT (Grand Rapids: Eerdmans, 1980), p. 557.

bound up and tied with a yoke around his neck in verse 8. However, Yahweh's deliverance is promised. Yahweh will break their yokes from off their neck and will tear off their bonds, so that strangers shall no longer make them their slaves (ולא־יעבדו־בו עוד זרים). It is at this point that we see the transition of Jacob's status from being "slaves of strangers" to the "servant of Yahweh" in verse 9. ועבדו את יהוה אלהיהם (But they shall serve Yahweh their God) is obviously in contrast to לא־יעבדו־בו עוד זרים. Since they are to serve Yahweh their God, Yahweh called them "Jacob, My servant" in verse 10. And the name "Jacob" is identified with "Israel" and used interchangeably in the same verse. Therefore, even Fohrer's isolation of verses 8-11 cannot be justified.[101] In addition, verse 11 contains a number of expressions that are found elsewhere in Jeremiah.[102] For example, "I am with you to save you" (1:8; 15:20); "I will not make a full end" (4:27; 5:10; 18:30; 30:11; 46:28); "the nations among whom I have scattered you" (9:16); "I will chasten you justly" (10:24). Therefore, we can find no reason to deny the unity of the book and the authenticity of Jeremianic authorship, and in that sense, O. Eissfeldt is correct in maintaining the genuineness of Jer. 30:5-21.[103]

However, we need to examine the similarity and dissimilarity of these passages as compared with the Isaiah passages in order to confirm our conclusion.

3) Isaiah 41–49

In Is. 41–49, we see many descriptions of Israel as Yahweh's servant. The expressions in this passage are very fresh and full of variety. However, we can find some evidence that these expressions are later than those of Jeremiah. First of all, the designation of Israel as a servant of Yahweh is always accompanied by stock election terms. For example, "Israel, My servant, Jacob whom I have chosen" (41:8; 43:10; 44:1,2); "My servant, whom I uphold; My chosen one in whom My soul delights" (42:1); " Israel, for you are My servant; I formed you, you are My servant" (44:21); "Israel My

101. Fohrer, *Introduction,* pp. 399-400.
102. J.A. Thompson, *Jeremiah,* p. 557; J. Bright, *Jeremiah,* p. 285.
103. O. Eissfeldt, *The Old Testament: An Introduction* (New York: Harper & Row, 1965), p. 361.

chosen one" (45:4); "You are My servant, Israel, in whom I will show My glory" (49:3), etc. Compared with the Jeremianic expression which is not followed by any possessive modifier, Isaiah's concept of "servant" shows evidence of sophisticated expansion and contains highly developed theological meanings. In particular, Isaiah's passages and contexts are mostly controlled and conditioned by the election theology which was prevalent in the later monarchic period. But in Jeremiah we do not find such a clear expression of the election idea. The concept of Yahweh's servant is transferred from the concept of being the slaves of strangers, viz., the Assyrians and Babylonians. Next, the specified mission or task of the servant in Isaiah is not found in Jeremiah. In Jeremiah, the Israelites were slaves of strangers, yoked and chained by bonds. But Yahweh delivered them to serve him. Neither task, nor mission, nor means to serve him is mentioned. In Isaiah, however, Israel as his servant was to be his witness (43:10) and to show forth his glory (49:3). Also, the usage of עבד appears more widely in Jeremiah than in Isaiah. Besides Israel in the book of Jeremiah, David (33:21,22,26), the prophets (7:25; 25:4; 26:5; 29:19; 35:15; 44:4), and Nebuchadnezzar (25:9; 27:6; 43:10; 46:26) are all designated as servants of Yahweh. In particular, prophets are designated as his servants in a collective sense. In Isaiah, however, the usage of עבד is limited to Eliakim (22:20), David (37:35), and Isaiah himself (20:3). In Deutero-Isaiah, "servant" is a designation for Israel alone, except for a few cases of singular usage which have been taken by some to refer to a promised Messiah. Therefore, the use of the term עבד can be said to be more wide-ranging in Jeremiah. In Jer. 34, we see Jeremiah's proposal to proclaim an emancipation of Hebrew slaves. In doing this, Jeremiah had recourse to the covenant which their forefathers made with Yahweh at Mount Sinai (Ex. 21:2-6). According to Lev. 25, the primary motivation for releasing the Hebrew slaves was based on the fact that Yahweh "brought them out of the land of Egypt" (Lev. 25:42), and this is completely in accord with Jeremiah's proposal (Jer. 34:13). The continuity of the idea between Lev. 25:42,55 and Jeremiah is maintained here. Therefore, we can safely conclude that the designation of Israel as the servant of Yahweh was initially Jeremianic. As Bright correctly pointed out,[104] the theory that Jer. 30:10 is a later insertion of a redactor who was

104. J. Bright, *Jeremiah,* p. 285.

influenced by Deutero-Isaiah does not stand. Rather, the author of Deutero-Isaiah seems to be heavily influenced by the election theology of the seventh- and sixth-century prophets of the southern kingdom.

In summary, we can say that the Yahweh-Israel relationship, expressed in terms of a master-servant metaphor, was known from an early date, perhaps as early as the settlement. However, Jeremiah was the first one among the prophets who employed the idea to describe the relationship between Yahweh and Israel. In particular, the deportation of Israel to Assyria, the consequent fate of Israel's enslavement, and the siege of Jerusalem by Nebuchadnezzar seem to be a setting from which the idea sprang. Jeremiah anticipates the future restoration of Israel as his servant and delivers the message of hope and comfort, even though his people were about to be sold as slaves. The expression of Deutero-Isaiah is obviously influenced by the election theology of the later monarchic prophets.

(7) Yahweh's Holy People

The designation of Israel as עם קדוש (holy people) does not necessarily carry the idea of ritual or ceremonial purity; rather its usage focuses on the relationship between Yahweh and Israel. This designation appears mostly in Deuteronomy (7:6; 14:2,21; 26:19), while a similar term (גוי קדוש, holy nation) is found in Ex.19:6. Besides its usage in the Pentateuch, עם קדוש is found in Is. 62:12 and Dan. 12:7.

1) Exodus 19:6

Many commentators do not distinguish between the meanings of עם קדוש and גוי קדוש.[105] However, there is much division regarding the problem of literary origins. On the one hand, Ex. 19:3b-8 as a literary unit is assigned to E by a group of scholars, such as Muilenburg, Wildberger, and Beyerlin, who argue for an early date. On the

---

105. J. Philip Hyatt, *Exodus,* NCBC (Grand Rapids: Eerdmans, 1980), p. 200; B.S. Childs, *The Book of Exodus,* OTL (Philadelphia: Westminster, 1974), p. 367.

other hand, Hyatt and Noth argue for a much later date, assigning the passage to the Deuteronomic redactor, or even later.[106] However, Childs maintains that these passages reflect the older covenant tradition of Moses as a covenant mediator, a tradition which is often found in the E source. While to him the poetic form is old, the vocabulary is not typical of Deuteronomy. Yet in their present position, he does not deny that these verses reflect the work of a redactor. Thus he concludes that, although the passage contains old covenant traditions, probably reflected through the E source, its present form bears the stamp of the Deuteronomic redactor.[107] If Childs's proposal is correct, the idea of "holy people" is not necessarily Deuteronomic and may therefore be regarded as an old one. However, we must examine the other passages in Deuteronomy.

2) Deuteronomy 7:6; 14:2,21; 26:19

Deuteronomy 7:6 is a perfect description of the election theology in its ideas and formula. According to Fohrer, this verse belongs to the content of Proto-Deuteronomy, which is presumably regarded as the law code of Josiah's reformation.[108] If this is true, we can again propose the early idea of "holy people." However, Dt. 14:2,21 must be understood from a different perspective, because the matter of concern is different from that of the previous verse. The main concern of Dt. 14 is not the election of Israel. It presupposes the election of Israel as a holy people to Yahweh, and requires them to keep themselves clean by eating clean animals. In particular, 14:21 prohibits the people from eating anything which dies of itself, since they are a holy people to Yahweh. Here we see a transition of thought from the holy people, set apart for the service of Yahweh, to the holy people who were to be ceremonially purified in order to meet the status of a holy people. In this sense, 26:19 is more akin to 7:6. Since 14:2,21 provides a reason for Israel's holiness, the whole section distinguishing between the clean and unclean animals (14:1-21) seems to be influenced by the election theology and associated

106. B.S. Childs, *Book of Exodus,* p. 360; M. Noth, *Exodus,* OTL (Philadelphia: Westminster, 1962), p. 157; J.P. Hyatt, *Exodus,* p. 200.
107. B.S. Childs, *Book of Exodus,* pp. 360-61.
108. Fohrer, *Introduction,* p. 169.

with the activities of priests. In that sense, Fohrer's assigning of this section to a later edition from the exilic period may be justified.[109] In relation to this, the separation term בדל is mostly found in the Holiness Code (Lev. 20:24, 26) and the post-exilic literature (Ezr. 6:21; 9:1; 10:11; Neh. 9:2; 10:29). פלה is also a characteristic term of the Priestly writings (Ex. 8:18 [E. 22]; 9:4; 11:17).

In sum, the idea of "a holy people to Yahweh" is an old one, perhaps originating in the period before Josiah's reformation, although it may very posssibly go back to the time of Moses. At first it was applied only to the Yahweh-Israel relationship. However, the priests' activities during and after the exilic period were responsible for the popular use of the idea as a theoretical basis for their separation from the gentiles and as a basis for ritual purity.

Summary

The later monarchic period was a new era in which the idea of election came into full bloom. Actually, except for the metaphors of the divine warrior and his levied army and the divine king and his people, the rest of the metaphors are the product of this critical period. The key theological concerns seemed to be focused on the relationship between Yahweh and his people.

Hosea saw the relationship in terms of a husband and his adulterous wife. His tragic experience of marriage with Gomer seems to provide a special insight into the apostasy of Israel, the consequent destruction of the kingdom, and the exile into Assyria. The concern for the land also grew in this period. Amos was the first to mention Israel's going into exile from its land (Amos 7:11,17). However, he did not give a theological explanation of it. Hosea took over this theme and related it to the sonship of Israel. For him the deportation of Israel from the land of inheritance was regarded as the rejection of sonship, because in the traditional faith Yahweh gave the land as an inheritance to his son, Israel. Hosea's metaphors, thus, were mainly drawn from family relationships such as husband-wife and father-son.

Isaiah's election idea was also a reflection of his age. The Syro-Ephraimite coalition against Judah, Ahaz's dependency on Assyria,

109. Ibid., p. 170.

Hezekiah's rebellion against Assyria, etc., were the international setting from which Isaiah's election theology had sprung. In this time of tumult, Isaiah sees Yahweh as the supreme ruler of world history (7:1-9; 10:23; 14:26-27; 23:8-9), the divine judge (26:8-9), and the king of kings (6:5; 8:21; 24:21,23; 33:22). He exhorted his people to total dependence on Yahweh alone for their national security. Therefore, belief in Yahweh as a divine warrior during the period of Sennacherib's siege of Jerusalem was realized under the guidance of Isaiah (Is. 36–37; 2 Kgs. 19). However, his idea of election is more clearly demonstrated in his concern for social justice. Isaiah compared the people of Judah who were corrupt and had no concern about social justice (Is. 1–4) to a vineyard which could not produce good fruits in spite of the farmer's special care, and he thus anticipated their final desolation because of their fruitlessness. Also, it is noteworthy that in Isaiah Yahweh is seen as the maker and creator of Israel (27:11), and Yahweh's judgment of his people is compared to a father's discipline of his son (10:24-25; 22:4).

Jeremiah portrays Yahweh as a shepherd, potter, and master. At the collapse of Jerusalem, he tried to explain the fall of the nation from Yahweh's point of view. And he argued that the fall of Jerusalem was brought about not because of Yahweh's weakness but because of his sovereignty over his creation. Therefore, Jeremiah portrays the Yahweh-Israel relationship in terms of a potter-clay analogy. The image of Yahweh as a shepherd and a master seemed to originate from the situation that the people were being taken into the exile as slaves, and even Jeremiah himself was among the exiles. However, we can observe that at the time of Jeremiah and Ezekiel the theology of election was much more developed and prevalent among the people, since these two prophets took up the former imageries or metaphors and expanded or developed them. For example, both Jeremiah and Ezekiel use Hosea's metaphor of marriage with more theological meanings and with a more refined and elegant style. Jeremiah's father-son imagery (Jer. 3:4,14,22; 31:19,20) was obviously borrowed from Hosea. It is also evident that Ezekiel was influenced by Jeremiah in his usage of the shepherd-sheep metaphor. In particular, the free use of a metaphor describing the Yahweh-Israel relationship in Jeremiah and Ezekiel seems to be a reflection of familiarity with the idea among the contemporary readers.

The basic difference between the monarchic idea as it developed and the previous one is that the former came into being out of the rejection environment. At the height of the national crisis, the prophets attempted to reawaken the people's relationship on the basis of Yahweh's eternal election. This was the nation's only hope for restoration.

4. CONCLUSION

The idea of election is an old one. The origin of the idea goes back to the time of the exodus event. As for the development of the idea throughout biblical history, we can see three important periods. First of all, in the pre-monarchic events the Yahweh-Israel relationship is mostly portrayed in terms of a divine warrior and his levied army. Israel perceived their election in the experience of war. The events of the exodus, conquest, and settlement provide background for this idea.

Second, Israel's main concern from the formation of the monarchy through the united monarchy was directed to the question of who was the real king. In the process of choosing Saul as their king, and then in the legitimizing of the Davidic dynasty, the people of Israel realized that Yahweh was their real king. In particular, the zeal of Samuel and David for Yahweh contributed much towards the election idea coming into prominence. And this climaxed in the erection and dedication of the Temple. Yahweh was believed to be enthroned in the Temple as the ruler of the world, dwelling among his people.

Third, we see the development of the prophetic idea at the close of both kingdoms. In terms of the national crisis, every prophet looked back to the events of Yahweh's salvation in the past, particularly to the exodus, and each portrayed these acts with their own characteristic election metaphors. On the basis of these analogies, they emphasized the indispensability of the national collapse and they further anticipated the future restoration. The listeners and readers of Jeremiah and Ezekiel seemed to have been very familiar with the idea of election. We also saw that their writings were influenced by the earlier prophets, such as Hosea and Isaiah.

Therefore, we can safely conclude that the various expressions and ideas of election sprang from the national concerns of each generation.

CHAPTER III

The Related Themes

The election theme is not separated from the other major themes of the Hebrew Bible. The concepts of covenant, mission, rejection, remnant, and restoration are indissolubly and organically related to one another, and together they convey the overall message of Scripture. Yet among these, the concept of election takes a prominent place in the biblical system of thought, because from this concept all the other themes are deduced and developed. Therefore, we need to examine these themes in relation to the election theme.

1. ELECTION AND COVENANT

Not all of the election metaphors are related to the idea of a covenant. Yet, because of their very nature, the practices of marriage and war necessarily entail the idea of a covenant. Therefore, the election metaphors here are extended to express the related ideas of covenant.[1] We will now examine the covenant idea with reference to marriage and war.

1. According to H.H. Rowley, "The election and covenant belonged together, so that loyalty to the covenant was essential to the continuance of the election" (*The Biblical Doctrine of Election* [London: Lutterworth, 1950], p. 68). Also G.E. Wright asserts that covenant is a device which explains the meaning and nature of Israel's election. And so covenant can not be treated independently of election, because it merely expresses in concrete terms the meaning of the relationship involved in election. Covenant is not in itself a redemptive act, but rather the expression and confirmation of this act (*The Old Testament Against Its Environment*, p. 55).

(1) Covenant with Reference to Marriage

Election was viewed from the perspective of marriage by most of the biblical writers. As a corollary idea, the covenant as well as the other themes mentioned above are also expressed by the marriage analogy. If betrothal is an initiation of a relationship between a man and a woman, the covenant can be viewed as a wedding that binds the couple legally. As a couple is legally bound through marriage, the covenant also carries legal force for both partners. Therefore, we can say that the covenant is a kind of act which puts the election into legal effect. It is an authoritative sealing of the election.

In Mal. 2:14, the human marriage is viewed as a covenant.[2] "Yet you say, 'For what reason?' Because Yahweh has been a witness between you and the wife of your youth, against whom you have dealt treacherously, though she is your companion and your wife by covenant [ואשת בריתך]." This verse clearly shows that by a covenant a couple enters the marriage union (cf. Gen. 31:50; Prov. 2:17), and because of the covenant a couple is required to act responsibly, i.e., in proper behavior toward each other so as not to deal treacherously.

This marriage covenant is also applied to the Yahweh-Israel relationship. In Ezek. 16, Yahweh explains the nature of his relationship with Israel from her birth and growth to the time when he took her for his bride. In verse 8, he said: "'Then I passed by you and saw you, and behold, you were at the time for love; so I spread

2. According to the Law of Hammurabi, marriage was a legal contract to be drawn up with the appropriate documents *(ANET,* p. 171, no. 128). Rivkah Harris agrees with Greengus in that the primary purpose of the so-called marriage documents was not to record marriage but to record important transactions which could effect the status and rights of husbands or wives ("The Case of Three Babylonian Marriage Contracts," *JNES* 33/4 [Oct., 1974]: 363-69). A papyrus document discovered at Thebes by the Eckley B. Coxe Expedition in 1922 shows that the writing of the marriage contract was a custom in ancient Egypt. See Nathaniel Reich, "Marriage and Divorce in Ancient Egypt: Papyrus Documents Discovered at Thebes by the Eckley B. Coxe Jr. Expedition to Egypt," *The Museum Journal* (University of Pennsylvania, 1924): 50-57. Among the Elephantine Papyri, marriage contracts are also found, see *ANET,* pp. 222, 223; Reuven Yaron, "Aramaic Marraige Contracts from Elephantine, *JJS* 3/1 (1958):1-39; B. Porten, *Archives from Elephantine* (Berkeley/Los Angeles: University of California, 1968), p. 206. See also J.C. Baldwin, *Haggai, Zechariah, Malachi,* Tyndale Old Testament Commentaries (London: Tyndale Press, 1972), p. 239. In Tobit 7:14, the father of the bride drew up a written marriage contract, which in the Mishnah is called *kᵉtûbâ.*

My skirt over you and covered your nakedness. I also swore to you and entered into a covenant with you so that you became Mine [ואשבע לך ואבוא בברית אתך ותהיי־לי],' declares the Lord Yahweh." Here, שבע is also a covenant term used exclusively of Yahweh (Dt. 4:31; 8:18). Since the election is Yahweh's sovereign choice of Israel, Yahweh's swearing to take Israel to be his is an oath affirming the characteristic divine grace. בוא בברית (1 Sam. 20:8; Jer. 34:10; 2 Ch. 15:12) and כרת ברית are synonymous. Both are used for divine-human covenants as well as for human treaties. Whereas כרת ברית emphasizes the act of making a covenant, בוא בברית puts more emphasis on the continuing status of a covenant that was once made. Yahweh acquired Israel by spreading his skirt over her and covering her nakedness. Thus, he possessed her and she become his. But this is not enough for marriage. A legal process was required to make a marriage effective in society, and the wedding ceremony was instituted for this very purpose. Yahweh took legal action in making Israel his by making a covenant.[3] Therefore, the Yahweh-Israel covenant is seen as a symbolic ceremony of a wedding.

We can see this picture more clearly in Jeremiah. When Jeremiah speaks of Yahweh's new covenant, he also mentions the old one. "'Behold, days are coming,' declares Yahweh, 'when I will make a new covenant with the house of Israel and with house of the Judah, not like the covenant which I made with their fathers in the day I took them by the hand to bring them out of the land of Egypt, My covenant which they broke, although I was a husband to them'" (Jer. 31:31-32).[4] Here, "My covenant which they broke" refers to the Sinai covenant, as seen in the preceding phrase: "the covenant which I made with their fathers in the day I took them by the hand to bring them out of the land of Egypt." According to this verse, Yahweh said that he was a husband to them at the very time that he made the covenant at Mount Sinai. Therefore, the Sinai covenant is understood as a wedding ceremony, and Yahweh is portrayed as a husband, with Israel, his covenant partner, as his bride.[5] If our

3. A. Weiser, "Glaube und Geschicht im Alten Testament," *BWANT* IV/4 (Stuttgart, 1931): 99-182.

4. For the exegesis of this verse, see Chap. 1 above, pp. 32-33.

5. For the covenant at Sinai as a wedding between God and Israel in the Midrashic literature, see L. Ginzberg, *The Legends of the Jews* (Philadelphia: Jewish Publication Society, 1928), 6:36 n.200. See also R.G. Rogers, "Doctrine of Election," p. 161.

premises are correct, the covenant meal in Ex. 24:9-17 can be also explained as a wedding feast.[6]

If the Sinai covenant carries with it in its nature the aspect of a wedding, what then is the content of the covenant? Jer. 11:2-5 gives us this clear interpretation of the Sinai covenant.

2   "Hear the words of this covenant, and speak to the men of Judah and to the inhabitants of Jerusalem;

3   and say to them,'Thus says Yahweh, the God of Israel, "Cursed is the man who does not heed the words of this covenant

4   which I commanded your forefathers in the day that I brought them out of the land of Egypt, from the iron furnace, saying, 'Listen to My voice, and do according to all which I command you; so you shall be My people, and I will be your God,'

5   in order to confirm the oath which I swore to your forefathers, to give them a land flowing with milk and honey, as it is this day."''" Then I answered and said, "Amen, O Yahweh."

Jeremiah was first commanded to listen to Yahweh's covenant words (דברי הברית) and then to speak to the people of Israel (v. 2). The words of the covenant are introduced here by the relative clause beginning with "which" (אשר) in verses 4 and 5. It was Yahweh's command and oath to the people (v. 5): "Listen to My voice and do according to all which I command you; so you shall be My people, and I will be your God." In order to confirm this covenant, Yahweh promised to give them the land of Canaan.

This covenant form (protasis: obedience to the word of God; apodosis: the Yahweh-Israel relationship) agrees exactly with the form of Ex. 19:3-6.

3   "You shall say to the house of Jacob and tell the sons of Israel:

---

6. According to D.J. McCarthy, a certain sort of sacrifice, such as a sacrifice of communion (זבח שלמים), produces a union between God and his people. And the covenant meal, sacrifice, and theophany were elements connected with and integral to the covenant (*Old Testament Covenant* [Atlanta: John Knox, 1972], pp. 30,31). However, Levine does not agree with McCarthy and proposes that "as far as the enactment of covenants is concerned, the use of sacrifice, where attested, represented only one of several means available for the celebration or sanctioning of a covenant." Furthermore, he asserts that "sacrifices were not the essential instrumentality by which covenants were put into force." See B.A. Levine, *In the Presence of the Lord* (Leiden: E.J. Brill, 1974), pp. 37-39. See also G. von Rad, *Genesis,* OTL, rev. ed. (Philadelphia: Westminster, 1972), pp. 184-85; Claus Westermann, *Genesis 12–36* (Minneapolis: Augsburg, 1985), pp. 222-23.

4 'You yourselves have seen what I did to the Egyptians, and how I
   bore you on eagles' wings, and brought you to Myself.
5 'Now then, if you will indeed obey My voice and keep My covenant,
   then you shall be My own possession among all the peoples, for all
   the earth is Mine;
6 and you shall be to Me a kingdom of priests and a holy nation.'
   These are the words that you shall speak to the sons of Israel."

First the commandments of Yahweh that Israel must keep and obey
are set forth (protasis), and then the covenant relationship between
Yahweh and Israel is promised (apodosis). Therefore, we can see
here that Jeremiah shared the exodus theology regarding the form
and content of the covenant. When Moses repeated the offer of
Yahweh to the people, they answered together saying: "All that Yahweh has spoken we will do!" (v. 8). All the people were commanded
to be consecrated and to gather together on Mount Sinai. "Then
God spoke all these words, saying, . . ." (20:1). Yahweh's words begin with the Ten Commandments and end with various ordinances
(Ex. 23:33). When Moses finished reading all the words of Yahweh,
all the people answered with one voice: "All the words which Yahweh has spoken we will do!" (Ex. 24:3). Then, the covenant between Yahweh and Israel was sealed with blood and they had the
covenant meal together. Here, "All the words which Yahweh has
spoken" (Ex. 19:8; 20:1; 24:3) does not necessarily refer to the Ten
Commandments alone. It encompasses all the ordinances given,
including the Ten Commandments, in Ex. 20:1–23:33. Jeremiah
gives us further evidence for this interpretation. The release of Hebrew slaves after six years of service is not mentioned in the Decalogue (Ex. 20:1-17), but is found in Ex. 21:2-11. However, in Jer. 34
Yahweh said that the Israelites transgressed his covenant because
they did not release the Hebrew slaves:

13 "Thus says Yahweh God of Israel, 'I made a covenant with your
    forefathers in the day that I brought them out of the land of Egypt,
    from the house of bondage, saying,
14 "At the end of seven years each of you shall set free his Hebrew
    brother, who has been sold to you and has served you six years, you
    shall send him out free from you; but your forefathers did not obey
    Me, or incline their ear to Me.
    . . . .
17 "Therefore thus says Yahweh, 'You have not obeyed Me in
    proclaiming release each man to his brother, and each man to his

187

neighbor. Behold, I am proclaiming a release to you,' declares Yahweh, 'to the sword, to the pestilence, and to the famine; and I will make you a terror to all the kingdoms of the earth.'" (Jer. 34:13-14, 17)

Verse 13 makes it clear that the ordinance regarding Hebrew slaves was given at the time of the Sinai covenant, and so Yahweh considered the release of Hebrew slaves after six years of service as one of the important covenant stipulations that Israel had to keep. But Israel did not keep it, and thus they are indicted for having transgressed his covenant (vv. 17, 18).

Therefore, we can see here two important characteristics of the Yahweh-Israel covenant. First of all, the form of the Yahweh-Israel covenant is basically different from the form of the ancient Near Eastern international treaty.[7] Second, the Decalogue alone is not to be seen as a full form of the Yahweh-Israel covenant.[8] Until now, research on the covenant has been mainly focused on the similarity or dissimilarity of its form as compared with that of the ancient Near Eastern international treaty.

The important point is not whether there is any clear resemblance, but rather how and from what perspective the people of Israel understood it. Robert M. Good refuses to accept the idea that the covenant formula (I will be your God, and you will be My people) is borrowed from the legal forms of marriage and adoption, and he suggests that the formula is fashioned instead after a client formula, the adoption of a tribe by an individual, as seen especially

7. Basing his work upon the study of V. Korošec, "Hethitische Staatsverträge," *Leipziger Rechtswissenschaftliche Studien* 60 (Leipzig, 1931), G. Mendenhall presents the outline of the Hittite treaty as follows: (1) preamble, (2) the historical prologue, (3) the stipulations, (4) the document clause providing for the preservation and regular re-reading of the treaty, (5) the lists of gods who witnessed the treaty, and (6) the curse and blessing formula *(Law and Covenant in Israel and the Ancient Near East* [Pittsburgh: Biblical Colloquium, 1955]). See McCarthy, *Old Testament Covenant,* pp. 11-12; and D.R. Hillers, *Covenant: The History of a Biblical Idea* (Baltimore: Johns Hopkins University Press, 1969), pp. 25-45. However, the lack of correspondence between the treaty form and the Israelite covenant has been pointed out by H.J. Kraus, *Worship in Israel* (Richmond: John Knox, 1966), pp. 136-40; and McCarthy, *Old Testament Covenant,* pp. 15-21.

8. The Decalogue is often treated as the text of a treaty in full form between Yahweh and Israel. However, McCarthy with J.J. Stamm points out that the Decalogue is far from perfect in terms of its resemblance to the treaty form, because even though there is a historical prologue, it lacks the essential curse and blessing formula of the treaties. For a discussion of this topic, see McCarthy, *Old Testament Covenant,* pp. 15-21.

in Arabic culture. According to him, in ancient times among the Arabs the rule of clientship was expressed by the phrase *aṭ-ṭunub biṭ-ṭunub* (tent rope touching tent rope). The joining of tents establishes a client relationship. Thus, the formula is drawn as "We encompassed their tents with our tents, and they became our 'cousins' (*banu ʿamm*)."[9] And he thinks that this client formula is associated with the concept of Yahweh's tabernacle. Thus he concludes: "That a client formula should circulate with a tent is entirely appropriate. The joining of Yahweh's tent to Israel accomplishes exactly what the Covenant Formula expresses: the adoption of a tribe by its new deity. The association of formula and tabernacle thus appears to be primary."[10] However, if we remember that marriage includes the duty of providing a domicile for the woman (ישׁב), and that election can be understood in terms of Yahweh's providing a dwelling place for Israel, as well as Yahweh's dwelling with his people (tabernacle, Lev. 26:11-12), then it can be seen that the formula of marriage and adoption is more akin to the covenant formula. The marriage union seems to reflect more precisely the Yahweh-Israel covenant relationship than does that of a client relationship.

From this same point of view, Z.W. Falk and M.A. Friedman correctly pointed out that the covenant formula ("You will be My people and I will be your God") was associated with Israel's marital-covenantal response ("You are my wife" and "You are my husband") which was to be declared by both partners (האמרת and האמירך).[11] In particular, Friedman's assertion is very persuasive that the covenant form of Dt. 26:17-19 ("You have declared the Lord, this day, to be your God . . . and the Lord has declared you, this day, to be his treasured people") is a reflection of mutual declaration in marriage.

As for the covenant form itself, it varies from case to case. Therefore, it is very hard to draw upon any one formula that can be applied to every case. However, we can hardly deny that the core of the covenant formula is the phrase that establishes the Yahweh-Israel relationship: "You will be My people and I will be your God." And this is primarily related to the concept of marriage.

9. R.M. Good, *Sheep of His Pasture*, p. 83.

10. Ibid., p. 84.

11. Z.W. Falk, *Hebrew Law in Biblical Times* (Jerusalem: Wahrmann, 1964), p.135; Mordechai A. Friedman, "Israel's Response in Hosea 2:17b: 'You are my Husband,'" *JBL* 99/2 (1980): 199-204; M. Weinfeld, "ברית," *TDOT*, 2:278.

(2) Covenant with Reference to War

In Ezek. 17, the covenant is understood with reference to the concept of an international treaty in the ancient Near East, and this concept is associated with war practice.

Ezekiel 17 portrays three stages of development that explain the reason for Yahweh's punishment of Israel for covenantal unfaithfulness. The first stage is seen in the parable of two eagles and a vine (vv. 1-10). The second one is both a parable and the interpretation of the parable, applying it to the contemporary international political situation (vv. 11-18). The third stage is the description of the Yahweh-Israel covenant relationship with reference to the first two stages, and it is parallel to an international treaty (vv. 19-21). In the first parable, the first eagle that planted a cedar and vine seems to be much stronger and more sublime in its appearance than the other one, since the descriptive modifiers, "long pinion," "(the plumage of) many colors," of the first eagle are omitted with regard to the second one. The first eagle certainly refers to Yahweh, the second one refers to other foreign gods, while the vine and tree are Israel. Now this description of Yahweh as an eagle (נשר) is also found in Yahweh's covenant proposal to Israel in Ex. 19:4 (cf. Dt. 32:11). The imagery of planting (שתל) a tree and sowing seed (ויתנהו בשדה־זרע) is typical of the imagery depicting Yahweh's election of Israel. Therefore, this parable emphasizes Yahweh's election of Israel and Israel's rebellion against Yahweh.

In the conclusion of this parable, Yahweh asks a rhetorical question regarding the fate of the rebellious vine: "Say, 'Thus says the Lord Yahweh, "Will it thrive? Will he not pull up its roots and cut off its fruit, so that it withers—so that all its sprouting leaves wither? And neither by great strength nor by many people can it be raised from its roots again. Behold, though it is planted, will it thrive? Will it not completely wither as soon as the east wind strikes it — wither on the beds where it grew?"'" (Ezek. 17:9-10).

To illustrate this concept of election and rebellion with even greater vividness, Ezekiel employs the contemporary international political scene in the second stage. The king of Babylon (Nebuchadnezzar) came to Jerusalem and took its king (Jehoiachin) and princes and brought them into Babylon (v. 12). He chose one of the royal families (Zedekiah, Jehoiachin's uncle) and made a covenant

with him (ויקח מזרע המלוכה ויכרת אתו ברית), putting him under oath
(v. 13). He also took away the mighty of the land, that the kingdom
might be in subjection, not exalting itself, but keeping his covenant, that it might continue (v. 14).

Babylon made a typical suzerain-vassal treaty with Israel.
However, Zedekiah rebelled against Nebuchadnezzar by sending
his envoys to Pharaoh of Egypt (Psammetichus II) that he might
give Zedekiah horses and many troops (v. 15). Again Yahweh asks
of the fate of Jerusalem and decrees its fall before Babylon, declar-
ing also the helplessness of Egypt (vv. 16-17). Here, the king of Babylon is compared to the first eagle, the king of Egypt to the second
(less splendid) eagle, and the vine to Jerusalem (Zedekiah). Thus,
the Yahweh-Israel relationship is viewed in the light of a suzerain-
vassal covenant. The order of events is noteworthy here. Nebuchadnezzar's selection (לקח) of Zedekiah and his making of a covenant with him (כרת ברית) show the relationship of election to
covenant.

This relationship is more clearly explained in the third stage.
Yahweh, the suzerain king, declares that Israel as his vassal despised his oath and broke his covenant, and so he is about to im-
pose sanctions on Israel. "As I live, surely My oath which he
despised and My covenant which he broke, I will inflict on his
head. And I will spread My net over him, and he will be caught in
My snare. Then I will bring him to Babylon and enter into judgment with him there regarding the unfaithful act which he has committed against Me" (Ezek. 17:19-20).

The main emphasis throughout these three analogies is on the
relationship between Yahweh and Israel, i.e., Yahweh's election of
Israel which then led to the covenant, Israel's despising her election
and breaking the covenant, and the following sanctions of Yahweh
against rebellious Israel.

As a summary of what we have found here in relation to our
topic, we can safely say that Yahweh's election of Israel is compared to Nebuchadnezzar's (a suzerain king) appointment of Zedekiah as his vassal king. The covenant is then understood as a legal
ratification of a suzerain's election of his vassal. Therefore, the covenant put the election into legal effect. Moreover, the ideas of election and covenant are closely associated with war. Babylon
conquered Jerusalem by force and made a covenant. Without the

submission of the less powerful king, either by military force or by any other means, the suzerain-vassal covenant could not be established.

The fact that Ezekiel viewed the election and covenant within the context of the Near Eastern international political treaties provides us with grounds with which to view the Yahweh-Israel relationship from the perspective of a suzerain-vassal relationship. Therefore, the covenant form of Josh. 24 can be said to have modified the ancient Near Eastern treaty form, while still being parallel to it.[12] That the vassal always had to be dependent upon his suzerain in his military defense against his enemies shows that Israel had to rely faithfully on Yahweh in war against the neighboring countries. Yahweh was a divine warrior who fought for Israel as well as a suzerain king who protected them as long as they were faithful to the covenant. When they betrayed Yahweh, however, he attacked and destroyed them. The fall of Israel and Judah is explained in terms of the sanctions of Yahweh against his vassal who broke the covenant (Is. 31:1-3).

Therefore, we can see here that the character of a covenant has two sides, i.e., the character of grace and the character of law. While the former emphasizes more the personal and intimate aspect of a relationship, the latter stresses the legal aspect of obligation and loyalty. The differences between the two aspects originate in the different understandings of the election idea. Since Ezekiel himself had these two different covenant ideas (Ezek. 16 and 17), we can see that the people of the Hebrew Bible had a broad view in their understanding of the covenant.

12. See D.R. Hillers, *Covenant*; D.J. McCarthy, *Old Testament Covenant*, pp. 11-12, 25-71. However, W.H. Schmidt points out that Josh. 24 shows a particularly close connection, but does not contain a blessing or curse, while the treaties on their part do not tell of the actual making of the treaty itself *(The Faith of the Old Testament*, pp. 104-5).

2. ELECTION AND MISSION

When Yahweh chose Israel for his people, he had a motive and purpose. As Vriezen mentioned,[13] election entails mission. These are not two separate themes. They are closely associated with each other. Therefore, we need to examine these themes here.

(1) The Motive of Yahweh's Election

1) The Love and Compassion of Yahweh

We have seen that the election term בחר is in almost all cases associated with love terminology (אהב, חשק, חמד, רחם, אוה, רצה, and חפץ), and this explains the reason for Yahweh's election of Israel. The fact that the idea of election is described by the marriage metaphor gives us further insight into the motive of Yahweh's election of Israel. Yahweh simply loved Israel, and that was the main reason for Yahweh's election of Israel. "Yahweh did not set His love on you nor choose you because you were more in number than any of the peoples, for you were the fewest of all peoples, but because Yahweh loved you" (Dt. 7:7-8a). Israel did not have any qualification in and of herself to be his people, and Yahweh also did not foresee any future redeeming quality in Israel (9:4-5). Yahweh's love for Israel simply caused him to choose her to be his. This love can be traced back to her forefathers (4:37; 10:15). Yahweh loved them, and that was the reason for his election of their descendants. Joined to this love, Yahweh's compassion for Israel is seen as another important motive for his election. Because Israel was the fewest of all peoples in number (7:7) and because they were groaning in Egypt (Ex. 2:24; 6:5), Yahweh said that he had chosen them. The parable of Ezek. 16:1-14, comparing Israel to a deserted baby in the open

---

13. "In the Old Testament the choice is always the action of God, of his grace, and always contains a mission for man, and of God" (Vriezen, "Die Erwählung Israels nach dem Alten Testament," *AThANT* 24 [1953]: 109). See also H.H. Rowley, *Biblical Doctrine of Election*, p. 45.

field, vividly shows Yahweh's sympathy for Israel, leading to her election.

If the basic motive for Yahweh's election has been understood as his love and compassion for Israel, this implies that the people of Israel acknowledged Yahweh's initiative and sovereignty in their relationship with him.

2) Yahweh's Covenant with the Patriarchs

Another reason for Yahweh's election of Israel is specified as Yahweh's keeping of his covenant with the patriarchs. Yahweh made a covenant with Abraham, "And I will make you exceedingly fruitful, and I will make nations of you, and kings shall come forth from you. And I will establish My covenant between Me and you and your descendants after you throughout their generations for an everlasting covenant, to be God to you and to your descendants after you" (Gen. 17:6-7). Yahweh is said to have remembered this covenant when he began the work of redeeming Israel from Egypt (Ex. 2:24; 6:5). He said to Moses that after the exodus he would take Israel for his people and he would be their God (Ex. 6:7). After the exodus, Yahweh said that he kept the oath which he swore to their forefathers by choosing them to be his people (Dt. 7:7,8).

Thus, Yahweh's motive in choosing Israel as his people was his faithfulness to keep the covenant he had made with their forefathers. Yahweh bound himself to the covenant with the patriarchs and chose their descendants, entering into a covenant relationship with them. Therefore, the basic attributes of Yahweh himself—love, compassion, and faithfulness—explain his motivation in choosing Israel.

(2) The Purpose of Yahweh's Election

Since Yahweh's motivation in election was found in his attributes, the purpose of election is not without relation to those same attributes. As R.M. Paterson mentioned, if God's election had no purpose other than to treat the people of Israel as his favorites, then it would be quite immoral and unjust.[14] But when Yahweh brought Israel out of Egypt and spoke to them at Mount Sinai, he made it clear: "If you will indeed obey My voice and keep My covenant, then you shall be My own possession among all the peoples, for all the earth is Mine; and you shall be to Me a kingdom of priests and a holy nation" (Ex. 19:5-6). Here, we can see that the intention of Yahweh for Israel was fellowship and service.

1) Election for Fellowship

Since the idea of election is viewed as Yahweh's establishing a relationship with Israel, Yahweh also wanted it to continue forever. This concept of fellowship is viewed in terms of Yahweh's dwelling with and walking among Israel.

ונתתי משכני בתוככם ולא־תגעל נפשי אתכם:
והתהלכתי בתוככם והייתי לכם לאלהים ואתם
תהיו־לי לעם:

Moreover, I will make My dwelling among you, and My soul will not reject you. I will also walk among you and be your God, and you shall be My people. (Lev. 26:11-12; cf. Ex. 33:16)

The symbolic expression of the fellowship of Yahweh with Israel in terms of his dwelling and walking among them is a part of the concept of election (Ex. 33:16). The building of the ark and its going before the Israelites during the period of exodus and conquest highlight this idea (Ex. 25:8; Dt. 23:14). Not only the ark but also the camp of Israel (Num. 5:3) and the land (Num. 35:34) were the places where Yahweh dwelt.

In order to have perfect fellowship with Yahweh, however, Israel was required to walk in complete conformity to Yahweh himself. Particularly, Israel was to be holy because Yahweh was holy.

והייתם לי קדשים כי קדוש אני יהוה ואבדל אתכם
מן־העמים להיות לי:

Thus you are to be holy to Me, for I Yahweh am holy; and I have set

14. R.M. Paterson, "Doctrine of Election," *The New Zealand Theological Review* 4 (Aug. 1966): 212.

you apart from the peoples to be Mine. (Lev. 20:26; cf. 11:44,45; 19:1; 20:7,24)

The characteristic expressions of Leviticus: "I am Yahweh your God, who has separated you from the peoples," "I have set you apart from the peoples to be Mine," "I am Yahweh who sanctifies you" (אני יהוה מקדשכם), etc., all emphasize Yahweh's requirement that Israel be holy. In order to be holy, Israel was to be separated from her neighboring countries in every area of life. The people were even commanded to cut off any relationships with the other nations so as not to follow their way of life. Rather, they were to live according to the law which Yahweh himself had given them to follow. Therefore, the Yahweh-Israel fellowship was maintained in so far as Israel conformed to the laws of Yahweh their God.

2) Election for Service

Yahweh elected Israel to be his servant. As a servant of Yahweh, Israel was to worship him, celebrate his feasts, and sacrifice to him.[15] Yahweh wanted Israel to be a kingdom of priests (Ex. 19:6). The phrase "a kingdom of priests" (ממלכת כהנים) does not necessarily imply "the priest as a representative of nations" here.[16] Rather, those services were exclusively committed to Israel among the nations.

However, Yahweh expected another important service from Israel when he chose her. It was the role of a witness.[17] Yahweh elected Israel to make himself known to the world through her. Israel was to show that "there is none like him in all the earth" (Ex. 8:10; 9:14; 14:4, 18), "the earth is Yahweh's" (9:29), and "Yahweh is greater than all the gods" (18:11). By doing miracles and wonders for Israel, Yahweh demonstrated his existence and power to Israel as well as to other, foreign nations. Thus, Yahweh used Israel as an instru-

15. See above, pp. 66-67.
16. Rather, it means that Israel has a responsibility of worship, celebration, and sacrifice to Yahweh among the nations.
17. This idea was strongly supported by H.H. Rowley, *Biblical Doctrine of Election*, pp. 45-68. In particular, he asserts that, "The election was only to be interpreted in terms of purpose and service" (p. 68). Again he says, "For the purpose of election is the service of God in the service of men, and the making known to all men of the character and will of God" (*The Missionary Message of the Old Testament* [Guildford: Billing and Sons Ltd., 1955], p. 55).

ment, to be his witness. Israel's exodus from Egypt, Israel's war against the Amorites, Israel's crossing the Jordan, etc., are the major events in which Yahweh declared himself God through Israel. Thus, Jethro, Moses' father-in-law, the priest of Midian, confesses: "Now I know that Yahweh is greater than all gods; indeed, it was proven when they dealt proudly against the people" (18:11). Rahab also made a similar confession when she received the Israelite spies into her house: "For we have heard how Yahweh dried up the water of the Red Sea before you when you came out of Egypt, and what you did to the two kings of the Amorites who were beyond the Jordan, to Sihon and Og, whom you utterly destroyed. And when we heard it, our hearts melted and no courage remained in any man any longer because of you; for Yahweh your God, He is God in heaven above and on earth beneath" (Josh. 2:10-11).

Since the demonstration of Yahweh's power in most cases originated in Yahweh himself, Israel was passive in the act of being his witness. It is hard to find any positive willingness on the part of Israel to proclaim Yahweh to the world until the time of the united monarchy. To the people of Israel, the foreign nations were only objects to conquer and destroy with the help of Yahweh. The Israelites tried to maintain the relationship with Yahweh in terms of the Law of Moses, and so it was unthinkable for them to be a positive witness of Yahweh to the gentile nations.[18] However, in Solomon's prayer of Temple dedication he mentions the concerns for the foreigner who is not one of Yahweh's people. "Also concerning the foreigner who is not of Thy people Israel, when he comes from a far country for Thy name's sake (for they will hear of Thy great name and Thy mighty hand, and of Thine outstretched arm); when he comes and pray toward this house, hear Thou in heaven Thy dwelling place, and do according to all for which the foreigner calls to Thee, in order that all the peoples of the earth may know Thy name, to fear Thee, as do Thy people Israel, and that they may know that this house which I have built is called by Thy name" (1 Kgs. 8:41-43). This prayer of dedication presupposes that foreigners will hear about the name and power of Yahweh and will ask him to show his generosity to them. This seems to be a significant

18. Quell and Altmann already pointed out the tension between particularism and universalism on this subject. See Quell, *TDNT,* 4:161; as well as Altmann, *Erwählungstheologie,* p. 9.

change in terms of Israel's attitude toward foreigners. Apparently, they came to regard the foreigners who called upon him as equal beneficiaries of Yahweh, as far as answers to prayer were concerned. The great diplomatic achievements during the reigns of David and Solomon seem to be responsible for this change. However, the modern sense of mission in which Israel became a positive witness to Yahweh is not yet found.[19]

The Servant Songs, however, provide an entirely different view of the servanthood of Israel.[20] First of all, Israel is appointed to be his witness.

"You are My witnesses" [אתם עדי], declares Yahweh,
"And My servant whom I have chosen,
In order that you may know and believe Me,
And understand that I am He.
Before Me there was no God formed,
And there will be none after Me.
I, even I, am Yahweh;
And there is no savior besides Me.
It is I who have declared and saved and proclaimed,
And there was no strange god among you;
So you are My witness," declares Yahweh,
"And I am God." (Is. 43:10-12)

Israel was his chosen servant to be his witness, to testify that Yahweh alone is savior and that he alone is God from eternity (Is. 41:8; 44:1-2, 8, 21; 49:3-6). In order to be so, Israel was to know him and believe him. And Yahweh has put his words into her mouth (51:16) to speak for him (51:16; 59:21) and to declare his praise (43:21). From this perspective of servanthood, Israel again can be called "a light to the gentiles."

He says, "It is too small a thing that you should be My servant,

19. G.E. Wright sees two traditions as to the mission of Israel. According to him, the Deuteronomic and priestly witness does not develop the universalism in which Yahweh's purpose of election is to use Israel for a universal blessing. Prophetic eschatology (e.g., Is. 2:2-4; Mic. 4:1-4), Second Isaiah, and the book of Jonah, however, do elaborate this meaning with reference to the role of Israel in Yahweh's universal blessing. See *The Old Testament Against Its Environment,* pp. 51-52.

20. See H. Eberhard von Waldow, "The Servant of the Lord, Israel, the Jews and the People of God," in *Intergerini Parietis Septum (Eph. 2:14). Essays presented to Markus Barth on his sixty-fifth birthday,* ed. Dikran Y. Hadidian, PTMS 33 (Pittsburgh: Pickwick, 1981), p. 360.

To praise up the tribes of Jacob, and to restore the preserved ones of
  Israel;
I will also make you a light of the nations
So that My salvation may reach to the end of the earth." (Is. 49:6)

Yahweh wants to save all the nations of the earth. For this purpose
he appoints Israel as a "light to the nations" to guide them to his
salvation (42:6; 60:3). "A light to the nations" is his word which he
has put into the mouth of Israel (59:21). Therefore, all the nations
will stream to Zion, to the mountain of Yahweh, to receive the word
of Yahweh, and on that day there will not be war between the nations any more (2:2-4; Mic. 4:1-3). "Then they shall bring all your
brethren from all the nations as a grain offering to Yahweh, on
horses, in chariots, in litters, on mules, and on camels, to My holy
mountain Jerusalem," says Yahweh, "just as the sons of Israel bring
their grain offering in a clean vessel to the house of Yahweh" (Is.
66:20). Thus, Israel as a servant of Yahweh plays a significant role
in his restoration of the earth — the role of guidance through the
word of Yahweh for all nations. In this sense, Israel will be a kingdom of priests on that day, for Yahweh has chosen Israel for that
purpose.

If we summarize what we have discussed here, we can find a
new aspect of the meaning of the exile. One can see two conflicting
purposes in Yahweh's election. As long as Israel continues to have
a sacred relationship with Yahweh, there is no room for her to be
Yahweh's witness to the world. Thus, the exile can be seen as the
period of creating a new sense of Israel's servanthood for the world.

3. ELECTION AND REJECTION

Israel's unfaithfulness to Yahweh brought about his rejection of her
as his people. The rejection terms, therefore, carry the opposite
meaning of the election terms. Since the idea of election is delineated in various metaphors, the concept of rejection is also depicted
in metaphors which accord with its opposite truths.

(1) Yahweh's Divorces His People

Since election is expressed by the marriage metaphor, rejection is described by the idea of divorce. As marriage terms are employed in representing the idea of election, divorce terms are used in explicating the idea of rejection. Hosea introduces a significant rejection formula: "You are not My people and I am not your God" (אתם לא עמי ואנכי לא־אהיה לכם, Hos. 1:9).[21] This has the exact opposite meaning of the election formula, and it is modified from the divorce formula in Hos. 2:4 (E. 2): "She is not my wife and I am not her husband" (היא לא אשתי ואנכי לא אישה). Besides this formula, we can see other concepts and terms for Yahweh's rejection of Israel.

1) Yahweh Writes a Bill of Divorce

In Dt. 24:1, when a wife finds no favor in her husband's eyes, her spouse is permitted to write her a certificate of divorce (כתב לה ספר כריתת; cf. 24:3). In the same way Yahweh says that he wrote a bill of divorce and gave it to Israel.

וארא כי על־כל־ארדות אשר נאפה משבה ישראל שלחתיה
ואתן את־ספר כריתתיה אליה ולא יראה בגדה יהודה
אחותה ותלך ותזן גם־היא:

And I saw that for all the adulteries of faithless Israel, I had sent her away and given her a writ of divorce, yet her treacherous sister Judah did not fear; but she went and was a harlot also. (Jer. 3:8)

The same expression is found in Is. 50:1. If we are correct in seeing the covenant on Mount Sinai as a wedding and the two tablets of stone as a marriage certificate, the bill of divorce correctly expresses the concept of Yahweh's rejection of Israel.

21. The divorce formula, "You are not my wife," "you are not my husband," can be found in Old Babylonian marriage documents. See Rivkah Harris, "The Case of Three Babylonian Marriage Contracts," *JNES* 33/4 (October, 1974): 363-69. In the Elephantine text, divorce, whether by husband or wife, is effected by utterance of the proper formula. The husband says, "I divorce X my wife" (*BMAP*, 2:7, p. 143; *AP*, 15:27, p. 46); *BMAP*, 7:21-22, p. 205, adds, "She shall not be to me a wife." The wife, if the divorce is by her initiative, says, "I divorce X my husband" (*BMAP*, 2:9, p. 143; *AP*, 15:23, p. 46). The formula in *BMAP*, 7:25, p. 207, is, "I divorce thee, I will not be to thee a wife." See Reuven Yaron, "Aramaic Marriage Contracts from Elephantine," *JSS* 3/1 (1958):14.

2) Yahweh Sends Israel out of His House

When a man took a woman to be his wife, he was to go and take
her into his house and provide a domicile for her. Thus, in election
Yahweh also went to Egypt and brought Israel out, providing her
with a dwelling place. Since divorce is the opposite idea of marriage, the phrase "sending out from the house" (שלחה מביתו) is a
peculiar expression of divorce (Dt. 22:19,29; 24:1,3,4). The same
expression is applied to describe Yahweh's rejection of Israel. In
Jer. 3:8, Yahweh said that he had sent Israel away and given her a
writ of divorce. Furthermore, in Jer. 15:1, Yahweh said:

אם־יעמד משה ושמואל לפני אין נפשי אל־העם הזה
שלח מעל־פני ויצאו:

> Even though Moses and Samuel were to stand before Me, My heart
> would not be with this people; send them away from My presence
> and let them go!

As a rough expression for this idea, sometimes גרש is used. גרש
means "to banish" or "to drive out." The Qal passive participle of
גרש is used for "a divorced woman" or "a widow" (Lev. 21:7,14;
22:13; Num. 30:10 [E.9]). When this verb is used in reference to
Yahweh, in most cases it refers to his driving out the nations from
the land of Canaan for Israel (Ex. 6:1; 23:30; 33:2; Num. 22:6;
Josh. 24:18; Judg. 2:3; Ps. 78:55). However, it is also used for Yahweh's driving Israel out of his house.

כל־רעתם בגלגל כי־שם שנאתים על רע מעלליהם
מביתי אגרשם לא אוסף אהבתם כל־שריהם סוררים:

> All their evils at Gilgal;
> Indeed, I came to hate them there!
> Because of the wickedness of their deeds
> I will drive them out of My house!
> I will love them no more;
> All their princes are rebels. (Hos. 9:15)

In relation to the concept of "sending out from the house," we
can think of "going back to her father's house." Since she was taken
from her father's house, she was to go back to the place where she
belonged when she was rejected by her husband, or when the marriage bond was no longer effective. Thus, Naomi's two daughters-

in-law were told: "Go, return each of you to her mother's house" (לכנה שבנה אשה לבית אמה, Ruth 1:8). This same expression is employed for Yahweh's rejection of Israel.

לא ישבו בארץ יהוה ושב אפרים מצרים ובאשור טמא יאכלו:

They will not remain in Yahweh's land,
But Ephraim will return to Egypt,
And in Assyria they will eat unclean food. (Hos. 9:3)

Since the marriage bond between Yahweh and Israel was broken because of Israel's playing the harlot, Israel was to return to the place from whence she was first taken (cf. Hos. 8:13; 9:3). At that time Yahweh will put his hook in her nose and his bridle in her lips, and he will turn her back by the way which she came (Is. 37:29; cf. Amos 4:2).

3) Yahweh Strips Israel

The placing of a garment over a woman is regarded as a symbolic claim to marriage (cf. Ruth. 3:9).[22] We can see a perfect picture of this idea in the election context of Ezek. 16. When Yahweh saw Israel, she had grown up, become tall, and reached the age for fine ornaments; her breasts were formed and her hair had grown. Yet she was naked and bare (ואת ערם ועריה, v. 7). And Yahweh said: "Then I passed by you and saw you, and behold, you were at the time for love; so I spread My skirt over you and covered your nakedness [אפרש כנפי עליך ואכסה ערותך]. I also swore to you and entered into a covenant with you so that you became Mine" (v. 8). Thus, we can see here that the spreading of the skirt and the covering of the nakedness of the woman are essential procedures for entering into the marriage relationship.

Since election is explained in terms of covering nakedness, the negative corollary of this leads us to see rejection as explained with respect to stripping (פשט) her of her clothing and leaving her naked.

I shall also give you into the hands of your lovers, and they will tear down your shrines, demolish your high places, strip you of your

22. Edward F. Campbell, Jr., *Ruth,* AB (Garden City: Doubleday, 1975), p. 123.

clothing [והפשיטו אותך בגדיך], take away your jewels, and will leave you naked and bare [והניחוך עירם ועריה]. (Ezek. 16:39; cf. 16:37; 23:10,26)

פן־אפשיטנה ערמה והצגתיה כיום הולדה ושמתיה כמדבר
ושתה כארץ ציה והמתיה בצמא:

Lest I strip her naked
And expose her as on the day when she was born.
I will also make her like a wilderness,
Make her like desert land,
And slay her with thirst. (Hos. 2:5 [E. 3]; cf. Jer. 13:22,26)

4) Yahweh Forsakes His People

Isaiah 54:6 describes rejected Israel as a wife forsaken (עזובה) and rejected (תמאס) in her youth.

כי־כאשה עזובה ועצובת רוח קראך יהוה ואשת נעורים
כי תמאס אמר אלהיך:

"For Yahweh has called you,
Like a wife forsaken and grieved in spirit,
Even like a wife of one's youth when she is rejected,"
Says your God.

Thus, we see that both עזב and מאס are used in the sphere of divorce. Since Yahweh was to forsake Israel, she would be called by the name "Forsaken" (עזובה) (Is. 62:4). As for מאס, Jer. 4:30 gives us a perfect description for the rejected Israel.

And you, O desolate one, what will you do?
Although you dress in scarlet,
Although you decorate yourself with ornaments of gold,
Although you enlarge your eyes with paint,
In vain you make yourself beautiful;
Your lovers despise you [מאסו־בם];
They seek your life.

In Jer. 6:30, even though the imagery is different from that of divorce, "rejected silver" (כסף נמאס) is used for rejected Israel, because "Yahweh has rejected them" (כי־מאס יהוה בהם).

(5) Yahweh Forgets (שכח) His People

The term שכח is used for Yahweh's response to Israel's forgetting (שכח) of Yahweh (Is. 49:14; Hos. 4:6). Since Israel forgot Yahweh (Jer. 2:32; 3:21; 18:15; Ezek. 22:12; Hos. 13:6; Is. 51:13), Yahweh has also forsaken and forgotten her (Hos. 4:6; Is. 49:14). However, the word "forget" was also used with reference to divorce. Israel is said to forget Yahweh because she followed her lovers (Hos. 2:15 [E.13]). Yet, Israel is described as rejected by her lovers. Thus, Jer. 30:12-14 portrays the misery of rejected Israel:

> For thus, says Yahweh,
> Your wound is incurable,
> And your injury is serious.
> There is no one to plead your cause;
> No healing for your sore,
> No recovery for you.
> All your lovers have forgotten you [שכחוך],
> They do not seek you.

Here, the verb שכח refers to Israel's rejection by her lovers. If we recall that Yahweh elected Israel because he remembered the covenant with their forefathers (Ex. 2:24), we can easily grasp this idea.

In addition to the above examples, as the negative counterpart to "Yahweh's loving Israel" are found the phrases: "to pour out My wrath on them" (לשפך חמתי עליהם, Ezek. 20:8,13, 21; 7:8; 14:19; Is. 42:25), "I set My face against them" (נתתי את־פני בהם, Jer. 21:10; 44:11, 27; Ezek. 14:8; 15:7; Amos 9:4), and "I have hidden My face" (הסתרתי פני, Jer. 33:5; Is. 54:8).

As we have seen, the rejection terms are borrowed from the divorce terms. Since Israel played the harlot and became an adulterous wife, Yahweh refused and forsook her. He stripped her of her garments and exposed her nakedness, and he wrote a certificate and gave it to her, sending her away to her parent's house. After that Yahweh forgot her.

(2) Yahweh's War Against His People

In election, Yahweh as a divine warrior chose Israel for his army against the nations and he fought for her. In rejection, however,

Yahweh chooses Assyria and Babylon as his agents against Israel and attacks Israel.[23] Yahweh proclaims war against his own people. He gives Israel into the hands of the enemy as punishment for her transgression of the covenant.[24] "For the same offenses Israel at one time was sent to punish other peoples by means of a holy war, for which Israel herself could now be punished by the same holy war with other peoples being used by Yahweh for this purpose."[25] The idea of a god's or goddess' rejecting his or her own people and fighting against them can be traced back to the early Mesopotamian period. The god Enlil killed the people of Kish and crushed the house of Erech and gave Akkad to Sargon. Akkad enjoyed prosperity under the guidance of Inanna, goddess of Akkad. However, she forsook her temple and city to fight against it. Thus came the catastrophe of Akkad.[26]

1) Yahweh Is Against Israel

Since Israel was not faithful to Yahweh, he no longer stood for her. Thus, in the rejection context is found the phrase הנני עליך ("Behold, I am against you," Ezek. 5:8; 21:8; 35:3; Jer. 21:13). And so Yahweh proclaims war against Israel.

ונלחמתי אני אתכם ביד נטויה ובזרוע חזקה ובאף
ובחמה ובקצף גדול:

And I Myself war against you with an outstretched hand and a mighty arm, even in anger and wrath and great indignation. (Jer. 21:5)

והמה מרו ועצבו את־רוח קדשו ויהפך להם לאויב הוא נלחם־בם:

Therefore, He turned Himself to become their enemy, He fought against them. (Is. 63:10)

Thus, Yahweh is no longer the divine warrior who fights for Israel. He has become an opponent of Israel.

23. G.E. Wright, *The Old Testament and Theology*, p. 129.
24. Millard C. Lind, *Yahweh Is a Warrior*, p. 110.
25. J. A. Soggin, "The Prophets on Holy War as Judgement against Israel," in *Old Testament and Oriental Studies*, BibOr 29 (Rome: Biblical Institute Press, 1975), p. 68.
26. "Like a maid who forsakes her chamber, the holy Inanna has forsaken her Agade [Akkad] shrine; like a warrior with raised weapons she attacked the city in fierce battle, made it turn its breast to the enemy." See Samuel N. Kramer, *From the Tablets of Sumer* (Indian Hills: Falcon's Wing Press, 1956), pp. 267-69.

2) Yahweh Employs the Agency of Babylon

In the context of rejection, Yahweh is still described in the figure of the divine warrior. He accompanies his strong and mighty agents: a storm of hail, a tempest of destruction (Is. 28:2-3; Jer. 23:19), a scorching wind (Jer. 4:12-13), a violent wind, a flooding rain, and hailstones (Ezek. 13:13). As Yahweh used those natural phenomena when he fought for Israel, he would now use them to fight against her. In addition, he employs a human army. As for the Assyrian army who destroyed Samaria, Yahweh said:

הוי אשור שבט אפי ומטה־הוא בידם זעמי:
בגוי חנף אשלחנו ועל־עם עברתי אצונו לשלל שלל
ולבז בז ולשימו מרמס כחמר חוצות:

> Woe to Assyria, the rod of My anger
> And the staff in whose hands is My indignation,
> I send it against a godless nation
> And commission it against the people of My fury
> To capture booty and to seize plunder,
> And to trample them down like mud in the streets. (Is. 10:5-6)

Assyria is introduced as the instrument of Yahweh's wrath to destroy the rebellious people of Samaria. As a divine warrior, Yahweh employed the Assyrian forces to pour out his anger on Israel.

Besides Assyria, Yahweh used Babylon to execute his judgment on Israel. He brings a nation from the north against Israel (Jer. 6:22; 13:20; 21:10).

> "Behold, I am bringing a nation against you from afar, O house of
>   Israel," declares Yahweh.
> "It is an enduring nation,
> It is an ancient nation,
> A nation whose language you do not know,
> Nor can you understand what they say.
> "Their quiver is like an open grave,
> All of them are mighty men.
> "And they will devour your harvest and your food;
> They will devour your sons and your daughters;
> They will devour your flocks and herds;
> They will devour your vines and fig trees;
> They will demolish with the sword your fortified cities in which
>   you trust." (Jer. 5:15-17)

In fact, Nebuchadnezzar king of Babylon is designated as the servant of Yahweh just as Israel was at the time of her election (Jer. 22:9; 27:6; 43:10).

לכן כה אמר יהוה צבאות יען אשר לא־שמעתם את־
דברי : הנני שלח ולקחתי את־כל־משפחות צפון נאם־
יהוה ואל־נבוכדראצר מלך־בבל עבדי והבאתים על־
הארץ הזאת ועל־ישביה ועל כל־הגוים האלה סביב
והחרמתים ושמתים לשמה ולשרקה ולחרבות עולם:
והאבדתי מהם קול ששון וקול שמחה קול חתן וקול
כלה קול רחים ואור נר: והיתה כל־הארץ הזאת לחרבה
לשמה ועבדו הגוים האלה את־מלך בבל שבעים שנה:

Therefore thus says Yahweh of hosts, "Because you have not obeyed My words, behold, I will send and take all the families of the north," declares Yahweh, "and I will send to Nebuchadnezzar king of Babylon, My servant, and will bring them against this land, and against its inhabitants, and against all these nations round about; and I will utterly destroy them, and make them a horror, and a hissing, and an everlasting desolation. Moreover, I will take from them the voice of joy and the voice of gladness, the voice of the bridegroom and the voice of the bride, the sound of the millstones and the light of the lamp. And this whole land shall be desolation and a horror, and these nations shall serve the king of Babylon seventy years." (Jer. 25:8-11)

Here we can see that the election term לקח is used for "all the families of the north" instead of Israel. These will be entrusted to Nebuchadnezzar to bring against Israel. The same expression is found in Jer. 34:2; 36:29; 38:3; Ezek. 23:28; 32:11-12. Thus, we see that Yahweh "is also the Master of the foreign armies, whose power is in no way limited by the boundaries of his own people. The hostile armies serve him as executioner of his judgment in Jerusalem."[27]

3) Israel Will Be Taken into Exile

In contrast to the idea of deliverance in the event of the exodus and taking captives in the war of the conquest, Israel in rejection will be the captives who are taken into exile. The Hebrew term גלה is widely used with the meaning "carry away captive" (Is. 5:13; Jer. 13:19; 29:7; 52:27; Lam. 1:3; Ezek. 39:23; Amos 5:27; 7:11,17; Mic. 1:16).

ואת־כל יהודה אתן ביד מלך־בבל והגלם בבלה והכם בחרב:

27. J.A. Soggin, "The Prophets on Holy War as Judgement against Israel," in *Old Testament and Oriental Studies,* p. 67, quoting A. Weiser, *Jeremia,* Alte Testament Deutsch (Göttingen: Vandenhoeck & Ruprecht, 1960), on Jer. 6:1-6.

> So I shall give over all Judah to the hand of the king of Babylon, and he will carry them away as exiles to Babylon and will slay them with the sword. (Jer. 20:4)

The verb שבה is also used to denote the same idea (2 Ch. 25:12; 28:17; Jer. 13:17; 50:33; Ezek. 6:9). שבי, a noun derived from שבה, is joined to a verb: הלך בשבי (to go into captivity, Is. 46:20; Jer. 20:6; Ezek. 30:18; Amos 9:4; Nah. 3:10), לקח בשבי (to take into captivity, Jer. 48:46), נתן לשבי (to deliver into captivity, Ps. 78:61). טול also carries a meaning similar to גלה and שבה.

> והטלתי אתכם מעל הארץ הזאת על־הארץ אשר לא
> ידעתם אתם ואבותיכם ועבדתם־שם את־אלהים
> אחרים יומם ולילה אשר לא־אתן לכם חנינה:

> So I will hurl you out of this land into the land which you have not known, neither you nor your fathers; and there you will serve other gods day and night, for I shall grant you no favor. (Jer. 16:13; cf. 22:26, 28)

The Deuteronomist's idea of exile agrees with this rejection concept explained in terms of Israel's being taken away captive (Dt. 21:10; 28:1-68).

4) Israel Will Be Spoiled (בזז, שדד, שלל)

In the election context, Israel as an army of Yahweh participating in his war enjoyed the dividing of the spoils (שלל) of her enemies (Num. 31:11-12; Dt. 20:14; Josh. 22:8). In the rejection context, however, Israel is spoiled. Yahweh proclaims that he will destroy his people (אבדתי את־עמי) because of what Manasseh did in Jerusalem (Jer. 15:7) and that he will bring the spoilers upon Israel.

> Their widows will be more numerous before Me
> Than the sand of the seas;
> I will bring against them, against the mother of a young man,
> A destroyer [שדד] at noon day;
> I will suddenly bring down on her
> Anguish and dismay. (Jer. 15:8)

Therefore, the people lamented and cried (Jer. 6:26; 4:13,20; 9:18 [E.19]; Is. 33:1; Hos. 10:14; Mic. 2:4). In Is. 10:5-6, Yahweh commissioned Assyria against Israel to capture booty and to seize

plunder (לשלל שלל לבז בז). The naming of Isaiah's son as מהר שלל חש
בז (swift is the booty, speedy is the prey, Is. 8:1-3) was Yahweh's
symbolic warning.

(3) Yahweh Apportions the Land to Nebuchadnezzar

Yahweh was depicted as the owner of all lands. He gave the land
flowing with milk and honey to his son, the people of Israel, as an
inheritance (Jer. 3:19). Since the land was indispensably associated
with the sonship and election of Israel, the idea of rejection was
also portrayed by Yahweh's depriving Israel of the land, casting
them out of the land, and desolating the land.

1) Yahweh Will Give the Land to Nebuchadnezzar

Since Israel betrayed Yahweh, he will withdraw from her the gift he
had bestowed on her. The land flowing with milk and honey will be
given to the one who is pleasing in his sight. Thus, Yahweh says
that now he has given the land to Nebuchadnezzar king of Babylon.
"Thus, says Yahweh of hosts, the God of Israel . . . 'I have made
the earth, the men and the beasts which are on the face of the earth
by My great power and by My outstretched arm, and I will give it
to the one who is pleasing in My sight. And now I have given all
these lands into the hand of Nebuchadnezzar king of Babylon, My
servant, and I have given him also the wild animals of the field to
serve him'" (Jer. 27:4-6). According to these verses, Yahweh is the
creator of the earth as well as the sovereign owner of all the lands.
Thus, he gives it to whomever he wants. But now (ועתה) he has given
it to Nebuchadnezzar.

We read more about this idea in Micah.

ביום ההוא ישא עליכם משל ונהה נהי נהיה אמר שדוד
נשדנו חלק עמי ימיר איך ימיש לי לשובב שדינו יחלק:

On that day they will take up against you a taunt
And utter a bitter lamentation and say,
"We are completely destroyed!
He exchanges the portion of my people;

How He removes it from me!
To the apostate He apportions our fields." (Mic. 2:4)

The basic idea of this verse is that Yahweh will withdraw the ownership of the fields from the people of Israel and give it to apostates.[28] Thus, the rejection of sonship involves Yahweh's withdrawal from Israel of the portion (חלק) which was given as an inheritance.

2) Yahweh Will Drive Israel out of the Land

Since Yahweh drove out (גרש) the Amorite, the Canaanite, the Hittite, the Perizzite, the Hivite, and the Jebusite from the land of promise in order to give it to Israel (Ex. 23:28-31; 34:11; Josh. 3:10; 24:18; 1 Ch. 17:21), now he is going to drive Israel out of the land so as to give it to Babylon. "And they went and served other gods and worshiped them, gods whom they have not known and whom He had not alloted to them. Therefore, the anger of Yahweh burned against that land, to bring upon it every curse which is written in this book; and Yahweh uprooted them from their land in anger and in fury and in great wrath, and cast them [שלך] into another land, as it is this day" (Dt. 29:25-27 [E. 26-28]). Here, שלך is used to denote "casting out" (cf. Jer. 7:15; 22:28). The Hiphil form of נדח is also used to convey the same meaning (Jer. 8:3; 16:15; 27:10; 29:14; 46:28).

כי נדחה קראו לך ציון היא דרש אין לה:

Because they have called you an outcast, saying: It is Zion; no one cares for her. (Jer. 30:17)

3) Yahweh Will Desolate the Land

The desolation (שממה) of the land is another feature of Yahweh's rejection of Israel as a son (Ezek. 6:14; 7:27; 12:20; 14:15-16; 15:8;

28. D.R. Hillers with many others proposes that the MT "apostate" is out of place. On the assumption that the lament has to do with the land's falling into enemy hands, perhaps Assyria, "apostate" would be the wrong word, and שובינו (our captors) would be preferred. See Hillers, *Micah,* Hermeneia (Philadelphia: Fortress, 1984), p. 32.

33:29). Yahweh's desolating the land expresses his vengeance for
Israel's defiling the land.

> Lift up your eyes to the bare heights and see;
> Where have you not been violated?
> By the roads you have sat for them
> Like an Arab in the desert,
> And you have polluted a land
> With your harlotry and with your wickedness.
> Therefore the showers have been withheld,
> And there has been no spring rain. (Jer. 3:2-3)

Yahweh made the land desolate either by stopping the rain (Jer. 3:3)
or by causing the wild beasts to pass through the land (Ezek. 14:15-
16). Thus, the land will be made more desolate and waste than the
wilderness (Ezek. 6:14). שחת also carries the same meaning as שמם
(Is. 36:10; Jer. 22:7; 36:29; Ezek. 5:16; 30:11).

(4) Yahweh Sells His People

In election, Yahweh as a master bought Israel to be his servant (Ex.
15:13, 16) to serve him. In rejection, however, Israel was to be sold.
Yahweh himself sold his people into the hands of their enemies,
because they forsook him (Dt. 28:69; Judg. 2:14; 3:8; 4:2,9; 10:7).

> Thus says Yahweh,
> "Where is the certificate of divorce,
> By which I have sent your mother away?
> Or to whom of My creditors did I sell you [מכרתי]?
> Behold, you were sold [נמכרתם] for your iniquities,
> And for your transgressions your mother was sent away." (Is. 50:1)

Again, in Is. 52:3, Yahweh says that Israel was sold for nothing
(חנם נמכרתם).

עבד is also used to describe the idea of rejection. Because Israel
forsook Yahweh and served foreign gods, Yahweh let them go their
own ways to serve idols.

> "Then you are to say to them, 'It is because your forefathers have
> forsaken Me,' declares Yahweh, 'and have followed other gods and
> served them and bowed down to them; but Me they have forsaken
> and have not kept My law.' You too have done evil, even more than

your forefathers; for behold, you are each one walking according to the stubbornness of his own evil heart, without listening to Me. 'So I will hurl you out of this land which you have not known, neither you nor your fathers; and there you will serve other gods day and night [ועבדתם־שם את־אלהים אחרים יומם ולילה], for I shall grant you no favor." (Jer. 16:11-13; cf. 5:19; Joel 3:6 [E. 4:6])

Yahweh caused Israel to serve other gods, as well as foreign kings, as their masters. Nebuchadnezzar is one whom they had to serve (Jer. 17:4; 27:4,17; 28:14; 40:9). Thus rejection is the result of Yahweh's allowing unlimited freedom to Israel which ultimately leads to their slavery to other gods and kings. In the same vein, לקרא דרור (to proclaim liberty) is used (Jer. 34:17).

(5) Yahweh Uproots His People

As the negative corollary to the election idea that Yahweh planted and sowed Israel in his land, the idea of rejection is portrayed as Yahweh's uprooting her and scattering her to the wind.

1) Yahweh Will Uproot Israel

The vineyard song of Yahweh in Is. 5:1-7 is one of the best illustrations of the Yahweh-Israel relationship. Yahweh the divine planter planted Israel with all enthusiasm and expectation for his vineyard. However, she produced only worthless grapes. Therefore, Yahweh was going to destroy her and leave her waste.

Ezekiel uses this motif in a slightly different way.

Your mother was like a vine in your vineyard,
Planted by waters [על־מים שתולה];
It was fruitful and full of branches
Because of abundant waters.
And it had strong branches fit for sceptors of rulers,
And its height was raised above the clouds
So that it was seen in its height with the mass of its branches.
But it was plucked up in fury [ותתש בחמה]
It was cast down to the ground [לארץ השלכה];
And the east wind dried up its fruit.

Its strong branch was torn off
So that it withered;
The fire consumed it. (Ezek. 19:10-12)

Two contrasting phrases are seen here: "planted [שתל] by the water"
and "plucked up [נתש] and cast down to the ground." The verb נתש
(to uproot) carries the idea of rejection with reference to Yahweh's
planting of Israel in his vineyard (cf. 1 Kgs. 14:15; Jer. 12:14-17;
2 Ch. 7:20). שרש (Ps. 52:7 [E. 5]) as a verb is identical with נתש in
its meaning. But the noun form שרש (root) is also used in the rejection context (Hos. 9:16; Is. 14:30; Mal. 3:19 [E. 4:1]). נסח (Ps. 52:7
[E. 5]; Prov. 2:22; 15:25; Dt. 28:63) also carries the same meaning
as נתש. "And it shall come about that as Yahweh delighted over you
to prosper you, and multiply you, so Yahweh will delight over you
to make you perish and destroy you; and you shall be torn from
the land [ונסחתם מעל האדמה] where you are entering to possess it" (Dt.
28:63).

2) Yahweh Will Scatter Israel to the Wind

Another image portraying the idea of rejection is Yahweh's scattering of Israel to the wind. The Hebrew verbs פוץ and זרה seem to be
used as an opposite concept of זרע (to sow).

ואפיצם כקש עובר לרוח מדבר:

Therefore I will scatter them like drafting straw
To the desert wind. (Jer. 13:24; cf. 18:17; Hab. 3:14)

וכל אשר סביבתיו עזרה וכל־אגפיו אזרה לכל־רוח
וחרב אריק אחריהם: וידעו כי־אני יהוה בהפיצי
אותם בגוים וזריתי אותם בארצות:

And I shall scatter to every wind all who are around him, his helpers
and all his troops; and I draw out a sword after them. So they will
know that I am Yahweh when I scatter them among the nations, and
spread them among the countries. (Ezek. 12:14-15; cf. Lev. 26:33; Jer.
49:32; 51:2; Ezek. 22:15; 29:12; 30:23,26)

The verb פוץ is mainly used for scattering sheep, but it also carries
the meaning of "scattering into the wind" (Jer. 18:17).

213

(6) Yahweh Devours His People

In election, Yahweh was described as a shepherd gathering his sheep into his pasture and feeding them. In rejection, however, Yahweh is compared to the one scattering the sheep and to a lion or bear tearing and devouring Israel.

1) Yahweh Will Scatter His Flock

As I mentioned above, פוץ denotes the idea of scattering the flock (Jer. 23:1-2; Ezek. 34:6; Zech. 13:7). Thus, it is used for the metaphorical description of Yahweh's rejecting Israel within the context of the shepherd-sheep relationship.

> Therefore thus says Yahweh of hosts, the God of Israel, "behold, I will feed them, this people, with wormwood and give them poisioned water to drink. And I will scatter them among the nations [והפצותים בגוים], whom neither they nor their fathers have known; and I will send the sword after them until I have annihiliated them."
>
> (Jer. 9:15-16)

This usage is also seen in Dt. 4:26,27; 28:64; Ezek. 12:15; 20:23; 22:15). In Jer. 50:17, פזר (to scatter) is used. "Israel is a scattered flock [שה פזורה], the lions have driven them away. The first one who devoured him was the king Assyria, and this last one who has broken his bones is Nebuchadnezzar king of Babylon."

2) Yahweh Will Devour Israel

As an image contrary to that of shepherd, Yahweh is compared to wild beasts such as lions, leopards, and bears which tear (טרף, Hos. 5:14; Jer. 5:6; בקע, Hos. 13:8), swallow (בלע, Is. 49:19; Lam. 2:2, 5; Hos. 8:7,8), and devour (אכל, Is. 9:12; Hos. 13:5-8) the flock.

> I cared for you in the wilderness.
> In the land of drought.
> As they had their pasture, they became satisfied,
> And being satisfied, their heart became proud;
> Therefore, they forgot Me.
> So I will be like a lion to them;

Like a leopard I will lie in wait by the wayside.
I will encounter them like a bear robbed of her cubs,
And I will tear open their chests;
There I will also devour them [אכלם] like a lioness,
As a wild beast would tear them [תבקעם]. (Hos. 13:5-8)

Since Israel was torn to pieces, she would be "just as the shepherd snatches from the lion's mouth a couple of legs or a piece of an ear" (Amos 3:12).[29] Also, טבח (to slaughter an animal, Is. 53:7) is used with reference to Israel (Lam. 2:21) and הרג (to slaughter an animal, Is. 22:13) with reference to Jacob (Lam. 3:43). In rejection, Yahweh is portrayed as the entirely opposite figure of the good shepherd of the flock.

(7) Yahweh Breaks His People

As a negative counterpart to the image of potter and builder, the image of Yahweh as the one who breaks and destroys is introduced in rejection. Yahweh is about to break his people as a potter breaks (שבר) his vessel (Jer. 14:17; 19:11; Hos. 1:5).

כה־אמר יהוה צבאות ככה אשבר את־העם הזה ואת־העיר
הזאת כאשר ישבר את־כלי היוצר אשר לא־יוכל
להרפה עוד ובתפת יקברו מאין מקום לקבור:

Thus says Yahweh of hosts, "Just so shall I break this people and this city, even as one breaks a potter's vessel, which cannot again be repaired; and they will bury in Topheth because there is no other place for burial." (Jer. 19:11)

הרס is used to denote the opposite of a builder (Jer. 31:28, 40; 45:4; Mic. 5:10 [E. 11]).

כה תאמר אליו כה אמר יהוה הנה אשר־בניתי אני
הרס ואת אשר־נטעתי אני נתש ואת־כל־הארץ היא:

Thus you are to say to him, "Thus says Yahweh, 'Behold, what I have built I am about to tear down, and what I have planted I am about to uproot, that is, the whole land.'" (Jer. 45:4)

29. According to ancient Near Eastern custom, the rescued pieces of a sheep were brought back as evidence of loss by the attack of wild beasts. See Ex. 22:12 (E. 13); Gen. 31:19; CH 266. See G.F. Hasel, *The Remnant* (Berrien Springs: Andrews University Press, 1980), pp. 180-81.

נתץ is also used within the sphere of building/breaking down (Jer. 39:8; 52:14; 2 Ch. 36:19). Sometimes אבד is used together with נתש, נתץ, and הרס (Jer. 1:10; 12:17; 18:7; 31:28).

ראה הפקדתיך היום הזה על־הגוים ועל־הממלכות
לנתוש ולנתוץ ולהאביד ולהרוס לבנות ולנטוע:

See I have appointed you this day over the nations and over the
    kingdoms,
To pluck up and to break down,
To destroy and to overthrow,
To build and to plant. (Jer. 1:10)

(8) Yahweh Defiles His People

"And you shall not profane My holy name, but I will be sanctified among the sons of Israel: I am Yahweh who sanctifies you" (Lev. 22:32) is the repeated pronouncement emphasizing the sanctity of Israel before Yahweh. However, the people of Israel defiled both themselves and Yahweh's name by serving other gods and following the customs of foreign countries. Therefore, Yahweh is going to profane them.

אמר לבית ישראל כה־אמר אדני יהוה הנני מחלל את־
מקדשי גאון עזכם מחמד עיניכם ומחמל נפשכם ובניכם
ובנותיכם אשר עזבתם בחרב יפלו:

Speak to the house of Israel, "Thus says the Lord Yahweh, 'Behold,
I am about to profane My sanctuary, the pride of your power, the
desire of your eyes, and delight of your soul; and your sons and
daughters whom you have left behind will fall by the sword.'"
(Ezek. 24:21)

In addition to חלל (Ezek. 7:21,22; 28:16), טמא (Ezek. 20:26), חנף (Jer. 3:2), and גאל (Is. 59:3; 63:3; Mal. 1:7,12) carry the same meaning.

The election term קדש is also used in a rejection context meaning "to set apart" the destroyer of Israel.

וקדשתי עליך משחתים איש וכליו וכרתו מבחר ארזיך
והפילו על־האש:

For I shall set apart destroyers against you,
Each with his weapons;
And they will cut down your choicest cedars
And throw them on the fire. (Jer. 22:7)

4. ELECTION AND THE REMNANT

The remnant theme of the Old Testament is inseparably linked to
the theme of election. Since Yahweh elected Israel by his sovereign
grace and not by her own merit, he does not completely nullify this
election because of her apostasy. Such is the character of election
that Yahweh's rejection of Israel is not a permanent and complete
one. Yahweh rejected his people for a brief moment in order to
discipline them.

> "For a brief moment I forsook you,
> But with great compassion I will gather you.
> In an outburst of anger
> I hid My face from you for a moment;
> But with everlasting lovingkindness I will have compassion on
>   you,"
> Says Yahweh your Redeemer. (Is. 54:7-8)

> "O Jacob My servant, do not fear," declares Yahweh,
> "For I am with you,
> For I shall make a full end of all the nations
> Where I have driven you,
> Yet I shall not make a full end of you;
> But I shall correct you properly
> And by no means leave you unpunished." (Jer. 46:28)

As the rejection is a temporary one, even Yahweh himself offers guidance to help escape the tragic moment. "Come, My people, enter into your rooms, and close your doors behind you; hide
for a little while until indignation runs its course" (Is. 26:20). Since
Yahweh would not utterly destroy Israel, there will be a remnant
through whom the restoration of Israel will occur.[30]

Because the nature of the remnant concept is closely inter-
woven with themes of election and rejection, its language and metaphors are also borrowed from their imagery.

(1) The Remnant, Those Who Escaped from War

שאר is most frequently used for denoting the concept of the remnant. The main usage of this word is in war contexts, in a primarily

---

30. G.F. Hasel sees the remnant as the bearers of the election (*The Remnant*,
p. 257). He also says that the goal of Yahweh's election of Israel which was frustrated by Israel's unfaithfulness can be realized in the remnant (p. 266).

negative construct.[31] When men of war finish attacking, the narrator will generally report: "So not a man was left" (ולא־נשאר איש בהם, Ex. 14:28; Josh. 8:17; Judg. 4:16; 1 Sam. 11:11), "they left no one" (לא השאיר שריד, Josh. 10:28, 30, 33, 37,39, 40; 11:14). Therefore, the term "remnant" (שארית) is a designation for those who have escaped from their enemies in war and have survived (2 Kgs. 19:31; 21:14; 1 Ch. 4:43).

If we remember here that Yahweh's rejection of Israel is described in terms of war imagery, it is natural to seek for the idea of the remnant in a war context brought about by Yahweh as a means of rejection. Is. 3:17-26 describes Yahweh's indictment of the daughters of Zion for their proud and sensual living. The ensuing declaration of war was the result of judgment that Yahweh brought about as a means of rejection.

> Your men will fall by the sword,
> And your mighty ones in the battle.
> And her gates will lament and mourn;
> And deserted she will sit on the ground. (Is. 3:25-26)

> For seven women will take hold of one man in that day, saying, "We will eat our own bread and wear our own clothes, only let us be called by your name; take away our reproach!"
> . . . .
> And it will come about that he who is left [הנשאר] in Zion and remains [והנותר] in Jerusalem will be called holy—everyone who is recorded for life in Jerusalem. (Is. 4:1-3)

Here, the remnant consists of those who, having escaped from war, now remain safe in Zion. Both the fall of Samaria before Assyria (2 Kgs. 17:18) and the fall of Judah before Babylon (2 Kgs. 24:14) were the result of war, and the remnant refers to those who escaped from the turmoil of war. This usage of שאר is also found in Jer. 34:7; 37:10; 38:22; Ezek. 17:21.

חמל portrays another aspect of the remnant idea. חמל is usually found in the sphere of slaughtering enemies or animals. חמל means "to have compassion on," or "to spare," referring mostly to one

---

31. Werner E. Müller suggests that the remnant motif originated from the Assyrian military practice (*Die Vorstellung vom Rest im Alten Testament,* Inaugural-Dissertation [Borsdorf-Leipzig, 1939], pp. 8-18). See also Hasel, *The Remnant,* pp. 18-19, 275-78, 373-74, 462; idem, "Semantic Values of Derivatives of the Hebrew Root *š'r,*" *AUSS* 11/2 (1973): 152-69.

who has compassion on a certain object and spares its life. So these
two meanings are used interchangeably. Saul and the people spared
(חמל) Agag and the best of animals and were not willing to destroy
them utterly (חרם, 1 Sam. 15:9). When David delivered Saul's family
to the Gibeonites to hang them, he spared (חמל) Mephibosheth
(2 Sam. 21:7). In the same way this term is used for Yahweh.

ויקנא יהוה לארצו ויחמל על־עמו:

Then Yahweh will be zealous for His land
And will have pity on His people. (Joel 2:18)

והיו לי אמר יהוה צבאות ליום אשר אני עשה סגלה
וחמלתי עליהם כאשר יחמל איש על־בנו העבד אתו:

"And they will be Mine," says Yahweh of hosts, "on the day that I
prepare My own possession, and I will spare them as a man spares
his own son who serves him." (Mal. 3:17)

In many cases, however, חמל is used in a negative construct, like
שאר, i.e., in a rejection context (Jer. 13:14; 21:7; Lam. 2:2; Ezek.
5:11; 7:4; 9:5,8,10).

As a remnant term, חוס carries exactly the same meaning as
חמל. Particularly in Deuteronomy, Israel is commanded not to have
pity on (חוס) their enemies around them and not to spare them (Dt.
7:16; 13:9 [E. 8]; 19:13,21; 25:12). In the rejection context this word
is used in a negative form, but in the remnant context it is reversed.

"And I will dash them against each other, both the fathers and sons
together" declares Yahweh. "I will not show pity [לא־אחמול] nor be
sorry nor have compassion [ולא־אחוס] that I should not destroy them."
(Jer. 13:14; cf. Jer. 21:7; Ezek. 5:11; 7:4,9; 8:18; 9:5,10; 24:14)

ותחס עיני עליהם משחתם ולא־עשיתי אותם כלה במדבר:

Yet My eye spared them rather than destroying them, and I did not
cause their annihilation in the wilderness. (Ezek. 20:17; cf. Neh. 13:22;
Joel 2:17; Jonah 4:10,11)

As a phrase that carries the remnant idea, לא־אעשה אתכם כלה (I
will not make of you a full end) is to be noted.

כי־כה אמר יהוה שממה תהיה כל־הארץ וכלה לא אעשה:

For thus says Yahweh,
"The whole land shall be a desolation,
Yet I will not execute a complete destruction." (Jer. 4:27)

219

כלה means "to end" or "to consume," representing the idea of total destruction of an entity. Thus the negative construct conveys partial negation. This usage is found in Is. 28:22; Jer. 5:10,18; 30:11; 46:28; Ezek. 11:13; 20:17; Nah. 1:8,9; Neh. 9:31; 2 Ch. 12:12.

Since the remnant is a designation for those who escaped the war that Yahweh brought against Israel, פליט (he who escaped) is also used in this sense.

והותרתי בהיות לכם פליטי חרב בגוים בהזרותיכם בארצות:
וזכרו פליטיכם אותי בגוים אשר נשבו־שם אשר נשברתי

However, I shall leave a remnant, for you will have those who escaped the sword among the nations when you are scattered among the countries. Then those of you who escape will remember Me among the nations to which they will be carried captive. (Ezek. 6:8-9)

The same usage of this word is found in Is. 4:2; 10:20;15:9; 37:31,32; Ezek. 6:8; 14:22; Joel 3:5; Ezr. 9:8,13.[32]

שריד is also found in the war context (Num. 21:35; Josh. 10:20,28,30,33,37,40) and carries the same meaning as שארית (Is. 1:9; Jer. 31:2; Joel 3:5 [E. 2:32]).

Though the usage of יתר covers a wider semantic range, it is still found in war contexts as a remnant term (Is. 1:8, 9; Ezek. 6:8; 12:16; 14:22; Jer. 44:7; Amos 6:9).

(2) The Remnant as the Stump of an Oak

Since Yahweh planted (נטע) Israel in election and uprooted it in rejection, the remnant imagery continues in this same line of thought. Yahweh spares a root for future restoration.

Yahweh has removed men far away,
And the forsaken places are many in the midst of the land.
Yet there will be a tenth portion in it,
And it will again be subject to burning,
Like a terebinth or an oak
Whose stump remains when it is felled [אשר בשלכת מצבת בם],
The holy seed is its stump [מצבתה]. (Is. 6:12-13)

32. Hasel (*The Remnant*, p. 265) notes that the Panamuwa Inscription (dated between 733/32 and 727 B.C.) uses a verbal form of *plṭ* with reference to the gods who "saved" (*plṭw'*) King Yaudi from ruin. See *KAI*, 2:223, 225, nr. 215:2.

During the course of rejection Yahweh will exterminate all but a tenth of remaining Judah. Thus the land will be forsaken. However, as when a tree is cut down the stump remains, Yahweh will spare the stump from which his new people will spring.

On another occasion, the surviving remnant of Israel is compared to a tree that will take root.

> And the surviving remnant of the house of Judah [פליטת בית־יהודה הנשארה] shall again take root downward and bear fruit upward. For out of Jerusalem shall go forth a remnant [שארית], and out of Mount Zion survivors. The zeal of Yahweh of hosts shall perform this. (Is. 37:31-32; cf. 2 Kgs. 19:30-31)

(3) The Remnant as Ears of Grain Left in the Field

Another image of the remnant is related to the harvest, the end result and climax of sowing. The remnant is compared to "ears of grain left in the field" after harvest.

> Now it will come about in that day that the glory of Jacob will fade,
> And the fatness of his flesh will become lean.
> It will be even like the reaper gathering the standing grain,
> As his arm harvests the ears [שבלים],
> Or it will be like one gleaning ears of grain [והיה כמלקט שבלים]
> In the valley of Rephaim.
> Yet gleanings will be left in it like the shaking of an olive tree,
> Two or three olives on the topmost bough,
> Four or five on the branches of a fruitful tree,
> Declares Yahweh, the God of Israel. (Is. 17:4-6)

Here, "ears of grain" (שבלים), "two or three olives on the topmost bough," and "four or five on the branches of a fruitful tree" all express the same remnant imagery, vividly depicting the fading glory of Jacob. After the harvest, a farmer is commanded to leave gleanings for the poor or orphans (Dt. 24:19-21; Jer. 44:9; Is. 24:13). This principle of "leaving" is then used to describe the idea of the remnant.

As we have seen, the imagery of the remnant is very limited because of the peculiarity of its subject matter, bridging the gap between rejection and restoration. However, we can safely say that the idea of the remnant basically has an organic unity with the concepts of election, rejection, and restoration in its theoretical description and in its employment of language and metaphors.

5. ELECTION AND RESTORATION

Since Yahweh's rejection of Israel was disciplinary in character, restoration was to follow in due course as a counterconcept of rejection. More precisely, it was Yahweh's restoring Israel to its original status as his people. Restoration, therefore, carries the concept or element of renewing and consolidating the former relationship between Yahweh and Israel. Thus most of its terms and metaphors are identical with those of election.

(1) Yahweh Will Take Israel Again

Even though Yahweh rejected Israel and sent her away because of her adultery, he could not stop loving her. He cries: "How can I give you up, O Ephraim? How can I surrender you [אמגנך], O Israel?" (Hos. 11:8). Thus, Yahweh is going to allure her (מפתיה) and bring her back to him (Hos. 2:16 [E.14]).

Isaiah 54:6 is more explicit; even though Jerusalem is here personified, it alludes ultimately to Israel.

"For Yahweh has called you,
Like a wife forsaken and grieved [עזובה ועצובת] in spirit,
Even like a wife of one's youth when she is rejected [תמאס],"
Says your God.

As he calls her back, Yahweh comforts and encourages her to come back to him without fear.

Fear not, for you shall not be put to shame;
Neither feel humiliated, for you will not be disgraced;
But you will forget the shame of your youth,
And the reproach of your widowhood you will remember no more.
For your husband is your Maker,
Whose name is Yahweh of hosts. (Is. 54:4-5)

Hosea 2:16-25 (E. 14-23) gives us a full description of this reunion. On the day of restoration, Yahweh will engage (ארש) himself to Israel forever (לעולם) (Hos. 2:21-22 [E. 19-20]). Here, לעולם (forever) is noteworthy. Since the Yahweh-Israel union was once broken, this word emphasizes the permanent, unchanging, and unbroken character of the reunion. Again, Yahweh will engage himself to Israel in righteousness (בצדק), in justice (במשפט), in loving-kindness (בחסד), in compassion (ברחמים), and in faithfulness (באמונה) (Hos. 2:21-22 [E. 19-20]). All these characteristics of the engagement were violated and rejected in the former failed union. In the first union, of course, Yahweh had shown all these virtues to Israel. But he had to confirm these again because Israel at this point definitely needed them more than at any time before. The marriage proclamation is described in verses 16 and 25 (E. 14, 23). Once a couple were united, a wife was to call her husband בעלי (my husband). However, "Baali" is a homonym of Baal, Israel's former lover with whom she played the harlot. Thus, Yahweh asks her to call him אישי (my husband) in order that he may remove the names of the Baals from her mouth and that she mention their names no more. The Yahweh-Israel reunion reaches its climax in the proclamation of the marriage oath sworn by both parties as in the case of human marriage. The phrase "You are My people, Thou art my God" (v. 25 [E.23]) is regarded as a modification of the marriage proclamation "You are my wife, you are my husband." In one aspect, this process of reunion is more formal and detailed than the original union.[33]

This renewed relationship is not without legal force. The bond of reunion has to be stronger and more permanent in its character so that it may not be broken or nullified again. The new covenant of Jer. 31:31-34 must be understood from this perspective of reunion.

33. R. Yaron proposed the possibility of the second marriage after divorce in ancient Israel and asserted that Dt. 24:1-4 is a device to ensure its stability and continuation. See Yaron, "The Restoration of Marriage," *JJS* 17 (1966): 1-11. Though G.J. Wenham does not deny the practice of remarriage, he proposes a different reason for the prohibition of reunion between the divorced couple in Dt. 24:1-4. According to him, marriage establishes a close and lasting relationship between a woman and her husband's family, a relationship that survives divorce or the death of one of the parties. In marriage a woman became a part of her husband's family, a sister to him and his brother. Thus, if a divorced couple wanted to come together again, it would be as bad as a man marrying his sister. See Wenham, "The Restoration of Marriage Reconsidered," *JJS* 29 (1978): 36-40.

31 "Behold, days are coming," declares Yahweh, "when I will make a new covenant with the house of Israel and with the house of Judah,

32 not like the covenant which I made with their fathers in the day I took them by the hand to bring them out of the land of Egypt, My covenant which they broke, although I was a husband to them," declares Yahweh.

33 "But this is the covenant which I will make with the house of Israel after those days," declares Yahweh, "I will put My law within them, and on their heart I will write it; and I will be their God, and they shall be My people.

34 "And they shall not teach again, each man his neighbor and each man his brother, saying, 'Know Yahweh,' for they shall all know Me, from the least of them to the greatest of them," declares Yahweh, "for I will forgive their iniquity, and their sin I will remember no more.

The days that come in verse 31 indicate the days of restoration (cf. v. 27). In those days Yahweh will make a new covenant with his people which will be entirely different from the old one that was made on Mount Sinai with their fathers. At that time Yahweh will not write the covenant document on stone but on their hearts so that it may not be broken. Thus, there will be no need to teach each other because every one will know (ידע) him. Here we can see the election formula (I will be their God and they shall be My people) as an aspect of the new covenant, especially since the marriage term ידע is used. Furthermore, a covenant is viewed as a marriage treaty. These facts lead us to conclude that even the new covenant is portrayed in terms of the marriage metaphor, and thus the legal bond of marriage through the new covenant is also one of the important parts of the Yahweh-Israel reunion. This new covenant also has a basic continuity with the old one (cf. Ezek. 16:60). In Jer. 50:5, this covenant of reunion is named "an everlasting covenant" (ברית עולם), and in Ezek. 37:26 it is identified with "the covenant of peace" (ברית שלום).

Since restoration metaphors carry the meaning of marriage reunion, "Yahweh's making Israel live in tents again" (Hos. 12:9) and "Yahweh's dwelling in the midst of Israel" (Ezek. 43:9; Joel 2:27) and "in the Tabernacle" (Ezek. 37:27) are noteworthy.

(2) Yahweh Will Bring Israel Back from Captivity

The return of Israel from her captivity is a conspicuous and prac-tical feature of her restoration as the people of Yahweh. The role of Yahweh in Israel's restoration from slavery in Babylon is also de-scribed in terms of the metaphor of the divine warrior. Again, Yah-weh is fighting for Israel against Babylon, and he chooses another agent, the Medes, to execute his plan of restoration.

1) Yahweh Will Be Against Babylon

Assyria and Babylon played a significant role as Yahweh's agents in his rejection of Israel. At the time of the restoration of Israel, however, they were to be forsaken and punished until desolate.

Isaiah 13–14 is the oracle concerning the fate of Babylon. This oracle begins with the description of Yahweh as a divine warrior who summons his consecrated ones for battles (13:1-16).[34] They are his mighty warriors and his proudly exulting ones (13:3). Yahweh is about to execute his anger through them. Verses 17-19 reveal more about the plan of Yahweh.

הנני מעיר עליהם את־מדי אשר־כסף לא יחשבו וזהב
לא יחפצו־בו: וקשתות נערים תרטשנה ופרי־בטן
לא ירחמו על־בנים לא־תחוס עינם: והיתה בבל
צבי ממלכות תפארת גאון כשדים כמהפכת אלהים
את־סדם ואת־עמרה:

Behold, I am going to stir up the Medes against them,
Who will not value silver or take pleasure in gold,
And their bows will mow down the young men,
They will not even have compassion on the fruit of the womb,
Nor will their eye pity children.
And Babylon, the beauty of kingdoms, the glory of the Chaldeans' pride,
Will be as when God overthrew Sodom and Gomorrah.

According to these verses, the mighty warrior that Yahweh has con-secrated is the Medes.[35] Yahweh's plan is to destroy Babylon through

---

34. See above, pp. 51-52.

35. Cf. Jer. 51:28. The Medes (מדי, Assyrian *Madai:* in a Persian inscription *Miâda*) were first mentioned by Shalmaneser II, in the ninth century B.C.; in the eighth century raids against Median chieftains were recorded by the Assyrian kings

the Medes, who do not take pleasure in booty and spoils but only in the taking of lives. In that day Babylon will be like Sodom and Gomorrah in the day of their destruction. Yahweh's first step in restoring his people was to break the power of Babylon under whose grip Israel was held captive.

After this doom is pronounced, Is. 14 begins with the description of Yahweh's restoration of Israel. "When Yahweh will have compassion on Jacob, and again choose Israel, and settle them in their own land, then strangers will join them and attach themselves to the house of Jacob. And the people will take them along and bring them to their place, and the house of Israel will possess them as an inheritance in the land of Yahweh as male and female servants; and they will take them as their captors, and will rule over their oppressors" (Is. 14:1-2). In these verses, the clause וּבָחַר עוֹד בְּיִשְׂרָאֵל (and [He] again will choose Israel) merits our attention. The restoration of Israel, according to Isaiah, is viewed in terms of re-election, and thus follows the idea of resettling and repossessing of the land by Yahweh as an inheritance. Furthermore, the situation is reversed in that they will now rule over their oppressors. In that day Israel will sing over the fallen tyrant, the king of Babylon (Is. 14:4-21).

The imagery portraying Yahweh as a divine warrior who sends his army against Babylon and destroys her is also one of the important themes of Is. 46–47, as well as of Jer. 50–51. In particular, Is. 44:28 and 45:1 reveal that Yahweh's anointed agent against Babylon is Cyrus, the king of Persia.

כה־אמר יהוה למשיחו לכורש אשר־החזקתי בימינו
לרד־לפניו גוים ומתני מלכים אפתח לפתח לפניו
דלתים ושערים לא יסגרו: אני לפניך אלך
והדורים אושר דלתות נחושה אשבר ובריחי ברזל אגדע:

Thus says Yahweh to Cyrus His anointed,
Whom I have taken by the right hand,
To subdue nations before him,
And to loose the loins of kings;
To open the doors before him so that gates will not be shut:

Tiglath-pileser and Sargon. In the seventh century they had a military alliance with the Babylonians in destroying Nineveh, and this friendly relationship continued until the end of the reign of Nebuchadnezzar (561 B.C.). It ceased to exist with the capture of Babylon by Cyrus in 538 B.C. See G.B. Gray, *The Book of Isaiah*, pp. 242-43.

I will go before you and make the rough place smooth;
I will shatter the doors of bronze, and cut through their iron bars.

(Is. 45:1-2)

Cyrus was appointed by Yahweh in order to subdue nations and to manifest the power of Yahweh to the whole world. Yahweh would use him to restore his people from the Babylonian captivity (Ezr. 1:1-11).

2) Yahweh Will Deliver Captive Israel

In the first stage of Israel's restoration, Yahweh destroyed Babylon through his agent, Cyrus, who held her captive. He then broke the bonds of the captives and delivered his people from them. Since Yahweh released Israel from captivity, they are commanded now to loose themselves from the chains around their necks.

Awake, awake,
Clothe yourself in your strength, O Zion;
Clothe yourself in your beautiful garments,
O Jerusalem, the holy city.
For the uncircumcised and the unclean
Will no more come into you.
Shake yourself from the dust, rise up,
O captive Jerusalem;
Loose yourself from the chains around your neck [התפתחו מוסרי
צוארך],
O captive daughter of Zion. (Is. 52:1-2)

As the counterconcept of "to be taken into captivity" (as a result of defeat in war), the release from captivity as a result of Yahweh's breaking the bonds of slavery is viewed as an image of Yahweh's restoration of Israel (cf. Jer. 30:8; 46:27-28). Having been released from the bondage of slaves, the Israelites were to come back to their homeland.

כי הנה ימים באים נאם־יהוה ושבתי את־שבות עמי
ישראל ויהודה אמר יהוה והשבתים אל־הארץ אשר־
נתתי לאבותם וירשוה:

"For, behold, days are coming," declares Yahweh, "when I will re-store the fortunes of My people Israel and Judah."[36] Yahweh says, "I

36. Here the NASB rendering of שבות עמי ישראל ויהודה as "the fortunes of My people Israel and Judah" is misleading. The literal meaning of "the captivity of My people Israel and Judah" is more acceptable. In the same way, "I will return" is a better translation for שבתי (NASB "I will restore").

227

will also bring them to the land that I gave to their forefathers, and they shall possess it." (Jer. 30:3)

3) Israel Will Plunder (נצל ,בזז)

At the time of rejection, Israel was plundered (בזז, Is. 10:6) and was taken into captivity by the nations who were the agents of Yahweh. In restoration, however, Israel will plunder them in return as in the time of the exodus (Ex. 3:22; 12:36).[37]

> "Therefore, as I live," declares Yahweh of hosts,
> The God of Israel,
> "Surely Moab will be like Sodom,
> And the Sons of Ammon like Gomorrah-
> A place possessed by nettles and salt pits,
> And a perpetual desolation.
> The remnant of My people will plunder them [שארית עמי יבזום]
> And remainder of My nation will inherit them."
>
> (Zeph. 2:9; cf. Jer. 30:16; 50:37)

(3) Yahweh Will Restore the Sonship of Israel

Yahweh's rejection of Israel was described by the metaphor of the rejection of sonship and the consequent deprivation of inheritance, viz., the land. The idea of restoration thus carries the imagery of restoring the relationship and bringing the people back to their inheritance.

1) The Restoration of Sonship

Even though Yahweh has rejected Israel because of apostasy and has driven the nation out of the land, he has not totally broken the ties of a father-son relationship between himself and Israel. Yahweh still is a father to Israel and Israel is his first-born.

> Behold, I am bringing them from the north country,
> And I will gather them from the remote parts of the earth,
> Among them the blind and the lame,

37. Here (Ex. 3:22; 12:36) נצל is used.

The woman with child and she who is in labor with child, together;
A great company, they shall return here.
With weeping they shall come
And by supplication I will lead them;
I will make them walk by streams of waters,
On a straight path in which they shall not stumble;
For I am a father to Israel [כי־הייתי לישראל לאב],
Ephraim is My first-born [ואפרים בכרי הוא]. (Jer. 31:8-9)

This poem describes the future scene of Israel's return from captivity. The wounded and afflicted are coming from the north with weeping. Yahweh again calls this people his first-born and he himself their father. In Jer. 31:20, Yahweh expresses his feelings for his people during this period of chastisement.

"Is Ephraim My dear son?
Is he a delightful child?
Indeed, as often as I have spoken against him,
I certainly still remember him;
Therefore My heart yearns for him;
I will surely have mercy on him," declares Yahweh. (Jer. 31:20)

In whatever situation Israel may be, Ephraim is still his dear son and delightful child. Yahweh could not forget him. The fact that Yahweh spoke against him so often is the evidence that he has not forgotten him, but rather has longed for him.[38] We can also find this same feeling of Yahweh for Israel in Hos. 11:8.[39]

---

38. Yahweh could not forget Zion either. Thus he compares himself to a woman with her nursing child in describing his feeling for his chosen city.

But Zion said, "Yahweh has forsaken me,
And Yahweh has forgotten me."
"Can a woman forget her nursing child,
And have no compassion on the son of her womb?
Even these may forget, but I will not forget you.
"Behold, I have inscribed you on the palms of My hands;
Your walls are continually before Me." (Is. 49:14-16)

Even though we can not directly identify the personified Zion with Israel here, the heart of Yahweh that longed for Zion during the period of rejection is the same toward his people.

39. The larger context of this verse refers to Yahweh's rejection of Israel. In 11:1, Israel is designated "My son" by Yahweh. In verse 3, Yahweh says that he taught Ephraim to walk and took him in his arms. Therefore, he cries in verse 8: "How can I give you up, O Ephraim? How can I surrender you, O Israel?"

2) A Better Name than That of Sons and Daughters

The promise of a new name is given to Israel at the restoration.

> And you will leave your name for a curse to My chosen ones,
> And the Lord Yahweh will slay you.
> But My servants will be called by another name. (Is. 65:15)

> And the nations will see your righteousness,
> And all kings your glory;
> And you will be called by a new name [שֵׁם חָדָשׁ],
> Which the mouth of Yahweh will designate. (Is. 62:2)

On the day of restoration, Yahweh promises to give a new name to Israel. According to T.D. Andersen's examination, the renaming in the biblical text is connected with the establishing and confirmation of a covenant between Yahweh and the person who is renamed, and the meaning of the new names, as seen in Abraham and Sarah, are directly connected to the covenant promises. Thus new names can be seen as a sign and guarantee of the covenant, and renaming is accompanied by a recitation of covenant promises.[40] However, Israel's being called by another name in the restoration context of Is. 65:15 is slightly different from the renaming in a covenant context. Since the name once given to Israel was defiled by their sin, Yahweh is about to give them a new and glorious name.

This new name will be better than that of sons and daughters, and it will be an everlasting name which will not be cut off.

> To them I will give in My house and within My walls a memorial,
> And a name better than that of sons and daughters;
> I will give them an everlasting name which will not be cut off [שֵׁם
> עוֹלָם אֶתֶּן־לוֹ אֲשֶׁר לֹא יִכָּרֵת]. (Is. 56:5)

---

40. T. David Andersen, "Renaming and Wedding Imagery in Isaiah 62," *Biblica* 67 (1986): 76. The renaming of Zion as חֶפְצִי־בָהּ (My delight is in her) or בְּעוּלָה לְאַרְצֵךְ (Your land married) in the context of restoration (Is. 62:2-4) may be seen in the same way, since Zion is the place where the people of Yahweh dwell and usually refers to the inhabitants. However, Andersen observed a very interesting point here. "The most common image is that of Zion as the mother of sons (49, 17-23; 51, 17-20; 54, 1-2.13; 60, 4-9; 66, 7-12). In 51, 17-20 the calamity which befell Israel is portrayed by a picture of Zion bereft of her sons who lie unconscious in the streets. The return from exile is portrayed by the sons' being brought back to their mother (49, 17-23; 60, 4.9)" (p. 79).

3) Israel's Return to Its Own Land

In election, the land was a gift of Yahweh to his son Israel, and in rejection, he withdrew it and drove him away from the land. Now in restoration, Yahweh brings him back and puts him in the land to possess it.

לכן הנה־ימים באים נאם־יהוה ולא־יאמר עוד הי־יהוה
אשר העלה את־בני ישראל מארץ מצרים: כי אם־חי־
יהוה אשר העלה את־בני ישראל מארץ צפון ומכל
הארצות אשר הדיחם שמה והשבתים על־אדמתם אשר
נתתי לאבותם:

> "Therefore behold, days are coming," declares Yahweh, "when it will no longer be said, 'As Yahweh lives, who brought up the sons of Israel out of the land of Egypt,' but 'As Yahweh lives, who brought the sons of Israel from the land of the north and from all the countries where He had banished them.' For I will restore them to their own land which I gave to their fathers." (Jer. 16:14-15)

Two epithets of Yahweh are introduced here. One is based on the context of past election and the other on that of future restoration. The parallel is that as Yahweh's redemptive act of exodus was a historical event in the past, so the return of Israel from exile by the help of Yahweh will be equally sure to come. At that time Yahweh will be worshiped on the basis of that future saving act from captivity, just as he had been worshiped till then on the basis of the past event of deliverance. Yahweh's future saving act for Israel is that he brings them back and restores them to their own land which he gave to their fathers. Therefore, we can see that the restoration is viewed as Israel's return to their own land from the dispersion. In Jer. 12:15, Yahweh clearly specifies that his restoration of Israel is his bringing Israel back to their inheritance, to their land. This idea can also be found in Jer. 30:3; 31:4; Ezek. 11:17; 34:27; 36:8, 24,28,35; 47:13-23; Amos 9:13-15; Joel 2:18; Ps. 105:43-45.

4) "My Delight Is in Her" (חפצי־בה), "Married" (בעולה)

In rejection, the land was to be desolated, defiled, and forsaken. In restoration, however, this aspect of rejection is reversed. Is. 62:4-5 presents a significant aspect of restoration with respect to the land.

לא־יאמר לך עוד עזובה ולארצך לא־יאמר עוד שממה
כי לך יקרא חפצי־בה ולארצך בעולה
כי־חפץ יהוה בך וארצך תבעל:
כי־יבעל בחור בתולה יבעלוך בניך
ומשוש חתן על־כלה ישיש עליך אלהיך:

It will no longer be said to you, "Forsaken,"
Nor to your land will it any longer be said, "Desolate";
But you will be called, "My delight is in her,"
And your land, "Married";
For Yahweh delights in you,
And to Him your land will be married.[41]
For as a young man marries a virgin,
So your sons will marry you;
And as the bridegroom rejoices over the bride,
So your God will rejoice over you.

This prophecy again presents new names for Zion (Is. 60:14) and the land which will replace the old ones. During the period of rejection, Zion was called "Forsaken" (עזובה). But at the time of restoration, it will be called "My delight is in you" (חפצי־בה). As for the land, it has been called "Desolate" (שממה), but hereafter it will be called "Married" (בעולה), because Yahweh delights in Zion as the young bridegroom rejoices over his virgin bride and the land accepts the inhabitants of Zion. The concept of the sons' marriage to the land is puzzling. However, the report of the tribal leaders of Israel who came back from spying out the land of Canaan provides a suggestion for understanding this imagery. They said: "The land through which we have gone, in spying it out, is a land that devours its inhabitants; and all the people whom we saw in it are men of great size" (Num. 13:32). According to this description, the land did not seem to be a place which would accept them as dwellers. Thus, during the period of rejection the mountains of Israel were called "a devourer of men and bereaver of the nation of children" (Ezek. 36:13). In the time of restoration, however, they will no longer be so called, because "you will no longer devour men, and no longer bereave your nation of children" (36:14). The land will be cultivated

41. The NASB insertion of "to Him" in verse 4 is totally misleading, since the context provides the notion of Yahweh's marriage to the land. But verse 5, "your sons will marry you," makes it clear that "your sons" indicates the people of the land and "you" refers to the land.

and sown and it will put forth branches and bear fruit for the people of Yahweh. Yahweh will multiply man and beast on that land and cause it to be inhabited as it was in former days (36:8-11). Thus, the concept of marriage between the inhabitants and the land in Is. 62:5 can be explained in terms of the land's acceptability of the inhabitants. In that day, "They will say, 'This desolate land has become like the garden of Eden; and the waste, desolate, and ruined cities are fortified and inhabited' " (Ezek. 36:35).

Therefore, Yahweh not only brings his people back to their own lands, but also renews the desolate wasteland for his people returning from the exile to inhabit.

(4) Yahweh Will Buy Back Israel

In rejection, Yahweh sold his people Israel as slaves and made them serve Nebuchadnezzar (Jer. 17:4; 27:4,17; 28:14; 40:9). In restoration, Yahweh buys back his people.

כי־כה אמר יהוה חנם נמכרתם ולא בכסף תגאלו:

For thus says Yahweh, "You were sold for nothing and you will be redeemed without money." (Is. 52:3).

Since גאל, which is rendered "to redeem," is in contrast to מכר (to sell) in the same verse, "to buy" would be a more accurate rendering here than "to redeem." קנה also carries the same meaning.

והיה ביום ההוא יוסיף אדני שנית ידו
לקנות את־שאר עמו אשר ישאר מאשור וממצרים
ומפתרוס ומכוש ומעילם ומשנער ומחמת ומאיי הים:

Then it will happen on that day that the Lord
Will again recover the second time with His hand
The remnant of His people, who will remain,
From Assyria, Egypt, Pathros, Cush, Elam, Shinar, Hamath,
And from the islands of the sea. (Is. 11:11)

On the day of restoration Yahweh will stretch out his hand again and will deliver his people. As he redeemed Israel out of Egypt, he will again purchase (קנה) it out of all the countries named. Therefore, this will be Yahweh's second redemption of Israel.[42]

42. KD, *Isaiah*, p. 289.

Even though Israel was sold for nothing (Is. 52:3), in restoration Yahweh will pay the ransom.

> For I am Yahweh your God,
> The Holy One of Israel, Your Savior;
> I have given Egypt as your ransom,
> Cush and Seba in your palce.
> Since you are precious in My sight,
> Since you are honored and I love you,
> I will give other men in your place and other peoples in exchange
>   for your life. (Is. 43:3-4)

Once Tyre, Sidon, and Philistia sold the sons of Judah and Jerusalem to the Greeks (Joel 3:3, 6). But Yahweh is going to arouse them from the place where they sold them, and return their recompense on their head. On that day Yahweh will sell their children into the hand of the sons of Judah. "'Also I will sell your sons and your daughters into the hand of the sons of Judah, and they will sell them to the Sabeans, to a distant nation,' for Yahweh has spoken" (Joel 3:8). The fortune of Israel is completely restored.

When Yahweh redeems Israel, they will be his servants. At that time Israel will be called his chosen servant.

ואתה ישראל עבדי יעקב אשר בחרתיך
זרע אברהם אהבי:
אשר החזקתיך מקצות הארץ ומאציליה קראתיך
ואמר לך עבדי־אתה בחרתיך ולא מאסתיך:

> But, you, Israel, My servant,
> Jacob whom I have chosen,
> Descendant of Abraham My friend.
> You whom I have taken from the ends of the earth,
> And called from its remotest parts,
> And said to you, "You are My servant,
> I have chosen you and not rejected you." (Is. 41:8-9)

The clause "You whom I have taken from the ends of the earth, and called from its remotest parts" suggests that this taking and calling refers to the future restoration of Israel. Yahweh's choosing of Israel is not a second one or a new one. He had already chosen them to be his servants before the time of their dispersal to the ends of the earth, and he did not reject them completely. Yahweh's choosing Israel was still effective even during the period of exile. When Yahweh restores them, however, he calls them again saying, "You are

My servant, I have chosen you and not rejected you." The Servant Songs of Isaiah are full of this idea (42:1; 43:10; 44:1-2,21; 45:4; 48:20; 49:3-6; 52:13; 54:17; 56:6; 65:8-16; 66:14; cf. also Jer. 46:27-28; Ezek. 28:25; 37:25).

One point to be noted here is that when Israel is introduced as Yahweh's servant in the context of restoration, Yahweh is sometimes presented as the king of Israel, the master (Is. 41:21; 43:15; 44:6). When Yahweh buys Israel back and restores the status of his people's servanthood, he will appoint them as "a light of the nations" (49:6) so that his salvation may reach to the ends of the earth, and he will use them as his witnesses through whom he shall show his glory (49:3). Therefore, at the time of restoration the task of Israel as his servant will become enlarged and universal in its character.

(5) Yahweh Will Plant Israel Again

Yahweh uprooted Israel in rejection. But now Yahweh plants them again in their land.

ושמתי עיני עליהם לטובה והשבתים על־הארץ הזאת
ובניתים ולא אהרס ונטעתים ולא אתוש: ונתתי להם
לב לדעת אתי כי אני יהוה והיו־לי לעם ואנכי אהיה
להם לאלהים כי־ישבו אלי בכל־לבם:

For I will set My eyes on them for good, and I will bring them again to this land; and I will build them up and not overthrow them, and I will plant them and not pluck them up. And I will give them a heart to know Me, for I am Yahweh; and they will be My people, and I will be their God, for they will return to Me with their whole heart.

(Jer. 24:6-7)

Yahweh's setting his eyes on them for good, bringing them again to this land, building them up, and planting them are all his works of restoring his people in the future. At that time the relationship between Yahweh as their God and Israel as his people will be reestablished. In particular, we can see here that the concepts of "building up" (בנה) and "planting" (נטע) are the opposites of the rejection ideas "to overthrow" (הרס) and "pluck up" (נתש) (cf. Jer. 42:10).

זרע carries the same idea of restoration as נטע in the future tense (Hos. 2:25 [E. 23]). In Jer. 31:27, Yahweh is said to sow the house of Israel and the house of Judah with the seed of man and the seed of beast. Hosea describes the scene on the day that Yahweh plants and sows Israel again as follows:

> I will be like the dew to Israel;
> He will blossom like the lily,
> And he will take root like the cedars of Lebanon.
> His shoots will sprout,
> And his beauty will be like the olive tree,
> And his fragrance like the cedars of Lebanon.
> Those who live in his shadow
> Will again raise grain,
> And they will blossom like the vine.
> His renown will be like the wine of Lebanon. (Hos.14:6-8 [E. 5-7])

When Yahweh heals the apostasy of Israel, he will be like "dew" to Israel, which promotes the life and growth of plants. On that day Israel will take root (ויך שרשיו), and his shoot will sprout and blossom. The fame of Israel will be restored again like that of the cedars and wine of Lebanon. The Song of the Vineyard will be sung again (Is. 27:1-7).

(6) Yahweh Will Gather His Flock Again

The imagery which portrayed Yahweh as a shepherd is also seen in the context of restoration. In contrast to rejection, Yahweh as a shepherd gathers together his dispersed sheep from the land of exile and feeds them.

> ואני אקבץ את־שארית צאני מכל הארצות אשר־הדחתי
> אתם שם והשבתי אתהן על־נוהן ופרו ורבו:

> Then I Myself shall gather the remnant of My flock out of all the countries where I have driven them and shall bring them back to their pasture; and they will be fruitful and multiply. (Jer. 23:3)

As a restoration term, קבץ is also found in Dt. 30:34; Is. 11:12; 40:11; 43:5; 54:7; Jer. 29:14; 31:8,10; Ezek. 20:34,42; 34:13; 36:24; 37:21; Mic. 2:12; 4:6; Nah. 3:18; Zech. 10:10.

אסף carries the same meaning as קבץ.

> אסף אאסף יעקב כלך קבץ אקבץ שארית ישראל
> יחד אשימנו כצאן בצרה כעדר בתוך הדברו תהימנה מאדם:

I will surely assemble all of you, Jacob,
I will surely gather the remnant of Israel.
I will put them together like sheep in the fold;
Like a flock in the midst of its pasture
They will be noisy with men. (Mic. 2:12)

Yahweh, assembling and gathering the remnant of Israel, is pictured as a shepherd who gathers his flock in the pasture. The same usage of אסף is also found in Is. 11:12; Jer. 21:4; Ezek. 11:17.

When Yahweh gathers his sheep, he will feed (רעה) and lead (נהל) them. He will not devour them; rather he will take care of them.

כרעה עדרו ירעה בזרעו יקבץ טלאים ובחיקו ישא עלות ינהל:

Like a shepherd He will tend His flock,
In His arm He will gather the lambs,
And carry them in His bosom;
He will gently lead the nursing ewes. (Is. 40:11)

According to Jer. 50:19, Yahweh will bring Israel back to the pasture lands of Carmel and Bashan, and they will be satisfied in the hill country of Ephraim and Gilead (cf. Ezek. 34:14,15; Mic. 7:14).

In contrast to the rejection imagery in which Israel became a prey for all the beasts of the field, Micah compares the remnant of Israel to a young lion among the beasts of the forest in restoration.

והיה שארית יעקב בגוים בקרב עמים רבים
כאריה בבהמות יער ככפיר בעדרי־צאן
אשר אם־עבר ורמס וטרף ואין מציל:

And the remnant of Jacob
Will be among the nations,
Among many peoples
Like a young lion among the beasts of the forest,
Like a young lion among flocks of sheep,
Which, if he passes through,
Tramples down and tears,
And there is none to rescue. (Mic. 5:7 [E.8])

(7) Yahweh Will Rebuild Israel

Since Yahweh is viewed as a builder of Israel in election, he is portrayed as her rebuilder in the context of restoration.

והשבתי את־שבות יהודה ואת שבות ישראל ובנתים כבראשנה:

I will restore the fortunes [i.e., captivity] of Judah and the fortunes of Israel, and I will rebuild them as they were at first. (Jer. 33:7)

The verb בנה implies the meaning of rebuilding in this context. In Jer. 31:3, עוד (again) is added to specify the meaning.

עוד אבנך ונבנית בתולת ישראל
עוד תעדי תפיך ויצאת במחול משחקים:

Again I will build you, and you shall be rebuilt,
O virgin of Israel!
Again you shall take up your tambourines,
And go forth to the dances of the merrymakers.

(8) Yahweh Will Cleanse Israel

In restoration, Yahweh cleanses his defiled people.

ולא יטמאו עוד בגלוליהם ובשקוציהם ובכל פשעיהם
והושעתי אותם מכל מושבתיהם אשר חטאו בהם וטהרתי
אותם והיו־לי לעם ואני אהיה להם לאלהים:

And they will no longer defile themselves with their idols, or with their detestable things, or with any of their transgressions; but I will deliver them from all their dwelling places in which they have sinned, and will cleanse them. And they will be My people, and I will be their God. (Ezek. 37:23)

Because the Israelites defiled themselves by worshiping foreign gods, Yahweh also defiled them. In restoration, the people will no longer defile themselves and Yahweh will cleanse (טהר) them from their sins of apostasy.

Ezekiel 36:24-28 describes Yahweh's cleansing and renewing of Israel:

ולקחתי אתכם מן־הגוים וקבצתי אתכם מכל־הארצות
והבאתי אתכם אל־אדמתכם: וזרקתי עליכם מים
טהורים וטהרתם מכל טמאותיכם ומכל־גלוליכם אטהר
אתכם: ונתתי לכם לב חדש ורוח חדשה אתן בקרבכם
והסרתי את־לב האבן מבשרכם ונתתי לכם לב בשר:
ואת־רוחי אתן בקרבכם ועשיתי את אשר־בחקי תלכו
ומשפטי תשמרו ועשיתם: וישבתם בארץ אשר נתתי
לאבתיכם והייתם לי לעם ואנכי אהיה לכם לאלהים:

> For I will take you from the nations, gather you from all the lands, and bring you into your own land. Then I will sprinkle clean water on you, and you will be clean; I will cleanse you from all your filthiness and from all your idols. Moreover I will give you a new heart and put a new spirit within you; and I will remove the heart of stone from your flesh and give you a heart of flesh. And I will put My Spirit within you and cause you to walk in My statutes, and you will be careful to observe My ordinances. And you will live in the land that I gave to your forefathers; so you will be My people, and I will be your God.

On the day that Yahweh brings the Israelites back to their own land, he will cleanse them. Sprinkling clean water on a sinful man is a required rite in the Law of Moses for purification (Num. 19:4ff.). By sprinkling, Yahweh is going to cleanse all the filthiness of the Israelites. Furthermore, he will remove the heart of stone from them and give them a new heart and he will put his spirit within and cause them to walk in his statues and keep his ordinances (Hos. 6:5 [E. 7:1]; 14:4; Joel 3:1 [E. 2:28]).

Yahweh is about to renew Israel entirely. After that, the Yahweh-Israel relationship will be reestablished. We can also note here the election formula "You will be My people, and I will be your God." Therefore, cleansing is one of the essential parts of Yahweh's restoration of Israel. Thus, they will be called "The holy people, the redeemed of Yahweh" (Is. 62:12).

CHAPTER IV

The New Testament Reflections

In describing the exclusive relationship between God and his people, the New Testament refers or alludes to many Old Testament texts. Many metaphors found in the Hebrew Bible are also used in the New Testament. However, their meanings are expanded or the objects of comparison in the metaphors are changed from the relationship between Yahweh and Israel to the relationship between Jesus and the disciples or between Jesus and believers.

1. THE BELIEVERS AS THE BRIDE OF JESUS

We have seen that one of the key election metaphors in the Old Testament was that of marriage. In the New Testament this metaphor is used by John the Baptist, by Jesus himself, and by Paul to describe the relationship between Jesus and believers. Jesus is portrayed as the bridegroom and those who believe in him as his bride.

(1) John 3:22-30

When Jesus begins to baptize people, many come to him. The disciples of John the Baptist seem to be frustrated, since Jesus attracts more people than their teacher does. Therefore, they come to him

241

and report the situation. John, however, makes it clear that he is not the Christ (v. 28) and casts himself in the role of a friend of the bridegroom and Jesus in that of the bridegroom (v. 29). "You yourselves bear me witness, that I said, 'I am not the Christ,' but, 'I have been sent before Him.' He who has the bride is the bridegroom; but the friend of the bridegroom, who stands and hears him, rejoices greatly because of the bridegroom's voice. And so this joy of mine has been made full" (Jn. 3:28-29). Here John makes two significant points. First of all, Jesus, not John, is both the Christ and the bridegroom, and the friend of the bridegroom is John himself. John describes himself as the groom's best friend who takes care of arranging the wedding.[1] Moses was given this role in the marriage between God and Israel, since the Sinai covenant was construed as a wedding between them, with Moses as the mediator. Paul also claims this role in 2 Cor. 11:2, "For I am jealous; for I betrothed you to one husband, that to Christ I might present you as a pure virgin."[2] The second point is that John describes the relationship between Jesus and his people in terms of the bridegroom-bride metaphor, where the bride refers to the people who came to Jesus and were baptized by him.[3] This analogy is obviously borrowed from the Old Testament theme of marriage between Yahweh and Israel.[4]

(2) Mark 2:19

In his answer to the question of John's disciples and of the Pharisees as to why his disciples did not fast, Jesus says: "While the bridegroom is with them, the attendants of the bridegroom do not fast, do they? So long as they have the bridegroom with them, they cannot fast" (Mk. 2:19; Mt. 9:15; Lk. 5:34). Jesus refers to himself

1. Raymond E. Brown, *The Gospel According to John,* 2 vols., AB (Garden City: Doubleday, 1966-1970), 1:152.

2. Ibid.

3. J.O.F. Murray interprets this: "In some real sense the Baptist testified that God Himself was in Christ betrothing His bride to Himself afresh" *(Jesus According to St. John* [London and Edinburgh, 1951]), cited by L. Morris, *The Gospel According to John,* NICNT (Grand Rapids: Eerdmans, 1971), p. 241.

4. Cf. A.J.H. Bernard, *A Critical and Exegetical Commentary on the Gospel According to St. John,* ICC (Edinburgh: T. & T. Clark, 1928), pp. 130-31.

as the groom, while the wedding guests represent his disciples.[5] Jesus does not identify, however, who the bride is. Nevertheless, the self-description of Jesus as a bridegroom hints at his understanding of the nature of the relationship between himself and his people.

(3) Ephesians 5:22-33

In this paragraph, Paul deals primarily with the husband-wife relationship and compares it with the relationship of Christ with his church. Paul suggests the following parallel points.

First of all, headship is one of the significant parallel points. As the husband is the head of his wife, Christ is the head of his church. This headship requires subjection of their counterparts (vv. 22, 24) in everything.

The second parallel point is love. Husbands are to love their wives as Christ loves the church and tenderly nourishes and cherishes her (v. 25). Christ gave up his life for the church and sanctified her by the washing of water. Thus, the church as well as the wives are required to be holy and blameless (v. 27).

Third, the union of husband and wife is parallel to the union of Christ and his church. As Gen. 2:24 indicates, the husband and wife become one flesh by marriage (Eph. 5:31), so Christ and his church constitute one body (v. 30). The head of the body is Christ and the members of the body are the members of his church. It is noteworthy that Paul views the Christ-church relationship in terms of the husband-wife relationship, particuarly in the headship, love, and union of the male figures with their counterparts. As M. Barth pointed out, Paul must have taken up the Old Testament imagery of husband-wife and developed it to a deeper level by means of the Christian's relationship to his savior.[6] According to this parallel-

5. οἱ υἱοὶ τοῦ νυμφῶνος means literally "the sons of bridal-chamber." It is a Hebraism, indicating the wedding guests who are most closely connected with the bridegroom (W. Bauer, *A Greek English Lexicon of the New Testament,* trans. and ed. W.F. Arndt and F.W. Gingrich [Chicago: University of Chicago Press, 1957], p. 547). See Norval Geldenhuys, *Commentary on the Gospel of Luke,* NICNT (Grand Rapids: Eerdmans, 1951), p. 197.

6. Markus Barth, *Ephesians,* 2 vols., AB (Garden City: Doubleday, 1974), 2:693. See also Francis Foulkes, The *Epistle of Paul to the Ephesians,* Tyndale New Testament Commentaries (Grand Rapids: Eerdmans, 1963), p. 156.

ism, the Christians of the New Testament replace the Old Testament people of Israel and Christ replaces Yahweh.

(4) Revelation 19:6-8

In his vision on the island of Patmos, John heard a great voice: "'Hallelujah! For the Lord our God, the Almighty, reigns. Let us rejoice and be glad and give the glory to Him, for the marriage of the Lamb has come and His bride has made herself ready.' And it was given to her to clothe herself in fine linen, bright and clean; for the fine linen is the righteous acts of the saints" (Rev. 19:6-8).

In the Johannine literature, the Lamb or the Lamb of God is a peculiar title for Jesus (ὁ ἀμνός [Jn. 1:29,36]; τὸ ἀρνίον [Rev. 5:7,9; 6:1]). His bride has made herself ready for the marriage by clothing herself in fine linen, bright and clean, which is the righteous act of the saints, according to John's explanation. Thus it is obvious that the "bride" of the Lamb refers to the saints.[7] And this figure of marriage denotes the intimate and indissoluble union of saints with Christ which is to be consummated at the end time.

Therefore, the marriage metaphor flows consistently from the Old Testament to the New to denote the intimate divine-human relationship. In the New Testament, however, Jesus is substituted for Yahweh and Christians replace Israel. This alludes to the divine lordship of Jesus and the continuity of Israel in the church. The role of John the Baptist and of Paul in establishing the relationship is also noteworthy as it parallels that of Moses in the Old Testament.

2. THE BELIEVERS AS THE SOLDIERS OF CHRIST

As Yahweh is portrayed as a divine warrior for his people in the Old Testament, Jesus is described as a warrior who fights for his saints in the New Testament. The Old Testament imagery, of course, persists in the post-exilic literature such as the books of Maccabees and the Dead Sea Scrolls.[8]

7. G.R. Beasley-Murray, *The Book of Revelation*, NCBC (Grand Rapids: Eerdmans, 1981), pp. 273-74; J. Massyngberde Ford, *Revelation*, AB (Garden City: Doubleday, 1975), pp. 310, 317.

8. 2 Macc. 3:22-30, 1QM12:6-11; 19:2-4. See Ford, *Revelation*, p. 319.

The ministry of Jesus is viewed as a kind of battle to establish his kingdom against the opposing forces. However, this battle is elevated to the spiritual level. Even though Jesus confronts the contemporary religious and political leaders, this is not his ultimate battle. We see his struggle reaching a climax on the cross, and through his victory over the satanic power, the saints are released from the bonds of death and bestowed with eternal life. We will examine below the nature of Jesus' ministry from the perspective of a divine warrior for the saints.

(1) Jesus, the Divine Warrior

The confrontation of Jesus with Satan and his exorcism are constantly observed throughout Jesus' earthly ministry. Mt. 12:22-31 is particularly significant for our thesis. When Jesus was accused of casting out demons by Beelzebul (Mt. 12:24), he explains the nature of his ministry as a battle against Satan. According to him, there are two opposing kingdoms: the kingdom of God (v. 28) and kingdom of Satan (v. 26). Each kingdom has its constituent members, whose warriors are Jesus and Beelzebul (v. 24). These two kingdoms confront each other in order to extend their own territories. Jesus presents himself as a warrior to fight for the demon-possessed against Beelzubul and to bring the power of the kingdom of God against him. Thus, Jesus' ministry can be said to be a kind of holy war against Satan,[9] and the cross can be understood as his last battle to establish the kingdom of God and deliver his people who are under the power of Satan.

Paul perceives this and proclaims that Christ disarmed the rulers and authorities by his cross.

> And when you were dead in your transgressions and the uncircumcision of your flesh, He made you alive together with Him, having forgiven us all our trangressions, having cancelled out the certificate of debt consisting of decrees against us and which was hostile to us; and He has taken it out of the way, having nailed it to the cross. When He had disarmed the rulers and authorities, He made a public display of them, having triumphed over them through Him.
>
> (Col. 2:13-15)

9. See O. Betz, "Jesu Heiliger Krieg," *Novum Testamentum* 2 (1958): 129.

As T. Longman indicated, "disarm" (ἀπεκδύομαι) is a military term.[10] The rulers and authorities, referring to Satan's armies, are subdued by Christ on the cross. As a result, sinners who are under the control of these powers are freed from their sin and death. We gain victory over death through Christ Jesus (1 Cor. 15:57) by whom God always leads us in triumph. Therefore, we find that salvation is explained in terms of the concept of a holy war and its language.

Particularly, the imagery of Jesus Christ as divine warrior in Revelation is noteworthy. Rev. 19:11ff. describes the second coming of Christ by employing the military imagery reminiscent of the divine warrior passages in the Old Testament. The white horse section begins with the appearance of Christ as a warrior. He wages war in righteousness (v. 11). His eyes are a flame of fire, and upon his head are many diadems (v. 12). He is clothed with a robe dipped in blood (v. 13).[11] From his mouth comes a sharp sword, with which he may smite the nations (v. 15). The heavenly armies, clothed in fine linen, white and clean, follow him on white horses. In contrast, the enemy forces designated as the beast[12] along with the kings of the earth and their armies gather together to make war against him who sat upon the horse and against his army (v. 19). In the battle, the beast is seized together with the false prophet and cast alive into the lake of the fire. The rest are killed by the sword of the rider on the white horse. Afterward the birds eat their flesh (vv. 19-21). This passage obviously describes Christ's second coming and his remaining battle against the hellish warrior.

Thus, Jesus' past earthly ministry as well as his remaining future ministry are basically seen as a holy war against Satan and his kingdom. By destroying this kingdom, Jesus establishes the kingdom of God. Since Jesus wages war against the hellish warrior, he

10. Tremper Longman III, "The Divine Warrior: The New Testament Use of an Old Testament Motif," *WTJ* 44 (1982): 303.

11. This is the imagery of Yahweh as a divine warrior in Is. 63:3; Joel 4:13 (E. 3:13).

12. This refers to the hellish warrior of Rev. 13, who is contrasted to Jesus Christ, the divine warrior, who has ten diadems (13:1) vs. Christ's many diadems; Christ's name as the "Word of God" (19:13) vs. the blasphemous name on the beast's head (13:1b), and the number of the beast that conceals a name. "P.W. Skehan argues that the beast has a number 666 which conceals his name and that Christ has a name (King of Kings and Lord of Lords) which when converted to Aramaic and added up results in 777" ("King of Kings, Lord of Lords, Rev. 19:16," *CBQ* 10 [1948]: 398; cited from Longman, *WTJ* 44 [1982]: 299).

levies his army and trains them to participate in a holy war. Therefore, his choosing the twelve disciples (Mt. 10:1-4; Mk. 3:14-19; Lk. 6:12-16), his sending out the seventy (Lk. 10:1-12), and Paul's exhortation for the saints to fight the good fight (1 Tim. 6:12) are to be understood in terms of this analogy.

(2) Jesus Chooses His Disciples

Since the focus of Jesus' ministry is the battle against satanic power, his choosing the twelve disciples is also closely related to battle. Jesus calls them for his earthly army as Yahweh called Israel in the Old Testament. In the call narrative of the Synoptic Gospels we can easily trace this interpretation.

First of all, the Greek terms προσκαλέω (Mt. 10:1; Mk 3:13) and προφωνέω (Lk. 6:13), which are translated as "to summon" or "to call," may be used as military terms clothed with the election idea, as in the Old Testament. These terms are employed when the military leader summons (קרא) his people as war breaks out. ἐκλέγω ("to choose," Lk. 6:13) and ποιέω ("to appoint," Mk 3:14) are election terms whose connotation may be traced back to the military usage of בחר and פקד we examined in chapter I.

Second, the purpose of Jesus' choosing the twelve disciples is to give them authority over demons and let them cast demons out (Mt. 10:1; Mk. 3:14; 6:7; Lk. 9:1). Preaching the kingdom of God (Mk. 3:14; Lk. 9:2) is also one of the main purposes of Jesus' choosing the twelve. However, we observed already that the kingdom of God was established by the victory of Jesus over satanic power and Satan's kingdom. It is, therefore, obvious that Jesus called his disciples to his holy war on earth.

Jesus is keenly aware of this aspect of holy war against demons and sends his disciples out as warriors. In Lk. 10:1, Jesus appoints seventy others and sends them to every city and place where he himself was going. He commands them to say, "The kingdom of God has come near to you" (10:9,11) and gives some other instructions (10:2-11). When the seventy return, they report with joy, "Lord, even the demons are subject to us in Your name" (10:17), and he responds that he was "watching Satan fall from heaven like lightning" (10:18). Further, he reminds them that he has given them "authority to tread upon serpents and scorpions, and over all the power of the enemy" (10:19). The coming of the kingdom of God brings the fall of Satan from heaven. Even though his disciples do not recognize that it was a holy war, they participate in it and enjoy the victory since he gave them authority and power to confront the enemy. Accordingly the disciples are called to a holy war.

(3) The Believers, the Soldiers of Christ

The idea that the disciples are the army of Christ is extended to the saints, particularly in Pauline literature. In 2 Tim. 2:3-4, Paul says that Christ enlisted the saints as soldiers and designated them as στρατιώτης Χριστοῦ 'Ιησοῦ (a soldier of Christ Jesus). Furthermore, Paul reminds the Ephesians that the Christian life is warfare. "For our struggle is not against flesh and blood, but against the rulers, against the powers, against the world forces of this darkness, against the spiritual forces of wickedness in the heavenly places" (Eph. 6:12). Even though πάλη ("struggle" or "wrestling") is not a war term, but rather a sport term meaning a hand-to-hand fight like wrestling,[13] the context clearly describes a "spiritual war" and "spiritual weapons." Furthermore, the parallel passage in 2 Cor. 10:3-4 should be understood in the context of war.[14] The enemy forces against which Christians should fight are rulers, powers, the world forces of this darkness, and spiritual forces of wickedness in heavenly places. These titles refer to the hosts of opponents against God and to the location of the devil's reign.[15]

In order to confront the devil, Paul exhorts the saints to put on the full armor of God (Eph. 6:11,13; cf. Is. 59:17; 1 Thess. 5:8): loins girded with truth, the breastplate of righteousness, feet shod with the preparation of the gospel of peace, the shield of faith, the helmet of salvation, and the sword of the Spirit, i.e., the word of God (Eph. 6:14-17).

Therefore, we can safely conclude that the New Testament

13. According to Barth (*Ephesians*, 2:764), just as Plato and Philo mixed the metaphors of sport and war, so Paul appears to have conflated them in order to avoid a tragic-dualistic worldview that life is a battle and war is the father of all things.

14. Ralph P. Martin, *2 Corinthians*, Word Biblical Commentary (Waco, Texas: Word Books, 1986), p. 305.

15. M. Barth, *Ephesians*, 2:764, 800-803.

writers took over the Old Testament motif of holy war to convey the nature of Christ's ministry, the relationship between Christ and believers, and the nature of the Christian life.

3. THE BELIEVERS AS THE FELLOW HEIRS WITH CHRIST

The imagery of father-son for the relationsip between Yahweh and Israel and its related idea of adoption are used to explain the basic doctrine of Christian salvation in the New Testament. In particular, John and Paul develop this idea of sonship and describe the relationship between God and the believer.

According to Paul, God's adoption of Israel as sons is a privilege bestowed upon the Israelites, his kinsmen (Rom. 9:4). Now this privilege is extended to the Gentiles by the will of the Father and through the mediation of the Son and the Holy Spirit. The overall plan of God's salvation is "the revealing of the sons of God" (Rom. 8:19). "But when the fulness of the time came, God sent forth His Son, born of a woman, born under the Law, in order that He might redeem those who were under the Law, that we [Gentiles] might receive the adoption as sons" (Gal. 4:4-5). Paul sees the Holy Spirit, who is the Spirit of God's Son (Gal. 4:6), as the agent in this process of adoption. Thus, he designates the Holy Spirit as the spirit of adoption (Rom. 8:15).[16] The spirit of adoption causes them to cry out to God, "Abba! Father!" and the Spirit bears witness that the believers are children of God (Rom. 8:15; Gal. 4:6). Therefore, we who are being led by the Spirit of God are sons of God (Rom. 8:14), and we are all sons of God through faith in Christ (Gal. 3:26). As in the Old Testament this adoption also entails the privilege of being heirs, heirs of God and fellow heirs with Christ (Rom. 8:17), so that the New Testament believers will inherit the kingdom of God (1 Cor. 6:9,10; 15:50; Gal. 5:21; Eph. 5:5).

Similarly, in Mt. 25:34, Jesus says that the kingdom is pre-

16. According to C.E.B. Cranfield, πνεῦμα υἱοθεσίας is "the Spirit who brings about adoption, uniting men with Christ and so making them sharers in His sonship" (*A Critical and Exegetical Commentary on the Epistle to the Romans,* 2 vols., ICC [Edinburgh: T. & T. Clark, 1975-1979], 1:397).

pared from the foundation of the world and is to be inherited by his sheep from the Father. In Luke this inheritance is mentioned in the context of election by saying that "your Father has chosen gladly to give you the kingdom" (Lk.12:32).

According to John, becoming a child of God is open to anyone who receives Jesus and believes in his name (Jn. 1:12). By his great love the believers are called the children of God, and it has not appeared as yet what they shall be, but when he appears, they shall be like him, because they shall see him just as he is (1 Jn. 3:1-2). In Revelation, John employs the Old Testament formula of election by describing Yahweh's adoption of Israel as his son: "I will be his God and he will be My son" (Rev. 21:7).

4. THE BELIEVERS AS THE SERVANTS OF CHRIST

The Old Testament metaphor of master-servant in describing the Yahweh-Israel relationship maintains its continuity with that of Christ and his saints. Christ is confessed as Lord and the concept of salvation is explained in commercial terms which we have observed in the Old Testament. However, we will limit our discussion to the buying-selling concept as a way of establishing a relationship between the Lord and his servants.

(1) Natural Men as Slaves of Sin

As Israel was a slave of Pharaoh in Egypt before Yahweh began his saving relationship, so "natural men" are described as "slaves" of sin. "However at that time, when you did not know God, you were slaves [ἐδουλεύσατε] to those which by nature are no gods" (Gal. 4:8). Gal. 4:3 says we are held in bondage (ἤμεθα δεδουλωμένοι) under the elemental things of the world. We are made slaves by being sold to sin. "For we know that the Law is spiritual; but I am of flesh, sold [πεπραμένος] into bondage to sin" (Rom. 7:14). The word πιπράσκω (to sell) is a typical commercial term, particularly used for the sale of humans.[17] Here in Rom. 7:14 it is used to denote the idea of a person losing independence and becoming subject to sin like a bondslave. Having been sold to sin, in Rom. 6:17 man is condemned to be a slave of sin. Thus, we can see that the Old Testament idea of מכר (to sell) is employed to describe the status of man who is under the power of sin.

(2) Christ Bought the Slaves of Sin

Since humans are sold to sin, they must be bought in order to be saved and freed. In relation to Christian salvation, the New Testament writers introduce the buying concept and use commercial terms such as ἀγοράζω, περιποιέω, λυτρόω.

ἀγοράζω is a common term used for the sacral manumission of slaves in Greek literature. In particular attested by the Delphic inscription, the god buys a slave to free him from his owner.[18] In 1 Cor. 6:20 and 7:23, Paul proclaims that "You have been bought [ἠγοράσθητε] with a price." And he exhorts us to glorify God in our body and not to become slaves of men. As F. Büchsel points out, Paul does not specify here who has bought us, or from whom we are bought, or at what cost.[19] In 2 Pet. 2:1 and Rev. 5:8, however, the one who purchased us is indicated as the Master (δεσπότης, 2 Pet. 2:1) and the Lamb (ἀρνίον, Rev. 5:8; 14:3,4), which clearly refer to Jesus Christ. Furthermore, John spells out the price Christ paid for his people, which is his blood.

περιποιέομαι carries the meaning "to preserve" (Lk. 17:33), "to obtain" (1 Tim. 3:13). But Acts 20:28 provides the meaning of pur-

---

17. πιπράσκω in the LXX, usually for the Hebrew מכר, may refer to the sale of humans (Gen. 31:15; Ex. 22:2; Lev. 25:39,42,47-48; Dt. 15:12; Esth. 7:4; Is. 52:3; Ps. 104:17). And in the NT, it is used for selling things and persons with the accusative of things (Mt. 13:46; Acts 2:45; 4:34; 5:4) or persons (Mt. 18:25) with the genitive of price (Mt. 26:9; Mk. 14:5; Jn. 12:5). See Herbert Preisker, "πιπράσκω," TDNT, 6:160.

18. In this case, the god does the slave no real favor, but simply mediates the freedom which he has mostly won for himself. Sacral manumission is for the most part only a legal form of self-manumission. See Friedrich Büchsel, "ἀγοράζω," TDNT, 1:124.

19. Ibid., p. 125.

chasing. Luke says that Jesus purchased (περιποιεῖσθαι) the Church of God with his own blood.

According to Büchsel, λυτρόω is used exclusively for the redeeming act of God or of Jesus. Its usage is basically the same as that of the LXX, and in later Jewish Rabbinic usage it corresponds to גאל and פדה.[20] Its basic meaning is "to free by ransom" and it is translated as "to redeem." However, Peter uses it in the meaning of "buying back by a ransom."[21] "Knowing that you were not redeemed with perishable things like silver or gold from your futile way of life inherited from your forefathers, but with precious blood, as of a lamb unblemished and spotless, the blood of Christ" (1 Pet. 1:18-19). Therefore, we have here the same idea of salvation as when Yahweh bought Israel, expressed by קנה and גאל in the Old Testament. Thus, we may conclude that the New Testament idea of buying and selling is deeply rooted in the Old Testament metaphor of Yahweh's buying and selling of Israel. As Yahweh bought Israel and proclaimed his ownership over them, Jesus also does so (Tit. 2:14; 1 Pet. 2:9).

5. THE BELIEVERS AS THE BRANCH OF THE VINE WHO IS THE CHRIST

In the Old Testament Yahweh is presented very often as the owner of a vineyard, while Israel is pictured as a vine or vineyard. Usually the imagery portrays Yahweh as planting Israel with the expectation of her producing good fruit in his land. This metaphor is also used in the New Testament in order to explain the relationship of God, Christ, and the believer. Jn. 15, Mk. 12:1-10, and Rom. 11 are the major texts to describe the relationship in terms of planter-plant imagery. However, we will focus our discussion mainly on Jn. 15.

At the outset of Jn. 15, Jesus says, "I am the true vine, and My Father is the vinedresser." In verse 5, Jesus explains his relationship to his followers: "I am the vine, you are the branches." Thus, he

20. "λυτρόω," *TDNT,* 4:350.
21. Cf. David Hill, *Greek Words and Hebrew Meanings: Studies in the Semantics of Soteriological Terms* (Cambridge: The University Press, 1967), pp. 70-71.

establishes the relationship between the three persons—the Father, Jesus himself, and the believers—by means of the allegorical features of the gardener, vine, and branches. The portrayal of God the Father as the vinedresser is the same as in the Old Testament. Jesus and his disciples can be identified with the people in the Old Testament who were to bear fruit. However, John develops the inseparable relationship between Jesus and his disciples through the analogy of vine and branches. Jesus identifies himself with his followers by describing himself as the vine and his disciples as branches: "Abide in Me, and I in you. As the branch cannot bear fruit of itself, unless it abides in the vine, so neither can you, unless you abide in Me" (v. 4). Through this metaphor, John emphasizes the organic union of Jesus with his disciples as a means of bearing fruit. It is to be noted that the place and function of Christ is more like a tree, rather than like God, the vinedresser. Jesus is viewed as the ideal Israel. Jesus fulfills the meaning and destiny of "Israel," and he is a "complete personality" replacing Jacob-Israel.[22] Therefore, this metaphor is basically similar to that of the Old Testament. John can be said to take up this imagery from the Old Testament and to develop the relationship of Christ and his disciples as vine and branches.[23]

However, the real point that John is trying to make in this chapter is how to bear much fruit on the basis of the established

22. Cf. John 1:51.

23. As for the background of the imagery of the vine and the branches, Bultmann maintains that John's imagery reflects the oriental myth of the tree of life, sometimes represented as a vine (*The Gospel of John* [Philadelphia: Westminster, 1971], p. 530 n. 5). S. Schulz, in *Komposition und Herunft der johanneischen Reden* (Stuttgart: Kohlhammer, 1960), thinks the best parallels are in the Mandean and Gnostic literature, even if there are Old Testament elements intermixed. The main reson for their rejection of the Old Testament as the background of the imagery of the vine and the branches is that the vine or vineyard stands for Israel, while John identifies the vine with Jesus and not with a people. Jesus is not a stalk but the whole vine, and the branches remain part of the vine. However, as Brown points out (*Gospel According to John*, 2:670), it is a feature of Johannine theology that Jesus applied to himself the terms used in the Old Testament for Israel and in other parts of the New Testament for the Christian community. R. Borig also rightly notes the Johannine transfer of OT collective imagery to a person: "In the OT the imagery of the vine was already associated not only with the community of Israel but also with the picture of an individual person, so that the Johannine transferral of a collective image to a person is already anticipated in Ezekiel's vine symbolism" (*Der wahre Weinstock* [Munich: Kösel, 1967], p. 101; cited from Brown, *Gospel According to John*, 2:671).

relationship between the vine and branches. For the disciples, maintaining a close relationship with Jesus is suggested as the fundamental requirement for bearing fruit. Along with this, Jesus mentions choosing his disciples in verse 16: "You did not choose Me, but I chose you, and appointed you, that you should go and bear fruit, and that your fruit should remain, that whatever you ask of the Father in My name, He may give to you." It is natural for John, who is well versed in the Old Testament imagery, to point out the theme of election here, since election is basically a matter of relationship in the Old Testament.

6. THE BELIEVERS AS THE SHEEP OF JESUS

In the Old Testament, Yahweh is described as a shepherd and Israel as his sheep, the sheep of his pasture. Particularly in Ezek. 34, Yahweh promises that he himself will be the shepherd of the flock and will seek, feed (v. 16), and lead them to rest (v. 15) in the context of future restoration. Surprisingly, in Jn. 10 Jesus alludes to himself as the one mentioned in Ezek. 34 and proclaims that he is the good shepherd (Jn. 10:11), comparing himself with Israel's leaders. He calls them thieves and robbers (v. 8), since they came only to steal, kill, and destroy the sheep. Jesus, however, claims to have come that they might have life and might have it abundantly. Furthermore, he calls them hirelings who leave the sheep when the wolf comes and snatches and scatters them, since they are not the shepherd or the owner of the sheep.

As Brown correctly points out,[24] the background of this imagery of Christ as shepherd can be traced to Ezek. 34. The parallel points between Ezek. 34 and Jn. 10 are numerous. First is the parallel in the characters in the metaphors. The relationship of Yahweh, his people, and the religious leaders is described in terms of the analogy of owner, sheep, and shepherd in Ezek. 34. This same analogy is applied to the relationship of Christ, his followers, and the Pharisees in Jn. 9–10. Second, the parallel language is noteworthy. In Ezek. 34, "slaughtering" (v. 3) and "scattering" (vv. 4, 5) of the sheep are the main accusations of Yahweh against the contem-

24. Raymond E. Brown, *Gospel According to John,* 1:396-97.

porary religious leaders. Christ also uses terms with similar meaning, such as "killing" (θύω), "destroying" (ἀπόλυμι), "scattering"
(σκορπίζω). Both Ezekiel and John use the very meaningful theological term "to know" (ידע, γινώσκω). In Ezek. 34:30-31, Yahweh
declares: "Then they will know [וידעו, καὶ γνώσονται] that I, Yahweh their God, am with them, and that they, the house of Israel,
are My people. . . . As for you, My sheep, the sheep of My pasture,
you are men, and I am your God." The relationship of knowing
described by the term ידע is not simply having knowledge about a
person. Rather, it describes the most intimate human relationship.
It is a theological term for election and covenant. Strikingly enough,
Jesus takes up this term and explains the relationship between him
and his followers, further himself and the Father: "I am the good
shepherd; and I know My own, and My own know Me, even as the
Father knows Me and I know the Father" (Jn. 10:14-15). Third, the
parallel ideas should be regarded as the most significant point. In
Ezek. 34, Yahweh denounces the shepherd of Israel (v. 10) and
promises that he himself will be a shepherd to feed the flock and to
lead them to rest (vv. 11-15). In Jn. 10, Christ condemns the Jewish
leaders and proclaims himself to be "the good shepherd" (v. 14).
Furthermore, he makes it clear that Yahweh's promise to be a shepherd and to set over them one shepherd, his servant David (Ezek.
34:23), is fulfilled in himself. Thus John obviously employs the
shepherd imagery of the Old Testament to picture Christ as the one
whom Yahweh promised to give in Ezek. 34.[25]

The imagery of the shepherd and his flock for the relationship
between Christ and his followers is extended to the apostles (or
church leaders) and the believers in the later stages. In Jn. 21, Jesus
commits his sheep to Peter to feed them. In Acts 20, Paul calls the
elders of the Ephesian church together and reminds them of the fact
that the Holy Spirit has made them overseers and shepherds of the
church of God. "Be on your guard for yourselves and for all the
flock, among which the Holy Spirit has made you overseers, to
shepherd the church of God which He purchased with His own
blood" (Acts 20:28). "The church of God" is implicitly designated
here as the flock or sheep.[26] Thus, the designation "shepherd" is
extended to the elders of the church.[27] Jesus is now called "the chief

25. Cf. ibid., p. 397, against Bultmann.
26. Cf. 1 Pet. 2:25.
27. Cf. 1 Pet. 5:2.

shepherd" (ἀρχιποίμην, 1 Pet. 5:4) and "the great shepherd of the sheep" (τὸν ποιμένα τῶν προβάτων τὸν μέγαν, Heb. 13:20).

At any rate, it is clear to us that the Old Testament picture of Yahweh as a shepherd is continued in the New Testament, particularly in picturing Christ as a shepherd. The New Testament writers force us to acknowledge that the promise of a shepherd in Ezek. 34 is fulfilled in Christ.

7. THE BELIEVERS AS THE HOUSE BUILT UP IN CHRIST

Yahweh is perceived as a maker, builder, creator, or molder of Israel in the Old Testament. Thus Israel is viewed as a house or a clay vessel. The New Testament writers use this imagery for describing either the nature of unity in the Christian community or the sovereignty of God over his people. However, the application of this imagery in the New Testament is slightly different from others which we have seen in the previous metaphors.

The relationship between Yahweh and Israel does not parallel exactly that between Christ and Christians. Israel does correspond to the believers, but Christ is identified as an indispensable member of the Christian body, the cornerstone of the building.

(1) Yahweh as a Builder

1) 1 Corinthians 3:1-23

The Corinthian church had strife among its members. They divided into parties, appealing to Paul, Apollos, Peter, or Christ. To deal with this problem, Paul teaches the nature of the relationship between preachers and believers. The preachers are the servants of the word working together with God for the salvation and spiritual growth of his people. Thus, Paul defines the relationship: "For we are God's fellow workers: you are God's field, God's building" (1 Cor. 3:9). Here, the metaphor of planting and the metaphor of building supplement each other. The primary meaning of οἰκοδομή is the act of building.[28] However, it is also found, as here, simply for a building itself. In this metaphor, the building refers to the Christian community, whose pattern is to be found in the Old Testament (Jer. 1:9ff.; 12:14-16; 24:6).[29] The building belongs to God and its foundation is Jesus Christ (1 Cor. 3:11). Further, in verse 16 Paul proclaims that the church is God's building: "Do you not know that you are a temple of God, and that the Spirit of God dwells in you?" (3:16). Orr and Walther translate ναός θεοῦ ἐστε as "you people are God's temple" in order to indicate that Paul refers to the church rather than individual Christians as a temple of God.[30]

2) Ephesians 2:19-22

By contrasting their status before and after they became Christians, Paul reminds the Gentiles that they were received into the house of God and were incorporated as the constituent parts of God's house (Eph. 2:1-19). In Eph. 2:20-22, as Barth points out,[31] three decisive parts of a building are mentioned: the foundation, the cornerstone, and the whole building. It is clearly specified in the context that the foundation refers to the apostles and prophets, the cornerstone to Christ, and the building to God's household, the saints (v. 19). Thus, the whole building consists of persons rather than of things or ideas. This building has not been completely built. It is under construction even now. The foundation and the cornerstone are laid, and each part is being fitted together into a perfect building. In the same way believers are also being built together into a holy temple in the Lord, a dwelling of God in the Spirit. Here, "God's household" (v. 19), "a holy temple in the Lord" (v. 21), or "a dwelling of God in the Spirit" (v. 22) are all used synonymously, referring to the church, the people of God. Thus, Paul obviously employs the

28. Hans Conzelmann, *1 Corinthians,* Hermeneia (Philadelphia: Fortress, 1975), p. 74.

29. Ibid., p. 75. Cf. Bertil Gärtner, *The Temple and the Community in Qumran and the New Testament: A Comparative Study in the Temple Symbolism of the Qumran Texts and the New Testament* (Cambridge: The University Press, 1965), pp. 56-60.

30. W.F. Orr and J.A. Walther, *1 Corinthians,* AB (Garden City: Doubleday, 1976), p. 168.

31. Markus Barth, *Ephesians,* 1:314.

Old Testament imagery of God's building of Israel for God's building of the church in the New Testament.[32]

3) 1 Peter 2:1-10

In this passage Peter links the imagery of a house with the idea of election.[33] He portrays Christ as "a living stone [λίθον ζῶντα] rejected by men, but choice and precious in the sight of God." God as a builder and the saints as living stones (λίθοι ζῶντες) are being built up into a spiritual house. It is to be noted here that both Christ and the saints are regarded as living stones, as parts of the building. Christ is not the builder of the house; rather he himself is the building. In this sense, Yahweh as the builder of Israel in the Old Testament is parallel to God as the builder of the spiritual house in the New Testament, with Christ as the cornerstone and the saints as its parts.[34]

In relation to this metaphor, Peter goes on to apply the designation of Israel as "a chosen race, a royal priesthood, a holy nation, a people for God's own possession" (Ex. 19:6), and "the people of God" (Hos. 1:10) to the New Testament believers (1 Pet. 2:9-10). All these titles are given by Yahweh exclusively to Israel in the context of election. Therefore, Peter is using the building imagery in association with the idea of election.

(2) Yahweh as a Maker

In the Old Testament, עשׂה is used for Yahweh as the maker of Israel. In Ephesians, Paul uses the corresponding Greek word ποίημα for God as a maker of the saints. "For we are His workmanship [ποίημα], created in Christ Jesus for good works, which God prepared beforehand, that we should walk in them" (Eph. 2:10). Ποίημα generally carries the meaning of "work" (ἔργον). However, it often connotes "a work of art." The addition of the verb κτίζω (to create) in verse 10 suggests that a creative act could be associated with it.[35]

---

32. Cf. Bertil Gärtner, *Temple and Community,* pp. 60-65.
33. Charles Bigg, *A Critical and Exegetical Commentary on the Epistles of St. Peter and St. Jude,* ICC (Edinburgh: T. & T. Clark, 1901), p. 135.
34. Cf. Bertil Gärtner, *Temple and Community,* pp. 72-88.
35. Markus Barth, *Ephesians,* 1:226.

As Yahweh is described as the maker of Israel in the OT,[36] God is here portrayed as the maker of the saints. The designation of the saints as God's creation (Eph. 2:10; Gal. 6:15; 2 Cor. 5:17) implies that the church is the new creation.[37] The building up of congregations and their membership is God's work: his work of salvation as well as of creation. The formula "the creator is savior, and the savior is creator" is one of the significant theological themes for restoration in Isaiah, and Paul seems to be aware of this connection here.[38]

(3) Yahweh as a Molder

The imagery of Yahweh-Israel as the divine potter-clay in the Old Testament is also used by Paul in Rom. 9:19-26 in order to show the sovereignty of God in his election of the Gentiles as his people despite Jewish complaints. Paul compares God to the molder (ὁ πλάσας) or to the potter (ὁ κεραμεύς) and the people, either Jews or Gentiles, to the thing molded (τό πράσμα) or to the clay (ὁ πηλός). He points out two things in this parable. First, the thing molded cannot complain to the molder, "Why did you make me like this?" (v. 20). Second, the potter has the right to make from the same lump of clay one vessel for honorable use and another for common use (v. 21). By the same principle, God can call and elect those who were not his people "My people," as in Hos. 1:10; 2:23.

The conclusion to be drawn from this is that God must be acknowledged to be free to appoint men to various functions in the ongoing course of salvation history for the sake of the fulfillment of his overall purpose.[39] The important point is that Paul employs the imagery of Yahweh as a molder or potter and Israel as the molded or clay and applies it to God and the believers in the New Testament.[40]

---

36. Hos. 8:2; Is. 44:1,2; 51:13; 54:5.
37. Markus Barth, *Ephesians,* 1:243.
38. Ibid.
39. C.E.B. Cranfield, *Romans,* 2:492.
40. Cranfield (ibid.) admits Paul was using a common biblical image of potter-clay here. However, he proposes that Wisd. 15:7 is more suitable background for the use of this imagery.

THE DIVINE ELECTION OF ISRAEL

8. THE BELIEVERS AS THE HOLY PEOPLE OF GOD

We observed that the idea of holiness' was closely associated with the idea of election in the Old Testament. Peter directly applies the typical Old Testament designation of Israel as "a chosen race, a royal priesthood, a holy nation, a people for God's own possession" to the New Testament believers (1 Pet. 2:9). Here, race (γένος), nation (ἔθνος), and people (λαός) are titles referring to the elect people of God, that is, Israel in the Old Testament (Ex. 19:6; Is. 43).⁴¹ The modifiers of those titles, ἐκλεκτόν, ἅγιον, and εἰς περιποίησιν supplement the idea of election. As Charles Bigg correctly points out, the nation is holy (ἅγιος) because it is separated from the other nations and consecrated to the service of God.⁴² The term does not necessarily carry any cultic, ceremonial, or ethical concept of holiness.

Then how are those titles shared with Gentile believers and closely associated with the idea of election in the New Testament? In the introductory paragraph of his epistle to the Romans, Paul states: "And you also are among those who are called to belong to Jesus Christ. To all in Rome who are loved by God and called to be saints . . ." (NIV Rom 1:6-7). The majority of Roman Christians were probably included among the Gentiles before they became Christians. But they were called to belong to Jesus Christ (κλήτοι Ἰησοῦ Χριστοῦ) and to be saints (κλήτοι ἅγιοι) and to be the loved ones of God (ἀγαπήτοι θεοῦ). Κλητός emphasizes the divine call (Rom. 1:1,6). The Romans were κλητοί ἅγιοι, i.e., ἅγιοι by virtue of having been called.⁴³ ,ccording to K.L. Schmidt, κλητός is a technical religious and biblical term which corresponds to מקראי (ὃν ἐγὼ καλῶ in Is. 47:12 LXX). Thus, he proposes for the origin of the New Testament κλητός that since κλητή ἁγία is found in Ex. 12:16 and Lev. 23:2ff. (for מקרא קדש), the combination of κλητός and ἅγιος may have been favored in the New Testament.⁴⁴

Paul's parable of grafting provides more clear hints that the New Testament concept of holiness is deeply associated with the

---

41. Bo Reicke, *The Epistles of James, Peter, and Jude,* AB (Garden City: Doubleday, 1964), p. 93.
42. Charles Bigg, *The Epistles of St. Peter and St. Jude,* p. 134.
43. C.E.B. Cranfield, *Romans,* 1:69.
44. K.L. Schmidt, "κλητός," *TDNT,* 3:494-96.

260

idea of election and is rooted in the Old Testament. "And if the first piece of dough be holy, the lump is also; and if the root be holy, the branches are too. But if some of the branches were broken off, and you, being a wild olive, were grafted in among them and became partaker with them of the rich root of the olive tree" (Rom. 11:16-17). The Gentile Christians, like the wild olive branches, are grafted onto Israel, the true olive tree. Thus the Gentiles owe their origin and their present status as "saints" to Israel. They share the privilege of election with Israel. Since Israel was the holy people of Yahweh (עַם קָדוֹשׁ לַיהוה), the Gentiles also became the saints of God (οἱ ἅγιοι τοῦ θεοῦ).

The moral principle of the saints is also established on the basis of this idea of election. Since the people of Israel were chosen, the ethical and ritual principle of holiness was applied to them. In the same way, the saints are required to be holy: "like the Holy One who called you, be holy yourselves also in all your behavior; because it is written, 'You shall be holy, for I am holy'" (1 Pet. 1:15-16; cf. Lev. 11:44).

Thus the major Old Testament metaphors for the relationship between God and his people are applied (sometimes with modification and enrichment) to the relationship between God or Christ and the church. Therefore, the identity of Christ and the status of the believers are closely connected with the election, rejection, and restoration of Israel. The New Testament use of Old Testament metaphors for Israel, the people of God, culminates in designating the church as "the Israel of God" (Gal. 6:16; cf. Phil. 3:3).

Conclusions

According to our study, the people of Israel were conscious of their exclusive relationship with Yahweh from the very earliest stages of their history, and they devoted their efforts to the portrayal of this relationship with imagery using a variety of terms and metaphors. Even though they did not use the modern theological term "election" (בחר) as we do today, the idea of election by Yahweh existed from the very beginning of their national history. Furthermore, the creation of the nation and the ensuing national unity seemed to generate faith in this idea. The election concept as a dominating theme in the Old Testament reached its climax among the Israelites at the rise of David's reign and at the building of the Temple under the leadership of Solomon. The activity of the prophets should be seen as a movement to awaken the minds of the people, who had departed from Yahweh, so as to renew the old faith in Yahweh's election of Israel. Therefore, the assertion that election is a product of the Deuteronomistic school, or even of the exilic community, must be rejected.

The idea of election has a variety of meanings. Since the idea deals with the relationship between a divine being and a human being, it was necessary to use metaphors from Israel's own life setting in order to describe it. A change in their life setting would then generate new and different expressions of this relationship. The terms and metaphors are drawn from the institution of the family (husband-wife, father-son), the experience of the battlefield (warrior-his levied army), the system of the royal court (king-servant), cultic practice (a holy people to Yahweh), as well as from motifs from nomadic (shepherd-sheep), agricultural (farmer-vineyard), and industrial (potter-clay) life. Therefore, the idea of election is a composite one. No single word or metaphor can convey the whole meaning.

Since the theme of election is closely associated with other key themes in the Old Testament, an organic unity and consistency of thought among the themes are found. The system of thought of election-rejection-restoration is carried through in each of the metaphors that are employed in election. The idea of rejection or restoration is not borrowed from entirely different and new metaphors, but from the previously coined descriptions of election. For example, marriage (including covenant)-divorce-remarriage (including new covenant) constitutes the thought chain of election-rejection-restoration. This same continuity of thought is found in the rest of the metaphors. Yahweh chooses and fights for Israel in election, but fights against Israel and sends them into exile in rejection. But in restoration he fights for them and brings them back again to their homeland. Yahweh adopts Israel as his son and gives the land to him as an inheritance in election, but he drives Israel out of the land and desolates it in rejection, while he has the Israelites returned to their own land to possess it again in restoration. Yahweh buys Israel in election, and sells them in rejection, but then buys them back in restoration. Yahweh sows and plants Israel in election, but uproots them in rejection, yet he plants them again in restoration. Yahweh is a shepherd of his flock in election, but he becomes a devouring beast in rejection, while he gathers them again in restoration. Yahweh makes and builds Israel in election, but he destroys them in rejection, and rebuilds them in restoration. Yahweh separates and sanctifies his people in election, but he defiles them in rejection, only to cleanse them again in restoration.

Therefore, it has been shown that the biblical writers were very consistent in their usage of terms and metaphors expressing these theological themes. This realization of a consistent linguistic usage in expressing these thoughts helps us to understand the messages of the prophets, particularly in the theology of exile and restoration.

In particular, the examination of the relationship between election and covenant is of special value. Until now, the covenant has been regarded as the dominant theme of the Old Testament by biblical scholars. However, it is now to be understood as the legal bond of Yahweh's election of Israel. It is a device to confirm the

Yahweh-Israel relationship. Thus, the covenant must be viewed in the context of election. Furthermore, our work has opened up a new theological meaning for the themes of the possession and dispossession of the land as well as the theme of redemption (purchasing and selling people). Only when we recognize Yahweh's ownership of the earth and his election of Israel as his son can we properly apprehend the concept of inheritance.

Finally, in the light of our study, the way has been made clear for a fruitful investigation into the continuity of the Old Testament election themes as seen in the New Testament, thus opening up new and previously untapped sources of biblical and theological understanding.

Bibliography

Ackroyd, Peter R. *Exile and Restoration.* OTL. Philadelphia: Westminster, 1968.

Albright, W.F. "The Song of Deborah in the Light of Archeology." *BASOR* 62 (1936): 26-31.

————. *From the Stone Age to Christianity.* Garden City: Doubleday, 1957.

————. *The Biblical Period from Abraham to Ezra.* New York: Harper & Row, 1963.

Altmann, Peter. *Erwählungstheologie und Universalismus im Alten Testament.* Berlin: Alfred Töpelmann, 1964.

Andersen, F.I., and Freedman, D.N. *Hosea.* AB. Garden City: Doubleday, 1984.

Andersen, T. David. "Renaming and Wedding Imagery in Isaiah 62." *Biblica* 67 (1986): 75-80.

Anderson, A.A. *Psalms.* 2 vols. NCBC. Grand Rapids: Eerdmans, 1981.

Audet, Jean-Paul. "Love and Marriage in the Old Testament." *Scripture* 10 (1955): 65-83.

Bächli, Otto. *Israel und die Völker: Eine Studie zum Deuteronomium.* Zürich: Zwingli, 1962.

Baldwin, J.C. *Haggai, Zechariah, Malachi.* Tyndale Old Testament Commentaries. London: Tyndale, 1972.

Barr, James. *Comparative Philology and the Text of the Old Testament.* Oxford: Clarendon, 1968.

————. *The Semantics of Biblical Language.* London: Oxford University Press, 1961.

Barth, Markus. *Ephesians.* 2 vols. AB. Garden City: Doubleday, 1974.

Bauer, W. *A Greek-English Lexicon of the New Testament and Other Early Christian Literature.* Trans. and ed. W.F. Ardnt and F.W. Gingrich. Chicago: University of Chicago Press, 1957.

Baumgartner, Walter. *Hebräisches und Aramäisches Lexikon zum Alten Testament.* 3 vols. Leiden: E.J. Brill, 1967-.

Beasley-Murray, G. R. *The Book of Revelation.* NCBC. Grand Rapid: Eerdmans, 1981.

Benedict, Marion J. *The God of the Old Testament in Relation to War.* New York: Columbia University, 1927.

Bernard, A.J.H. *A Critical and Exegetical Commentary on the Gospel According to St. John.* ICC. Edinburgh: T. & T. Clark, 1928.

Betz, O. "Jesu Heiliger Krieg," *Novum Testamentum II* (1958): 116-37.

Beyerlin, Walter. *Near Eastern Religious Texts Relating to the Old Testament.* OTL. Philadelphia: Westminster, 1978.

Bigg, Charles. *A Critical and Exegetical Commentary on the Epistles of St. Peter and St. Jude.* ICC. Edinburgh: T. & T. Clark, 1901.

Blau, J., and Greenfield, J.C. "Ugaritic Glosses." *BASOR* 200 (1970): 11-17.

Blenkinsopp, Joseph. *A History of Prophecy in Israel.* Philadelphia: Westminster, 1983.

Boecker, Hans Jochen. *Law and the Administration of Justice in the Old Testament and Ancient East.* Minneapolis: Augsburg, 1980.

Boling, Robert G. *Judges.* AB. Garden City: Doubleday, 1975.

Botterweck, G.J., and Ringgren, Helmer. *Theological Dictionary of the Old Testament.* 6 vols. Grand Rapids: Eerdmans, 1979-.

Brichto, Herbert Chanan. "Kin, Cult, Land and Afterlife—A Biblical Complex." *HUCA* 44 (1973): 1-54.

Bright, John. *A History of Israel.* 2nd ed. Philadelphia: Westminster, 1972.

———. *The Kingdom of God.* Nashville: Abingdon, 1953.

———. *The Authority of the Old Testament.* Nashville: Abingdon, 1967. Repr. Grand Rapids: Baker, 1980.

———. *Jeremiah.* AB. Garden City: Doubleday, 1965.

Brown, F., Driver, S.R., and Briggs, C.A. *Hebrew and English Lexicon of the Old Testament.* Oxford: Clarendon, 1907.

Brown, Raymond E. *The Gospel According to John.* 2 vols. AB. Garden City: Doubleday, 1966-1970.

Bruce, F.F. *Israel and the Nations.* Grand Rapids: Eerdmans, 1969.

Brueggemann, Walter. "Amos IV 4-13 and Israel's Covenant Worship." *VT* 15 (1965): 1-15.

———. *The Land.* OBT. Philadelphia: Fortress, 1977.

Büchsel, Friedrich, "ἀγοράζω." *TDNT,* 1:124-28.

———. "λυτρόω." *TDNT,* 4:349-56.

Burrows, Millar. "The Ancient Oriental Background of Hebrew Levirate Marriage." *BASOR* 72 (Dec. 1939): 2-15.

Buttenwieser, Moses. *The Psalms.* New York: KTAV, 1969.

Campbell, Edward F., Jr. *Ruth.* AB. Garden City: Doubleday, 1975.

Carley, Keith W. *Ezekiel among the Prophets.* SBT 2/31. London: SCM, 1974.

Carroll, Robert P. *When Prophecy Failed.* New York: Seabury, 1979.

Childs, B.S. "A Study of the Formula 'Until This Day'." *JBL* 82 (1963): 279-92.

———. "The Etiological Tale Re-Examined." *VT* 24 (1974): 388-97.

———. *Introduction to the Old Testament as Scripture.* Philadelphia: Fortress, 1979.

———. *The Book of Exodus.* OTL. Philadelphia: Westminster, 1974.

Christensen, Duane L. *Transformations of the War Oracle in Old Testament Prophecy.* Harvard Dissertations in Religion 3. Missoula: Scholars Press, 1975.

Clark, W. Malcolm. "The Origin and the Development of the Land Promise Theme in the Old Testament." Ph.D. Dissertation, Yale University, 1964.

Clements, R.E. *Prophecy and Tradition.* Atlanta: John Knox, 1975.

———. *One Hundred Years of Old Testament Interpretation.* Philadelphia: Westminster, 1976.

———. *Old Testament Theology.* Atlanta: John Knox, 1978.

Clines, David J.A. *The Theme of the Pentateuch.* JSOTSup 10. Sheffield: JSOT, 1978.

Cohen, S. "Ezekiel." *IDB*, 2:203-13.

Conzelmann, Hans. *1 Corinthians.* Hermeneia. Philadelphia: Fortress, 1975.

Coogan, M. David. *Stories from Ancient Canaan.* Philadelphia: Westminster, 1978.

Cooke, Gerald. "The Israelite King As Son of God." *ZAW* 73 (1961): 202-25.

Coppes, Leonard J. "חשׁק." *TWOT,* 1:332.

Craigie, Peter C. *The Book of Deuteronomy.* NICOT. Grand Rapids: Eerdmans, 1976.

———. *The Problem of War in the Old Testament.* Grand Rapids: Eerdmans, 1978.

———. *Ugarit and the Old Testament.* Grand Rapids: Eerdmans, 1983.

Cranfield, C.E.B. *A Critical and Exegetical Commentary on the Epistle to the Romans.* 2 vols. ICC. Edinburgh: T. & T. Clark, 1975-1979.

Cross, F.M. "The Song of the Sea." *JTC* 5 (1968): 1-25.

———. *Canaanite Myth and Hebrew Epic.* Cambridge: Harvard University Press, 1973.

Cross, F.M., and Freedman, D.N. *Studies in Ancient Yahwistic Poetry.* SBLDS 21. Missoula: Scholars Press, 1975.

———. "The Song of Miriam." *JNES* 14 (1955): 237-50.

Dahl, Nils Alstrup. *Das Volk Gottes: Eine Untersuchung zum Kirchenbewusstein des Urchristentum.* Darmstadt: Wissenschaftliche Buchgesellschaft, 1963.

Dahood, Mitchell. *Ugaritic-Hebrew Philology.* BibOr 17. Rome: Pontifical Biblical Institute, 1965-1970.

———. *Psalms.* 3 vols. AB. Garden City: Doubleday, 1965-1970.

Danell, G.A. "The Idea of God's People in the Bible." In Anton Fridrichsen et al. *The Root of the Vine.* New York: Philosophical Library, 1953.

DeRoche, Michael. "Jeremiah 2:2-3 and Israel's Love for God during the Wilderness Wanderings." *CBQ* 45 (1983): 364-76.

Driver, S.R. *An Introduction to the Literature of the Old Testament.* Rev. ed. New York: Charles Scribner's Sons, 1923.

———. *A Critical and Exegetical Commentary on Deuteronomy.* ICC. Edinburgh: T. & T. Clark, 1895.

Dus, J. "Gibeon: Eine Kultsätte des ŠMŠ und die Stadt des Benjaminitischen Schicksals." *VT* 10 (1960): 353-74.

Dustin, G.R. "The Marriage Covenant." *Theology* 78 (April 1975): 244-52.

Eaton, John H. *Kingship and the Psalms.* SBT 2/32. Naperville: Allenson, 1975.

Eichrodt, Walther. "Covenant and Law: Thoughts on Recent Discussion." *Interpretation* 20 (1966): 301-21.

———. *Theology of the Old Testament.* 2 vols. OTL. Philadelphia: Westminster, 1961-1967.

Eissfeldt, Otto. "Partikulismus und Universalismus in der Israeli-tisch-Judischen Religionsgeschichte." *Theologische Literaturzeitung* 79 (1954): 283-84.

————. *The Old Testament: An Introduction*. New York: Harper and Row, 1965.

Falk, Z.W. *Hebrew Law in Biblical Times*. Jerusalem: Wahrmann, 1964.

Fisher, L., ed. *Ras Shamra Parallels*. 2 vols. Analecta Orientalia 49-50. Rome: Pontifical Biblical Institute, 1972-1975.

Fohrer, Georg. *Introduction to the Old Testament*. Nashville: Abingdon, 1968.

Ford, J. Massynberde. *Revelation*. AB. Garden City: Doubleday, 1975.

Forshey, H.O. "The Construct Chain *Naḥᵃlat YHWH/ᵉlōhim.*" *BA* 20 (1957): 51-53.

Foulkes, Francis. *The Epistle of Paul to the Ephesians*. Tyndale New Testament Commentaries. Grand Rapids: Eerdmans, 1963.

Frankfort, Henri. *Kingship and the Gods*. Chicago: University of Chicago Press, 1978.

Freedman, D.N. "Early Israelite History in the Light of Early Israelite Poetry." In *Unity and Diversity*. Ed. H. Goedicke and J.J.M. Roberts. Baltimore, London: Johns Hopkins University Press, 1975. Pp. 3-34.

————. *Pottery, Poetry, and Prophecy: Studies in Early Hebrew Poetry*. Winona Lake: Eisenbrauns, 1980.

Friedman, Mordechai A. "Israel's Response in Hosea 2:17b: 'You are my Husband'." *JBL* 99/2 (1980): 199-204.

Friedman, Richard Elliot, ed. *The Poet and the Historian: Essays in Literary and Historical Biblical Criticism*. HSS 26. Chico: Scholars Press, 1978.

Gärtner, Bertil. *The Temple and the Community in Qumran and the New Testament: A Comparative Study in the Temple Symbolism of the Qumran Texts and the New Testament*. Cambridge: The University Press, 1965.

Geldenhuys, Norval. *Commentary on the Gospel of Luke*. NICNT. Grand Rapids: Eerdmans, 1951.

Geller, Stephen A. *Parallelism in Early Biblical Poetry*. HSM 20. Missoula: Scholars Press, 1979.

Gevirtz, Stanley. *Patterns in the Early Poetry of Israel*. Chicago: University of Chicago Press, 1973.

Gibson, J.C.L. *Canaanite Myths and Legends.* Edinburgh: T. & T. Clark, 1978.

Ginzberg, L. *The Legends of the Jews.* 7 vols. Philadelphia: Jewish Publication Society, 1909-1938.

Glueck, Nelson. *Ḥesed in the Bible.* New York: KTAV, 1975.

Good, Robert M. *The Sheep of His Pasture: A Study of the Hebrew Noun ʿAm(m) and Its Semitic Cognates.* HSM 29. Chico: Scholars Press, 1983.

Gordis, Robert. "On Adultery in the Biblical and Babylonian Law— A Note." *Judaism* 33 (1984): 210-11.

Gordon, Cyrus H. *Ugaritic Textbook.* Analecta Orientalia 38. Rome: Pontifical Biblical Institute, 1965.

Gray, G.B. *A Critical and Exegetical Commentary on the Book of Isaiah, I-XXVII.* ICC. Edinburgh: T. & T. Clark, 1912.

Gray, John. *The Biblical Doctrine of the Reign of God.* Edinburgh: T. & T. Clark, 1979.

———. "The Kingship of God in the Prophets and Psalms." *VT* 11 (1961): 1-29.

Greenberg, Moshe. *Ezekiel, 1-20.* AB. Garden City: Doubleday, 1983.

———. "Hebrew *Sᵉgullā:* Akkadian *sikiltu.*" *JAOS* 71 (1951): 172-74.

Greengus, S. "The Old Babylonian Marriage Contract." *JAOS* 89 (1969): 505-32.

———. "Sisterhood, Adoption at Nuzi and 'Wife-sister' in Genesis." *HUCA* 46 (1975): 5-31.

———. "Old Babylonian Marriage Ceremonies and Rites." *JCS* 20 (1966): 55-72.

Grossfeld, Bernard. "The Translation of Biblical Hebrew פקד in the Targum, Peshitta, Vulgate and Septuagint." *ZAW* 96 (1984): 83-101.

Gunkel, H. "Der Micha-Schluss." *ZS* 2 (1924): 145-78.

Hallo, William W., and Simpson, William Kelly. *The Ancient Near East: A History.* New York: Harcourt Brace Jovanovich Inc., 1971.

Halpern, Baruch. *The Constitution of the Monarchy in Israel.* HSM 25. Chico: Scholars Press, 1981.

Harris, R. Laird. "גאל." *TWOT,* 1:144.

———. "חסד." *TWOT,* 1:305-7.

Harris, Rivkah. "The Case of Three Babylonian Marriage Contracts." *JNES* 33/4 (October, 1974): 363-69.

Harrison, R.K. *Introduction to the Old Testament.* Grand Rapids: Eerdmans, 1969.

Hasel, Gerhard F. *The Remnant.* Berrien Springs: Andrews University Press, 1980.

———. "Semantic Values of Derivatives of the Hebrew Root שאר." *AUSS* 2 (1973): 152-69.

Hayes, John H., ed. *Old Testament Form Criticism.* San Antonio: Trinity University Press, 1977.

Herrmann, Siegfried. *A History of Israel in Old Testament Times.* Philadelphia: Fortress, 1981.

Hill, David. *Greek Words and Hebrew Meanings: Studies in the Semantics of Soteriological Terms.* Cambridge: The University Press, 1967.

Hillers, Delbert R. *Covenant: The History of a Biblical Idea.* Baltimore: Johns Hopkins University Press, 1969.

———. *Micah.* Hermeneia. Philadelphia: Fortress, 1984.

Huffmon, Herbert B. "The Treaty Background of Hebrew *Yāda'.*" *BASOR* 181 (1966): 31-37.

———. "The Covenant Lawsuit and the Prophets." *JBL* 78 (1959) 286-95.

Huffmon, Herbert B., and Parker, Simon B. "A Further Note on the Treaty Background of Hebrew *Yāda'.*" *BASOR* 184 (1966): 36-38.

Hyatt, J. Philip. *Prophetic Religion.* New York: Abingdon-Cokesbury Press, 1947.

———. "Deuteronomic Edition of Jeremiah." In *A Prophet to the Nations.* Ed. Leo G. Perdue and Brian W. Kovacs. Winona Lakes: Eisenbrauns, 1984. Pp. 247-67.

Irwin, W.A. "Israel." In H. Frankfort et al. *The Intellectual Adventure of Ancient Man.* Chicago: University of Chicago Press, 1946.

Jacob, Edmond. *Theology of the Old Testament.* New York and Evanston: Harper & Row, 1958.

Jagersma, H. *A History of Israel in the Old Testament Period.* Philadelphia: Fortress, 1983.

Jenkins, Alan W. *The Elohist and North Israelite Traditions.* SBLMS 22. Missoula: Scholars Press, 1977.

Johnson, A.R. "The Primary meaning of the the Root גאל." VTSup 1 (1953): 66-77.

Jones, Gwilym H. "'Holy War' or 'Yahweh War?'" *VT* 25 (1975): 642-58.

Kaufmann, Yehezkel. *The Religion of Israel.* New York: Schocken Books, 1972.

Keil, C.F., and Delitzsch, F. *Commentary on the Old Testament in Ten Volumes.* Grand Rapids: Eerdmans, repr. 1980.

Kelly, J.N.D. *A Commentary on the Epistles of Peter and Jude.* London: Adam & Charles Black, 1969.

Kidner, Derek. *Psalms.* 2 vols. Tyndale Old Testament Commentaries. Downers Grove: IVP, 1975.

Kitchen, K.A. *Ancient Orient and Old Testament.* Downers Grove: IVP, 1968.

Klein, Ralph W. *Textual Criticism of the Old Testament: The Septuagint after Qumran.* Philadelphia: Fortress, 1974.

Kline, Meredith G. *The Structure of Biblical Authority.* Grand Rapids: Eerdmans, 1972.

Koch, K. "Zur Geschichte der Erwährungsvorstellung in Israel." *ZAW* 67 (1955): 205-28.

Kramer, Samuel N. *From the Tablets of Sumer.* Indian Hills: Falcon's Wing Press, 1956.

Labuschagne, C.J. *The Incomparability of Yahweh in the Old Testament.* Leiden: E.J. Brill, 1966.

Lang, Bernhard. *Monotheism and the Prophetic Minority.* Sheffield: Almond, 1983.

LaSor, William Sanford, Hubbard, David Allan, and Bush, Frederic William. *Old Testament Survey.* Grand Rapids: Eerdmans, 1982.

Lemke, E. "Nebuchadrezzar, My Servant." *CBQ* 27 (1966): 45-50.

Levine, Baruch A. *"Mulūg/melûg*: The Origins of a Talmudic Legal Institution." *JAOS* 88 (1968): 271-85.

———. "Priestly Writers." *IDBSup.* Pp. 683-87.

———. *In the Presence of the Lord.* Leiden: E.J. Brill, 1974.

———. "In Praise of the Israelite *Mišpāhâ*: Legal Themes in the Book of the Ruth." In *The Quest of the Kingdom of God: Studies in Honor of George E. Mendenhall.* Ed. H.B. Huffmon et al. Winona Lake: Eisenbrauns, 1983. Pp. 95-106.

Lewis, Jack P. "ידע." *TWOT,* 1:388.

L'Heureux, Conrad E. *Rank among the Canaanite Gods: El, Ba'al, and Repha'im.* HSM 21. Missoula: Scholars Press, 1979.

Limburg, J. "The Root ריב and Prophetic Lawsuit Speeches." *JBL* 88 (1969): 291-304.

Lind, Millard C. *Yahweh Is a Warrior.* Scottdale: Herald Press, 1980.

Lindblom, J. *Prophecy in Ancient Israel.* Philadelphia: Fortress, 1962.

Loewenstamm, Samuel E. "נחלת ה." In *Studies in Bible.* Scripta Hierosolymitana 31. Ed. Sara Japhet. Jerusalem: Magnes Press, 1986. Pp. 155-92.

Longman, Tremper III. "The Divine Warrior: The New Testament Use of an Old Testament Motif." *WTJ* 44 (1982): 290-307.

McCarter, P. Kyle, Jr. *1 Samuel.* AB. Garden City: Doubleday, 1980.

McCarthy, D.J. "Notes on the Love of God in Deuteronomy and Father-Son Relationship between Yahweh and Israel." *CBQ* 27 (1965): 144-47.

———. *Old Testament Covenant: A Survey of Current Opinions.* Atlanta: John Knox, 1972.

———. *Treaty and Covenant.* AnBib 21A. Rome: Biblical Institute Press, 1978.

———. "Compact and Kingship: Stimuli for Hebrew Covenant Thinking." In *Studies in the Period of David and Solomon and Other Essays.* Ed. Tomoo Ishida. Winona Lake: Eisenbrauns, 1982. Pp. 75-92.

McComiskey, T. E. "ברא." *TWOT,* 1:127.

———. "קרש." *TWOT,* 2:786-87.

McCurley, Foster R. *Ancient Myths and Biblical Faith: Scriptural Transformations.* Philadelphia: Fortress, 1983.

McKay, J.W. "Man's Love for God in Deuteronomy and the Father/Teacher-Son/Pupil Relationship." *VT* 22 (1972): 426-35.

Martin, Ralph P. *2 Corinthians.* Word Biblical Commentary. Waco, Texas: Word Books, 1986.

Mendelsohn, I. "A Ugaritic Parallel to the Adoption of Ephriam and Manasseh." *Israel Exploration Journal* 9 (1959): 180-83.

Mendenhall, G.E. "Election." *IDB,* 2:76-82.

Mettinger, Tryggve N.D. "YHWH SABAOTH—The Heavenly King on the Cherubim Throne." In *Studies in the Period of David and Solomon and Other Essays.* Ed. Tomoo Ishida. Winona Lake: Eisenbrauns, 1982. Pp. 109-38.

Meyers, Carol. "The Roots of Restriction: Women in Early Israel." *BA* 41 (1978): 91-103.

Mihaly, Eugene. "A Rabbinic Defense of the Election of Israel: An Analysis of Sifre Deuteronomy 32:9, PIQA 312." *HUCA* 35 (1964): 104-43.

Millard, A.R., and Wiseman, D.J., eds. *Essays on the Patriarchal Narratives.* Winona Lake: Eisenbrauns, 1980.

Miller, Patrick D. *The Divine Warrior in Early Israel.* HSM 5. Cambridge: Harvard University Press, 1973.

Miscall, Peter D. *The Workings of Old Testament Narrative.* Philadelphia: Fortress, 1983.

Montgomery, James A. *A Critical and Exegetical Commentary on the Books of Kings.* Ed. H.S. Gehman. ICC. Edinburgh: T. & T. Clark, 1951.

Moore, George F. *A Critical and Exegetical Commentary on Judges.* ICC. Edinburgh: T. & T. Clark, 1895.

Moran, William L. "The Ancient Near Eastern Background of the Love of God in Deuteronomy." *CBQ* 25 (1963): 77-87.

Morgenstern, J. "Jubilee." *IDB,* 2:141-44.

———. "Sabbatical Year." *IDB,* 4:1000-1001.

Morris, L. *The Gospel According to John.* NICNT. Grand Rapids: Eerdmans, 1971.

Mowinckel, S. *The Psalms in Israel's Worship.* Nashville: Abingdon, 1962.

Muilenburg, J. "Jeremiah, the Prophet." *IBD,* 2:823-35.

Mullen, E. Theodore, Jr. *The Assembly of the Gods.* HSM 24. Chico: Scholars Press, 1980.

Muller, Valentine. "The Prehistory of the 'Good Shepherd.'" *JNES* 3 (1944): 87-90.

Muller, Werner E. *Die Vorstellung vom Rest im Alten Testament.* Inaugural-Dissertation. Bordorf: Leipzig, 1939.

Murray, J.O.F. *Jesus According to St. John.* London and Edinburgh, 1951.

Napier, David. *Song of the Vineyard.* Philadelphia: Fortress, 1982.

Nelson, Richard D. *The Double Redaction of the Deuteronomistic History.* JSOTSup 18. Sheffield: JSOT Press, 1981.

Newsome, James D., Jr. *By the Waters of Babylon: An Introduction to the History and Theology of the Exile.* Atlanta: John Knox, 1979.

Noth, Martin. *The Deuteronomistic History.* JSOTSup 15. Sheffield: JSOT Press, 1981.

Ogden, G.S. "Time, and the Verb היה in O.T. Prose." *VT* 21 (1971): 451-69.

Oppenheim, Leo, gen. ed. *The Assyrian Dictionary.* Chicago: University of Chicago Press, 1964-.

Orlinsky, Harry M. *Essays in Biblical Culture and Bible Translation.* New York: KTAV, 1974.

Orr, W.F., and Walther, J.A. *1 Corinthians.* AB. Garden City: Doubleday, 1976.

Oswalt, John N. "כון." *TWOT,* 1:433-34.

Otzen, Benedikt, Gottlieb, Hans, and Jappesen, Knud. *Myths in the Old Testament.* London: SCM, 1980.

Parker, Simon B. "The Marriage Blessing in Israelite and Ugaritic Literature." *JBL* 95 (1976): 23-30.

Paterson, R.M. "Doctrine of Election." *The New Zealand Theological Review* 4 (Aug. 1966): 211-18.

Paul, S.M. "Adoption Formulae." *Eretz-Israel* 14 [H.L. Ginsberg volume] (1978): 31-36.

———. "Adoption Formulae: A Study of Cuneiform and Biblical Legal Clauses." *MAARAV* 2/2 (April, 1980): 173-85.

Philips, Anthony. "Another Look at Adultery." *JSOT* 20 (1981): 3-25.

Phythian-Adams, W.J. *The Call of Israel: An Introduction to the Study of Divine Election.* London: Oxford University Press, 1934.

Polzin, Robert. *Moses and the Deuteronomist.* New York: Seabury, 1980.

Porten, B. *Archives from Elephantine.* Berkeley/Los Angeles: University of California, 1968.

Preisker, Herbert. "πιπράσκω," *TDNT,* 6:160.

Priest, J.F. "Etiology." *IDBSup.* Pp. 293-95.

Pritchard, J.B. *The Ancient Near East.* 2 vols. Princeton: Princeton University Press, 1958.

———. *ANEP.* 2nd ed. Princeton: Princeton University Press, 1969.

———. *ANET.* 3rd ed. Princeton: Princeton University Press, 1969.

Quell, Gottfried, "Election in the Old Testament." *TDNT,* 4:145-68.

Rad, Gerhard von. *Old Testament Theology.* 2 vols. New York: Harper & Row, 1962-1965.

———. *The Message of the Prophets.* New York: Harper & Row, 1965.

———. *Der Heilige Krieg im Alten Israel.* 3rd ed. Göttingen: Vandenhoeck und Ruprecht, 1969.

———. *Genesis.* OTL. Rev. ed. Philadelphia: Westminster, 1972.

Raitt, Thomas M. *A Theology of Exile.* Philadelphia: Fortress, 1977.

Reich, Nathaniel. "Marriage and Divorce in Ancient Egypt: Papyrus Documents discovered at Thebes by Eckley B. Coxe Jr. Expedition to Egypt." *The Museum Journal* (University of Pennsylvania, 1924): 50-57.

Reichert, Andreas. "Israel, The Firstborn of God: A Topic of Early Deuteronomic Theology." In *Proceedings of the Sixth World Congress of Jewish Studies.* Jerusalem: World Union of Jewish Studies, 1977. 1:341-49.

Reicke, Bo. *The Epistles of James, Peter, and Jude.* AB. Garden City: Doubleday, 1964.

———. "Micah 7:7-20." *HTR* 60 (1967): 347-67.

Riemann, P.A. "Mosaic Covenant." *IDBSup.* Pp. 192-97.

Riesener, Ingrid. *Der Stamm עבד im Alten Testament.* Berlin, New York: Walter de Gruyter, 1979.

Roberts, J.J.M. "Zion in the Theology of the Davidic-Solomonic Empire." In *Studies in the Period of David and Solomon and Other Essays.* Ed. Tomoo Ishida. Winona Lake: Eisenbrauns, 1982. Pp. 93-108.

Rogers, Robert G. "The Doctrine of Election in the Chronicler's Work and the Dead Sea Scrolls." Ph.D. Dissertation, Boston University, 1969.

Ross, J.P. "Jahweh צבאות in Samuel and Psalms." *VT* 17 (1967): 76-92.

Rowley, H.H. *The Biblical Doctrine of Election.* London: Lutterworth Press, 1950.

———. *The Missionary Message of the Old Testament.* Guildford and London: Billing and Sons Ltd., 1955.

———. *The Faith of Israel.* London: SCM, 1979.

Rummel, Stan, ed. *Ras Shamra Parallels.* Vol. 3. Analecta Orientalia 51. Rome: Pontifical Biblical Institute, 1981.

Sawyer, John F.A. *Semantics in Biblical Research.* SBT 2/24. Naperville: Allenson, 1972.

Schafer, B.E. "The Root *bḥr* and Pre-Exilic Concepts of Chosenness in the Hebrew Bible." *ZAW* 89 (1977): 20-42.

Scharbert, J. "Das Verbum פקד in der Theologie des Alten Testaments." *BZ* 4 (1960): 209-26.

Schedel, Claus. "Bund und Erwählung." *ZKT* 80 (1958): 493-515.

Schmidt, K.L. "κλητός." *TDNT,* 3:494-96.

Schmidt, Werner H. *The Faith of the Old Testament.* Philadelphia: Westminster, 1983.

Seebass, H. "בחר." *TDOT,* 2:73-87.

Senior, Donald, and Stuhlmueller, Carroll. *The Biblical Foundations for Mission.* Maryknoll: Orbis Books, 1983.

Seters, John van. "Joshua 24 and the Problem of Tradition in the Old Testament." In *In the Shelter of Elyon: Essays on Ancient Palestinian Life and Literature in Honor of G. W. Ahlström.* Ed. W. Boyd Barrick and John R. Spencer. JSOTSup 31. Sheffield: JSOT, 1984. Pp. 139-58.

Silva, Moises. *Biblical Words and Their Meaning: An Introduction to Lexical Semantics.* Grand Rapids: Zondervan, 1983.

Smend, Rudolf. *Yahweh War and Tribal Confederation: Reflection upon Israel's Earliest History.* New York: Abingdon, 1970.

Smith, Henry P. *A Critical and Exgetical Commentary on the Books of Samuel.* ICC. New York: Charles Scribner's Sons, 1899.

Smith, J.M.P. "The Chosen People." *AJSL* 45 (1928-29): 73ff.

Soden, Wolfram von. *Akkadisches Handwörterbuch.* 3 vols. Wiesbaden: Otto Harrassowitz, 1965.

Soggin, J. Alberto. *Introduction to the Old Testament.* OTL. Philadelphia: Westminster, 1976.

———. "The Prophets on Holy War as Judgement against Israel." In *Old Testament and Oriental Studies.* BibOr 29. Rome: Biblical Institute Press, 1975.

Speiser, E.A. *Genesis.* AB. Garden City: Doubleday, 1964.

Spriggs, D.G. *Two Old Testament Theologies.* SBT 2/30. Naperville: Allenson, 1974.

Stade, B. "Micah 7. 7-20, ein Psalm." *ZAW* 23 (1903): 164-71.

Staerk, D.W. "Zum Alttestmentlischen Erwählunsglauben." *ZAW* 55 (1937): 1-36.

Szikszai, S. "Kings, I and II." *IBD,* 3:26-35.

Terrien, Samuel. *The Elusive Presence.* New York: Harper & Row, 1978.

Thomas, D. Winton. *Documents from Old Testament Times.* New York: Harper & Row, 1958.

Thompson, J.A. "The Significance of the Verb *LOVE* in the David-Jonathan Narrative in Israel." *VT* 24 (1974): 334-38.

Thompson, Thomas L. *The Historicity of the Patriarchal Narratives.* BZAW 133. New York: Walter de Gruyter, 1974.

Tigay, Jeffrey Howard. "Adoption." *Encyclopaedia Judaica.* Jerusalem: Keter, 1971. 1:298-301.

Tucker, Gene M. "Covenant Forms and Contract Forms." *VT* 15 (1965): 487-503.

Vannoy, J. Robert. *Covenant Renewal at Gilgal: A Study of I Samuel 11:14-12:25.* Cherry Hill: Mack Publishing Co., 1978.

Vaux, Roland de. *Ancient Israel.* 2 vols. New York: McGraw-Hill, 1961.

Vriezen, Th. C. *Die Erwählung Israels nach dem Alten Testament.* Zürich: Zwingli, 1953.

————. "Die Erwählung Israels nach dem Alten Testament." *AThANT* 24 (1953): 109.

————. *An Outline of Old Testament Theology.* Oxford: Basil Blackwell, 1970.

Waldow, H. Eberhard von. "The Servant of the Lord, Israel, the Jews and the People of God." In *Intergerini Parietis Septum (Eph. 2:14). Essays presented to Markus Barth on his sixty-fifth birthday.* Ed. Dikran Y. Hadidian. PTMS 33. Pittsburgh: Pickwick, 1981.

Ward, James M. "The Message of the Prophet Hosea." *Interpretation* 23/4 (1969): 387-407.

Watts, John D.W. "The People of God: A Study of the Doctrine in the Pentateuch." *The Expository Times* 72 (1955-56): 232-37.

Weinfeld, Moshe. *Deuteronomy and the Deuteronomistic School.* Oxford: Clarendon, 1972.

————. "ברית." *TDOT,* 2:253-79.

————. "Davidic Covenant." *IDBSup.* Pp. 188-92.

Weippert, M. "'Heiliger Krieg' in Israel und Assyrien: Kritische Anmerkungen zu Gerhard von Rads Konzept des 'Heiligen Krieg im alten Israel.'" *ZAW* 84 (1972): 460-93.

Weiseman, Ze'eb. "The Nature and Background of BĀḤUR in the Old Testament." *VT* 31 (1981): 441-50.

Weiser, A. "Glaube und Geschichte in Alten Testament." *BWANT* 4/4 (1931): 99-182.

Weiss, David Halivni. "The Use of קנה in Connection with Marriage." *HTR* 57 (1957): 244-48.

Weiss, Meir. *The Bible From Within.* Jerusalem: Magnes, 1984.

Wenham, G.J. "The Restoration of Marriage Reconsidered." *JJS* 29 (1978): 36-40.

Westermann, Claus. *Genesis.* 3 vols. Minneapolis: Augsburg, 1984-1986.

―――. *Isaiah 40-66.* OTL. Philadelphia: Westminster, 1969.

Wharton, J.A. "People of God." *IDB,* 3:727-28.

White, Hugh C. "The Divine Oath in Genesis." *JBL* 92 (1973): 165-79.

Widengren, Geo. "Yahweh's gathering of the Dispersed." In *In the Shelter of Elyon: Essays on Ancient Palestinian Life and Literature in Honor of G.W. Ahlström.* Ed. W. Boyd Barrick and John R. Spencer. JSOTSup 31. Sheffield: JSOT, 1984. Pp. 227-45.

Williamson, H.G.M. *Ezra, Nehemiah.* Word Biblical Commentary. Waco, Texas: Word Books, 1985.

Wiseman, D.J., ed. *Peoples of Old Testament Times.* Oxford: Clarendon, 1973.

Wolff, Hans Walter. *Anthropology of the Old Testament.* Philadelphia: Fortress, 1974.

―――. *Hosea.* Hermeneia. Philadelphia: Fortress, 1974.

Wood, Leon J. "חפץ." *TWOT,* 1:301-2.

Woudstra, M.H. *The Book of Joshua.* NICOT. Grand Rapids: Eerdmans, 1981.

Wright, G.E. "Erwählung." *Die Religion in Geschichte und Gegenwart.* Ed. Kurt Galling. 6 vols. 3rd ed. Tübingen: J.C.B. Mohr (Paul Siebeck), 1958. 2:610-12.

―――. "The Good Shepherd." *BA* 3/1 (Feb. 1940): 44-48.

―――. *The Old Testament Against Its Environment.* SBT 1/2. London: SCM, 1968.

―――. *The Old Testament and Theology.* New York: Harper & Row, 1969.

Yaron, Reuven, "Aramaic Marriage Contracts from Elephantine." *JSS* 3/1 (1958): 1-139.

————. "The Restoration of Marriage." *JJS* 17 (1966): 1-11.

Young, E.J. *The Book of Isaiah.* 3 vols. Grand Rapids: Eerdmans, 1972.

Zimmerli, Walther. *Man and His Hope in the Old Testament.* SBT 2/20. Naperville: Allenson, 1968.

————. *The Old Testament and the World.* Atlanta: John Knox, 1976.

————. *Old Testament Theology in Outline.* Atlanta: John Knox, 1978.

————. and Jeremias, J. *The Servant of God.* SBT 1/20. Rev. ed. London: SCM, 1965.

Zobel, Hans-Jürgen. "Ursprung und Verwurzelung des Erwählungsglaubens Israels." *Theologische Literaturzeitung* 93 (1968): 1-12.

Name Index

Scripture Index

23:3	112, 122	14:2	32	12:20-25	125
23:10	112, 122	14:3	21	12:22	91, 125, 137
23:13	93	14:16	37	13:13	132
24	192	16:15	37	13:14	137
24:13	81	19:1	31	14:20	35
24:18	201, 210	19:2	39	14:37	61
24:22	112	19:22-23	16	14:45	132
		20:18ff	61	15:1	35
Judges		20:25	50	15:2	166
2:3	201	20:31	50	15:9	219
2:8	75	20:37	155	15:21	13
2:14	211	21:7	29	16:1-13	126
3:8	211	21:19-24	12	16:5	96
4:2	80, 211	21:22	12	17:1	46
4:6-7	155			17:2	50
4:9	211	*Ruth*		17:7	74
4:15	111, 124	1:4	21, 31	17:18	109
4:16	218	1:8	202	17:21	50
4:18	50	3:7	202	17:26	59, 127
4:22	50	3:8	202	17:34-36	85
5:1	113	3:9	202	17:36	59, 127
5:1-31	113	4:10	18, 19, 29	17:45	59
5:2-5	114	4:13	27	17:45-47	127
5:3	114, 116			17:48	50
5:3-4	118	*1 Samuel*		17:55	109
5:3-5	122	1:15	37, 78	18:7	126
5:5	114, 116	1:19	24	18:17	59, 127, 137
5:6-8	114, 115	2:8	36	20:6	52
5:9-11	115	2:16	13	20:8	185
5:11	35, 116, 122	2:28	47	20:31	132
5:12-22	116	4:1	50	21:11	126
5:13	55, 118, 122	4:2	50	21:19-20	13
5:20	118	4:8	56	23:2	61
5:20-21	111	4:9	74	25:15	52
5:21	118	7:3-4	123	25:18	59
5:23	118, 122	7:10	111, 123	25:25-39	21
5:24-27	118	8:5	76, 124	25:28	128
5:24-31	118	8:7	124	25:40-41	27
5:28-30	118	8:7-8	76	25:43	27
5:30	11	8:11-17	75	28:6	61
6:35	50	8:19-20	76	29:5	126
7:7	120	8:20	124	30:4	35
7:15	119	9:16-17	35	30:8	61
7:17-18	119	11:1	74		
7:20b	119	11:11	218	*2 Samuel*	
7:22	119	12:1-5	124	5:12	132
7:24	50	12:1-25	124	6:13	114
8:27	42	12:6-12	124	7:1	137
8:33	42	12:8	24	7:7-8	131, 137
9:45	82	12:10	76	7:10	81, 137
10:7	211	12:12	76, 124	7:10-11	131
11:18	35	12:17	125	7:12-13	132
11:20-21	35	12:19	125	7:14	63

35:20	50	60:8-9	58	145:1	77
36:19	216	60:8-11	129, 130	149:2	90
36:23	54	60:12-14	130		
		68:25	77	*Proverbs*	
Ezra		69:36	36	1:17	16
1:1-11	227	74:2	79	2:17	184
2:61	67	74:12	77	2:22	213
6:21	95, 179	74:17	89	4:12	114
9:1	95, 179	77:16-18	111	7:8	114
9:2	31	77:20	85, 87	11:18	82
9:8	220	78:52-55	87	15:25	213
9:13	220	78:55	201	22:8	82
10:11	95, 179	78:61	208	23:2	16
		78:68	48	31:16	81
Nehemiah		78:70	47		
5:8	80	79:13	84	*Ecclesiastes*	
9:2	179	80:2	87, 163	2:4	81
9:31	220	80:3	163	2:5	81
10:29	95, 179	80:5	163	10:20	16
10:31	31	80:7	163	11:16	82
13:22	219	80:8	163		
13:27	23	80:9	81, 163	*Song of Solomon*	
		80:9-20	162	*(Canticles in the text)*	
Esther		80:15	163	1:13	141
2:7	14, 64, 65, 66	80:16	81, 163		
2:15	14, 64, 65, 66	80:18	163	*Isaiah*	
2:17	37	80:20	163	1–4	159, 180
		84:4	77	1:2	68
Job		89:28	65	1:8-9	220
7:18	52	90:2	92	1:9	220
18:7	114	92:14	83	1:29	48
31:15	132	94:9	81	2:2-4	199
31:39	16	95:3	77	2:6-8	140
		95:5	89	2:20	140
Psalms		95:6	125	3:1	78
1:3	82	95:6-7	84, 90	3:17-26	218
2:3	155	97:5	78	3:25-26	218
2:7	92	100:3	90	4:1	37
5:3	77	105:6	75	4:1-3	218
7:3	88	105:42	75	4:2	220
8:2-3	78	105:43-45	231	5	81
18:14	111	107:37	81, 82	5:1-7	159, 160, 212
24:1	71	108:8-9	58	5:1a	160
24:8	56	108:8-10	130	5:1b-2	160
33:12	47	114:6	111	5:2	80, 81
44:3	81	119:73	132	5:3	80
44:5	77	119:90	132	5:3-6	160
47:5	48	119:111	36	5:5	80
47:8	77	132:13	49	5:7	160, 161
52:7	93, 213	135:4	36, 47	5:13	207
60:3-7	129	135:5	78	6:5	180
60:3-14	128	136:3	78	6:12-13	220
60:7	130	140:12	132	7:1-9	180

290

THE DIVINE ELECTION OF ISRAEL

62:2	69, 230	5:18	220	16:13	158, 208
62:4	69, 203	5:19	212	16:14-15	231
62:4-5	17, 231	6:4	61	16:15	72, 210
62:5	233	6:22	206	17:4	212, 233
62:11-12	98	6:26	208	18:1-10	93
62:12	69, 97, 177, 239	6:30	203	18:1-11	168, 169
63:3	216	7:10	69	18:1-12	170
63:10	205	7:11	69	18:4	89, 93, 170
63:11	87	7:15	210	18:5-6	170
63:16	68	7:25	76	18:6	89, 93
64:7	68, 90, 93, 170	7:30	69	18:7	93, 125, 216
64:7-8	171	7:34	158	18:7-10	170
65:8-15	174	8:3	210	18:9	81
65:8-16	235	8:16	158	18:11	170
65:12	49	9:8	166	18:12	170
65:15	78, 230	9:15	87	18:14	125
65:17	91	9:15-16	214	18:15	72, 204
65:21	81	9:16	175	18:16	158
66:3-4	49	9:18	208	18:17	87, 213
66:14	235	10:5	114	18:30	175
66:20	199	10:16	99	19:11	215
		10:21	87	20:4	208
Jeremiah		10:24	175	20:6	208
1:5	25, 89, 96	11:2	186	21:4	237
1:8	175	11:2-5	186	21:5	205
1:9ff	257	11:4-5	186	21:7	219
1:10	54, 81, 93, 216	11:5	186	21:10	204, 206
2:2-3	22	11:17	81	21:13	205
2:21	80, 81, 160, 162	12:2	81	22:7	61, 211, 216
2:26-27	149	12:7-8	72	22:9	207
2:32	72, 204	12:13	82	22:26	208
3:2	216	12:14	125	22:28	208, 210
3:2-3	211	12:14-15	83, 157	23:1	86
3:3	211	12:14-16	257	23:1-2	85, 87, 214
3:4	68, 180	12:14-17	213	23:1-4	165, 167
3:14	180	12:15	72, 125, 231	23:2	166, 168
3:22	180	12:17	93, 125, 216	23:3	168, 236
3:6-10	147, 149, 152	13:14	219	23:4	86, 168
3:8	34, 43, 200, 201	13:17	208	23:8	158
3:14	22, 34	13:19	207	23:19	206
3:16	52	13:20	206	23:27	72
3:19	65, 68, 71, 157,	13:22	203	24:6	82, 84, 92, 93,
	209	13:24	87, 213		164, 257
3:21	72, 204	13:24-25	72	24:6-7	158, 235
4:12-13	206	13:25	72	24:7-8	157
4:13	208	13:26	203	25:4	76
4:20	158, 208	14:17	215	25:8-11	207
4:26-27	158	15:1	201	25:11	158
4:27	175, 219	15:7	93, 208	25:15	93
4:30	141, 203	15:8	208	25:29	69
5:6	88, 214	15:20	175	27:4	212, 233
5:10	175, 220	16:11	158	27:4-6	209
5:15-17	206	16:11-13	212	27:6	207

8:7-8	214	9:13-15	72, 231	1:7	216
8:10	86	9:14	81	1:12	216
8:13	202	9:15	82, 83, 84, 179	2:10	91
8:14	90, 125			2:14	184
9:3	202	*Jonah*		3:17	36, 219
9:15	201	4:10-11	219	3:19	213
9:16	213				
10:11	155	*Micah*			
10:12	82	1:16	207		
10:14	208	2:4	208, 210		
11:1	51, 67	2:12	236, 237	**NEW TESTAMENT**	
11:1-4	154	3:5	61		
11:1-11	153	4:1-3	199	*Matthew*	
11:2	154	4:6	236	9:15	242
11:5-7	155, 156	4:13	78	10:1	247
11:8	222, 229	5:5	85	10:1-4	247
11:8-9	156	5:7	237	12:22-31	245
11:8-11	156	5:8	88	12:24	245
11:10-11	156	5:10	215	12:26	245
11:11	24	5:12-14	140	12:28	245
12:9	224	7:14	237	25:34	249
12:10	24				
13:4	25	*Nahum*		*Mark*	
13:5-8	214, 215	1:8-9	220	2:19	242
13:6	204	2:13	88	3:13	247
13:8	88, 214	3:10	208	3:14	247
14:4	239	3:18	236	3:14-19	247
14:6-8	236			6:7	247
		Habakkuk		12:1-10	252
Joel		2:18	89		
1:18	37	3:3	114	*Luke*	
2:17	219	3:14	213	5:34	242
2:18	219, 231			6:12-16	247
2:27	224	*Zephaniah*		6:13	247
3:1	239	1:13	81	9:1	247
3:3	234	2:9	228	9:2	247
3:5	220	3:17	56	10:1	247
3:6	212, 234			10:1-12	247
3:8	234	*Haggai*		10:2-11	247
3:9	61	2:23	16	10:9	247
				10:11	247
Amos		*Zechariah*		10:17	247
2:7	72	1:6	76	10:18	247
3:2	25	4:14	78	10:19	248
3:12	215	6:5	78	12:32	250
4:2	202	9:13	58	17:33	251
4:13	89	10:3	85		
5:11	81	10:9	82	*John*	
5:27	207	10:10	236	1:12	250
6:9	220	13:7	214	1:29	244
7:11	179, 207			1:36	244
7:17	179, 207	*Malachi*		3:22-30	241
9:4	204, 208	1:2	48	3:28	242